Serial Killers

Beyond Evil
True Crime Case Files
Vol. 1

Jack Smith

ISBN: 9781983237713

Printed in the United States

MAPLEWOOD
– PUBLISHING –

Contents

The Casanova Killer
John Paul Knowles

November 7, 1974

As she entered her home in Milledgeville, Georgia, all Ellen Carr probably had on her mind was going to bed. She was a registered nurse who worked a night shift, and although the small family welcomed the money, the job was a demanding one.

Inside, the house was unnaturally quiet. She found that odd. Her husband, forty-five-year-old businessman Carswell Carr and fifteen-year-old daughter Amanda usually greeted her when she came home from the hospital.

That wasn't the only sign that something was seriously amiss. As an investigator later put it, "The (place) looked as if it had been attacked by an animal." Mirrors were smashed. Slashed furniture lay everywhere, some of it in pieces. Books from the bookshelves littered the floor.

Had they been robbed? Where were Carswell and Mandy? Heart pounding, Mrs. Carr ran from room to room, calling out. Minutes later, she was back outside, screaming hysterically. Neighbors called the police to what was obviously the scene of a gruesome double homicide.

Carswell Carr's nude corpse was lying face down on the couple's bed, hands bound behind his back and twenty-seven stab wounds, inflicted by scissors, all over his body. The medical examiner later determined that he had died of a heart attack, likely brought on by the torture. Down the hall, Amanda was also face down in her room, one nylon stocking tied tightly around her neck and the other shoved down her throat. To compound the horror, she appeared to have been raped after death.

When Mrs. Carr regained her senses, she went through the house with the police and identified several things that were missing: Carswell's briefcase, shaving kit, credit cards, identification, and most of his clothing.[1]

While detectives searched for more clues, the murderer, wearing his victim's clothes, was in an Atlanta bar, flirting with a lady reporter. He told her his name was Daryl Golden, but his real name was Paul John Knowles, and he was destined to be remembered as one of the most vicious and unpredictable serial killers of his generation.

******

Whenever and wherever a story appears about the murder spree of Paul John Knowles, it is accompanied by one news photo in particular. It shows a brooding, handsome man with tousled hair and a cigarette dangling casually from his mouth. He bears a striking resemblance to the

---

[1] *Augusta Chronicle*, November 7, 1974

actor Robert Redford, whose rugged good looks have always sent women flocking to the theaters whenever one of his movies debuted.

"(Knowles') easy charm and an indefinable air of danger made him catnip to women and eventually earned him his homicidal nickname, the 'Casanova Killer'," crime historian Harold Schechter wrote in *The Serial Killer Files*.[2]

The label was rather misleading. Paul John Knowles was not cut from the same cloth as Ted Bundy, a charismatic but sadistic lady killer who preyed exclusively on women. A criminal lowlife who degenerated into a serial slaughterer, Knowles wasn't choosy when it came to victims. Men, women, children of all ages – he murdered them all. He was a one-man crime wave who killed at least eighteen people, with some sources putting the final body count at thirty-five.

Knowles became the stuff of American nightmares in July 1974, when he escaped from a Jacksonville, Florida jail after being arrested for fighting. That same night, he broke into the home of a retired schoolteacher named Alice Curtis, tied her up, and ransacked the place for money. The sixty-five-year-old woman choked to death on her gag, but Knowles saw that as no reason to leave town. He drove around Jacksonville in the dead woman's car until the police connected him with the crime and a manhunt began.

So did a lot of killing.

By the time he was captured in November 1974, Paul John Knowles had left a string of bodies throughout the southern U.S. In addition to Carswell and Amanda Carr, his victims included two sisters aged eleven and seven, a housewife who was strangled with a phone cord while her toddler looked on, and a Florida State trooper who he handcuffed to a tree and shot execution-style.

After his capture, Knowles basked in his newfound celebrity, giving several media interviews and describing himself as "the most successful member of my family." He chuckled that the only thing he would regret about being executed was that he would be unable to keep watching the police make fools of themselves.

The rape and murder spree of Paul John Knowles has not been remembered to the same extent as the crimes of Ted Bundy, John Wayne Gacy, or Jeffrey Dahmer. The female journalist who met (and slept with) Knowles in Atlanta wrote a book about her short-lived relationship with him, and in 2005, New Dominion Pictures produced a docudrama titled *Dangerous Pursuit*, but otherwise, he is a footnote in the history of American serial murders.

Until now. This book examines the life of Paul John Knowles in detail: his turbulent childhood, the broken engagement that turned him from petty criminal to rampaging killer and the four-month rape and murder marathon that may have claimed up to thirty-five victims.[3]

---

[2] Schechter, H. *The Serial Killer Files: The who, what, where, how, and why of the world's most terrifying murderers*, p. 169
[3] https://donmcclellan.wordpress.com/2011/12/23/serial-killer-killed-by-an-angel/

Traces of his rampage continue to surface. In December 2011, police investigators in Georgia identified the remains of Ima Jean Sanders, a thirteen-year-old girl who went missing in 1974 and was likely a Knowles victim. Although he has been dead for forty-one years, Paul John Knowles continues to make headlines.

Paul John Knowles (Author's Collection)

One Night in Georgia

November 7, 1974

British journalist Sandy Fawkes needed a drink. Badly. So she wandered into a Holiday Inn bar in Atlanta, Georgia and started ordering.

Fawkes, a forty-five-year-old redhead, had botched an assignment for the *National Enquirer* in Washington, DC, which left her discouraged and desperately in need of diversion. The liquor helped. So did the sight of the handsome stranger at the other end of the bar.

"His gaunt good looks made him stand out from the crowd," she remembered years later. "He looked like a cross between Robert Redford and Ryan O'Neal."

The man, who appeared to be in his mid- to late twenties, was over six feet tall, broad-shouldered and narrow-hipped, and had rugged facial features that Fawkes found attractive. His suit and tie were conservative yet classy, providing no hint that they were actually the clothes of a murdered man.

She was still checking him out when he noticed her too. Coming over, he asked her to dance. She politely declined, saying that she had to work. Fawkes left for the local *Enquirer* offices to wrap things up but soon returned to the bar on impulse and found the man still there.

This time she accepted his invitation, and things started to happen. They talked for hours, went out to dinner, and finished the night in her bed. As his hands wandered over her body, she had no idea that the night before, they had snuffed out the lives of Carswell and Amanda Carr.

******

He told her his name was Daryl Golden. During the week they spent together, he slowly integrated himself into her life. However, he remained so attentive, considerate, and protective that she barely noticed the intrusion at first. He insisted on paying for everything and drove her everywhere that she needed to go in a white Chevrolet Impala that looked brand new.

With Golden's expensive wardrobe and vehicle, he looked rich to Fawkes, although she did notice some oddities. He paid for everything with credit cards but didn't have enough cash on him to buy a newspaper. Perhaps she was too smitten to care. When he volunteered to drive her to Miami where he claimed to have an appointment, she agreed at once.

By all accounts, the couple had a great time. They went clubbing, with Fawkes glowing with pride whenever her new paramour stepped onto the dance floor. "He was a spectacular dancer," she recalled, and indeed he was. Golden was such a performer than once he started moving, everyone else on the dance floor stepped aside to watch. He clearly loved it, too.

At one point he asked her if she had ever written a book and if she would consider writing one about him. Like most writers, Sandy Fawkes was used to being inundated with book ideas, but she humored him by asking why his life would make a good subject.

To her amazement, Golden replied that he did not have long to live. "Within a year, I will be dead," he stated, adding that he expected to be killed for something he had done.

While Fawkes stared at him with disbelief and growing alarm, he said that his attorney in Miami had been given some tapes for safekeeping and their contents would be revealed after his death. "It will make world headlines," he promised.

That conversation signaled the end of their time together. "After a week, I just had a feeling I wanted to get away from him," Fawkes recalled.[4]

Days later, Sandy Fawkes was approached by police detectives who had questions about her former lover. They told her who he really was; Paul John Knowles, an ex-convict suspected of committing a series of rapes and murders over the last four months. They grilled her about the liaison and even hinted that she could be charged as an accomplice.

"Police in Macon, Georgia make Rod Steiger look like a fairy," she shuddered afterward.

When the detectives showed her photos of items taken from the Carr residence, any doubt about "Golden's" guilt dissolved. She recognized several pieces of clothing that Knowles had been wearing. She was doubly shocked to learn that their original owner had been murdered the day before she met Golden. The police also informed her that the sleek white Chevrolet Impala belonged to a businessman named William Bates whose strangled corpse had been dumped outside Lima, Ohio last September.

The kill list sickened her. Two young girls strangled and dumped in a swamp outside Jacksonville. A Texas woman raped and murdered, with her corpse being dragged through a barbed wire fence afterward. What must have been especially alarming was the murder of Ann Dawson, a beautician from Birmingham, Alabama. Knowles met her on September 23 and traveled with her until the 29th, at which point he disposed of her.

It took Sandy Fawkes a long time to recover. She was no lightweight when it came to bloodshed. In 1973, she had covered the Yom Kippur War in the Middle East. But never before had she come so close to a violent death, and she constantly wondered why Knowles had spared her.

Perhaps she indirectly answered that question three years later, when *Killing Time*, an account of her fling with Knowles, was published. (The book was republished in 2004 as *Natural Born Killer: In Love and on the Road with a Serial Killer*.) Knowing that she was a journalist, Knowles must have decided that she was his ticket to the infamy he craved so desperately.

Sandy Fawkes was lucky. At least eighteen others weren't.

---

[4] "Sandy Fawkes." The Telegraph. Accessed April 8, 2015.
http://www.telegraph.co.uk/news/obituaries/1506578/Sandy-Fawkes.html.

The Year of Fear

The 1970s were marked by exuberance, creativity, and breakthroughs. People disco-danced to infectious Bee Gees beats, kept pet rocks, and watched beautiful lady cops take down bad guys on *Charlie's Angels*. On May 14, 1973, NASA launched Skylab, the first American space station, taking mankind one step closer to living and working in space. Five years later, on July 25, 1978, another scientific landmark took place when Louise Brown, the first "test tube baby," was born.

Like every era before and after it, the 1970s also had its dark side. There were two assassination attempts on President Gerald Ford in 1975. In November 1979 Islamic militants stormed the U.S. Embassy in Tehran and took over 60 American diplomats and citizens hostage for 444 days, a debacle known as the Iranian Hostage Crisis. There was also a frightening increase in the number of serial killers. According to a homicide database at Radford University, 450 of these mass murderers were at work during the 1970s, compared to 156 the decade before.[5]

There has been a lot of speculation over why serial killer activity spiked so sharply during the 1970s. Some experts propose that murderers who grew up and warped their psyches during the drug-polluted, cult-ridden 1960s were old enough to act on their impulses the following decade. Others suggest that the pool of available victims grew exponentially after the free-wheeling Sixties. More young people (especially women) lived on their own, hitchhiked, had sex with strangers, and indulged in other pursuits that put them at risk.

If there were a "banner year" for serial killers in the United States, it would be 1974. It later became known as the "Year of Fear" because the best of the worst either got their start or made further inroads in their respective reigns of terror.

- In January, John Wayne Gacy killed his second victim, a teenaged boy, and stashed the corpse in his closet prior to burial. When blood leaked from the victim's nose and mouth and stained his carpet, Gacy "plugged" future kills using cloth rags or the victim's own underwear.

- On January 15, Dennis Rader, alias BTK (Bind-Torture-Kill), kicked off his decades-long murder spree by annihilating four members of the Otero family in Wichita, Kansas. He capped the morning of mass slaughter by hanging 11-year-old Josephine Otero from a pipe in the basement and masturbating while she died.

- Ted Bundy, who would rape and murder several women across multiple states before being executed, claimed his first documented victim on January 31. He broke into the basement bedroom of 21-year-old Lynda Ann Healy, a senior at the University of Washington, battered her unconscious, and carried her away. Her decapitated and dismembered remains were not found until a year later.

Paul John Knowles also began to kill in 1974. Like Ted Bundy, a failed romance factored in his breaking point. But where Bundy was focused and goal-oriented enough to be accepted into law school and work at a suicide crisis center, Knowles didn't bother trying to fit in anywhere. All he cared about was being famous and feared, although not necessarily in that order.

---

[5] Dimond, Diane. "The Year We Began to Understand Serial Killers." The Huffington Post. Accessed May 22, 2015.

A Killer Is Born

Paul John Knowles was born on April 17, 1946, in Orlando, Florida, and grew up in Jacksonville. He had two older brothers and sisters. His father was a hard-working carpenter. Knowles was apparently an intelligent but destructive child, defying his parents, Thomas and Bonnie, and ignoring schoolwork in favor of running wild and showing off. Like-minded boys clustered around him like flies, impressed by his nerve and the way he talked back to adults without fear.

Their admiration fuelled his vanity and inspired him to act out in ways that exceeded mere childish mischief. In 1953, when he was seven, he started breaking the law by stealing bicycles. In view of the crimes he would later commit, this was a trivial incident, but it created a criminal record that would only get worse.

Thomas and Bonnie Knowles tried to control him, but Paul was incorrigible. If restrained or confronted, he would explode into a murderous rage. The system didn't fare any better with him. By the time he was seventeen, Knowles had been sent to the Florida School for Boys six times on charges ranging from breaking and entering to grand larceny. He showed no interest in reforming. Each time he was released, Knowles would head back to Jacksonville, meet up with old friends, and resume his routine of joyriding, burglary, and stealing until the law caught up with him again.

Even as a young man, Knowles dreamed of becoming a criminal celebrity. He devoured books about John Dillinger, Bonnie and Clyde, Baby Face Nelson, and other outlaws who swept across America and left bloody devastation in their wake. He wasn't as inspired by Al Capone and the more regimented world of organized crime, seeing it as too tame in comparison, although he appreciated the money and power that professional gangsters had at their disposal.[6]

Although there is no proof that Knowles murdered anyone before 1974, his violence toward women was well-established. Kathy Hardy[7], whose brother ran with the future killer during the late 1960s, says that he could be terrifying.

If he liked a girl, and she rejected him, watch out. He had a real temper and would punch a woman without even thinking. I remember him being beaten up by the boyfriends or brothers of these girls a few times, but it didn't change him.[8]

Surprisingly, Kathy got along with Knowles.

I knew how to handle him, I guess. He loved being flattered and told how "bad" he was. He used to say that one day he would be this big, famous, bad guy. When I said, "Better give me your autograph now then" Paul was tickled. I was never scared of him but then again, he liked me.

In March 1965, when he was nineteen, a policeman stopped him while he was driving a stolen car. Knowles grabbed the officer's gun, forced him into the vehicle, but released him two hours

---

[6] Interview with Kathy Hardy
[7] A pseudonym
[8] Interview with author

later unharmed. He was soon picked up, convicted of kidnapping, and sentenced to one to five years in the state prison.

Although the Florida School for Boys was no holiday camp, prison was edgier, more vicious. The food was bad. So were hygiene standards. Outside, gay liberation was in progress, but for Knowles, homosexuality was the only available outlet for his sexual urges. Because he was now having sex with men more than women, he would soon find it difficult to achieve orgasm with a female partner, which added to his agitation.[9]

Two years and eight months later he obtained parole. He was far from rehabilitated. In April 1968, Duval County police caught him attempting a break and enter, which sent him back to Raiford prison to complete his sentence. He was released on May 10, 1970, with, as a parole official later put it, "$25 in his pocket, a new suit, and no responsibilities."[10]

He did have a girlfriend, though. Jackie Knight, a tiny brunette, had met Knowles after his 1967 parole. Her husband at the time introduced them. Soon Knowles was visiting the Knights regularly. He was especially fond of their three children. Jackie would later remember how much he enjoyed taking them to local fairs and winning prizes for them. Soon after he went back to prison for violating parole, the Knights separated, and Jackie started writing to Knowles. A romance bloomed, and he vowed that after getting out of prison he would marry her and go straight.

He and Jackie married as soon as he left Raiford, but the relationship floundered. No one wanted to employ an ex-convict, so Knowles gave up on looking for honest work and went back to his drinking buddies. Alarmed, Jackie took the children and moved to Macon, Georgia. Although she succeeded in getting the marriage annulled, she remained in touch with Knowles thereafter.

It did not take him long to get in trouble again. On September 15, 1971, Knowles was convicted of breaking and entering with intent to commit a felony and sentenced to three years. It is unclear why he got off so lightly given the existence of a previous record. In 1971, the maximum penalty for that offense was fifteen years.

Equally mysterious is why Knowles received furlough privileges after a year. The outcome was predictable. He simply left one day and failed to return. When the police caught up with him on December 6, 1972, he fought like a cornered wildcat, punching out one officer and nearly taking down another before they overpowered him and returned him to Raiford.

It looked as if nothing could ever convince him to give up his violent ways. Then he met the woman who would change his future.

---

[9] In *Killing Time*, Sandy Fawkes reported these difficulties. There was also no semen collected from the bodies of the women that Knowles assaulted.
[10] *Ocala Star-Banner*, January 10, 1975

Star-Crossed Lovers

During his nearly nine years in the Florida prison system, Knowles was a loner. Other inmates referred to him as a "rat," although there's no evidence that he was ever an informer. One prison official described him as "antisocial, profiting neither from experience nor punishment."[11] Records show that he scored 125 on an intelligence test, which was above average for the population at large and considered amazing for a prison inmate.

He may not have passed the time by making friends, but he did have other interests, one of which was astrology. He read his daily horoscope and let it affect his mood. A positive outlook left him giddy to the point of mania, while a negative or cautious prediction made him withdraw and keep to himself. This obsession with the mysterious soon extended to tarot cards, which he became quite adept at reading.

In late 1972 or early 1973, Knowles began exchanging letters with twenty-six-year-old Angela Covic, a San Francisco cocktail waitress whose name he had found in *American Astrology* magazine. Covic's mother was a renowned local psychic so she, like Knowles, loved the esoteric and found his handwriting especially alluring.

Angela Covic. (Author's Collection)

She responded to him enthusiastically, beginning each letter with "Hi, Mad Dog Knowles!" This delighted him. He called her "my Yiddisher angel" and decorated each letter with crayon drawings of astral symbols, flowers, and chubby devils with the initials "P.J." between their horns. The fact that he was a prison inmate didn't faze her. Her former husband was currently serving time in a California prison. Also, Knowles concealed his violent history, telling her that he had been busted for drug dealing.

---

[11] "Paul John Knowles was 'considered a rat' by inmates." *The Evening Independent*, November 25, 1974.

When she traveled across the country to visit him at Raiford in September 1973, they hit it off so well that he proposed marriage. Mrs. Covic accepted, and even hired a Florida lawyer, Sheldon Yavitz, to secure his release on parole so he could join her in California.

Knowles now had an incentive to toe the line. He earned a high school diploma and began some college courses. When the Parole Commission agreed to hear his case, he vowed that if released, he planned to go to California, where Angela Covic and a sign-painting job awaited him. Knowles conceded that he had been angry and aimless before. Now he had a reason to abandon his old ways.

Chairman Ray Howard later recalled that they agreed to his parole for two reasons: he was due for release in a year anyway, and California officials had agreed to supervise him. There was likely a third reason. Knowles would be leaving his hometown of Jacksonville where he kept falling off the straight and narrow. Another prison officer told the press, "He has too many friends and acquaintances in Jacksonville who kept on getting him into trouble."

Upon his release on May 14, 1974, Knowles flew to San Francisco. But when he turned up at Angela Covic's home, the reception was not quite what he had expected. She didn't say it right away, but she had changed her mind about marrying him. A psychic had warned her that a dangerous man was entering her life, and she was now afraid.

Knowles stayed for less than a week, sleeping at her mother's place each night. Finally, Angela told him that she had changed her mind about getting married and decided to reconcile with her former husband.

Paul John Knowles was more than stung by the rejection. Angela's worship had raised him on a pedestal and had made him feel powerful. From her, he had gotten the sense of celebrity that he'd craved all his life. The crash landing left him disoriented and furious.

Knowles returned to Jacksonville in a state of extreme agitation. He got into a bar fight, pounded the bartender into a bleeding pulp, and found himself in jail. Rather than go back to Raiford prison for violating parole, Knowles picked a lock and escaped on July 26, 1974.

His killing spree began that night.

Both Young and Old

July 26, 1974

Knowles was on the run and needed to get away fast. That required money and a vehicle, neither of which he had access to, so he invaded the Jacksonville Beach home of Alice Curtis, a sixty-five-year-old retired schoolteacher. It is not known whether he actually broke in or was invited inside after using a ruse. He would employ both strategies in the months to come.

After overpowering and tying up the elderly woman, Knowles ransacked her home looking for money and valuables. Focused on collecting what he could and getting away quickly, he was unaware that Mrs. Curtis' dentures had been dislodged by her gag and forced down her throat. By the time he went to check on her, she had choked to death.

Something must have shifted in Knowles as he stared down at the elderly woman's corpse. He had never killed anyone before.[12] Sandy Fawkes, who came to know him somewhat during their short time together, speculated on what must have gone through his head.

"I believe that in the first killing... he sensed his own power for the first time in his life," she wrote in *Killing Time*. "The man who had always been... dominated by judges, juries, and jailers had found revenge, a source of emotional satisfaction."[13]

As an ex-convict, Knowles would also have known that killers had status in the prison hierarchy. As a petty thief, he'd been relegated to the lower rungs of the ladder. Abducting a police officer would have elevated him somewhat, but as a loner doing time for non-violent offenses, he remained at the bottom echelon.

Now things were different. If he ever went back to prison, it would be as a murderer. But not just *any* murderer. He wanted to be the "biggest of them all," as he later told his attorney. If the only way to keep himself in funds and stay free was to kill, he wouldn't hesitate.

After leaving the scene in Mrs. Curtis' white Dodge Dart, Knowles drove west to Jacksonville and hid out with friends. It wasn't long before he killed again. This time it would be a double murder.

******

August 1, 1974

At 6:00 p.m., Elizabeth Anderson, accompanied by her thirteen-year-old daughter, left her residence in Jacksonville's Pumpkin Hill area to visit a sick relative. Two younger girls, 11-year-old Lillian, and 6-year-old Mylette, remained at home, but they weren't expected to be alone for long. Mrs. Anderson's husband, Jack, a commercial fisherman, was due home at 7:00 p.m.

---

[12] Although Knowles would later claim that he killed three people in San Francisco after Angela rejected him, this has never been substantiated.
[13] Sandy Fawkes, *Killing Time*, p. 165

She called the residence shortly before 7:00 p.m. to check on the girls, and they assured her everything was fine. But when Jack Anderson arrived home at 7:20 p.m., delayed by a problem with his boat, the girls were gone.[14]

The Andersons were convinced that Lillian and Mylette had been kidnapped. "Our children wouldn't do anything they weren't told," Jack Anderson insisted. "I feel someone broke into the house and took them away. We are just praying they will be returned."[15]

With assistance from the public, the police conducted a 140 square mile search of northeastern Duval County, but nothing was found. Jack and Elizabeth Anderson were beside themselves with anxiety. Lillian had a thyroid condition, and Mylette suffered from asthma and a weak heart. Both required medication.

The sisters' fate was not revealed until the following January when authorities listened to a tape-recorded "diary" that Knowles kept.

He said that he had been in the middle of abandoning Mrs. Curtis' car on a quiet residential street when he noticed the Anderson girls watching him curiously. They weren't strangers to him. In fact, Elizabeth Anderson was a friend of Bonnie Knowles, his mother. Convinced that they would tell their parents they had seen him, Knowles coaxed Lillian and Mylette into the white Dodge dart, drove them to a remote location, and strangled them both. Afterward, he dumped their bodies in a swamp.

Acting on the information, the police searched all the swamps in the area but failed to turn up the missing girls. Although Knowles claimed credit for their disappearance, the case officially remains open.

---

[14] *Sarasota Herald-Tribune,* August 4, 1974
[15] Ibid

Road Kills

August 2, 1974

After deciding to drive to Macon, Georgia to hide out at Jackie Knight's place, Knowles made another stop to replenish his money stores. He broke into the Atlantic Beach home of Marjorie Howie, strangled her with a nylon stocking, and escaped with cash and valuables. One of the latter was a television set that he proudly presented to Jackie when he arrived at her home.

It was while en route to Macon that he met and murdered his fifth victim.

August 1974 – date unknown

Although only 13 years old, Ima Jean Sanders was strong-willed and independent. After her parents' divorce in 1968, she went to live with her father in Beaumont, Texas but ran away frequently. Her disappearances were so common that Mr. Sanders rarely notified the authorities. He knew that she always turned up sooner or later.

In July 1974, Ima Jean hopped on a bus to Warner Robins, Georgia, where her mother Betty and stepfather lived. Upon arriving, she called Betty from the bus station, announced her arrival, and asked if someone could come to pick her up.

Ima Jean's four-year-old sister, Sharron, was thrilled to see her. Six months earlier, Sharron had watched in horror when another sister, Charlotte, fell off the family's houseboat in Florida and drowned.[16] Since then, she had clung to her older sister whenever they were together.

On August 1, Betty left the family's mobile home for a few hours. She asked Ima Jean to babysit Sharron. However, soon after Betty's departure, a group of Ima's older friends pulled up in a conversion van. After ordering her sister to go inside and lock the doors, Ima Jean left with them.

"I remember being upset," Sharron said in 2011.

It was the last time she saw her sister.

In his taped reminiscences, Knowles would remember that sometime in August 1974, he picked up a teenaged hitchhiker named "Alma" not far from Warner Robins. After taking her to a wooded area, he raped and strangled her and left her body between some trees. For reasons he never explained, Knowles returned to the location two weeks later and found that animals had dragged the barely-recognizable corpse a short distance away.

The girl's jawbone had been detached from her skull during the feeding frenzy over her remains. For some reason, this bothered Knowles enough for him to bury the small piece of bone. Then he departed.

---

[16] Purser, Becky. "Sister of girl killed by serial killer recalls fateful day in Warner Robins". *The Telegraph*, December 22, 2011.

August 23, 1974

By the last week of August, Knowles was running low on funds, and despite the television and other gifts, Jackie Knight had hinted that he was overstaying his welcome. So on August 23, he went to Musella in Crawford County and knocked on the door of 24-year-old divorcee Kathy Sue Woods Pierce, who was home alone with her three-year-old son, Joel.

Once the door closed, Knowles demanded money. Mrs. Pierce tried to scream, which enraged him. Ripping the telephone out of the wall, he wrapped the cord around her neck and pulled tight, until it was practically buried in her flesh. While Joel watched helplessly, Knowles dragged his mother's body into the bathroom, left it on the floor, and departed after taking whatever cash he could find. He left the boy unharmed.

The carnage was discovered by the father of Pierce's boyfriend, who called the police. Georgia Bureau of Investigation officers tried to talk to Joel, but the boy wasn't much help.

September 3, 1974

After leaving Jackie's place, Knowles headed north. There doesn't appear to have been a strategy to his itinerary. He simply wanted to put as much distance between him and each crime as possible.

On September 3, he was in Lima, Ohio. That evening he entered the bar at Scott's Inn and struck up a conversation with William Bates, a 32-year-old account executive for the Ohio Power Company. The bartender, who knew Bates, watched with mild interest as the executive chatted with a man he later described as tall, young, and redheaded. The two men left together, and Bates was never seen alive again.

Mrs. Bates soon reported her husband missing. The police detectives investigating his disappearance found an abandoned white Dodge Dart near Scott's Inn and traced it back to the deceased Alice Curtis. The link confirmed their suspicion that the account executive fell victim to foul play. On Thanksgiving Day, a hunter found his nude body in the woods outside the city. He had been bound and gagged with electrical tape before being strangled to death.

Given the fact that Bates was naked when discovered, Knowles almost certainly lured him out of the bar with the promise of homosexual favors. Sandy Fawkes later marveled over his ability to detect men who were open to such proposals. In *Killing Time*, she recalled sitting in a bar with Knowles and watching one man come in, look around, and then saunter up to a man in an armchair. The two exchanged words before leaving together.

"Homosexuals," said Daryl with satisfaction in his voice, "or 'poofs', as you would call them."

"How could you tell? They looked like respectable businessmen."

"Lots of highly respectable businessmen in this country are gay. You'd never guess to look at them, all that backslapping hides a lot."[17]

---

[17] Sandy Fawkes, *Killing Time,* p. 83

Knowles took his victim's money, credit cards, and white Chevrolet Impala. Then he headed west for California, once again leaving the site of his latest murder far behind.

September 12, 1974

A later examination of credit card transactions confirmed that after he left Lima, Knowles drove east to Missoula, Montana and then south into Utah. On September 12, he ended up in Ely, Nevada, a growing city in the east-central part of the state. He had run out of money, and Bates' credit cards were now maxed out, so he went hunting.

Knowles had picked up a gun in his travels and used it to overpower Emmett and Lois Johnson, a San Pedro couple in their sixties who were vacationing in their camper. He tied them up, shot both of them behind the left ear, and escaped with their cash and credit cards. Their bodies were not discovered until September 18, long after he'd left the state.

September 21, 1974

Driving through Seguin, Texas, Knowles spotted Charlynn Hicks, a 42-year-old widow, outside a rest stop on US 10. According to one account, her car had broken down, and he pulled over to ask if she needed help. Another version states that Hicks, who was on her way to a chili-cooking contest in San Marcos, had paused during her journey to admire the rest stop's view.

When Mrs. Hicks failed to show up in San Marcos, her family contacted the Guadalupe County Sheriff's Department. A search commenced. Her car was found at the rest stop, so police hunted through the surrounding countryside. On September 25, a deputy found her nude body in some brush near the highway. She had been strangled to death, and her skin was torn in places after Knowles dragged the corpse through the barbed wire fence that separated the brush area from the road.[18]

The Houston *Post* offered a $1000 reward, but Mrs. Hicks' murder remained unsolved until Knowles took credit for it two months later.

September 23, 1974

Two days after murdering Charlynn Hicks, Knowles was in Birmingham, Alabama. There he met Ann Dawson, an outgoing 49-year-old beautician. He must have found her more intriguing than his previous victims, because he traveled with her for six days before killing her on September 29. All he would say afterward was that he had "tired" of her and dumped her corpse in the Mississippi. Dawson's body was never found.

October 16, 1974

For the next few weeks, Knowles traveled through Oklahoma, Missouri, Iowa, and Minnesota, leaving no known bodies behind. Then, on October 16, he walked up to a home in Marlborough, Connecticut and knocked on the door. When 16-year-old Dawn Wine, who was home alone, answered, Knowles, forced his way inside, tied her up, and raped her.

---

[18] *Del Rio News-Herald*, September 26, 1974

When Dawn's mother, 35-year-old Karen Wine, came home, he subjected her to the same treatment. Then he strangled them both with silk stockings and left, taking money, a tape recorder, and some records from Dawn's collection. He gave the latter to Jackie Knight's children when he visited them again.

October 19, 1974

Three days after leaving Connecticut, Knowles made another deadly stop. Arriving in Woodford, Virginia, a small community in Caroline County, he persuaded or forced 53-year-old Doris Hovey to let him into her home. He told her that all he wanted was a gun, and as soon as he got it, he would leave.

Mrs. Hovey believed him. She led the way into the study and retrieved her husband's rifle. As soon as he loaded it, Knowles shot her through the head. Before leaving, he wiped his prints from the weapon and left it beside her cooling corpse.

******

As he drove to Florida, Knowles knew that he had taken enough lives to guarantee his infamy. But only if someone knew what he had done. Someone who he could count on to not turn him in.

In Key West, he picked up a pair of young hitchhikers and volunteered to drive them to Miami. He later said he'd planned to kill them but hadn't gone far before a policeman stopped him for a traffic violation. The officer let him go with a warning, but Knowles was forced to change his intended course of action. There was no way he could murder the couple after a policeman had seen him with them.

No matter. There would be more opportunities to augment his bloody glory later. After dropping his passengers off in Miami, he went to see his lawyer, Sheldon Yavitz and presented him with two things: a set of audio tapes and a shocking proclamation.

"I have something to tell you. Brace yourself. I'm a mass murderer."

Sheldon Yavitz

By 1974, Sheldon Yavitz's criminal law practice was booming.

"I was too antisocial to have other clients," he said in 1993. "I liked professional criminals. I wasn't judgmental."[19]

When Angela Covic retained him to secure Knowles' release on parole, Yavitz was a criminal defense pro. Clients included Cuban extortionists who attacked their victims with hand grenades, a gang of marijuana smugglers that delivered to customers using Federal Express, and a man who loved to rob adult bookstores. When a jewel thief paid his fees using precious stones, Yavitz didn't bat an eye, and when a burglary ring offered him a Cobra sports car in lieu of money, he happily accepted. He even had a convicted drug dealer work for him as a secretary.

Yavitz automatically assumed that his clients were guilty, so he was never shocked by their crimes. Whenever they called him, he only asked for details of their arrest and how to reach them by phone. He rarely if ever secured their release using actual facts, convinced that the truth would always be damning in their cases. Instead, he got them off on continuances and technicalities such as improper search and seizure by the police.

In October 1974, when Paul John Knowles visited his office, Sheldon Yavitz was making more than $100,000 a year. He operated his practice out of a small office at the side of his huge ranch house in Coral Gables. His non-judgmental attitude toward his clients' crimes was as well-established as it was lucrative, but even he was surprised by Knowles' admission.

He listened as Knowles described his audiotape diary and called all the murders "successes." He wanted Yavitz to make sure that the press and public knew about them after his death so he could, in his words, "become as famous as Bonnie and Clyde."[20]
Michael Newton, author of *The Encyclopedia of Serial Killers*, wrote that Yavitz recommended surrender, but Knowles insisted that he would rather be shot down in a blaze of glory like John Dillinger or Bonnie and Clyde. Because he had committed murder in several death-penalty states, he knew that his days were numbered. He intended to live what time he had left as wildly as possible.

Yavitz agreed to keep the tapes, without listening to them, until after Knowles' death. Happy, the self-proclaimed "success story" headed back to Jackie Knight's home in Macon. While there, he may have killed Edward Hilliard and Debbie Griffin, another pair of teenaged hitchhikers who had been traveling from their hometown of Gainesville, Florida to Love Valley, North Carolina. Hilliard was found outside Macon on November 2, body punctured by five bullets. Although Debbie Griffin remained missing, searchers came across her purse, keys, and some articles of clothing not far from her companion's body.[21]

---

[19] *Sun-Sentinel,* January 24, 1993
[20] Ibid
[21] Griffin's body has never been found.

Although Knowles never took credit for Hilliard's murder or Griffin's disappearance, he was definitely in the area when they were found, so chances are high that he killed them. Perhaps he was making up for the young couple he'd been forced to release in Miami. At any rate, the police were still actively searching for Griffin's body when Knowles struck again.

Murder in Milledgeville

Early on the morning of November 7, Assistant Police Chief Charles Osborne of the Milledgeville, Georgia police department was informed that something had happened at a house in one of the town's suburbs. Osborne, accompanied by some of his officers, found the place easily. People were milling about on the front lawn, looking frightened and confused at the same time.

As a police officer, Osborne was no stranger to violent crimes. But when he stepped out of the crisp fall air into the attractive home, he was instantly chilled. The place had been ransacked, and two murder victims were in the bedrooms, killed in a manner reminiscent of nightmares.

Carswell Carr, aged 45, was lying on the bed he had shared with his wife, Ellen. He was naked, his hands bound behind his back, and his body covered with drying blood. The doctor who examined him at the scene stated that the cause of death appeared to be a heart attack, as the wounds were not deep and had probably been inflicted with scissors as a form of torture.

The second victim was 15-year-old Amanda Carr. She had been strangled with unspeakable violence, with a nylon stocking knotted around her neck and another shoved so far down her throat that a doctor had to extract it. Her killer had attempted to rape her at some point but failed, as no semen was present.

Judging by the degree of rigor mortis in both bodies, the doctor estimated that father and daughter had been killed sometime between 11:30 p.m. the night before and 3:00 a.m. that morning. The police initially believed that two people had committed the murders, given the extensive damage to the house and the complications presented by overpowering two healthy victims alone.

Osborne directed his detective team to search for clues. The scissors used to stab Mr. Carr were found but contained no fingerprints. (A sweep of the crime scene failed to turn up a single usable print.) Once she calmed down, Mrs. Carr helped the police compile a list of items that were missing from the house. Most of her husband's stylish wardrobe had been taken, along with his brown leather briefcase, shaving kit, credit cards, and house keys. A plastic watch and digital clock radio were also missing from Mandy's room.

The police later learned that Carswell Carr had been seen the night before in the Pegasus, a bar known to be frequented by homosexuals. The bartender noticed him talking to a tall, young man with reddish hair, but he couldn't recall if they left separately or together.

Helen Ray, a sales clerk at Zayre department store in Macon, came forward to say that after the murders, a young, redheaded man had bought a tape recorder and four blank tapes from her and paid for the items with a credit card issued to Carswell Carr. When Miss Ray read about the gruesome death of the real Mr. Carr, she contacted the police and gave them a thorough description. A call immediately went out for all police departments to be on the lookout for a tall, good-looking, young man with red hair and a Zapata mustache.[22]

******

Despite the carnage he had committed, Paul Knowles did not leave Georgia immediately. Instead, he drove Carr's white Chevrolet Impala to Atlanta and booked a room at a Holiday Inn using the dead man's credit card. After settling in, he headed back out and eventually ended up at the Holiday Inn in the city's core. There he met the woman who would eventually write about him, ensuring the posthumous glory he craved.

Sandy Fawkes

Hard-drinking, British journalist Sandy Fawkes noticed Knowles immediately. Impressed by his rugged good looks and stylish attire, she let him buy her a drink when he approached.

Knowles told her that he was a businessman from New Mexico, visiting Atlanta to oversee a court case involving a restaurant chain his father owned. He added that he identified with the central character in *Jonathan Livingston Seagull.* She got the impression that he had a "desperate anxiety to be liked."

Fawkes initially resisted his advances, joking at one point, "You could easily be another Boston Strangler for all I know."

They both burst out laughing. Then, eyes glittering with excitement, Knowles said, "But the Boston Strangler is dead."

At the end of the night, they ended up in Sandy's hotel room. After using Carswell Carr's shaving kit to remove his Zapata mustache, Knowles followed her into bed. Although they kissed and made out, he was unable to achieve an erection. He apologized, but Fawkes reassured him. He'd had too much to drink, she said. Before turning out the light and cuddling beside him, she joked, "So you're not really another Boston Strangler after all. What a disappointment."

The journalist assumed they would go their separate ways in the morning, but Knowles blocked all of Sandy's efforts to leave him. He drove her to a scheduled interview instead of letting her take a cab. She made plans to fly to her next assignment in West Palm Beach, Florida that afternoon, while he was supposedly attending court on his father's behalf. To her surprise he

---

[22] A type of moustache in which both ends extend down to the chin, as worn by Marlon Brando in the 1952 film *Viva Zapata!*

approached her as she was leaving the hotel, saying that the matter had been settled out of court.

Fawkes was due to fly to Florida at 6:20, so he proposed that they spend her remaining time in Atlanta together. While they had drinks at a revolving bar called the Polaris, Knowles told her his name was Daryl Golden. Gazing out the window at some men working on a giant crane, he became pensive.
"Would you write a book about me? You see, I haven't got long to live."

Her jaw dropped. "You what?"

She assumed that he was about to admit to being terminally ill, but instead, "Golden" explained, "I am going to be killed. Soon. It might be in two days or two months. I don't know when. But within a year I will be dead. I am going to be killed by someone."[23]

While Sandy Fawkes struggled to digest this incredible announcement, Knowles went on to say that he would be killed for something he had done in the past. He couldn't tell her what it was, but he had made some audio tapes that explained everything and left them with his Miami attorney. They would be revealed after his death, and he promised that they make world headlines.

Half-convinced he was joking, she commented lightly that perhaps he had a morbid obsession with death and should see a psychiatrist. Knowles smiled back and said that he'd actually seen one once.

"He told me I had the perfect criminal mind."

Fawkes didn't know what to think, but she was intrigued enough to postpone her flight. The journalist in her wondered if he was a hitman on the run or something else that could one day translate into the scoop of a lifetime. She claimed in her book, *Killing Time*, that there were times when she detected something odd about him and was genuinely afraid, but it was apparently never enough to make her actively flee him.

They ended up driving to Florida together. During the ride, he told her that he wanted to get married one day but didn't think he ever would. He told her that he'd been engaged to a San Francisco divorcee but that she had gone back to her husband. Another engagement, this one to a girl in Macon, Georgia, failed when she married someone else. Now he was going to die soon, so it didn't matter.

Fawkes tried repeatedly to get him to tell her what he'd done, but he refused. Once she caught him tearing a story from the local newspaper about the Carr murders and asked him about it, but he dismissed her questions by claiming that he had friends who lived where the events took place.

---

[23] Sandy Fawkes, *Killing Time*, p. 33

Fawkes took it all in, not sure what to make of any of it. She had mixed feelings about Golden. On one hand, his strange proclamations and possessive behavior were disconcerting. But on the other, she found him easy to talk to, even sympathetic.

She had been raised in an orphanage until the age of four and a half and suffered institutional indignities like being forced to wear different colored underwear to let everyone know she was a bed wetter. Her foster parents had been alarmed when she learned to read more quickly than their own kids and forbade her to touch any books in the home except the Bible. When she told "Golden" all of this, he seemed to understand.

In what has to be a supreme example of irony, Knowles drove Fawkes to a scheduled interview with William J. Saxbe, the United States Attorney General. Her editor wanted her to ask Saxbe about the slew of early parolees who were being released before completion of their sentences, a situation that was arousing considerable public indignation. Knowles must have loved it.

They finally parted ways nearly a week later. Knowles wanted to stay with her longer. She had introduced him to highly placed journalist friends who made him feel important by proxy. However, she was insistent and managed to evade him each time he called her room or hung out in the bar of whatever hotel she was staying at. At last, he seemed to give up.

Paul John Knowles was out of her sight, but once Sandy Fawkes found out who he was and what he had done, he would never be out of her life.

On the Run

After Sandy Fawkes left him, Knowles met James and Susan MacKenzie, a British couple who knew Sandy and felt sorry for Knowles because he now seemed so alone. When Susan, an attractive blonde, mentioned that she had a hair appointment the next day, Knowles offered to drive her and she accepted. James MacKenzie had no objection to the arrangement. He and his wife both found the lonely young man to be polite and respectful.

Once Susan was in his vehicle, Knowles pulled over after driving a short distance and asked her for sex. Shocked, she refused, so he pulled out a pistol. Instead of cowering or crying, she fought back, knocking the weapon aside and screaming. When she got the car door open Knowles grabbed a fistful of her hair but she broke loose, ran into the road, and hailed a passing motorist.

Susan went straight to the police and told them what happened. A bulletin went out immediately, containing descriptions of the attacker and the car and requesting all police officers to watch for "Daryl Golden." Soon afterward, a West Palm Beach policeman recognized the white Chevrolet Impala and pulled him over. Knowles drew a sawed-off shotgun.

"Hold it right there," he warned.

The officer, who had opened his car door, dropped to the pavement and stayed there until Knowles drove away.

Knowing that the police would be watching for his car now too, Knowles ditched it and sought to steal another. That afternoon, a wheelchair-bound woman named Beverly Mabee heard a knock at the door of her West Palm Beach home. She opened it to a good-looking young man who identified himself as Bob Williams from the Internal Revenue Service and asked if he could come in.

Puzzled but not wanting to be perceived as uncooperative, Miss Mabee consented. Once he was inside, Knowles dropped the act and told her that he needed a hostage and a getaway car because the police were after him.

The young woman remained calm. "I knew if I screamed he would get violent. So I just kept quiet," she said afterward.

She told him that she did not own a car, but her sister, Barbara Tucker, did. When she added that Barbara was actually en route, Knowles sat down and waited.

"He knew his business," Miss Mabee would remember. "He didn't talk much. He just sat down, and we waited for Barbara."[24]

When Mrs. Tucker arrived, accompanied by her six-year-old boy, Knowles pounced. He tied up Beverly Mabee, told the child to go play in another room, and forced Barbara to drive with him to Fort Pierce in her beige Volkswagen.

Mrs. Tucker, who was a redhead like Sandy Fawkes, didn't scream or do anything to antagonize her captor. She remained calm, kept him talking, and did everything he ordered. Instead of killing her, Knowles left her tied and gagged in a motel room on Friday night before escaping in her car.

When Beverly Mabee wriggled out of her bonds, she called the police and reported Barbara's abduction. Her description of their assailant tallied so closely with that of Daryl Golden that detectives suspected they were dealing with more than an attempted rapist.

Anxious to see if he was already in the system, the police dusted Miss Mabee's home for fingerprints and showed her some mug shots. The two identification tactics soon yielded a positive result, and an all-points bulletin went out requesting area patrols to be on the lookout for Paul John Knowles. His photo was also televised, along with the warning to residents that he was armed and dangerous.

The net was closing in.

******

---

[24] *Ocala Star-Banner*, November 17, 1974

Detectives tracked down Sandy Fawkes and questioned her about "Golden." Because the Carr murders were initially thought to be a two-person job, they were also trying to determine if she had been an accomplice in any of his crimes. When Fawkes realized that her strange companion had been a rapist and suspected murderer, she was shocked. Any doubt was erased when the detectives showed her some photographs of items taken from the Carr residence, and she recognized shirts and suits that "Golden" had been wearing.

Asked if he had given her any gifts, Sandy showed them a Mickey Mouse watch. They checked it against the inventory of missing items and determined that it had once belonged to Mandy Carr, which sickened her further. As a journalist who specialized in challenging and even violent assignments, not much rattled her, but the realization that she had been riding in a murder victim's car and enjoying luxuries paid for by a dead man's credit cards nearly did her in.

Until her death in 2005, Sandy Fawkes never stopped wondering why Knowles spared her. She suspected that it was because he wanted her to write that book about him and guarantee his place alongside other famous killers. In *Killing Time*, she also speculated that he might have seen her as a kindred spirit, given their rough childhoods and their sense of having been abused by "the system." Whatever the reason, she would forever be tagged as the one who got away.

Another Double Execution

By now law enforcement officials all over the state were on the alert for Barbara Tucker's stolen Volkswagen. On November 16, a 35-year-old Florida Highway Patrol trooper named Charles Eugene Campbell noticed a car of the right make and color traveling on US 19 near the North Florida city of Perry.

Turning on his siren, he overtook the vehicle and stopped the driver for questioning. Knowles, who had been en route to Georgia, drew his gun before Campbell could even reach for his. After ordering the trooper to cuff himself and get in the back of the patrol car, Knowles abandoned the Volkswagen and drove off in Campbell's vehicle.

A passing motorist witnessed the kidnapping and hurried to the nearest phone to call the police, but by the time they arrived, Knowles and his victim were long gone.

******

Knowles knew that he needed to abandon Campbell's black and yellow patrol car at the first available opportunity. It was too conspicuous, and by now law enforcement everywhere would be on the alert for it. Using the siren, he tricked James Meyer, a businessman from Delaware, into pulling over near a wooded area southwest of Perry. After herding Campbell and Meyer into the back seat of the latter's blue Ford Gran Torino and making sure both were secured, he resumed his trip.

Later that day, he pulled into a gas station in Lakeland, Georgia, to buy a package of cigarettes. The proprietor briefly wondered why a uniformed policeman was in the back seat of the car, but when Campbell gave no indication that something was wrong, the man promptly forgot the matter. Later, when details of the kidnapping were televised, he notified the authorities and gave them a description of Knowles' new vehicle.

The following day, November 17, two Georgia sheriff's deputies spotted the blue Ford traveling along Highway 42. Roadblocks went up everywhere, but Knowles evaded them until 1:10 that afternoon when he encountered a police blockade near Stockbridge, Georgia. Instead of surrendering, he stepped on the gas and crashed through it. The impact sent the car careening into a tree. Bloody and battered but still mobile, Knowles jumped out and ran into the Henry County woods, firing a snub-nosed revolver to keep the police at bay.

Meyer's vehicle after Knowles crashed through the roadblock.
(*Author's Collection*)

Inside the smashed-up car, Georgia police officers found Campbell's hat and empty gun belt. There was no blood on the back seat to suggest that the hostages had met with foul play there, so hope persisted that they might be found alive.

Orders went out to take Knowles alive so that the fate of the missing men could be determined. For several hours, the police searched the woods of Henry County using tracking dogs and helicopters. Finally, Knowles emerged from a clearing at the woodland's edge and was spotted by David Clark, a local resident and Vietnam War veteran.

David Clark (*Author's Collection*)

Seeing the bleeding, exhausted man step into view, Clark grabbed his hunting shotgun and approached. Knowles, who had run out of ammunition and wrapped a scarf around his injured head to staunch the bleeding, simply gazed at him and said, "Please help me."

The bespectacled young man escorted him to a neighbor's house where the police were called. When squad cars showed up and officers took Knowles into custody, Clark admonished them gently.

"Don't hurt him."

Because their prisoner was already hurt – his head was bloody and a gunshot wound to his leg left him limping – the police took him to the office of Dr. Joseph A. Blissit for a quick examination. When the doctor assured them that the injuries were minor, Knowles was delivered to the Henry County Jail.

******

Word of the capture traveled fast. When Knowles spotted the crowd of reporters around the jail, he laughed in delight. Those present later likened his face to that of a grinning, satisfied jackal. He loved the way they closed in on him like he was a celebrity, shouting questions and taking his picture. He had never felt so important in his life.

Determined to prolong the experience and hold the upper hand, Knowles refused to tell his captors whether the hostages were dead or alive. He did toy with them, saying that "one word would reveal where the men were," but kept the word to himself.

"The guy's not having anything to say. He holds all the cards in that respect," one official told the press. "His attorney is supposed to be driving up from Miami now."

25

A widespread search was conducted, with off-duty officers, game and fish rangers, and citizen volunteers joining in. Night temperatures were frigid, and if Meyer and Campbell were not found soon, they risked death by exposure. The authorities even arranged to have Sandy Fawkes come in, hoping that she could get some information out of their prisoner, but that plan was abandoned when they learned that she had offered an exclusive to the *Atlanta Constitution*.

The fate of the two missing men remained a mystery until November 21, when deer hunters in Pulaski County made a gruesome discovery inside a pine thicket. Meyer and Campbell had been handcuffed to a tree and shot in the head execution-style. Their bodies were cold, indicating that they had been dead for days.

When informed that the search was over, Knowles beamed. Then he told his keepers what the magic word had been: Pabst. There was a Pabst brewery near where the men were found. Pleased with himself, he laughed again.

Famous at Last

Sheldon Yavitz arrived from Florida. During his first meeting with Knowles, he noticed that his client, while buoyed by a sense of accomplishment, was unnerved at the prospect of being put to death for his crimes.

"I don't want to be electrocuted," Knowles insisted. "I don't want them to fry me. That's a bad way to die."

Yavitz indulged him, personally believing that nothing would stand between Knowles and Death Row. "Well, how about if they hung you? That be all right?"

"No, I don't want to be hung either."

"Maybe a firing squad. You could have a cigarette and a blindfold. That more your style?"

Knowles seemed intrigued by the idea. "No. Well, I don't know."

"How about poison?"

"Sure. I'd take poison. But I want you to do what it takes to keep me alive."

For someone who didn't want to be executed, Knowles certainly tempted fate. When Douglas County Sheriff Earl D. Lee, who later described him as "intelligent and mean as hell," asked him how many people he had killed, Knowles just smiled and traced a figure 18 on his left palm. "Where did you kill them?"

Knowles wrote down the following on a piece of scrap paper: *Texas, Florida, Georgia, Ohio, Virginia, Connecticut, Mississippi.*

To others he gave different answers, claiming 35 murders at one point. But investigators would only ever be able to link him to the 18 he admitted to Sheriff Lee.

When photos of him were published in newspapers all over North America, Knowles' good looks earned him a new nickname: "the Casanova killer." His easy laugh, quick smile, and devil-may-care demeanor alternately fascinated and repelled people. His comments to the media were flippant, self-obsessed, and thoroughly typical of someone who was reveling in the attention.

At one point he mentioned the tapes that he had given to his attorney, saying that the contents would make him famous. Federal Judge Wilbur Owens ordered Sheldon Yavitz to hand them over but the lawyer refused, citing attorney-client privilege. They were in his personal safe, but he would not divulge its location or combination to U.S. marshals. Nor would his wife, Patsy, so Judge Owens jailed them both on contempt charges.

Yavitz finally gave in, primarily to get his wife released, and surrendered two packages containing tapes and documents. The latter included Knowles' will, which left everything to his parents and directed Yavitz "to make my life story, record, and history known to the world for the good of society." He suggested "books, movies, and television" as ideal mediums for getting his story to the masses.

Judge Owens freed Patsy and ordered Yavitz to appear in court later to show why he should not be held in criminal contempt for refusing to divulge the tapes in the first place. Unable to post the $15,000 bond, Yavitz remained in jail along with his client.

Yavitz's mentor, famed defense attorney Ellis Rubin, arrived from Miami to represent his former protégé. He petitioned to have the subpoena for the contempt hearing quashed, citing the Fourth Amendment, which guaranteed the inviolability of attorney-client privilege. Judge Owens denied the petitions instantly.

Knowles was having a much better time than his attorney. When he was taken to the Baldwin County courthouse in Milledgeville to be arraigned for the murders of Carswell and Amanda Carr, he was thrilled by his reception. People lined the streets outside the courthouse, and those especially eager to catch a glimpse of him climbed onto roofs or hung off balconies. Nothing spoiled his good mood, even the hostile presence of Carr family relatives and friends in the courtroom. Manacled and wearing a bright orange jumpsuit, he smiled at everyone as Charles Marchman, a local attorney appointed to his defense team, addressed the judge.

Georgia Governor Jimmy Carter appointed State Attorney General Arthur Bolton to prosecute Knowles for the numerous killings he had committed in Georgia. Florida also wanted him for the murders of Marjorie Howie (whose color television had been retrieved from Jackie Knight's home by federal agents) and Alice Curtis, his elderly first victim. Although he never named Alabama as one of his hunting grounds, state authorities there planned to question him about the torture murder of Ben Sherrod, a Miami native whose knife-slashed body had been found in a Brewton motel room on October 22.

With so many murder charges both laid and pending, the execution of Paul John Knowles appeared to be a certainty. It was only a question of when.

End of the Road

On December 4, Knowles was secretly transferred to the Douglas County jail in Douglasville because the facility was considered more equipped to contain a veteran escapee. Local residents later expressed shock that the now-infamous Casanova Killer had been a guest of the city lockup. An attorney with offices less than 20 yards from the building said he had had no idea. An attractive young woman at an office supply store on the next block shuddered, "I would have been scared out of my wits if I'd known he was back there."

Knowles bided his time, answering questions with a cocky smile or maddeningly cryptic response. Then, in mid-December, he agreed to show Sheriff Lee where he had disposed of Trooper Campbell's service revolver. It is unclear whether Knowles was offered an incentive to cooperate, or if he was simply toying with the police. The gun was an important piece of evidence as he'd allegedly used it to murder the trooper and James Meyer, so his keepers were willing to indulge him.

On December 18, Sheriff Lee and Georgia Bureau of Investigation agent Ron Angel put Knowles in a car for transport to Henry County where he had assured them that they would find the weapon. Lee drove while Angel sat up front beside him and Knowles reclined in the back, manacles securing his wrists and ankles.

Ron Angel *(Author's Collection)*

The vehicle was on US 20 near Lee Road when Sheriff Lee noticed that Knowles had lit a cigarette. Slowing down the car, he asked the prisoner to hand it over. Instead of complying, Knowles put out the cigarette and lunged, one of his wrists free while the handcuffs dangled from the other. He leaned over the seat and grabbed the sheriff's gun, which went off through the holster.

While Lee fought to control the careening car and push his attacker back, Ron Angel drew his own weapon and shot the prisoner three times. One bullet entered Knowles' chest, hit a bone, and exited out his right side. The second hit him under the right arm, and the third lodged in his brain.

"I'm sure he died instantly," the coroner said afterward. "Either the head or chest wound would have done it at that close range."

The car skidded off the highway, went down a small embankment, and stopped against a barbed-wire fence post. After confirming that Knowles was beyond medical aid, Lee radioed the news to headquarters. A pathologist arrived and pronounced the prisoner dead at the scene.

The mystery of how Knowles had undone his handcuffs was soon solved. A broken piece of paperclip was wedged in the right cuff's lock. If he had succeeded in grabbing Lee's gun, another double execution would almost certainly have followed.

James Campbell, brother of the murdered trooper, was thrilled by the news. "I'm just tickled to death that he died. I was afraid he could go into court, get declared insane, and go into a mental hospital. So I'm glad that it happened this way."

The personal effects taken from his jail cell included a photograph of an electric chair that he had ripped out of a magazine and a letter to Angela Covic in which he likened himself to Bonnie and Clyde, John Dillinger, and other outlaws who had died in a hail of bullets.

"When this is over," he wrote, "I will be more famous (or even more so)."

Scrawled on the cell wall in fading pencil was: *Paul John Knowles, December 4, 1974, til?*

Knowles' corpse was taken to the Whitely and Tidwell funeral home. Owner Steve Tidwell was instantly besieged with requests to see the bullet-riddled remains. One teenaged girl pleaded, "I've never seen a mass murderer before." Tidwell refused all of them and breathed a sigh of relief when he obtained the clearance to place the body in a wooden casket and convey it to the Atlanta airport. From there it was flown to Knowles' father in Jacksonville for burial.

******

Given his history of escape attempts, the inquest jury believed that Knowles had conned his keepers into taking him out of the jail so that he could break loose. His Florida attorneys thought otherwise.

"The least they could have done is wait until he was convicted to execute him," Ellis Rubin declared.

Sheldon Yavitz agreed. "I can't believe he attempted to escape. He didn't want to die. Where would he go with chains on?"

Both men refused to attend the inquest, saying that the result would be "a foregone conclusion." They insisted that their client had been set up for execution, and Charles Marchman, the dead killer's Georgia attorney, seemed to agree. He claimed to have a letter from Knowles' former cellmate, who swore that Knowles believed he would be killed before trial.

The letter was probably genuine, as Knowles made the same prediction to a lot of people. He had really appeared to believe that his deeds made him the Jesse James or John Dillinger of his generation, and that, like them, he would never live to face justice.

After the inquest jury absolved them of wrongdoing in connection with Knowles' death, Sheriff Lee and Agent Ron Angel received near-universal acclaim for taking out one of the country's worst serial killers to date. Sheila McGuire, the sheriff's secretary, told reporters that the office phone was ringing off the hook, with most of the callers wanting to congratulate her boss. Even if the killing had been pre-planned, some said, it was nothing less than such a monster deserved.

******

When Angela Covic got the news about her former lover's death, she jumped in a car and drove across the country, intending to see Knowles' parents and in her words, "try to see that he gets a decent funeral." Reporters interviewed her during a stopover in Atlanta.

"Paul was deeply religious," she claimed. "He believed deeply in life after death... He was very spiritual." Although her rejection of him the previous summer appeared to have played a contributing role in his rampage, she said, "I loved him. If he had escaped this time, I would have gone with him."

Knowles was buried in Jacksonville, Florida, with only his family and Angela in attendance. The Baptist minister who conducted the funeral service expressed popular sentiment when he refused to pray that the dead killer's soul would rest in peace.

Aftermath

Paul John Knowles was dead, but the families of his victims continued to suffer. Jack Anderson, the father of Lillian and Mylette, sued Knowles' estate for damages in excess of $2,500. He stated in his complaint that he and his wife, Elizabeth, had undergone and would continue to undergo severe mental pain and suffering.[25]

Anderson died in 1994. According to his wife, he was never able to accept that his daughters were dead, and the failure to recover their bodies added to the illusion that they were not dead. The family never moved and their phone number remained unchanged for years because as Elizabeth put it, he "thought the babies were coming home."

Interviewed in 1998, Elizabeth confirmed that the years after Lillian and Mylette's disappearance were "horrible." She admitted to having spells in which she retreated within herself and refused to come out. When her husband died, she bought "memorial" headstones for her daughters and erected them in the family cemetery plot.

"My heart says they're in heaven. They're with Daddy now," she said. "But I'd like to have bodies so I could really say goodbye."[26]

******

In April 1976, the skeletal remains of a young woman were found in a patch of woods off Highway 96 in Peach County, Georgia. Because they would not be identified, the bones were sent to the Georgia Bureau of Investigation Crime Laboratory in Atlanta, where they remained unclaimed for 37 years.

Then, in January 2011, the mother and sister of Ima Jean Sanders, who had run away from Warner Robins in August 1974, submitted samples of their DNA to the Austin County, Texas, Sheriff's Office. They had never stopped wondering what had happened to her, and while they hoped that she had made a new life for herself elsewhere, they also needed to know if the worst had come to pass.

The Sheriff's Office sent the samples to the Office to the University of North Texas Center for Human Identification (UNTCHI), where they were in turn uploaded into the Relatives of Missing Persons index of the Combined DNA Index System (CODIS), a database containing DNA of convicted criminals, missing persons, and unidentified bodies.

A result was soon found. The genetic data from Ima Jean's mother and sister matched the DNA from the Peach County remains, which the GBI had entered into CODIS. Aware that Paul John Knowles had been at work in the area around the time Ima Jean vanished, investigators spoke with current and retired members of all agencies involved in the original investigations of Knowles' crimes. When they asked about the infamous audiotape diary that had been

---

[25] *Boca Raton News*, April 18, 1975
[26] "Their Families Are Still Healing" 11/23/98 | Jacksonville.com. Accessed May 22, 2015.

surrendered to Judge Owens, court officials advised that the only copies of the tapes and their transcripts had been destroyed years ago, when the federal courthouse in Macon was flooded.

A search of the GBI archives, however, yielded a letter written in 1975 by the U.S. Attorney. It summarized Knowles' taped confession of his Georgia murders. One passage read:

"Sometime in August 1974, Knowles picked up a white, female hitchhiker named Alma who represented her age as 13 or 14 but who appeared to be in her late teens. He carried this girl to a wooded area some distance from Macon, possibly west. He raped her and then strangled her and left her body in woods between trees. Approximately two weeks later, he returned to the location and found that the body had been moved eight or ten feet away apparently by animals. The body was greatly deteriorated and barely identifiable as a human being. Knowles found her jawbone and buried it in the area."

Consistent with Knowles' claim, the jaw bone was missing from Sanders' skeleton.

Captain Chris Rooks of the Warner Robins Police Department flew to Texas to deliver the news to Ima Jean's relatives personally. When she received her daughter's ashes from the state of Georgia, the former Betty Sanders (now Wisecup) fought to control her emotions.

"After 38 years of waiting to know, you feel like the walls closed in. I carried her home from the hospital, and I get to carry her home today."

*****

As a serial killer, Paul John Knowles is difficult to categorize. He had no real victim profile: men, women, children, and seniors all died during his four months in action. He sexually assaulted some of his victims but left others untouched. Although he claimed that he killed the Anderson girls to prevent them from identifying him to their parents and the police, Knowles left Beverly Mabee, Barbara Tucker, and Barbara's six-year-old son unharmed. Perhaps he himself had no idea what type of victim he would kill next, or how.

In several respects, Knowles matches the classic profile of a thrill killer. For him, outsmarting the police was a form of amusement, and he loved the media attention that followed his capture. He kept detailed records of his killings, or "successes", as he called them, by tearing out newspaper pages and reliving everything in his audiotaped diaries. Although he doesn't appear to have enjoyed killing in the classic sense, murder was his ticket into the spotlight, giving him the fame that he craved.

Author Harold Schechter dismissed him as a "nihilistic lowlife who degenerated from a petty criminal into a homicidal drifter, randomly killing anyone unlucky enough to get in his way." Sandy Fawkes, herself a longtime inmate of dehumanizing public institutions, commented, "Paul John Knowles was as much a victim as any of the eighteen people he killed... May his poor, demented soul rest in peace." Knowles himself would probably have preferred Sheldon Yavitz's assessment of him as "the most heinous killer in history."

The Cross Country Killer
Tommy Lynn Sell

Some serial killers seem to have such ideal lives that it's almost impossible to understand the motivation for their crimes. Then there are killers who had such rough childhoods that it's easy to see why they turned out the way they did. Killers like Tommy Lynn Sells.

Tommy was born to Nina and William Sells on June 28, 1964, in Oakland, California, along with a twin sister, Tammy Jean. The twins had two older siblings, Timothy Lee and Terry Joe, and they were soon joined by another set of twins, both boys, and later by a brother – Jerry Kevin, Jimmy Keith, and Randy Gene respectively.

Although William was listed as the father on the birth certificates, Tommy would later swear that the biological father of all the children was a man named Joe Lovins. William had regular employment, with benefits, but when he fell into serious financial trouble, he turned to Joe Lovins to help. Tommy claimed that Lovins took advantage of William's debt to force him to claim the kids as his. Nina never denied the claim.

Joe Lovins is the man who gave Tommy Sells the words that were his motto during his decades of killing: "Dead men tell no tales."

The Early Years

William Sells gave Tommy his surname, but not much else. Shortly after Randy Gene was born, he abandoned Nina and the children and was never heard from again.

The rest of the family moved to Missouri, and not long after, Tammy Jean – Tommy's twin sister – developed a high fever. Nina took her daughter to the hospital shortly after six AM. The doctors quickly diagnosed her with pneumonia. She was immediately admitted and placed in an isolation tent for treatment.

Nina stayed by her daughter's side until six thirty that evening, when Tammy Jean succumbed to the illness. Nina demanded an autopsy, not believing it was pneumonia, and she was proved correct: Little Tammy Jean had contracted spinal meningitis. Tommy later commemorated the death of his twin sister with a tattoo on his upper left arm. It was a tombstone with her name.

Tommy stayed with his mother's aunt while the rest of the family attended the funeral. As the service started, Nina received an urgent message that Tommy had developed a high fever, too. He was taken to the same hospital as his sister, and the same doctor gave the same diagnosis. Not trusting the hospital and fearing that her son would also die, Nina took Tommy to another hospital ninety miles away. Halfway there, Tommy sat up as if nothing was wrong; his fever had broken. Regardless, he spent five days in the hospital before he was released.

Soon after he recovered, his mother decided to rent a house from her aunt. When she checked out the place with her son in tow, the aunt offered to keep Tommy until the rest of the family was settled into their new home. For two and a half years, Tommy stayed with his Aunt Bonnie. He would later say they were the best two and a half years of his childhood.

Tommy received all the attention he needed from his aunt's two daughters, twelve-year-old Sandy and eight-year-old Kathie. Each day they went to school, he would walk out to meet them as they came home. The three of them would play until it was dinnertime, eat as quickly as they could, and then play some more until it was bedtime.

Bonnie and her girls loved Tommy so much she decided to offer to adopt him to make it a legally binding and permanent solution. Nina didn't agree. She yanked her son out of the only home he had felt safe in and brought him back to hers. Up until that point, she had acted as if he didn't exist.

Bonnie repeatedly tried to visit Tommy, but Nina refused to let her see him. Bonnie decided not to hire a lawyer to pursue the matter further – a decision she would later regret.

At seven, Tommy started abusing alcohol, drinking bourbon he found under his grandfather's truck seat. His attendance at school became sporadic. Tommy felt school was too much of a challenge, and so he did whatever he could to avoid it.

When he was eight, Tommy met a man from Frisbee, Missouri. The man started a systematic seduction of Tommy Lynn Sells. He took Tommy to Kennett, where he taught him to shoot pool and bought him gifts. The visits to the man's house lasted only a few days at a time at first. Then they steadily became longer and longer. Tommy would throw a fit each time Nina insisted he return home, and he wouldn't stop begging to go back. She gave in, and eventually, Tommy started living with the man full-time.

The man provided Tommy with an allowance. He loved that he had money to spend each day, but the money always came with a price; that price was sexual favors. The man sexually abused Tommy for years. After the first time, Tommy curled up in a ball and cried. He wanted to tell someone, but he didn't know who to tell. When the man was questioned in 2000, he denied the allegations.

At the age of ten, Tommy started smoking marijuana. Lovins, his biological father, died when Tommy was just eleven. He attended the funeral, and when he tried to tell his biological father he missed him, his grandmother told him to be quiet and sit down. They would have none of that.

At the age of thirteen, Tommy was staying at his grandmother's home overnight. She was asleep when she felt a movement in her bed. Tommy was naked and slipping beneath the covers with her. She told him to get out, and Tommy did as he was told. He never tried to climb into her bed again.

Later on, Tommy walked from his grandmother's house to his family's trailer to see his mother and brother. When he pulled on the knob, it was locked. When he knocked, no one responded. He looked inside the window and saw there was nothing inside. They had left without him.

Just a few days after he learned that his mother had left without him, he pistol-whipped a woman who angered him.

Tommy hit the road to live his life how he wanted when he was just fourteen years old. He had vivid memories of the places he'd visited, such as the Grand Canyon, Vegas, and Niagara Falls.

However, his memory of his first murder was vague. He wasn't sure who the victim was or what state the killing occurred in. He did recall that the first life he took was in self-defense, in Mississippi, but that was never proven.

Wherever it started, his murder spree would last for decades.

The Murder Spree Begins

On July 5, 1979, just outside Port Gibson, Mississippi, Kathleen Cade phoned her husband and arranged for him to meet her at their son's tee-ball game at 5:30 that evening. She loaded her two sons, Richard and John Jr., into the car and left their home.

The game went late, and Kathleen fell asleep in an easy chair in the living room when the family returned home. When she woke after midnight, Richard had fallen asleep in his own bed, and John and John Jr. were watching television in the master bedroom. Kathleen walked down the hall to her room and snuggled into bed.

Sometime during the wee hours of the morning, a young man put a stool from the patio beneath a window at the front of their house. He quietly removed the screen, climbed through the open window, and lowered himself down to the floor without making a sound. In his possession was a .32-caliber gun.

He hid, listening to be sure the residents were asleep. A little while later, he moved into the kitchen. He got a gallon jug of milk from the refrigerator and drank from it as he moved around the family home. He set the milk down on the floor in the den.

Kathleen heard rustling and some scuffling noises, but she couldn't quite wake up. She heard something that sounded like popping popcorn or the sound of a car backfiring, and then her husband shouted. She came fully awake, and the first thing she saw was her digital clock on her nightstand. It read 3:01 AM. Then she saw her husband, who turned on the light and told her he was bleeding.

He stumbled into the bathroom, where his terrified wife and son watched him as he tried to wash his hands in the sink. Then he toppled backward, dead.

Investigators were flabbergasted. Nothing was missing from the home, they couldn't find any fingerprints, and Kathleen passed a polygraph test and was cleared. They found no reasonable explanation as to why someone would kill 39-year-old John Cade, who was the chairman of the church board and didn't appear to have any enemies.

***

In Oakland, California, in 1980, Tommy killed a man with an ice pick. He didn't stick around to be sure his opponent was dead, but he got picked up by the police anyway. When he was asked by one Lieutenant Pope if he'd killed the man, Tommy said he sure should have, because he'd stabbed him so many times.

He himself had been seriously injured during the fight. The ice pick had narrowly missed his spine, and he had bleeding in his kidneys. While he was lying in a hospital bed, a nurse came in and lifted the sheet to insert a catheter. Tommy wasn't having it, and a fight ensued. Against medical advice, he left the hospital and hitchhiked to St. Louis, where his mother was living. It took forty-nine hours for him to reach her home. She let him in and nursed him back to health.

***

In the early 80s, he lived in Little Rock, Arkansas, where he spent some time at a youth home behind McClellan High School. He and his girlfriend then rented an apartment at 6 Portsmouth Drive, but the relationship didn't last. Tommy had a string of women who would come and go, so many that his mother took to calling him her 'little whore'.

In May of 1981, Nina and her remaining boys were living in Arkansas too. While she was taking a shower in the morning before she went to work, she heard the bathroom door open. The shower curtain pulled back, and Tommy joined her in the shower stall. Nina told him to get out. She kicked his shins, hit his shoulders with her fists, and finally convinced him to leave. He put on his clothes and fled the house.

He was admitted to the Community Mental Health Clinic in Jonesboro for the attempted sexual assault of his mother. He attended his first appointment even though he was confused about why he was there. He didn't know why he'd attacked his mother.

It became obvious to the counselor that he was a volatile young man, and as they progressed in the sessions, it also became evident that Tommy had had a troubled childhood. He felt unloved and unwanted. He believed himself to be the cause of all the problems in the household, and he was unhappy about his current life. He wanted to hurt someone else in order to relieve his pain.

During the diagnosis process, it was revealed that he was involved in cannabis and alcohol abuse, and that he suffered from aggression, conduct disorder, and under-socialization. He was advised to attend regular therapy sessions to help him explore his anger and his emotions. He attended five of those sessions, and then on June 18, he called and canceled the sixth appointment. He never returned.

***

March 27, 1982, Tommy was arrested in Little Rock for public intoxication after a disturbance on Geyer Spring Road. At the time, he worked at the Kinney Shoe Store on that same street.

Later that year he became the father of a boy with Cindy Hanna. Cindy had been his first love, but her father strongly disapproved of Tommy. Considering that Tommy had robbed the church the family attended, it would be hard to blame him.

He later confessed to committing two different murders in the area during this time. One incident has been confirmed, although it had a slightly different outcome than what Tommy believed and confessed to.

Tommy snuck up to a home in a wooded area just south of the Pulaski-Saline county line at 14715 Chicot Road. He hadn't planned on hurting anyone; he just wanted to break in and steal what he could find. Unfortunately, Hal Akins was home when Tommy broke in. When he was caught in the act, Tommy ran from the scene, and Hal followed him. Without warning, Tommy turned and shot Hal. Hal fell to the ground and held his breath, pretending he was dead, and it worked. Tommy believed he'd killed the man and left.
Tommy claimed that the second, unconfirmed, murder took place when he and an accomplice kidnapped a woman seven miles southwest of Little Rock. They took her down a dirt road to a hundred-foot bluff that overlooked an old quarry. They tormented her, raped her, and killed her. Then they threw her into the water-filled quarry.

***

In 1983, Sells was pretty stationary. He lived near St. Louis, Missouri, in Breckenridge Hills, and received three traffic tickets in the area that year.

Colleen and Thomas Gill lived with their two children in the West End of St. Louis. They were the owners of Colette & Thomas on Hair, Ltd., a beauty salon in Des Peres. They had bought a fixer-up home at Washington Terrace in January of 1983.

On July 31, Thomas Gill was pulling into the driveway when he saw a man matching Sells' description leaving the home. When Gill went inside, he discovered the bloody bodies of his wife and four-year-old daughter. He ran upstairs to check on his one-year-old son, Sean, who was unharmed and still sleeping peacefully in his crib.

At first, Thomas believed it to be a robbery gone wrong. The neighborhood had been plagued with break-ins, but his wife was still wearing her diamond ring. For their part, the police were suspicious of Thomas, who'd purchased a $600,000 life insurance policy on Colleen three weeks prior to her murder. However, no evidence of his guilt was ever found, so Thomas Gill was never arrested.

On May 8, 1984, Sells was arrested by the Scott County Sheriff's Department in Benton, Missouri, on charges of stealing a Ford Mustang. He pled guilty to the crime and was sentenced to two years in the state penitentiary by a judge who happened to be the father of one of Sell's grade school classmates. While he served his sentence, his daughter was born to Nicole Snow.

He entered Jefferson City Correctional Center on September 18, 1984. The convicts referred to the place as 'God's bloodiest forty acres on earth'. Minor infractions landed him at Algoa Correctional Center, then Booneville, and then back to Algoa. From Algoa, he was paroled on February 18, 1985.

In July of that year, he stole another vehicle and drove to Rolla, Missouri, where he abandoned it at a doughnut shop. On July 19, he checked into the New Horizons Rehabilitation Center in Vichy, Missouri, fifteen miles north of where he'd left the vehicle. Three days later, his mother told the police where he was, and an officer interviewed him about the car theft.

Worried he would have to go back to prison, he fled the rehab center. Just days later, a woman and her five-year-old boy were killed when Tommy flew into a violent rage.

Killings without Discrimination

July 26, 1985 was a Friday, and Rory Cordt was going to be turning five in eight days. He was over the moon excited about going to kindergarten in the fall, but he was even more excited because he was going to the fair with his mother, Ena, that day. Ena was a small, pretty woman with dark hair and dark eyes.

Life can get lonely for a divorced woman in a small town. After years as a janitor at Skaggs Hospital in Branson, Ena now worked at a car wash in Forsyth throughout the day and cared for her son in the evenings. At the county fair, she flirted with a man by the Ferris wheel. She probably thought it was harmless, but the man would turn out to be the last person she saw on earth.

Ena's yard was littered with toys that night. Inside, the rooms were clean but a little disorganized. When Sells arrived, Rory was in bed. According to Sells, the visit was pleasant enough. Until, that is, he went to the bathroom and returned to find Ena looking through his bag.

Whether it was fear that she might find and steal his cocaine, or just anger about her rummaging through his things, no one will ever really know. After all, serial killers are notorious for lying. However, the story of Ena's death is not a fabrication.

When Tommy came out of the bathroom, he spotted her bent over his bag. He immediately flew into a blind rage, grabbed Rory's baseball bat from the hall, and lifted it high in the air. He beat Ena viciously over the head, on the arms she raised to defend herself, across her back, and on her head again. She screamed, begged, and prayed for someone to hear, but no one did. Not anyone who could help her, anyway.

Little Rory stood in the doorway, watching Tommy beat his mother to death. Not satisfied with beating her with the bat, he grabbed one of her kitchen knives and slit her throat, ending it once and for all for Ena Cordt. And because Joe Lovins had told Tommy Sells that no witnesses could ever be left alive, he grabbed little Rory and dragged him into the living room, beating him over the head with the baseball bat the entire time. He then slit Rory's throat just like he'd slit Ena's, and then he proceeded to wipe away all the fingerprints and evidence left behind.

Once he was done cleaning up after his rampage, he gathered his belongings and took Rory's bat with him. He forced his way out through a rarely used door and fled into the night. Carnies tend to disappear on a whim, so his absence from the fair he'd been working at that night didn't raise suspicions.

Ena and Rory's bodies lay cold in their home for three days before someone found them. On July 30, 1985, at seven in the evening, Ena's parents made the gruesome discovery of their daughter and grandson. Her red car had been parked out front all this time, but when they knocked, no one answered. They pushed the door open, and the smell of the decaying bodies hit them immediately.

The day Rory should have been celebrating his fifth birthday, he was buried in the ground beside his mother at Snapp's Cemetery in Taney County. Ena's other child, eight-year-old Peggy, was still alive. She'd been spending her summer vacation visiting with her father.

Law enforcement had no motive, no suspects, and no solution for the double homicide. Tommy Sells had gotten away with it, so far.

***

It became obvious that Sells' stint in rehab was not a success. On September 4, 1985, on drugs and drunk, he was driving down the road with two underage girls in his vehicle. He lost control of it, flipped it, and rolled it three times. All three occupants walked away with only minor injuries, but Sells was arrested for driving under the influence and charges related to the girls. Thirty days later, the court dropped all charges for the girls and sentenced him to time served.

However, on October 15, his parole was revoked, and he returned to Missouri State Penitentiary. On October 29, he went back to Boonville Correctional Center. His violations in prison were infrequent and minor – self-mutilation and making a disturbance. He was released on May 16, 1986, with his full sentence served.

After leaving prison, he worked for Atlas Towing in St. Louis for a short time. He hauled vehicles and made emergency roadside repairs. While so employed, he met and married a woman named Sandy, who has since died of breast cancer.

One night he was repairing a vehicle around five minutes from the Arch off-Broadway in downtown St. Louis. Without provocation, Sells claimed, the owner kicked him. Sells pulled out his gun and shot the man, leaving him for dead. Before he could get out of the area, he was arrested in Pagedale Township for stealing the light bar from a tow truck. But the charges were dropped, and he continued to cross the country nomadically.

***

Sells wandered south until he landed at Aransas Pass, Texas, a tiny fishing town separated from the Gulf of Mexico by Mustang Island. There, he found a job with Gulf Team Shrimp. Their boats went out to sea for thirty days at a time. On one of these trips, Sells overdosed on heroin. He turned blue and passed out before he was able to inject all the heroin. He was found with the needle still stuck in his arm.

When the rig man found him, his breathing was labored. Since the boat was two and a half days out, Sells' survival was questionable. The captain called the Coast Guard but Sells regained consciousness before they arrived.

After the bad experience at sea, he never went back. Instead, he wandered across the nation, going wherever he wanted. There were violent encounters along this journey. Sells may be the one who murdered nineteen-year-old Michelle Xavier and twenty-year-old Jennifer Duey in Fremont, California in 1986. Their bodies were found off Mill Creek Road. One had been shot in the head while the other had had her throat slit.

***

In April of 1987, Sells hopped onto a freight train and rode as far north as possible. He got off in Lockport, New York, close to Niagara Falls.

On May Day, Susan Korcz was at a local bar fighting with her boyfriend, Michael Mandell. She left the bar angry, heading in a direction that wouldn't take her home. She was never seen again after that and was listed as a missing person.

Leads were followed up and suspects were questioned without result. Susan didn't show up or call the hair salon where she worked, and there wasn't any activity on her credit cards or her bank account. She never contacted her family. Within weeks, she was presumed dead. The police conducted a search of the waterways and canal, but they never found her body.

In the center of the town is the Niagara escarpment. Some of the hillsides off this escarpment take a fifty-to-sixty-foot drop. Near there is a canal with locks that gives the town its name. More than seven years after Susan disappeared, a worker was sent up onto the hill to clear off some debris. He saw what he first thought was a piece of trash, but when he picked it up, he realized it was a human skull.

Susan's body was finally found eight hundred feet from the canal near a railroad trestle. She'd been buried in a shallow grave that had been covered with debris. Due to the advanced state of the body's decomposition, the cause of death wasn't determinable.

***

On May 3, 1987, two days after Susan disappeared and two states away, Tommy Sells woke up with blood all over his clothes.

He wandered aimlessly toward the southwest until he stopped in Humboldt County, Nevada. Humboldt County is a desolate area where the largest employers are in the mining industry. From the early 1800s on, they have mined copper, silver, molybdenum, iron, tungsten, clay, bauxite, and mercury. The countryside is spotted with hot springs and abandoned mines. To the south is the small town of Winnemucca. The population in 1987 was close to thirteen thousand.

Upon arrival, Sells landed a job for Raymond Lavoie Roofing Company. However, his expenses were greater than his paycheck. He passed a bad check on October 28, and then on the 30th he stole a bank bag and a handgun from one of his company's trucks and used Raymond Lavoie's credit card to rent a hotel room for a woman.

Twenty-year-old Stefanie Stroh was a college student at Reed College in Oregon, but she was a long-time resident of San Francisco. She'd just returned from a ten-month trip to Europe and Asia, and when she arrived in New York, she decided to fulfill her lifelong dream of hitchhiking across the United States with a friend. They traveled as far as Salt Lake City together. She called home almost daily to speak to her mother, who was tracking her trip across the country. She wasn't worried, because Stefanie had never told her that she was hitchhiking.

On October 15, Stefanie Stroh went to a payphone to call her parents. After she had described the sights she'd seen since her last call, she told them where she was and assured them it would only be a few days until she arrived home.

The following day, she was at the Motel 6 in Winnemucca. There were no rooms available, and she asked whether there might be any in Reno, farther down Route 80.

Tommy Sells later told the Texas Rangers that he found the young woman alongside the road. She looked like a knockout as he drove closer. She was five-foot-five, well-endowed, and had sun-bleached brown hair. She was wearing hippy clothing and carried an orange sleeping bag roll with a gray backpack. She stuck out her thumb as Sells drove up, presenting him with an opportunity he just couldn't resist. Coming to a stop, he pushed the passenger door open, and she ran over to his pickup truck.

She asked him where he was going, but it didn't really matter. Sells would have told her he was going anywhere she wanted. She got into the vehicle.

Stefanie was relieved she had found a ride, so when Sells told her he had some acid and asked her to drop it with him, she didn't think twice. After all, she was hitchhiking across the country. What better time to experiment with drugs?

High on LSD in the desert, Sells choked her to death. In the stolen truck he was driving were a washtub and a bag of concrete. Sells put Stefanie's feet in the tub, mixed up some concrete, and left her hanging off the tailgate of the truck overnight as the concrete hardened.

In the morning, he dragged her body and belongings to a thirty-foot wide hot spring. It wasn't a tame body of water, and anyone who stuck their feet in would regret it. He dropped her in feet first, and then he drove out of the desert.

Three days after Stefanie was killed, when she hadn't arrived home and hadn't called, her mother and stepfather called the Winnemucca Police Department and filed a missing person report. When they found out she'd been hitchhiking across the country, it was easy to assume she'd been abducted and transported across states lines, and so the FBI was put on the case in November.

Stefanie's biological father rushed to the scene with nine family members and friends. They went straight from the airport to the Chrysler dealership. Stroh purchased eight jeeps and set out to find his missing daughter. Because they had received the last call from Wells in Elko County, they began there. Word traveled that she'd been spotted in Winnemucca, so they turned their attention to Humboldt County.

Amazed by the emptiness of Nevada, they drove for days – through the desert and down Route 80 to Reno. Along the way, they put up posters and asked questions at hotels, restaurants, and everywhere else they stopped. They finally began to focus on Reno, asking low and moderately priced hotels if Stefanie had made it that far.

The fliers were posted everywhere in Winnemucca and Reno, as well as up the interstate. The Motel 6 where Stefanie had stopped and asked for a room provided the names and addresses of everyone who'd stayed there on October 16, in the hopes that someone had seen her after she'd left. They asked questions everywhere else they thought Stefanie might have stopped. Her stepfather made a television appearance pleading for information about his stepdaughter.

Finding no answers, they returned to the dealership and sold the jeeps back. Then they flew back to the West Coast.

However, law enforcement agencies were still on the case, and their task was nearly impossible. Between thirty-two thousand and thirty-six thousand vehicles traveled Route 80 every day. The desolate terrain complicated the search even further.

San Francisco offered a ten-thousand-dollar reward for information leading to Stefanie, or to the person or persons responsible for her disappearance.

The Strohs hired a psychic to aid them in their search. They were told they could find her body at the bottom of a mine or a well in eastern Nevada near a town with four syllables in the name. Battle Mountain and Winnemucca fit that description. There would be a white building and a strip mine nearby. Finally, the psychic told them that she saw Stefanie's feet in concrete.

Authorities scouted that area. They found an old roadhouse that matched the profile from the psychic, and an abandoned dry well. Mike Curti, the chief of police, called in the city's fire rescue truck to shine powerful lights down into the well. He looked down with binoculars, but the light couldn't penetrate all the way down.

Curti then called the sheriff's department, and they brought over a video camera. They lowered it down the old well and recorded images sharp enough to identify junk that had been thrown down there, but there wasn't any sign of Stefanie's body.

The family then requested an aerial search of the area. A pilot on his way to pick up a prisoner in California was willing to do the job. With the camera rolling, low and slow, he scanned the area between Lovelock and Winnemucca on the chance that Stefanie's body might have been thrown off the highway somewhere.

In November, a female resident of Winnemucca reported an incident that had taken place around the same time Stefanie had disappeared. The resident was traveling along the frontage road when she spotted a young woman matching Stefanie's description. She was scuffling with a man driving a truck alongside the highway. The resident stopped and asked if the woman needed help, but the woman never responded. The man jumped into his truck, and the woman walked westward on the highway.

A few days later, another woman said she'd seen the same event. She claimed the man had been walking along the highway and the woman had been driving the rig. The new witness had gotten the name of the truck company, making it possible for the police to track the identity of the driver. Soon, the FBI had a name from the Arkansas-based trucking company. However, the man was no longer employed at that business, and his location wasn't known.

The residents of Winnemucca couldn't stop talking about the case, even though none of them knew the girl who had disappeared. On several occasions, people had come across unidentified remains in the desert. The buzz would pick up again and, every time, Stefanie's family would come out to see if it was her. But the remains were never hers, and she was never found. Some law enforcement officials believe Sells' confession that he murdered Stefanie, but others don't.

Neither his employers nor his friends knew of his plans to leave Winnemucca, but on November 3, he was heading out of town. In a matter of days, he made it to Illinois.

More Gruesome Murders

Nothing terrible ever occurred in Ina, Illinois. The small town in the south of the state was home to a bank, gas station, store, post office, and a fire station. There were just enough trailers and houses for the 475 residents. On November 17, 1987, a deadly fear entered their hearts.

Of the four people who were at a house on the southern edge of town that evening, only Sells was left to tell the tale of what happened, and he couldn't get the story straight. He told three different versions over the years. In one, he met Keith Dardeen while he was hitchhiking, and Keith brought him home. In another, he and Keith met at a pool hall and Keith invited him home. In yet a third account, he was never invited inside; he broke down their door. In the first two versions, Sells told investigators that Keith had made homosexual advances toward him. However, Keith was not known for picking up hitchhikers, and he was very protective of his family. It's unlikely that either of the first two versions is true.

Through Sells' stories and the physical evidence, the investigators pieced together the most likely path of the events that night.

Riding the rails through Illinois, Sells jumped off a train in Ina near Route 57, a major highway that ran north to south through the entire state. To the north, it passed by Champaign-Urbana and Kankakee, and then went to Chicago. From where Sells disembarked, the highway passed south through a series of small whistle-stop towns until it ended near the Kentucky state line.

45

Like any serial killer, Sells was constantly looking for open doors of opportunity or vulnerability in his victims. The modest trailer looked perfect to him. The 'For Sale' sign beckoned to him. The Dardeens rented the property and farmed the land near the house. They owned the trailer, but it was starting to feel too small for their growing family.

Sells sat in the dark, watching the home and waiting as he drank one beer after another. When he figured it was time, he approached the home cautiously with a gun in his hand. He'd stolen the gun in Nevada. He knocked on the door. Keith opened it and asked Sells what he wanted. Sells said he was interested in purchasing the mobile home.

Keith Dardeen had not heard a vehicle pull up, and when he looked over the stranger's shoulder, he would have seen only his vehicles in the driveway. Aware of his responsibility to his pregnant wife, Eileen, and his young son, Peter, he suppressed his desire for a sale and refused to allow Sells into the home. But as he closed the door, Sells threw his body into the open gap and pulled out his gun. He pointed it directly at Keith's head.

Sells shouted obscenities and threats as Keith backed up with his hands raised above his head. A few yards away, Eileen was clutching Peter to her side in fear. At a shout from Keith, she turned to run to the bedroom with her son. Sells was quick, and he grabbed Peter from his panicking mother. He held the gun to the three-year-old's head.

According to one of Sells' stories, he asked Keith for rope, and when Keith said he didn't have any, Sells told Keith to find something with which to tie up his wife and son.
After he had fumbled through the drawers in the kitchen, Keith found a roll of duct tape. Without moving the gun away from Peter's head, Sells bound his feet, mouth, and hands with the tape. Dragging the boy with him, he ordered Eileen Dardeen to the floor. He then repeated the process with her. This would be their last chance to see one another. Sells told Eileen that if she moved, he would kill her husband.

Sells then turned to Keith and threatened to kill his wife and child if he didn't do as he was told. With the gun to his head, Keith drove his vehicle a mile away to an empty field. When the vehicle stopped, Keith knew he had to get the gun away from Sells. If he didn't, he'd be dead. If he died, there would be no one to protect his family. He made his move, but it wasn't fast enough. Sells shot him in the cheek. Keith slumped back.

Sells dragged his body from the car and threw him down onto the ground. Keith protested weakly and tried to struggle, but it was no use. Sells unzipped Dardeen's pants and pulled out his genitals, cutting them from his body. Then he shot him twice, once in the side of his head and once in the side of his face.

Engulfed in the bloodlust of that moment, Sells jumped into Keith's car and drove back to the Dardeen home. When the door opened, Eileen's eyes looked hopeful momentarily. However, when she saw who walked through the door, her hope turned into horror.

Sells unbound her feet so that he could rape her. He used scissors to cut off her clothes, and when she struggled, he threatened to kill her son if she didn't cooperate. Instantly, she was still and accepted the assault without a sound.

As she lay on the floor, Sells roamed through the trailer. Peter was crying uncontrollably and Sells couldn't take it any longer. He raised a baseball bat and bashed in the toddler's head. Eileen rushed Sells just as he raised the bat again to pummel her son, and he only grazed Peter's head.

He shoved Eileen back, and with her hands bound, she lost her balance and fell to the floor. He raised the bat and struck the toddler multiple times until he was sure the boy was dead. Sells then turned his attention back to Eileen, but when he raised the bat again, he saw something strange happening. Eileen had gone into labor. A small baby girl was born right before his eyes. He watched coldly.

Sells turned to Eileen, saw the desperation in her eyes, and picked up a knife. He sliced into her breasts, turned to the baby, and bludgeoned it to death with the baseball bat. Then, he turned to Eileen Dardeen and fractured her skull with the bat. As her final breaths were leaving her, he sexually assaulted her with the baseball bat and left it lodged inside of her.

With the Dardeens dead, Sells carried the bodies of Eileen, Peter, and the infant into the master bedroom and laid them in the bed very carefully. He removed the duct tape from their bodies, stuffed the pieces into his pockets, and cleaned up after himself. He wiped down surfaces for fingerprints, cleaned up the puddles of blood, and sanitized all areas where he had touched to remove any evidence. It was a slow and meticulous process.

When he knew he'd erased all evidence of his crime, he climbed into Keith's blood-spattered 1981 Plymouth and headed south on Highway 57.

When Keith did not show up for work on Wednesday, his supervisor called his home. Keith was a dependable employee, so missing work was very concerning. That evening, the supervisor called Keith's father, Don Dardeen. Don was just as confused as the supervisor, so he went over to the home of his ex-wife, Joeann.

His daughter, Anita Knapp, and her two sons had come over for pizza. Joeann knew an unexplained absence wasn't in character for Keith, so she called the sheriff's office, and Don drove to Ina to meet them with a house key.

What they found at the home sent waves of fear through the village of Ina. There was only one adult body in the bed, not two. The missing person was Keith Dardeen, and he instantly became a suspect. Many minds in the community leaped to the obvious conclusion. It was only natural considering that Keith was missing, and his family was dead.

The murder also reminded the residents of Ina of something that had happened just four and half years before, only ten miles up Route 57 in Mount Vernon. Nineteen-year-old Thomas Odle had murdered his parents and his three siblings. He'd quietly ambushed them as they arrived home from work and school, and many wondered if another man had erupted into a rage and done the same thing.

***

When the doorbell rang at Joeann's house, her grandsons Robbie and Eddie ran to answer it. When they opened the door, they were looking into the muzzles of guns held by four police officers. Upon hearing the news, Joeann immediately wanted to know where Keith was.

So, did the police. Officers escorted her to her bedroom and questioned her about his location. They asked her about the baby, and she insisted that there was no baby in the household. She was unaware of the brutal birth of her granddaughter.

No matter how much the pushed and accused her son, she and her family friends were adamant that Keith had done nothing. They knew it was impossible for him to have committed such a disgusting crime. They urged the police to find him, hoping he was still alive. Late the following night, hunters found Keith's body.

His vehicle was found later. It was as if the killer was taunting the community and the police. The bloodstained Plymouth was parked near the police station in Benton, about eleven miles away from the crime.

There was a basketball game at the high school that night, which usually would have meant a gaggle of teenagers making plans with each other outside afterward. Not tonight. When the game ended, all the students were kept inside the gym. They weren't allowed to leave until their parents arrived to escort them to their vehicles.

Rumors spread like wildfire through the area. There was a serial killer in southern Illinois. It had to have been a satanic ritual because of what had been done to the mother and baby. It was someone they knew and trusted. There was a killer amongst them, and it could be their neighbor.

***

In the aftermath of the murder, thirty local and state detectives were assigned to the case. They interviewed hundreds of potential witnesses, but they never found a suspect. Their clues were limited. No money had been stolen, a portable movie camera and VCR had been left in plain sight, no evidence pointed to a specific suspect, and there was no reason for this quiet family to be victims of this brutal crime. No one who had been questioned recalled anything out of the ordinary.

Their only lead was a dead family. They had a mother and father so devoted to their son that they never allowed a milestone to pass without videotaping it. They were a couple so eager for the birth of their second child that they wrapped a present for Peter's third birthday with a card that read 'Happy Birthday, big brother, from January 10th.'

Peter had received the baseball bat that birthday, even though Keith knew his son was too little for it. He believed his son would have the chance to grow into it, and he could teach Peter how to hit the ball. Keith had dreamed of the day they could play ball together.

Joeann Dardeen never gave up hope on finding the killer of her son and his family. She gathered more than three thousand signatures in her community in 1994 and sent them to the Oprah

Winfrey show. The producers weren't interested because the crime was too gruesome for television.

Other shows were reluctant to present the story when there weren't enough details to assemble a profile of the suspect. America's Most Wanted was one of them, but in 1998, they had a change of heart. Joeann Dardeen pinned her hopes on the show's remarkable success at closing cases and bringing criminals to justice. The show aired in November, but it never produced a single suspect or any credible leads.

Drifting and Killing

Knowing he had to get out of the area fast, Sells took a job with R.B. Patasnic, a Cape Girardeau, Missouri company. They wanted men to work construction on a two-lane state road in Florida. It was Road 84, also known as Alligator Alley. When it was finished, it was renamed Interstate 75. It went directly from the Atlantic Coast to the Gulf Coast through the Everglades.

As Sells was working in Florida, his legal father passed away, a fact unnoticed by Sells. Hip-deep in the murky water and holding a measuring rod, Sells stood very still as a snake swam past his legs. That was the end of his working with the construction crew. He wasn't willing to risk his life like that.

In St. Louis, he was arrested again for stealing a vehicle on January 13th.

In September of 1988, he headed north. That same month, Melissa Ann Trembley disappeared. She was eleven years old and lived in Salem, New Hampshire. She had last been spotted at a convenience store parking lot talking to a man with dark hair who was in desperate need of a shave.

They found her body face down on the railroad tracks between two trains at a Boston and Maine freight terminal in Lawrence, Massachusetts, on September 12. She'd been sexually assaulted before she was stabbed to death. Blood and footprints sixty-five feet from where her body had been found suggested she'd struggled with her attacker.

Unfortunately, a slow-moving freight train had rolled across her body, destroying much of the evidence.

***

That fall, in Salt Lake City, Utah, a woman and her three-year-old son fell under Tommy Sells' spell. He put them out on the streets by his side as they held signs that said 'Homeless and hungry. Please help.' He coached the boy to make sad faces and sad smiles, and after a few weeks, it was time for them to go on a road trip. The mother and child piled into the back of a stolen Dodge van and went to Idaho to spend the night along the Snake River in Gooding County. The mother and her son never returned from that trip. Sells confessed to killing them both and dumping their bodies in the river. He walked away with his pockets lined with the cash he'd accumulated from the passersby who had taken pity on the woman and small child.

***

Tucson drew Sells south. In mid-December, he crossed paths with a homeless man by the name of Kent Alan Lauten, a native of Phoenix who was bouncing back and forth between the two cities.

Sells sold a bag of marijuana to Kent, who promised to give Sells money later that day. When they met up again, Kent taunted Sells and refused to pay. Sells couldn't do anything about the taunts at the time because Kent's friends were around, and he was outnumbered. However, he knew where Kent slept.

Sells crept up to Kent's sleeping quarters that night and found him in the arms of another man. Sells was on top of Kent in no time with a pocketknife in his hand. The other man fled from the scene in the dark, and Kent locked eyes with Sells. Sells stabbed him multiple times, and Kent bled to death alone.

With his pocketknife and hands, Sells scratched a shallow grave in the ground and rolled the body in. He scattered a pile of dirt over it, and then piled dead leaves and other debris on top. He covered it all with a tarp and tamped it down with his feet.

Then he slunk off into the night and slept.

Two days later, a twelve-year-old boy wandered into the homeless camp to find a good spot to dig sand for his grandfather. His quickly forgot his plans when he found Kent's remains poking out from beneath the ground. Sells was in San Bernardino, California by that point.

He was arrested on Christmas Eve for assault with a deadly weapon, but the police were unable to locate the victim, so Sells was released.

He went north on Interstate 5, stopping in Berkeley next. On January 27, 1989, he got into a fight with a ticket agent at a BART train station. The police report of that incident confirms he was in the area and Sells later claimed to have killed a twenty-year-old prostitute while he was there.

According to his story, it was a drug deal gone bad. He originally thought he was bargaining with a man, and when he discovered the prostitute's gender, he killed her. Police found an unidentified body near the area where he claimed to have left her, just north of Lake Tahoe in a town called Truckee.

Sells made a trip to Colorado in March, and then continued north on Route 5 until he came to Roseburg, Oregon, a small town an hour south of Eugene. He worked for a small woodcutting business and lived at a local couple's home.

He spent his workdays chopping felled trees into firewood for his employers' roadside stand. He said that while he was in the area, he kidnapped a girl with long hair who was in her twenties, and then he raped and killed her.

On May 9th, he met a hitchhiker who was looking to go up to Washington State. When she tried to steal his drugs, he murdered her, too. He left both the bodies in the forest where he was cutting trees. Later that day, he was arrested for second-degree theft for stealing thirty dollars from the firewood stand.

He served fifteen days in the Roseburg jail, and then he was a free man again.

***

Sells had made a short stop in Berkeley before he journeyed east to Arkansas. On August 16, 1989, he was charged with theft and arrested in North Little Rock. On the 23rd, the charges were dropped, and he was free again.

He went back to Oakland for a brief time and then went to Montana for a short visit with a girlfriend in Missoula.

He returned to Oakland in time to experience the earthquake on October 17. Shortly before it happened, he got off the commuter train and went into a restroom to shoot up some heroin. He was standing outside the facilities when the tremors hit, and the lights went out. He grabbed a pole and hung on, thinking at first that his years of alcohol and drug abuse had finally caught up with. Then he noticed that the light pole was swaying back and forth and heard the sound of the roads and buildings collapsing.

He didn't wait for the aftershocks. He hurried south to Reno, where he was arrested the following night and put into a detox center.

Once again, the rehabilitation was a wasted effort. He was soon arrested in Carson City, Nevada, and put into another rehabilitation center for thirty days. In December, he overdosed on heroin and was hospitalized in Phoenix for two days.

In January of 1990, he returned to Salt Lake City, where he was arrested for possession of cocaine and for stealing a vehicle on the 7th. When the crime lab results showed the substance wasn't cocaine, he was released, and he headed off to Wyoming. His activities there earned him an extended stay in prison.

On January 12, in Rawlings, Wyoming, he struck up a conversation with a young couple. Both were around eighteen. The woman was very pregnant, and the tires on their truck were very bald. Sells offered to help them with their transportation issue.

He looked around the area until he found a 1978 Dodge pickup truck with the proper sized tires, and then he stole the truck. The owner, Bobby Daniels, bolted from his house in pursuit of the runaway vehicle, and when it drove out of sight, he returned to the house where he and his wife lived. He called the police to report the theft.

Sells took the tires off the stolen pickup truck and put them on the desperate couple's truck. Taking a duffle bag from the interior, he abandoned Bobby's truck and went in search of his own transportation.

While Bobby and his wife were describing the man wearing a green shirt and red hat they'd seen just before their truck was stolen, Tony Selzer was protecting his own pickup truck. He confronted a similarly dressed man carrying a dark duffel bag who had been climbing into the cab. Sells made a retreat, ditching the duffel bag on his way.

Police spotted the couple's truck with the new tires in no time. They told their tale and offered a third description of the truck thief.

Sells hid four blocks away from the scene of the crime, waiting for a train to come through and give him a ride out of town. An hour after the truck theft, he ran out to jump a freight car. Officer Anderson saw him before he made the getaway and arrested him for public intoxication.

Once the car theft came to light, they held him on a ten-thousand-dollar bond. Deeming him needy, the Carbon County judge appointed a public defender, John Hoke. On February 2nd, Hoke filed a motion to suspend proceedings until the accused could be examined for mental illness or deficiency. The court complied and ordered Sells to be transported to the Wyoming State Hospital.

The medical personnel had thirty days to assess and evaluate his mental condition and file a written report about any deficiency they discovered.

In his intake report, Dr. Howard Winkler described Tommy Lynn Sells as a well-nourished, well-developed twenty-five-year-old white male who looked like Charles Manson with his black beard, shoulder-length brown hair, and dirty complexion. He listed Sells' mood as flat. He described Sells' thoughts as bizarre. Sells stated that he heard the tattoos on his arms – a bird, a wolf, and a dragon – talking to him, telling him to do things. Dr. Winkler concluded that Sells did not understand that anything was wrong with him and that his outlook was poor.

On March 1, Sells asked to be put back on Thorazine, stating that he was having trouble dealing with the difficulties of life and didn't know if he could handle them. Hospital records indicated that he was a heavy user of drugs and alcohol before he was arrested. He was almost always drunk or high on something. Total withdrawal could result in psychosis, the evaluation warned.

Sells had a history of mood swings over the years. His personality was labeled as being antisocial, self-destructive, and unpredictable. Outbursts of temper came from small provocations, and he was easily frustrated and impulsive. He couldn't read or write.

One Dr. Heinbecker issued a diagnosis of depressive disorder, severe alcohol and drug dependency, and personality disorder with antisocial, borderline schizoid features. After evaluation, he was prescribed five milligrams of Cogentin and five milligrams of Haldol. The first was to control his tremors, and the second was an antipsychotic.

Sells returned to the Carbon County jail in early March. Dr. Heinbecker's official report to the judge was that the defendant had the capacity to comprehend his position, understand the nature and object of the proceedings, and conduct his defense in a rational manner. He concluded that Sells could stand trial despite being mentally ill and that he would remain competent for the foreseeable future, even in the absence of specific treatment for his mental illness.

On March 12, Sells was rushed from the jail to the emergency room. He'd been having shakes and said he felt like he was bouncing off the walls. He was diagnosed as having a severe anxiety attack.

On the 18th, an ambulance raced him to the emergency room yet again. He was shaking again, but this time it was worse. His speech was slurred, he was having spasms, and he was stuttering uncontrollably. This time, suspicion fell on his medication. They changed his prescription to twenty-five milligrams of Elavil and eighty milligrams of Inderal SR for hypertension. Later, they added one hundred milligrams of Mellaril, an antipsychotic, and twenty-five milligrams of Valium for anxiety.

In custody, Sells was a model inmate. There were no disciplinary actions taken against him. He completed a 265-hour course in barbering and worked in the leather shop as an outside trustee at the Wyoming Honor Conservation Camp. In January 1991, he was released, and then he wandered first to Colorado and then back to Florida.

***

On December 9, in Marianna, Florida, the Christmas season was being celebrated with the annual parade. Twenty-five-year-old Teresa Hall attended the parade with her daughter Tiffany, who was five at the time.

The girl was exhausted by the end of the evening, and she was almost asleep by the time they returned home. The railroad tracks were a hundred feet from their front door. Teresa prepared her daughter for bed.

Their front door was kicked in, and all dreams of Christmas were gone. Sells raged through the home, knocking everything out of his way. He lifted a table above his head and smashed it on the floor, splintering it. Then he jerked loose one of the legs and bludgeoned Teresa to death. Her daughter suffered the same fate not long after. Sells fled the home still holding the table leg in his fist.

Obviously, Teresa didn't report to her job the following day. The owner of the store she worked at tried to contact her at her home, but the phone rang unanswered all day. Concerned, Teresa's boss called her mother, who sent Angus Mitchell, Teresa's stepfather, to check on her and her daughter. When he saw the broken down door, he knew something was wrong. He entered the home and discovered the two bodies.

A few minutes later, Teresa's husband returned home. He'd been working a job in Georgia and had been gone for two days. His alibi was air-tight, and the police didn't have any other suspects or answers.

Angel Maturino Resendiz came under suspicion after his arrest by the Texas Rangers in 2000. He'd been dubbed the Railway Killer and had been linked to a string of murders that happened near railroad tracks across the south. Sells admitted that he was the one who murdered Teresa, but authorities were never sure as there was no evidence to link him to the crime.

On March 4, 1992, Sells was arrested in Charleston, South Carolina, for public intoxication. He received a thirty-day sentence. On April 2, he was arrested again on the same charges. As soon as he was let out, he left. The mountains of West Virginia embraced Sells next. Their primitive, rugged beauty fueled his next act of violence.

Going Back to Prison

At the age of twenty, Fabienne Witherspoon thought she could take care of herself. At five-foot-eight, with a solid, athletic body, she had physical prowess many women lacked. She looked tough, too: She had an attractive face, but her dark brown eyes held just enough of an edge that no one accused her of being cute. She had thick, curly brown hair that fell below her shoulders, and her uninhibited style tended to suggest a streak of wildness that lay just beneath the surface.

On May 13, she was house-sitting at 906 Grove Avenue in Charleston, West Virginia. It was an ordinary neighborhood where bad things didn't tend to happen, although she was nervous that day as she walked to the women's health clinic for a pregnancy test.

On her way back to the house, though, she felt at peace with the world. She was relieved that the test had been negative.

Then she saw a man in his mid-twenties with unkempt, matted hair and intriguing eyes. He was standing on the corner of Washington Street and Pennsylvania Ave. He held a sign that read 'Hungry, will work for food.'

He told Fabienne a tale of misery and woe in a soft voice with a hint of a southern accent. He told her his name was Tommy Sells, and that he and his wife were living under a bridge. His children were very hungry.

Fabienne felt a wave of compassion for the man, and she felt a bit of sexual attraction to him, too. She brought him to her house to find some food he could take back with him. She grabbed two trash bags and filled them both with food and clothing for him to take back. She smiled and asked if he needed anything else.

Sells told her his wife really needed some underwear, so she went back to her bedroom to find some clean ones. When she turned around, he was standing behind her with a knife from the kitchen in his hand. Sells immediately brought the knife to her throat and told her to take off her clothes.

Fabienne hesitated, but with the knife under her chin, she really had no choice. She removed her shirt and unfastened her bra, kicked off her shoes and pushed off her socks, and reached for the waistband of her pants. Then she froze.

Sells had the knife clenched between his teeth. He pushed her hands away and pulled down her pants. As soon as he began to remove his clothes, she looked away and stared at the floor. Then he smacked, shoved, and threatened her into the bathroom and down onto her knees, where he forced her to perform oral sex.

Sells then pushed her back onto the floor and spread her legs, raping her. She lay there, praying he would finish and leave.

He stopped, rose to his feet and ordered her to get into the shower. There, he raped her again. Then he pulled her from the shower and shoved her onto her knees, once more demanding she give him oral sex.

Still not sated, he jerked her over to the toilet and bent her over it. Just as he was about to sodomize her, she grabbed a ceramic duck from the back of the toilet. She grabbed it and smashed it over his head, and shards of the duck flew around the room. She kept hitting him over and over again with the remains of the figurine.

As they struggled, she was able to get the knife out of his hands. She stumbled from the bathroom to the front door, but he grabbed her and tried to manhandle her back into the bedroom. She stabbed him, and he grabbed her wrist and regained possession of the knife. He stabbed at her, but she jumped back and received only a deep slice across her skin. She also got control of the knife again.

They wrestled around the room, trading blows until he finally got her down on the floor with him on top of her. He strapped her ankles and wrists together with tape and secured the bindings with strips of sheets from the bed.

He raised a piano stool over his head and beat her bloody until the seat broke loose from the base. Then he tried to slit her throat – but this time, he panicked. The cut he made would only require a few stitches.

He grabbed a boom-box and a VCR and escaped from the home. He left behind the gifts she had stuffed into the bags.

As soon as Fabienne became conscious again, she fought her way out of the bonds. She wrapped herself up in a blanket, picked up her cordless phone, and hurried outside to call the police. Her descent down her front steps left a trail of blood and tape.

Before Fabienne left in the ambulance, she informed the investigators that the man who had assaulted her was Tommy Sells, and that he was sleeping by the river.

Sergeant Westfall and Detective H.S. Walker processed the crime scene as Detective Rollins and Lieutenant Epperhart searched the riverbank for their suspect. Sells wasn't unknown to the investigation division. He'd been observed for a few weeks holding up signs at the corner of

Clendenin and Quarrier Streets. It didn't take long for one Detective Hammons to obtain an address for Sells, and then he and Westfall went to an apartment on Bigley Avenue and questioned Sells' former roommates – Rebecca Gibson, Curtis Sizemore, and Karin Pamela Young.

When the officers started the interview, they believed they were talking to two women and one man. They were wrong. Karin Young wasn't a woman. By the end of the interview, they were aware that Karin was a transvestite whose transformation was so complete that she'd fooled two men with extensive investigative experience.

When Sells had first met Karin, he'd been deceived too. So much so, that the first time he was intimate with Gina, Karin's sister, he'd had a moment of doubt about her. He threatened to kill her if he found out she was really a man, and she'd laughed it off as a joke at the time.

Rebecca, Curtis, and Karin told the investigators that Sells had come to the apartment around five in the afternoon. He told them he'd been in a fight and was bleeding, but he wasn't going to the hospital. While he was there, he'd removed his shirt and stuffed it into a garbage bag. Westfall found the shirt and bagged it as evidence.

When they were asked if they knew where Sells had gone, Curtis told them to try a place where Sells had been living for the past week. It was Gina Young's apartment.

***

After Sells arrived at Gina's place, he called his mother to ask her how he could butterfly bandage a cut. She asked him what kind of cut and how many, and he told her around twenty-three, but some of those were superficial. His mother told him how to bandage the cuts, and then told him he had to get to a hospital. Rather than seeking medical attention, he told his girlfriend to purchase some dope and a fifth of Jim Beam.

When she came back, he told her that if he died, he wanted his body to go back to Missouri.

An hour later, Hammons and Westfall arrived at the apartment door. Gina stepped back and let the officers in. They found Sells lying on the living room floor in serious pain, with multiple stab wounds to his abdomen. His external bleeding had slowed, but his internal bleeding was profuse. His kidney and spleen had been nicked, his lung had partially collapsed, and his testicles had been sliced. The detectives called for an ambulance and rushed him to the hospital, where he received immediate trauma surgery and then spent a week in recovery.

In the beginning, it looked like the case against Sells would be cut and dried, but when the prosecutors were preparing for trial, they found a few issues. It hadn't been long since Fabienne had filed another sexual assault charge that wasn't prosecuted. To the jury, the questionable nature of that charge might cast doubt on her current claim. To make everything worse, the defense uncovered some psychological reports that reflected poorly on Fabienne. They threatened to use the newfound information in court in defense of Tommy Sells.

In light of the revelations, the prosecution wasn't confident it could find Sells guilty and put him in prison. They were ready to deal. They felt that some jail time was better than the chance of none. The two sides agreed to a plea bargain. The sexual assault charges were dropped, and on June 25, 1993, Sells was sentenced to an indeterminate term of not less than two years but not more than ten years for malicious wounding. The judge gave him credit for four hundred and two days of time served. He was placed in the Northern Correctional Facility just south of Wheeling.

***

Sells had a friend waiting for him behind bars. Gina's heterosexual brother, Billy Young, watched Sells' back from the moment he arrived to the moment he left the jail.

Sells started out as a model prisoner who did nothing wrong. He earned the designation of trustee, but he soon abused that position. Sells and another inmate, Gregory Carter, found a .357 pistol inside the prison. They planned to trade the gun for marijuana, but for safe keeping, Sells hid the weapon in the warden's office. Another trustee caught him and reported him. Charges were filed but then dropped when Sells was moved to maximum security at Mt. Olive Prison.

During this prison stint, he taught himself to read with the help of the Bible. He hadn't been able to read anything when he'd dropped out of ninth grade at the age of sixteen. He worked very hard at his self-education, pushing himself to reach his goal, and sent his first letter of his life from prison.

In 1994, he struck up a friendship with a new inmate by the name of John Price. John was a nurse who'd been working for a home health service company in Logan, West Virginia. Three of his friends were found deceased after they'd injected themselves with a narcotic drug that was ten to a hundred times more powerful than heroin. John had undoubtedly been the source of the drug, but evidence of a more active role in their deaths was pretty weak. Facing the possibility of going to prison for life for the deaths of his friends, he pled guilty to providing the drugs but denied having administered the injections.

He told Sells about his sister, Nora, who was twenty-six years old and a bit slow. She was the product of special education classes in the public school system. She received a social security income check every month and visited her brother often. John introduced her to Tommy Sells.

***

Nora Price sat on the other side of the glass with the telephone receiver pressed to her ear. It was her first visit with Tommy Sells. The cold barrier didn't provide much of a romantic ambiance, but romance blossomed anyway. Later on, they were allowed contact visits that sealed Nora's fate. Sells took advantage of her intellectual deficiency and sweet-talked her into falling in love. She was easy for him to manipulate. She'd had a rough childhood and couldn't recall anyone being nice to her like Sells was. They wrote and talked about the day he'd get out and all of the things they could do then. He conned her out of small amounts of cash while she was there, and then he moved in for the prize.

He informally proposed to her through a letter, and then came the big day. Mt. Olive's prison had an annual event where visitors were able to spend an entire day with a prisoner. On the prison lawn, on a spring day, Sells asked Nora if she would marry him.

57

While Sells was still in prison in April of 1996, they were married. From that day on, seventy-five percent of Nora's checks went to Sells. As a sign of his gratitude, he had two tattoos done with her name written on them. One was a rose on his neck, and the other was a motorcycle with a dragon on his right upper arm. She was infatuated with him.

During his time at the prison, mental health professionals diagnosed him with bipolar disorder, but his illness wasn't treated. He was released in May of 1997.

***

Within days of being released, he left West Virginia and Nora behind. On June 1, though, he called her from Michigan and told her he wanted to get back together with her. She agreed, and he returned. Together, they hitchhiked and rode trains to Tennessee. They settled down in the town of Cleveland, and Sells got a job at a car wash. On July 29, local police gave him a ticket for driving without a license.

Sells abandoned Nora again on August 18 and went west. Nora, unable to cope on her own, went back to her home state of West Virginia.

On September 5, Sells called his mother from Oregon, and then he called Nora's mother. He traveled east again, picked up Nora in West Virginia, and took her to his mother's home in Missouri. By that time, Nora was pregnant.

In October, Sells got a job as a mechanic. He managed to stay off drugs for three weeks, and the family had high hopes he would finally be able to settle down. However, neither Nora nor his job could keep him drug-free for long. He came home one night high, and in no time, there were tracks up his arms.

Nothing could keep him tied to his home, and by mid-October, he was stalking his next victim.

***

Sells admitted to the murder of Joel Kirkpatrick in private conversations, but he never confessed to the authorities, and there was no investigation into his possible involvement. The following account was obtained by interviewers who spoke to Tommy Sells, but none of it has ever been proven.

Sells stated that he traveled east from St. Louis on Interstate 64. When he arrived at Lawrenceville on October 13, 1997, it felt like it would be an uneventful evening. However, it turned out to be one of the community's most memorable nights.

Sells first met Julie Rea at a convenience store, where she treated him rudely, according to Sells. From that moment, he wanted revenge.

Anger drove him to the front door of a house he'd never been in before. He carefully broke a window, making no more noise than he had to in order to get inside. He went directly to the kitchen, where he picked up a knife. He went to the first bedroom and found ten-year-old Joel Kirkpatrick asleep.

Sells plunged the knife into Joel, who managed to scream and wake up his mother. He left the boy lying at the foot of his bed and slipped from the room and away from the approaching mother. She raced to the room yelling her son's name.

She looked through the doorway and didn't see her son at the foot of his bed, so she turned, and that's when she saw Sells. He had the hood of his sweatshirt drawn up around his face, the drawstring pulled tight to conceal his features. She ran toward him, confronting the monster who'd stabbed her son. She chased him through the glass doors and into the backyard, screaming for help.

Outside, she tripped over something in the yard, and the intruder took the opportunity to turn around and hit her in the head.

She was too dazed to move or think for a moment. When she finally raised herself up on her arms she saw the man fleeing again. He pulled the hood down and revealed his face to her under a streetlight. She came to her feet again and rushed to a neighbor's house on the other side of the street. Once inside, she called the police to report her son's abduction.

In minutes, officers arrived at the scene and found Joel Kirkpatrick in his bedroom, deceased. He had suffered multiple stab wounds. Julie was taken to the emergency room to be treated for a black eye, scratches, and abrasions on the tops of her feet, as well as inside her legs and her knees, wounds on her shoulders, internal bruising, and a laceration on her right arm that required five stitches.

While Tommy Lynn Sells never told authorities he committed the heinous crime against Joel Kirkpatrick and his mother, he admitted it in private to several people.

The Carnival and a Second Wedding

Sells was on the move again, heading for Springfield, Missouri. As he walked the streets, he spotted a young woman with brown hair and followed her home. His unfruitful stalking drove him to a fever pitch. From his vantage point in a parked van, he sought someone who was a little more vulnerable. He saw a man with three children enter an apartment. The oldest was a thirteen-year-old girl with auburn hair, freckles on her nose, and a pretty grin. Her name was Stephanie Mehaney. Sells turned his focus and fantasies on this potential victim.

Suzette Carlisle, the mother, wasn't at home. She'd been admitted to the hospital with life-threatening pneumonia. Her fiancé, Rob Martin, had taken the children to the hospital to visit her that night. Once they returned home, he played video games with them and stayed in the apartment until they were asleep. Stephanie was so tired she collapsed on her bed in her clothes.

At eleven that evening, Sells saw the man leaving by the back door. Rob locked it behind him and then left to return to Suzette's side, assuming that the rarely used front door was already locked.

He was wrong.

Sells crept silently through the dark and then slipped through the front door into the quiet home. He went from room to room, looking for his next victim. He looked in on the eight-year-old and the nine-year-old, and then he found Stephanie.

Her eyes flew open as he slapped tape across her mouth, blocking her nose and making it hard for her to breathe. He jerked her out of bed and dragged her to the front door. With her glasses left behind on her nightstand, the world was blurry for Stephanie.

She tried to free herself from Sells' grip but just ended up making him angrier. He threw her into the front seat of the van, and Stephanie immediately tried to escape by grabbing for the door. Sells struck her across the face with the back of his hand, and she quieted down. She was afraid to make another attempt at escape as they drove through the countryside.

Sells finally parked off Missouri 266 on Road 99. To make her easier to handle, he injected Stephanie with a large dose of cocaine. He pulled off her shoes and jeans, hitting her when she struggled. When he brought his hand to her face, she cringed, and tears came to her eyes when he ripped off the tape. He raped Stephanie, and then he took her life by choking her to death.

He gathered her clothing and abused body and walked toward a cow pasture. He unlatched the gate, moved further from the road and dropping her jeans and shoe along the way. When he reached a pond, he dropped her body into the water.

Rob returned to the apartment at five thirty the following morning to make breakfast for the kids and make sure they got to school on time. He unlocked the back door, heard the sound of an alarm clock, and went to Stephanie's room to turn it off. When he went into the room, he found she wasn't there. He checked on the other two kids, and they were both asleep. He looked in all the rooms, and then woke the other two children to question them, but he wasn't able to find out where she'd gone.

Within hours, Stephanie's mother filed a missing person report. She didn't believe her daughter would have run away; Stephanie had been a homebody. She took care of her younger siblings while her mother wasn't around, and rather than running around with friends, she was more likely to sit with her siblings on the front porch. For a thirteen-year-old girl, she was pretty responsible. At the time, she was one of twenty-six runaway or missing girls who'd been reported in the area.

In the weeks following her disappearance, investigators talked to more than thirty people and searched six residences. They weren't able to confirm a reported sighting of Stephanie.

Thirty-four days passed without word from Stephanie. Then, on November 18, 1997, a group of hunters were walking through a field and discovered the partially clothed body of a teenage girl submerged in a pond. When police arrived at the scene, they found a shoe and a pair of jeans nearby.

The body was too decomposed to make a visual identification. Investigators called the families of all twenty-six missing girls to inform them of the discovery, and then they obtained dental records of all the girls.

Using those records, the unknown body was identified as Stephanie Mehaney the very next day. There was very little other information about her disappearance. Investigators received fifteen phone calls after the body was found, which was an all-time low.

Twenty members of the sheriff's department, accompanied by volunteer high school students, returned to the scene to do a grid-by-grid search. The line would stop when someone shouted 'stop', and the evidence would be bagged. Then, the line would move forward again.

On Christmas Eve, the results of Stephanie's autopsy were made public. Her body was too decomposed to determine whether she had been sexually assaulted.

A picture of Stephanie became the sole permanent fixture on the bulletin board of Detective Jim Arnott. It was the only unsolved murder in Greene County in more than twenty years. Arnott carried another picture of her in his notebook and yet another in his vehicle. He never stopped thinking about what had happened to her.

***

However, Sells did stop thinking about her. He brushed away the memories and returned to his mother and wife in St. Louis, where he worked at the same auto shop until he left again.

On December 15, Tommy Sells was back in Winnemucca, Nevada. He stayed only one night at the Overland Hotel, but before he left the area, he drove to the desolate location where he'd left Stefanie Stroh's body in 1978, reliving the fond memories of that night. He was back in St. Louis in time to get another traffic ticket on December 29, 1997. That day, he left town, and Nora never saw the father of her unborn child again.
Sells wasn't happy when he left St. Louis. Nora was going to give birth to his son in three months, and he didn't feel equipped or inclined to take care of a baby or a wife. He'd hoped his younger brother would raise the child, but Randy didn't want any children, either. He feared that if he took Sells' child, then his brother might hit him up for cash and favors all the time.

Nina knew that Nora couldn't care for a baby alone, and Sells wasn't responsible enough to help. At her age, she didn't feel capable of raising a child either, not even if it was her grandchild. With the help of her sister in Arkansas, she contacted an attorney to arrange for the child to be adopted. He came to her home with a schoolteacher to evaluate Nora and make certain she wanted to give up the baby.

In April of 1998, in Jonesboro, Nora gave birth to a little boy. She never saw the baby. He was immediately placed with a family in that town, where he lived for the following four years.

Nina was determined that she wasn't going to go through the process again, so she made sure Nora had her tubes tied.

Nora went back to St. Louis to live with her mother-in-law. Sells was nowhere near the area when his son was born. He'd sold his mechanic's tools in Little Rock and, on January 19, 1998, he traveled south.

***

Carnival season begins early in Texas, and Sells got a job driving the truck that hauled the Ferris wheel for Heat of America in Aransas Pass. He operated the ride, too.

The second week the carnival was in the town of Del Rio, on the evening of March 5, 1998, Jessica Levrie brought her kids to the fair. It was a cool night for March. While the kids rode the Ferris wheel, she stood on the sidelines enjoying their smiles. Her green eyes and her welcoming face caught Sells' interest.

He suggested it'd be a nice night for a cup of hot cocoa. The children got off the ride and begged to go on it again. While they went back into the air, Jessica invited Sells back to her home for a warm drink. Sells ended up spending that night and many other nights at her home while he finished up his tour in Del Rio. On the day the carnival packed up to leave, Jessica went to the grounds and grabbed a word here and there with Sells as he worked with the crew to prepare the caravan for travel.

Sells was sitting in the rig in the parking lot, ready to go with the rest of the crew, when Jessica showed up one final time. Enamored with her beauty and the love that seemed to emanate from her, he asked her if she wanted to ride with him to Corpus Christi.

Jessica told him yes, and they both climbed into the truck for the fourteen-hour drive to the Gulf Coast. She spent two days in the city, and then Sells put her on a bus back to Del Rio. She returned two days later. With her hands on her hips, she asked him if he was ready to come home. Sells was ecstatic and told her that yes, he wanted to go home with her.

They went back in her vehicle and began living together with her two teenaged daughters and two younger boys in Del Rio. On March 31, he reported to the local unemployment office to look for work.

Sells found a job as a salesman and mechanic at Amigo Auto Sales, and Jessica worked at a Chinese restaurant waiting tables. In his off time, Sells drew pictures of roses for Jessica. Just a few short years after he had learned to read and write, he was penning love poems for her.

Following her lead, he managed to shape an inkling of a normal life. They took turns driving the kids to school, and Sells took the boys fishing or worked on craft projects with them. He even ironed their clothes for school from time to time.

Pets were a big part of their family. At one point, they had two cats, three dogs, six birds, a guinea pig, two hamsters, a snake, and a turtle. With Jessica's encouragement, Sells managed to avoid drugs and alcohol for some time.

However, on June 28, Sells set off on another road trip north to Sonora, Texas. Then he went east to Beaumont. While he was in northeast Texas, he racked up two more traffic tickets. They were still outstanding a year and a half later when he was arrested for Kaylene Harris' murder.

Then he returned home, attempting to hang onto the normalcy of domestic existence. It only took one family crisis to undo Jessica's good influence and set him back on his usual path.

In August of 1998, twenty inches of rain fell quick and hard. The lights went out at 505 Andrade Street, and outside, a woman yelled. The San Felipe Creek had crested and was destroying the small neighborhood.

The woman, Jessica's mother Virginia, grabbed a flashlight and pointed it across the street to her daughter's house. Finally, her shouts caught the attention of the family. She pleaded with them to come over to her home, but Jessica said they would be okay.

Virginia insisted they would be safer with her, and the family relented. Sells and Jessica stood in the water, passing the children across the street. Virginia would put them safely indoors. Ten minutes later, she opened her front door to discover there was water in her yard. Jessica and Sells joined her on the porch and watched as the water rose.

In the street, a woman was grabbing for fences, bushes, and poles as she was swept away by the water. Sells jumped off the porch in an attempt to save her, but his clothing snagged on the front-yard fence, and the woman slipped away. He pulled himself back to safety.

The river running down the street carried the woman beneath a truck whose motor was running. They all screamed, fearing the truck would move and run her over. A man inside the truck heard the desperate warning and jumped out, struggling through the water to drag the woman to safety.

Many residents of the neighborhood were forced into the trees or up onto their roofs as the water consumed everything in its path. Inside Virginia's home, the children were put into the room that was highest above the ground. No one knew it was the most dangerous room in the house at the time.

Water was swirling around the garage and around a shack. The shack was swept away by the flood, and when Sells stepped out the front door to get cigarettes from a shop next door owned by Virginia's father, he closed the door and collapsed against it. He told them it was gone.

Screams erupted from the children when they heard the sound of a trapped cat. They thought it was beneath the washer at first, but it was beneath the floor where the water was rising. Sells desperately tried to save the cat by prying up the floorboard to get to it, but he wasn't quick enough. The four children had to listen to the cat drowning, screaming in terror.

The water kept rising, forcing the children to move to the back of the room. It didn't stop rising until it reached the level of Virginia's hips. Then it receded, leaving muck in its wake. Her bed was up high, and there was a dry spot on it where the children could lie down and go to sleep.

Exhausted, Virginia collapsed onto the sofa and instantly fell asleep. Sells and Jessica found spots on the floor and settled down in the quiet.

The following morning, the water had receded further, bringing hope that the danger was over. But at around four in the afternoon, the Border Patrol went from door to door to warn the residents more water was coming. They transported everyone to the high school gym, but the shelter wasn't the refuge they thought it would be.

The water rose there, too. All the refugees were then sent to the civic center, which was on higher ground. Virginia, her ninety-year-old father, and her daughter's family stayed at the civic center for two weeks. Then they were moved to the Siesta Motel for a few days, and after that they were moved from place to place as they waited for the waters to recede.

The flood was traumatic for the entire community, this family included. Looking back, Sells stated that he knew the moment he was carrying those kids out of the flood that nothing would be the same with Jessica again.

Sells and Jessica eventually settled more permanently in a trailer at the American Campgrounds, about ten miles west of their original home. Soon after they moved in, Jessica and Sells were driving down Route 90. Sells pulled to the side of the road abruptly, and when Jessica asked him what was wrong, he asked her if she'd marry him.

She said yes. Plans for their wedding raced ahead, and they were married in a church in Del Rio on October 22, 1998. In late 1998, Sells worked for a few months at Ram County as a mechanic.

However, the aftereffects of the stress from their ordeal in the flood started to bear down on them. Again, Sells was abusing alcohol and drugs, and his work hours were erratic. Jessica couldn't understand the behavior, and it was intolerable.

Her nagging turned into arguments, which turned into fierce fights. On February 22, 1999, Sells left Del Rio. By March 5, he was in Pensacola, Florida. After a phone call from Jessica, he made his way home. He got his job back, but on March 28, he was thrown out again. Jessica demanded he get clean before he came home again, and Sells hit the road once more.

The Horrific Spree Continues

Jamie and Debbie Harris and Debbie's eight-year-old, Ambria Halliburton, moved into a rental trailer in Gibson County, Tennessee, in January of 1999. Their new home was in the Caraway Hills area, a sparse community where thick clusters of trees separated the neighbors and provided them with privacy.

By the end of February, marital issues drove the two into separation. They moved out of the trailer; Jamie moved to Gibson, and Debbie thought she had another place to live. However, it didn't work out, so she ended up going back to their former landlady. Debbie wanted to move back into the trailer, but she didn't have enough money. The landlady, Dawn, agreed to accept the deposit money and let her pay the rent the following week. Debbie and Ambria settled back into the trailer on March 15.

Dawn last saw Debbie on Monday, March 29, when she brought the rent payment by. She was twenty-five dollars short, and Dawn agreed to let her have a few more days. Debbie thanked her and left, saying she was going to interview for a second job.

***

Sells related the events of that night to the Texas Rangers who had arrested him. He said he took a twenty-mile detour off Route 40 when he reached Jackson. Around midnight on March 30, he approached a small trailer. He knocked on the door, and it opened. He slipped inside quietly and found a knife in one of the kitchen drawers. As he crept down the hall to Debbie's room, he spooked a calico cat. It leaped off the bed and scurried into a hiding place.

Just past the dresser, Sells noticed an overturned bucket next to the bed that was serving as a makeshift nightstand. It had a picture and an alarm clock on it. He eased into the bed and put the blade of the knife to Debbie's throat.

Debbie didn't resist. She knew that she had to be quiet if she wanted her daughter to live. After he had raped her unresponsive body, Sells stabbed her multiple times. He stepped across the hall into the bathroom, holding the knife. He set it down beside the sink, picked up a bar of soap from the soap dish, and then cleaned the blood off his hands and arms.

When he turned and looked into the hall, Ambria was standing there silently. He chased her into the living room, where he caught her and slammed the knife into her tiny body with so much force it lifted her off her feet. He stabbed her again, and then she went limp. He shoved the knife into her a third time, loosening his grip, so she slumped to the floor.

Thinking he heard a noise from Debbie's room, he went back to the bedroom to be sure she was dead. He stabbed her one last time in the chest and left the knife there.

The neighbors noticed that Debbie's vehicle had been sitting in her driveway without moving for several days, but it was Easter weekend, and holidays often put people's regular schedules off track. For her part, the landlady had decided not to hassle Debbie when she didn't show up with the rest of the rent.

However, on Easter Sunday, a friend decided to pay a visit to Debbie's trailer. She opened the door, and what she found inside wasn't pleasant. The decay was in such an advanced state that it forced the arriving investigators to tack up a sign that read Danger, Biohazard.

At two in the morning on Monday, agents from the Tennessee Bureau of Investigation arrived to process the scene. They worked until mid-morning to gather all the pieces of potential evidence. But they found nothing suspicious in the trailer – no DNA, fingerprints, or forensic evidence that pointed to the identity of the person who had done this. The bodies were then sent out for autopsy.

On the Thursday, Debbie and Ambria were both laid to rest in the Salem Church Cemetery in Gadsden.

A $2,500 per victim reward was issued by the governor for any information that led to the arrest, indictment, and conviction of the person or people responsible for the murders. More than twenty suspects were put forward, but all were exonerated.

Before the bodies had even been found, Sells was already states away. He hired on with a carnival in Greensboro, North Carolina. That job was to take him to San Antonio, where a nine-year-old girl would be his next victim.

***

Fiesta is a ten-day celebration in San Antonio, Texas, that begins in April. It features events that raise money for charitable programs, but for most residents, it's just an excuse for an extended party.

The 1999 festivities kicked off a story below street level, down on Riverwalk. Any place where the narrow walkway was broad enough, chairs were set up and tickets were sold. At the Arenson River Theatre, spectators squeezed into the long tiers of benches cut into the hill, and faces watched out the windows of apartment buildings along the San Antonio River. The Cavaliers rode on floats that glided down the waterway through the cheering crowd of close to 225,000 people.

Halfway through Fiesta, the Battle of Flowers Parade took place in downtown San Antonio. The floats were adorned with flowers, and high school bands dominated the festivities as they marched. They wound through the streets, issuing a siren call to everyone. Then, like modern day Pied Pipers, they led the spectators to the Alamo Stadium, where 3,600 high school band members would compete.

Fiesta in San Antonio would never be complete without a carnival, and working at this carnival in 1999 was Tommy Lynn Sells.

One of the largest celebrations was Fiesta del Mercado, which ran daily from the late morning until midnight. On April 18, Mary Bea Perez, a nine-year-old girl, went to El Mercado with her extended family. Like all the Fiesta events, this one was heavily patrolled by police officers on foot, bicycles, and horseback. It was considered a safe venue for families.

Around ten that night, Mary Bea and her uncle went to a booth where he bought a round of beer for the adults. He didn't realize she'd trailed behind him, and when he returned to the group, the third-grader was gone.

In the middle of the music and the heady aroma of food, Sells snatched Mary Bea and whisked her away. He hustled her into his truck and told her they were going to take a little ride. He then forced her onto the floorboard, where she huddled in fear.

A mile and a half from El Mercado, they came to a stop near the stockyards. Sells pulled Mary Bea out of the vehicle and led her through a hole in the fence. In that isolated area, he laid her down on a queen-sized mattress and forcibly undressed her as she fought back. When he finished raping her, he wrapped her t-shirt around her neck and strangled her to death.

At the fair, her family was frantic. They searched for her in the square for two hours. Then they went home in the hope they would find her there, safe. But she wasn't there either. They called the police to report her disappearance.

The entire city went on high alert. This type of thing just didn't happen at Fiesta. Families with small children thought twice about taking their children to the event after that. Prayers for her safe return came from pulpits across the town.

In the middle of their pleas, rain fell. It was heavy enough to wash Mary Bea's body downstream from the place where she'd been discarded.

Ten days after that night in El Mercado, a man who was fishing with his son in Azalan Creek found Mary Bea's body.

Her life had been almost as sad as her death. Her mother hadn't had enough food to feed her daughter, and so Mary Bea would be seen wandering around the neighborhood looking for handouts. No suspects were ever found, and Mary Bea was put to rest.

By the time she was, Tommy Sells was already in Kentucky.

A Community Devastated

Riding on trains, Sells traveled to Lexington, Kentucky, and signed up at Labor Ready. He lived on the streets for a few weeks, sometimes renting a home for a day or two from a woman who worked at a fast-food restaurant on the next street over from the Labor Ready office. He eventually found jobs at Excel Building Services and the Lexington recycling center. On May 13, he clocked in at Transylvania University.

Haley McHone was thirteen years old, and she was rather troubled, although most people didn't know it. Outside her family home, she was known to be a sunny girl who would always lend a stranger a helping hand when necessary. She approached life with boundless energy and seemed to get along with everyone but her family. There, she felt alienated.

Her incompatibility with her family left her feeling isolated, hurt, and alone. Luckily, refuge was nearby. She'd ride up the road to her grandmother's house, and her grandmother, Anne Walker, told her she could move in after school was over for the summer.

To make some spending money, Haley babysat, walked dogs, and pulled weeds in the neighborhood near the University of Kentucky. When her grandmother became ill and went into the hospital, she would ride miles on her bicycle to visit her. She always picked flowers to bring to her grandmother, whatever was in bloom.

Haley's real problems at home began after she stayed at Charter Ridge, an adolescent psychiatric facility. Since then, she'd been under the care of a psychiatrist and was taking anti-depressants. Authorities recorded the reason for her stay as emotional damage caused by sexual abuse.

On May 13, she was not in school due to an appointment she had with her psychiatrist. First thing in the morning, she went to her grandmother's house to have breakfast. Afterward, she stopped to play some games at her home. Then she got on her bike and went to Elizabeth Street Park.

As she rode to the park, she kept her eyes peeled for stray dogs. She'd been bitten by one about a month earlier and was nearing the end of a series of painful shots.

She placed her bike against the end of a set of swings, pushed off into the dirt beneath a swing, and pumped her legs as hard as she could to get as high as she could. Lost in the sensation of the ride, she was unprepared for what happened.

Sells' base instincts were ignited when he saw the teenage girl on the swing alone. He looked around the park to make sure no one was there, and then he crept up to the girl. He shoved her off the swing, slapped his hand over her mouth, and held her tight. His other arm squeezed her tightly to his side as she struggled with him, and he dragged her kicking and squirming from the park to a wooded lot behind it.

He demanded oral sex, telling her that he wouldn't hurt her if she complied. Afraid of what he might do to her, she agreed. While Sells was removing his shirt, he heard the sound of a couple walking through the park, and he put his hand over Haley's mouth to keep her quiet. She didn't make a noise or struggle, thinking she'd be safe if she didn't put up a fight.

Once the couple was out of earshot, Sells yanked off Haley's clothes and pushed her into the dried leaves, where he raped her. Again, she didn't struggle, thinking he would leave her alone when he was finished. However, he didn't just use her and walk away like her previous molester had.

Sells strangled her with her own shirt, twisting it tight and cutting off her air supply. She tried to aim for his eyes as she defended herself, but he managed to hang on and kill her.

Sells pushed her into a depression in the ground and shoveled debris over her body. Brushing the leaves off his clothes and running his hands through his hair, he emerged from the wooded lot. He took her bike and pedaled his way to the projects, where he sold her bike to a man for twenty dollars.

The time for Haley's psychiatric appointment came and went, and when her mother couldn't find her, she contacted Haley's grandmother. The rest of the day, Haley's father and mother and her three older siblings scoured the neighborhood for her. They walked the streets until well after it was dark.

At 11:52 that evening, a Lexington police officer found Sells passed out drunk, lying in a heap at the foot of a lamppost. He woke him up and arrested him for public drunkenness. He was released the following morning. Without picking up his paycheck, he hopped onto a freight train and got off near the Indiana border. He stole a truck that was parked near the tracks and drove away. When it broke down, he broke into a local business office, stole cash and another truck, and went north.

For ten days, Haley's family and the police stuck up posters about her everywhere. Sightings of her were reported, and everyone had a swell of hope each time, but none were confirmed.

Then one day a man was walking his dog near Elizabeth Street Park, and the dog picked up a scent. The owner didn't know what had gotten into his dog, but he allowed the animal to lead him into the woods. No amount of scolding could have kept the normally well-behaved dog away from his mission. By the time they reached the source of the dog's excitement, the smell was overwhelming. The man ran home to call the police. He had found Haley's body.

The neighborhood lit up with red and blue lights from police vehicles, and police bicyclists were soon patrolling the park.

Once the scene was processed and the body was removed, flower bouquets, notes, and potted plants were placed where Haley had died. On May 27, a crowd of two hundred neighbors, teenagers, faculty, college students, family, and friends all gathered at a candlelight vigil for Haley.

Her body had been found just a hundred yards from the spot on the railroad tracks where another body had been found 21 months before. Christopher Maier, a twenty-one-year-old college student, had been beaten to death and left on the tracks. His girlfriend had been raped, beaten, cut across her neck and discarded. She'd survived. At the time of Haley's death, this case had not been solved. Then, in June, Christopher's murderer was identified as Angel Maturino Resendiz – the Railway Killer.

There was naturally speculation that Resendiz was guilty of Haley's murder, too. The police department pursued that angle, but they found no evidence to support it.

In the coming weeks, the community joined hands to landscape the park and put up a fence. They created a neighborhood watch to improve safety for the children who visited.

Anne Walker grieved for Haley. Even after Haley's body was found, she continued to spend part of each day talking to her granddaughter. In an irony that went unnoticed at the time, a photo of Anna in Elizabeth Street Park was published in the Lexington Herald-Leader seven weeks after Haley was discovered. The t-shirt she wore read 'Tommy Girl'.

Before the body was even found, Sells was under arrest again. He had been picked up in Madison, Wisconsin, on a drunk and disorderly charge. He'd been waving a box-cutter around threateningly. The weapon earned him more than the usual overnight stay in the drunk tank, and while in custody, he assaulted another inmate.

When he came down from the frenzy that had overcome him when he'd attacked his fellow prisoner, he gave his jailer a handmade hangman's noose and told him he wanted to kill himself.

Released on June 24, he went home to Del Rio. His arrival was not as welcome as he would have hoped. He couldn't get his job back at Ram Country, and he had such a ferocious fight with Jessica that one of her daughters called the police to their home. Sells ended up accused of molesting Jessica's daughter, Samantha. The social worker made it clear that Jessica and her four children could not stay in the trailer with Sells.

Jessica took her family to her mother's home, and on July 3, Sells drove north to Oklahoma.

Pure Evil

1998 was an awful year for Susan Wofford and her family in Oklahoma. Susan and her husband Fred had been living in the rural area for twelve years after moving there from the southern outskirts of the city of Norman, where all three of their children had been born.

Ricky was seventeen, Michael was fourteen, and Bobbie Lynn – their daughter – was thirteen when their troubles started. A phone call from the hospital brought bad news. Ricky had been sitting in the back seat of a vehicle driven by his friend when they were in a car accident. The entire seat had flown forward through the windshield on impact, and the broken glass had ripped Ricky's face to shreds, permanently altering his features.

He'd healed enough two months later to go out to a basketball game with Michael. Fred dropped them off at the high school gym – and then he disappeared. For two weeks, Susan wondered and worried about her husband. She didn't know if he was dead or alive. Her mind went over every scenario. Then the police found his car on a dead-end street close to their home. His body was behind the steering wheel with a gunshot wound to his head. He'd committed suicide.

A month later, Michael was sitting in the passenger seat of a van while it drove down the highway. The driver lost control, and the van rolled over the median strip and slid to a stop upside down. The roof was smashed down to the tops of the seats. Michael survived only because he'd been thrown out before the van rolled over. Nevertheless, he sustained some serious injuries – a fractured collarbone, broken ribs, and punctured lungs. He was barely able to breathe when the paramedics arrived, and he was rushed to the hospital in critical condition.

Throughout this turmoil, Bobbie Lynn was the bright spot in Susan's life. She was creative, joyful, and a straight-A student. She played the trumpet and baritone in the school band and was on the basketball team.

At home, she liked to play with her cats and read. There were many semi-feral cats prowling around the neighborhood, and Bobbie Lynn knew each one by name. She was more than willing to nurse kittens back to health when the mother disappeared, feeding them from a bottle until they were ready for solid foods.

After the misery in 1998, Susan deserved a break. She wasn't going to get one in 1999.

Bobbie Lynn hit puberty in the spring of that year, and her relationship with her mother changed. Susan was used to her daughter following her around the house and talking about everything in her life the second it crossed her mind. To Susan, it seemed the change in her daughter happened overnight. She was quiet and wanted to spend more time alone in her room. Socializing with her friends was suddenly much more important than hanging around her family and caring for the cats.

On July 2, fourteen-year-old Bobbie Lynn told her mother she was going with friends to Canton Lake in Blaine County over the weekend. Susan gave her daughter ten dollars in spending money for the trip, even though she hated the thought of her get into an automobile after what had happened to her sons.

Bobbie Lynn didn't make it to the lake. As planned beforehand, she and her friends embarked on a reckless adventure they knew wouldn't have received their parents' approval.

***

That same weekend, Tommy Sells arrived at Kingfisher. As he was driving up from Del Rio, he was drinking heavily and taking cocaine throughout the day and night. Despite his altered state of mind, he remembered the details of that night vividly. His memory matched the evidence investigators had found.

Sells drove up Route 81 north of Oklahoma City and into the town of Waukomis, where he abruptly turned around and began heading south. During the early hours of July 5, he pulled into a convenience store to inflate a leaky tire on his '79 Dodge. He also wanted to take a look under the hood. The truck was a wedding present from his bride, and it was one of his most valued treasures, an impressive vehicle by Oklahoma standards.

At four in the morning, after he sold some cocaine to an older couple in the parking lot, he saw a young woman. She was about five-foot-five, with blonde hair and blue eyes and many earrings. She was using the telephone and complaining that she wasn't able to reach anyone.

He saw his opportunity and approached the seventh grader. He asked her why such a pretty woman was making such a fuss, and she told him she needed a ride home and couldn't get one. He told her he'd give her a ride and, dropping his tools to the floor, invited her into his truck. Bobbie Lynn made herself comfortable on the passenger seat. Her relief at going home was tinged with the guilt of where she'd been all weekend. She hoped her mother wouldn't find out.

Sells smiled at her and asked her if she wanted some coke. She told him she didn't have any money, and he told her she had something worth much more than money. When she told him to take her back to the convenience store, he backhanded her and told her to shut up.

Intimidated by his brutality, Bobbie Lynn didn't dare move or make a sound. She stared straight ahead as Sells drove northwest of Kingfisher and pulled over onto a dark and isolated road. There, he forced her to perform oral sex, fondled her, and began trying to rape her. Before he could penetrate her, her desperation overcame her fear. She slapped and scratched at him, and then she aimed a kick at his genitals.

That's when his rage took over. He grabbed a ratchet from the floor and rammed it inside of her.

Bobbie Lynn opened the truck door and tried to flee, but Sells had a gun. He shot her in the head, and she fell to the ground dead.

It was time to clean up the mess he'd made, so Sells grabbed her purse and duffle bag from his truck and threw them as far as he could. The pair of earrings she was wearing caught his eye, so he plucked them from her earlobes and slid them into his pocket.

He removed the ratchet and pulled her clothing back into place before he lifted her lifeless body. He lost her tennis shoe in the weeds before disposing of her body in an inconspicuous location further off the road. Although she was disheveled, she was still dressed in the clothes she'd been wearing at the convenience store.

With his rage satisfied and the evidence well hidden, he began driving back toward Texas.

***

At first, Bobbie Lynn's mother was angry her daughter had violated her trust and not returned home when she was expected to. In the beginning, the authorities treated her disappearance as a runaway case. The community gathered around the distraught mother and helped her search for her daughter, passing out fliers and reassuring her that everything was going to be okay.

When Bobbie Lynn was listed as a missing person, her mother's hope all but disappeared, to be replaced by an unending anxiety. The waiting game began. July went by too slowly, with too many false alarms. Susan's phone would ring with people letting her know Bobbie Lynn had been seen riding with someone in a truck. There were reports that her body had been found at Canton Lake. None of it had any basis in the facts.

Susan did whatever she could to distract herself from her worries about her missing daughter. She paced from one end of her house to another, wearing a path in her carpet.

Unconfirmed sightings of Bobbie Lynn continued to pour into the Kingfisher County Sheriff's Department. The months passed by, and finally, a witness came forward saying he'd seen a man talking to a girl who looked like Bobbie Lynn. It had been in a convenience store parking lot. Forensic artists drew a sketch of the suspect.

The following day, hunters stumbled across a library card and some lipstick. The library card bore the name Bobbie Lynn Wofford. They ended the hunting trip early and reported their findings to the authorities.

Bobbie Lynn had never been to that location, but it was known as a spot where teenagers commonly gathered to drink and party after dark.

Her yellow duffle bag, tennis shoe, and her black purse were all found, and the police kept searching until they found her decomposed body. It wasn't held together with much other than her clothes. The advanced decomposition made it difficult to tell, but head trauma led them to suspect that she'd died of a gunshot wound to the head.

***

Susan's phone rang again, and someone else was on the other end to tell her what had happened to her daughter. This time the information was accurate, but it wasn't the news she wanted to hear.

Once the body was found, girls in Bobbie Lynn's age group were afraid. They wouldn't walk to school anymore, and their parents didn't even try to make them. They were terrified their children would be next, so they were extra-vigilant about where their children were and what they were doing.

It was December before DNA tests verified that the bones belonged to Bobbie Lynn. No one knew how Susan would continue to function after the fourth tragedy in her family. Local churches were too small to hold the large number of people who wanted to stand by her as she mourned for her daughter. Ultimately, the funeral was held in the school gymnasium to accommodate the large crowd.

An anonymous tip led investigators to focus their attention on Deb's Sports bar, a tavern in Kingfisher. They interviewed the co-managers and confiscated drugs, hair samples, ammunition, and adult videos, but it was a fruitless effort.

Bobbie Lynn's killer was long gone.

***

Sells had returned to Del Rio, and after two rounds of interviews, the charge that he'd molested Jessica's daughter was dismissed as unfounded. Jessica and her children moved back in with Tommy Sells, and he stuck around for a few months while he worked for Amigo Auto Sales.

Bill Hughes, his employer, invited Sells and Jessica to go to Grace Community Church services with him. Crystal and Terry Harris and their children Katy and Lori were at those services, too.

When Terry Harris needed a new vehicle, he wanted to go somewhere he could trust. He chose Amigo Auto Sales because a fellow church member owned the establishment. The salesman that assisted him was Tommy Lynn Sells.

One evening, Sells showed up at Terry's home, and he invited Sells inside. Crystal took a single look at Sells' appearance – scraggly hair, beard, and tattoos – and was immediately uneasy. Chiding herself for her judgmental nature, she joined the men in the living room to listen to their conversation.

Sells admitted to having been in prison. He also admitted to having an alcohol problem that was tearing his marriage to shreds. He confessed he didn't know what he could do to save his relationship with Jessica, and then he told Terry how lucky he was to have a wife who was nice and children that listened to him.

Down the hall from the adults, Katy confided to Lori that she didn't like the way Sells looked at her. Lori told her sister that she ought to tell their father, but Katy argued that her father would get into a fight with the man, and she didn't want her father to get in trouble.

While Crystal sat with the men in the living room, she developed a fascination with Sells' tattoos. She knew that prison tattoos usually mean something, so during a lull in the conversation, she asked him what his represented. Sells told her she didn't want to know.

***

Route 44 goes through Joplin, Missouri, and across the state line into Oklahoma. State Route 59 goes west to the small town of Welch just ten miles from the border.

Down a long driveway off a country road, less than five miles north of Welch, was the modest trailer of Daniel and Kathy Freeman. They lived in this trailer with their daughter, Ashley. Daniel had built an addition that had doubled the size of the original trailer, and a rock foundation and a walkway dressed up the home's appearance. They had electricity and telephone service, but they didn't have running water, and they used a wood stove for heat.

Christmas of 1999 was a somber affair for the Freeman family. It was the first one they were celebrating since the death of their son, Shane. Earlier that year, their seventeen-year-old son had been shot to death in a confrontation with a Craig County deputy.

74

Ashley turned sixteen on December 29. That night, Jeremy Hurst, her boyfriend, delivered a present to her and stayed for a short visit. Her best friend, Lauria Bible, was spending the night.

While the four occupants were sleeping, Tommy Sells crept up to the trailer. He dodged between the animal pens on their property, moving closer to the home. When he was inside, he found a gun easily. Ashley and her father had been hunting since she was a child, and there were more than fourteen guns in the home. Sells picked one of them.

He stalked into the adults' bedroom, where they were sleeping, and rammed the butt of Daniel's own shotgun into his collarbone to get his attention. Sells wanted him awake when he died. When Daniel opened his eyes the barrel was pointed at his head, and the gunshot that followed a split second later blasted his body from the bed. The second shot, to Kathy's head, killed her where she lay. Sells slid a knife across her nude abdomen, disemboweling her. He did the same happened to Daniel, and he still wasn't finished. He cut off Daniel's arms and his right leg with an ax.

In the other bedroom, the first shot had awakened Lauria and Ashley. When the second shot blasted down the hall, Ashley recognized the sound. They huddled together, too afraid to move from where they were. They struggled to silence their gasps and tried to hear every sound to identify the noises they heard, but none of them made sense.

In the kitchen, Sells was pouring gasoline in a puddle on the floor in front of the wood stove. He splashed some of it on the heater itself, and smoke rose from the surface instantly. The flames followed within seconds.

Just as the girls smelled the first faint whiffs of the fire, a figure appeared in the doorway. He lunged at them with his hands clutching the shotgun, which he aimed at their heads. He ordered them out of the room and into the cold night. Shoving, cursing, and hitting, he herded them into the van. They took off into the darkness before dawn arrived.

Barreling down Route 44, Sells tortured both girls and then ended their lives. He claimed that he brought the van to a halt somewhere near the Red River and dumped the two girls in an isolated area before he kept heading south. Their bodies were never recovered.

On December 30, a neighbor on his way to work at six thirty in the morning noticed the fire at the trailer and called the police. The fire department raced to the scene, but the home was a complete loss. The only portion still intact was the floor of the master bedroom. There, the waterbed had doused some of the flames.

When the home was searched, only a single body was found – Kathy Freeman's. She was lying on the remains of the waterbed. In addition to the absence of bodies, two other items were missing. Daniel had a collection of arrowheads and Indian tools he'd been amassing since he was a child, and his rarest pieces were framed in glass boxes. The more common ones were stored in plastic buckets. Of the thousands of items in his collection, only a handful were ever found.

The second item never recovered was Ashley's savings. She'd been working at a Roscoe convenience store and saving every penny she could. She'd had between $1,100 and $4,000.

That cash had been wrapped in foil and stored in a Tupperware container tucked in the freezer amongst packages of frozen meat. Lauria's purse with her $200 worth of Christmas money was found at the scene.

All day, the family's neighbors searched every inch of the forty-acre lot on foot and on horseback. They found no signs of Daniel, Lauria, or Ashley.

At 5:30 in the afternoon, the home was released to Daniel's half-brother. At the time, the theory was that Daniel had murdered his wife, torched his home, and abducted the two children. Amid the confusion, there was one detail that caused doubt, though. All the vehicles, including Lauria's, were still on the premises.

Lauria's parents, Lorene and Jay, were not satisfied with the search of the home, and they were determined to find out what had happened to their daughter. As they trudged through the ashes and rubble early the following morning, it took them only five minutes to make a shocking discovery. Ashley's Rottweiler was lying on the blackened floor next to the waterbed. When she stood to greet Lauria's parents, they saw that she'd been lying on the remains of Daniel's shattered head. When Lorene pulled back the carpet at that spot, they saw the outline of a second body.

When the sheriff's department returned, they ordered Lorene and Jay off the scene. However, they refused to leave until every piece of debris had been sifted through.

Daniel Freeman was removed from the list of suspects. Investigators even entertained the idea that the two girls were the perps they were looking for; however, the families disagreed with this theory. After all, Lauria's purse, car, money, and identification were all at the scene. Interviews of those who knew the girls and an investigation into their histories further diminished the credibility of the idea that they were involved.

Speculation now centered on three different approaches. The relatives of the Freemans were convinced that the crime was connected to Shane's death and Daniel's threatened civil suit against the Craig County Sheriff's Department. Even after the deputy and his brother passed a polygraph test, the family's remained suspicious.

Jay and Lorene believed that the tragedy had been tied to drug trafficking in some way. However, while Daniel was known to have smoked marijuana, and it was suspected he'd grown some for his personal use, he didn't have a record of drug offenses, and law enforcement had no evidence he'd sold drugs.

The investigators finally settled on Steven Ray Thacker, a known killer who'd been on the run. He was caught in early January and put on death row in Tennessee for stabbing someone in Dyersburg. He was charged with other murders in Missouri and Oklahoma as well. However, they couldn't connect him to the murders in Welch.

No matter how much they searched, none of their leads came up with a good explanation as to what had happened to the Freeman family and Lauria Bible.

The Last Murder

When Sells went home, he came face to face with Jessica's wrath the second he pulled open the door. He'd been gone with her van for days, he'd missed work, and money was needed to pay the bills. The two of them drove to the Pico Convenience Store, where Sells attempted to get in contact with Bill Hughes on a pay phone. He wanted to arrange a pickup for his final paycheck. He went into the store for some smokes and ran into Terry Harris. The two of them talked for five minutes. Back home, the fight continued and Sells left to escape Jessica's anger.

He sought refuge at Larry's Lakefront Tavern, where he drank Coke and Jim Beam and talked to the waitress. According to the waitress, Noel Houchin, Sells was a major nuisance that night. He asked her for sex, asked where she lived, and then asked her for sex again. When she mentioned that her car was broken down, he offered to pay to have it repaired if she had sex with him. Finally, he told her he owned Amigo Auto Sales, and she could have any vehicle on the lot if she would just have sex with him.

According to Sells, he told her worked at Amigo Auto, not that he owned it. He also said he wasn't interested in her himself, but told her Bill Hughes was interested, and if she batted her eyes at him, he'd help her out.

At one point, Sells took a break from drinking. He paid his tab, collected his change, and left the bar to change from the shorts he was wearing to a pair of pants. When he emptied the pockets of his shorts, he realized that he must have grabbed someone else's money, too, when he scooped up the change.

He went back to the tavern and realized the money belonged to Sonny, a friend and a neighbor of his. He turned it over to Sonny and sat down for another Jim Beam and Coke. He was one of the final two patrons to leave the bar when it closed around two in the morning.

He stopped on his way home near a flea market where an older woman had an outdoor refrigerator. He reached inside to pull out some beer and venison. While he ate, he decided he would go to Terry Harris' home to get the money he believed was owed to him. Sells insisted, after his arrest, that he'd fronted cocaine to Terry Harris in exchange for five grand, but no evidence that corroborated this claim was ever found.

He left the property when the woman's son pulled up to the house. He then stopped by his trailer and picked up one of the long-bladed knives that he kept outside. Jessica was never aware he was home.

***

In the wee hours of December 31, 1999, six residents of a double-wide trailer were fast asleep. The man standing outside the residence attempted to trip the lock on the back door with his knife blade, but he failed. The family dog had begun barking in its pen, so he let it smell his hand and patted it on the head until it was quiet. Then he removed the screen from the window above an air conditioner and attempted to push up on the sash, but the drawn latch held the pane in place.

Tommy Sells moved quietly to the front of the house, to the window of fourteen-year-old Justin Harris' room. It was raised to allow the coolness of the mid-December air inside. The open window was the perfect entry point for Sells. He removed the screen, set it to the side, and eased himself inside the window.

Justin Harris had been blind since birth, so when he heard a noise, he thought his sister and her friend were teasing him again. He told them to stop coming into his room and promptly fell back asleep.

Sells walked into the next bedroom and used his lighter to see the occupant. Seven-year-old Marque Surles was fast asleep in her bed. Sells stood and stared at her in the flickering light, and then he turned away.

He walked down the hall to the opposite end of the trailer where he saw Crystal Harris – the mother – and Lori Harris – her twelve-year-old daughter – fast asleep. He touched Crystal on the leg. She didn't stir, so he left her alone.

He walked back down the hall to explore the final bedroom. Walking over the threshold, all he heard was the quiet breathing of the two people inside.

He pulled the door closed behind him as he caught the scent of children in the room. Ten-year-old Krystal Surles stirred on the top bunk. Sells froze, unable to identify the source of the noise because the room was pitch black. His right hand squeezed the knife handle, and in two steps, he was leaning over Kaylene 'Katy' Harris on the lower bunk bed. He told her to wake up, then lay down next to her with his hand on her throat. His other hand held a twelve-inch boning knife.

When she asked what he was doing there, he didn't respond. Instead, he slit open her shorts and her panties, slit her bra in two, and returned the knife to her throat while his free hand fondled her. She jerked free and tumbled out of bed to the side closest to the wall. She ran for the door, shouting for someone to go get her mother, but Sells was already there, blocking her path. He stabbed at her and drew first blood.

She said he'd cut her, and he flipped on the light and looked at the wound on her arm, pulling her toward him. Above, Krystal woke with a start and peered through the slats of the top bunk bed. First, she saw Katy, and then she saw a man she recognized as Tommy Lynn Sells with his hand clasped over Katy's mouth.

Without warning, Sells slit Katy's throat, and Krystal watched as the blood raced down Katy's neck. Sells pulled the knife back and sliced again, deepening the wound in the thirteen-year-old girl's neck. Then he lost control, and as Katy slid to the floor, he stabbed her multiple times. Then he turned and looked at Krystal, who had her hand at her throat. He told her to remove her hand, and she asked him not to hurt her, but that didn't matter to Tommy Sells. He slit her throat anyway.

As quietly as he had come in, he left the premises. Unaware that the other occupants were still alive, Krystal waited until she heard a car start and leave. She felt her way to the bedroom door and fled into the night.

***

About a quarter of a mile down the street, Herb Betz woke to his alarm clock going off at 4:45 that morning. He'd wanted to get up early so he could watch the world's first New Year's celebration, which would happen in New Zealand at five o'clock Texas time. When he heard the alarm, he changed his mind and went back to bed.

Outside, in her plaid boxers and a t-shirt, Krystal was stumbling down the road. There were no streetlights and no moon, and the road dipped and turned. She stepped onto the front porch of the nearest trailer, but then remembered that Terry Harris had had a dispute with this neighbor and ordered them not to go to this home.

So she turned and went further up the road to a white trailer with brown and green trim. It was the home of Herb and Marlene Betz. She rang the doorbell and waited. Herb glanced at the clock. It was two minutes before five in the morning. He pulled on his pants, wondering who was at his door. Krystal leaned on the doorbell again, and by the time Herb reached the door, the pounding of a fist echoed through his trailer.

Herb asked who was there, but Krystal wasn't able to speak because her voice box had been cut. Herb turned on the light and looked outside to see Krystal on his porch. She raised her chin and pointed at her bloodied throat, and Herb immediately called for his wife to call the police.

When the police arrived at the Harris home, they woke up Crystal Harris and her daughter when they entered. When asked if anyone else in the residence was hurt, Crystal had no idea what they were talking about. When she was asked if anyone was sleeping in the east side of the trailer, she told them that her daughter was back there with her friend.

When the officers reached Katy's room, they found her battered corpse. She was nude from the waist down. The cut in her neck was obscene, but they checked for a pulse anyway. They couldn't find one.

The family was removed from the trailer, and the investigation began.

The Arrest

Tommy Sells took the bloody knife with him when he left the trailer. He stopped outside to grab the two screens he'd removed from the windows, and then he drove further down Route 90, to the lake. On the bridge, he threw the screens as far as he could and listened until he heard them hit the water.

When he got home, he washed the blood from his hands, undressed, and crawled into his waterbed. He pleaded with Jessica to hold him that night, and she wrapped her arms around his body and held him tight until he drifted off to sleep.

He woke at noon. Jessica was already gone. He arranged to sell the truck, but he would need to wait until the credit union opened on Monday to get the money. He figured there was one more thing he had to do before he left town. He had to get back at Frances Cuzak, an attorney and federal public defender who'd made him angry.

A short time before, he'd met her son at a bar and gone with him to Frances' home. He'd used the phone all evening until she told him she needed to make some calls. Her attitude had offended him greatly, and he planned to kill her on Sunday night.

With his future settled in his mind, he walked over to the house of Sonny, the friend he'd seen at the bar the previous night. They drank beer and whiskey and used cocaine. He eventually staggered home from Sonny's, but an angry Jessica threw his clean clothes into the yard and told him not to come back until he was sober. She slammed the door and locked it. Sells went back to Sonny's home.

After he did, the sheriff set up surveillance of the trailer where he lived. Not wanting to make him aware of their presence, they stayed on the other side of the street. Ironically, Sonny's place was on the same side of the street where the officers had set up to watch Sells' home.

Sells got busy on the phone. He made a few threatening phone calls to his mother-in-law, Virginia Blanco. She called the sheriff's department to report these messages, and the deputies asked if they should move in and take Sells down. However, they were told to put Virginia up in a motel and park her car elsewhere.

A few hours later, Sells once again returned home. While he was still under the influence of alcohol and drugs, this time Jessica unlocked the door and let him inside. A deputy placed a call to the lead investigator, letting him know that a scream had been heard inside the trailer. Again, they were told not to go in. The reasoning was that if it was just one scream, someone might have just stubbed their toe – either that or their throat had been slit and they were already dead.

Unaware that the deputies were outside, Sells went to bed. He would later be woken up by the deputies with an arrest warrant.

The Conviction

The trial to convict Tommy Lynn Sells was not long or drawn out. It was a pretty open and shut case. After all, there was an eyewitness to the murder of Katy Harris. It wasn't difficult for the jury to come to the conclusion that Sells should be put to death, and so he landed on death row forthwith. What followed was not so simple. There would be many years of heartache relived and old cases closed.

On November 8, 2000, Tommy Sells was admitted to death row in the Polunsky Unit in Livingston, Texas. He was given the number 999367. He found the accommodations and regulations more confining than his time at Val Verde Corrections Center. He didn't have a television to watch, couldn't call people, and wasn't allowed to smoke.

He was held in a section of a pod that had fourteen prisoners overall, and he had to spend twenty-three hours a day in his cell. It was a six-foot wide space that had a toilet, sink, and bed. Sometimes he'd sleep on the floor and use his bed as a desk for writing or drawing desk.

At one point he became part of a small protest on death row. The inmates refused to eat dinner on the nights Texas executed one of their number, and they wouldn't speak between six and seven that day. Of the eighty-four prisoners, only seven received a meal tray.

Sells was allowed to shower every three days. Before he was able to leave his cell, he had to put his hands behind his back and stick them through a hole while cuffs were put on. The shower room was seven feet long by two feet wide. After he stepped inside, he would stick his hands through another hole, and the guard would release the cuffs. On a good day, a guard would return to take him back to his cell within ten to fifteen minutes. On bad days, he had to wait in there as much as an hour.

However, Sells quickly adapted to the lifestyle of men who were living on borrowed time. In one of his statements, he said prison was his home. It was the one thing in his life that never changed. He could rely on prison to offer the same routine day in and day out, and he knew exactly what his relationship was with everyone inside.

There were no unknowns for Sells when he was in prison.

Sells had been physically removed from his wife, but even in his absence, he made problems for her. Her children were teased and isolated at school by their teachers and peers alike. She herself suffered as a powerless witness to the incessant bullying.

She fought to keep her boys in her home. After rarely visiting them for the past five years, her ex-husband now wanted custody of them. In court, the judge was very upfront. She needed to stop all communication and visits to Tommy Sells, or the boys were going to be taken from her.

Jessica ended all contact with her husband. One by one, his family members stopped sending letters or calling. Only his Aunt Bonnie kept writing him with regularity. One of her letters let him know that his grandmother had passed away.

The television show 48 Hours flew Texas Rangers Coy Smith and Johnny Allen to New York to view the first episode of a two-part series on the crimes of Tommy Sells. On February 1, 2001, they appeared on The Early Show on CBS.

Following a clip of Harold Dow talking to Sells, Jane Clayson interviewed the officers. That night's showing of 'Dead Men Tell No Tales' interested more of the nation's law enforcement agencies than the Rangers had anticipated. When they returned to their offices, they had more than nine hundred phone calls and six hundred emails to return.

They asked the same questions over and over again – did anyone have any fingerprints, DNA evidence, or physical evidence to connect their perp to the other crime?

It was obvious that not all of these crimes were the work of Tommy Sells, but the volume of cases still frightened them.

The same day the 48 Hours show aired, the district attorney for Bexar County, Texas, Susan Reed, took the Mary Bea Perez case to a grand jury in San Antonio. She secured a capital murder indictment against Tommy Sells. The documents alleged that he choked the nine-year-old girl to death with his hands to keep her from testifying against him.

The indictment was based purely on Sells' confession. While forensic technicians had tested items found at the crime scene, they hadn't come up with anything, and they had all the evidence they were ever going to find.

That same night, the phone rang in Kathleen Cowling's home in Clinton, Mississippi. It was a friend of hers who had watched the show and believed she had identified the murderer of Kathleen's first husband, John Cade. She told her that Sells had liked to climb into windows to get into people's homes.

Kathleen told her friend she'd watch the second part of the show, but she thought Sells was an unlikely suspect because he would have been too young. It had been more than twenty-one years since the murder of her husband, but she still thought of him. She wanted answers about his death, so in preparation for watching the second episode, she pulled out a forensic artist's sketch of a suspicious man who'd been spotted near the home five hours after John had been killed.

A woman who had been visiting Grand Gulf State Park with her two children around eight in the morning on July 6, 1979, had been frightened by a young man who appeared to be on drugs. When he ran at her, she grabbed her children and put them into the car. She slammed down the door locks and had to wait for the young man to get out of her way before she could leave.

She described this young man as having acne scars, a dark complexion, and short, dark hair. He drove away in a white Chevrolet with a black interior and Mississippi tags. However, the most frightening thing was his shirt. It had been splattered with blood. The forensic artist had worked with her to render a likeness of the unknown man. He was a suspect in Cade's murder, but he'd never been found.

Kathleen made herself comfortable to watch the second episode of 'Dead Men Tell No Tales' with the sketch at her side and skepticism in her heart. But as she compared the man on the screen to the picture in her hand, her heart leapt to her throat and she clutched the drawing with white-knuckled fingers. There were similar curves in the jaw line. The eyebrows had the same pointed growth in the same places. Sells and the drawing both had a distinct line on the chin, and the same oval-shaped face and wavy hair. In every photograph that flashed on the television, there were the same tightly closed lips as those in the drawing.

Kathleen had been hoping for an answer to her husband's murder, and it looked like Tommy Sells was it.

She wrote Tommy Sells in prison and asked him if he'd been in Mississippi in 1979. He wrote back that he had been in Arkansas, Mississippi, Tennessee, and perhaps California, too.

Her next letter asked if he had acne when he was fifteen, if he was driving that summer and if he remembered the July Fourth holiday weekend. He admitted that his face had had pretty bad eruptions at that age, and that not only was he driving cars by then, but he was also stealing them. He couldn't remember where he was on that particular weekend, though.

She wrote him again, wanting to know if he remembered any of the cars he'd stolen and driven for a bit. She enclosed a copy of the forensic sketch, asking if he thought that resembled him when he was fifteen. His response mentioned a white Chevrolet that summer.

An investigator visited Kathleen and told her that Sells said he'd committed a murder in Mississippi. She was excited, but she wasn't foolish. She wanted to believe she'd found her husband's killer, but first Sells needed to provide her with unpublished details about the crime scene and the events that took place that night. She wanted to visit him with a lawman at her side to record and confirm the confession. She didn't want any charges filed, she assured Sells, she just wanted closure.

Sells agreed to talk to her and tell her everything, but stipulated that she couldn't bring law enforcement with her. Her skepticism was great, but she decided to go anyway.

Over the years, Sells admitted to many murders. When someone came forward to ask if he had been involved in an abduction or murder, he would tell them whether he had been or not. When he was asked why he was so forthright, he said it was because he believed these people deserved closure. However, he was never charged with all the murders he admitted to, and some bodies still have not been found.

On reason for this is that Texas does not allow death row inmates to leave the state to participate in further investigations.

Tommy Lynn Sells was executed by lethal injection on April 3, 2014.

The Happy Face Murderer
Keith Hunter Jesperson

Stories about serial killers are incredibly popular. Tracking down a mass murderer is a constant plot line in films, television, and literature. But these stories are often based on real life. In certain circumstances, however, real life goes a step beyond what we could imagine happening in fiction. Sometimes, the actions of a serial killer can seem so extreme and strange and their motivations so twisted and evil that we struggle to comprehend exactly how they fit into the modern world. In the case of Keith Hunter Jesperson, the truth behind his murder spree is more horrific than anything Hollywood's best screenwriters could have dreamed up.

After a disturbing childhood left the giant of a man riddled with emotional and psychological scars, Jesperson traveles across Canada and spent time strangling and killing women whom he met along the way. While he was only convicted of eights murders, his own boasts suggest that total could have reached as high as 160. As a truck driver, he had the perfect cover story for traveling from town to town without having to put down roots. Often leaving an unsuspecting family at home, he was out in the wilderness committing heinous acts without anyone from the authorities coming close to suspecting his guilt.

Jesperson, annoyed by the lack of attention he was receiving, began to leave messages to the public. Scrawled onto the walls of truck stop bathrooms, he signed each confession with a happy "smiley face." This led the media to christen him the Happy Face Killer. It was decades before the investigators came close to catching the killer. Read on to discover just how Keith Hunter Jesperson managed to get away with way too many horrific murders. This is the story of the Happy Face Killer.

Early Life in Canada

Tracing the life of a serial killer can be a daunting task. Many of the more famous killers, such as John Wayne Gacy or Jeffrey Dahmer, exhibit similar traits and can help point towards a future of deviant behavior. Psychological trauma, abuse, and an inclination towards violence can all hint at what might lie ahead for the young person. In the case of Keith Jesperson, a journey into his childhood can be illuminating, chilling, and prophetic. As we begin to look into exactly what shaped him into the man he became, it becomes increasingly obvious just how distressing a childhood he experienced.

On the 6th of April, 1955, Leslie and Gladys Jesperson gave birth to their third child. The couple lived in a town named Chilliwack in British Columbia, Canada. The boy was named Keith and would eventually be the middle child of five, with two brothers and two sisters. Leslie Jesperson was a stoic man, an alcoholic whose emotional distance from his family would be noted in later years. The distant and often remote Northwest district of Canada has a habit of breeding strong men, but the cold of the climate was bred into Leslie's bones. Out in the wilderness, it was not uncommon to have to endure zero temperature chilling gales, with blizzards regularly forcing the locals indoors. The son of a blacksmith, Leslie Jesperson's father had moved to the region in the 1930s. A failed move to the warmer, more agricultural pastures of Saskatchewan resulted in a humiliating failure for the family, who were some of the millions affected by the aftershocks of the Great Depression. Forced back to the cold, Leslie's family was used to going hungry and to the cold.

The family patriarch, Leslie's father, Arthur, was unfamiliar with the concept of defeat. The failed move to the east and the resigned move back to British Columbia was said to have broken him, embittering him, and forcing him to come to terms with the idea of failure. In the family – descended, they said, from warrior Danes – such losses were abhorrent and not to be tolerated. Arthur's own brother – Keith's great uncle – was committed to an insane asylum around this time. Not wanting to face the idea, he decided to kill himself. Lacking the traditional means, the man took a nail measuring three and a half inches and hammered it into his own skull. This was the family atmosphere in which Leslie was raised and which he would imprint on the young Keith.

The family's blacksmith shop was always busy. There were two forges, and the kids would help out when they weren't in school. Leslie would grow up swinging the hammer against the red hot iron as his father made horse shoes and other metal works for the locals. He worked to the point of exhaustion every day just to help the family put food on the table. By the time Keith was born, the old blacksmith Arthur was relegated to a looming presence in the corner of the room. Rather than the strong-armed iron worker remembered by Leslie and the family, Keith recalled a "tough guy" who never showed emotion to anyone, much less spent time talking to the kids in the family. Women were, to Arthur, seeming wastes of space. The ideas and concepts were impressed upon Leslie and Keith from a young age.

Forever shocked by the failure in Saskatchewan, old Arthur was tainted by the idea that he was forced to sometimes go out and shoot gophers just to feed his family. It was a work ethic and approach to life that left a huge imprint on Keith's father. Leaving school in the tenth grade, Leslie found himself doing anything he could to put together money. Not only was he a plumber and blacksmith, but he took to teaching himself Morse code, mechanical and hydraulic engineering, electronics, and how to manufacture items. During a particularly difficult time, he became a coffin maker for the local native tribes who were suffering from an epidemic. His hard work and creativity left Leslie with a string of clever inventions designed to simplify logging in the area and make it more efficient. Turning his skills to anything, he was able to teach himself how to play the accordion and the keyboard, as well as write poems. Friends of Leslie remembered him as the six-foot-tall life of any party, but the man never topped five foot eleven. The soft rural accent belied a furious anger known only to those closest to him.

Having seen his own father's struggle to piece together a living, Leslie was determined not to let himself be caught in such a rut. As well as being named the Master of the Fraser River Dikes, he took on a number of jobs and started a number of businesses. This time spent on his career impacted the family and the time he was able to spend with his wife and five children. Added to this and above all else, he drank.

To Keith, however, the man was still an icon, a figure demanding respect. Leslie was an engineer, a trusted member of the community, a friend to all who knew him, and he was the family's authority figure. As Keith remembered it at a later date, however, his father would "work and eat and then drink himself to sleep." Just like in the blacksmith's forge, Leslie encouraged – practically demanded – that the children help their father when they could. Every day was a work day, and if the children showed any signs of laziness, they were beaten.

Leslie was a master of both physical and psychological abuse. Keith would remember the sarcastic put-downs, the insults, and the wisecracks made by his father. One incident involved a young Keith asking his father whether an electric fence was working. Leslie encouraged his son to urinate on the fence and laughed uproariously when the boy received a sharp electric shock. He pulled a similar trick with one of the girls, encouraging her to touch the fence while he laughed. As a learned and practical man, Leslie would get angry when his children couldn't replicate his own capacity for learning. He was emotionally and physically distant from the children. Drinking, working, and missing school plays, for example, were all par for the course. Women, too, were also seemingly not deserving of Leslie's respect, with him telling Keith on numerous occasions that he was only still with his wife, Gladys (Keith's mother,) because of her cooking. It was an attitude that Keith would absorb.

Gladys herself was an equally hard worker, but was at least present for the raising of the children. Having been brought up in a strict, puritanical household, she found even the slightest mention of sex abhorrent. When she had been growing up on a farm, the women and girls of the household were not even allowed to be present when the animals were being encouraged to breed. There was not a single member of the Jesperson family – including Leslie – who was ever permitted to see Gladys without her clothes. In her own house, Gladys would allow no discussion of sex, sexuality, or any associated matter. To her, it was an entirely taboo subject. It was a known fact that she preferred the two girls, Jill and Sharon, while Leslie favored two of his boys, Brad and Bruce. Keith was left alone, the forgotten middle child.

For Keith, childhood was not a happy time. Between his father's alcoholic beatings, his mother's staunch religious approach to child-rearing, the indifference by both of them, he was encouraged to find his own way in the world. Recognized as the least bright of all of the Jesperson children, Keith's earliest memory is of a day at the park. Standing at the top of the slide and noticing his younger brother Brad sitting at the bottom, he took a decent-sized rock and balanced it at the top of the chute before letting go. The rock rolled down the plastic and caught the younger boy in the head. Blood was drawn, and Brad erupted into a barrage of tears. It would be Keith's sister Sharon who took the blame, however, and he was happy to let her.

People have come forward with memories of Keith's early childhood as being fairly normal. He was a quiet and obedient young boy, but one who was prone to day-dreaming. Facing a lot of teasing about his inability to focus and his lack of mental athleticism, Keith was a ponderous, sluggish young boy. The only area where he showed any capacity was in the family's favorite game, cribbage, which he was able to play before he could read.

During the time of Keith's childhood, Chilliwack was a rural area. Though the family would later move to the larger town of Selah, they would always own animals, including chickens, horses, ducks, sheep, and dogs. Leslie, ever the handyman, built a wooden water wheel to help trap salmon in the stream that would run through their land. As the children were out helping and working, they would be scattered across the several acres the family owned. When it was time for dinner, Gladys would pull the cord on a huge orange whistle, and the children would come running back to the kitchen table.

Keith was also a shy boy. Happy to play alone, even before he started school, he could be found digging tunnels and building forts. His mother thought that he was never happier than when playing alone. Daydreaming and imagining his life as a hunter in Africa or a sailor in the navy, Keith played out heroic fantasies in his mind, but always on his own.

But sometimes, it was impossible to escape his father's attention. Speaking after his imprisonment, Keith could recall one day when he was forced into hiding under the kitchen table from the leather belt that Leslie used to whip the children. As his father screamed, "Don't you run away from me!" the then four year old attempted to hide amid the chair and table legs. Grabbed and dragged out, Leslie laid the belt repeatedly across his son's backside, punishment for some long-forgotten indiscretion. Stop crying, Keith was told, or he would be given something to cry about.

One incident that Keith remembered incurring his father's wrath involved a duck that Leslie kept as a pet. Keith had been playing outside when he came across the bird, a favorite of his father's various menagerie. Suddenly struck by a violent impulse, Keith took a rock and killed the bird. His father found out, and despite Gladys's attempts to intervene, Keith received a whipping with the belt. The drink consumed by Leslie gave the beating an extra edge and made him almost impossible to reason with when his temper flared.

Keith would find a friend before he was five years old. A brown Labrador named Duke arrived in the house just before Keith's birthday and soon became firmly attached to the middle child. Sharing a room with Brad, Duke could often be found sleeping on Keith's bed during the nights. For once, Keith had a topic he was happy to discuss with anyone. He would animatedly chat about Duke with anyone who would listen. The dog would chase salmon along the stream and cars along the road, taking a few blows in the process. Duke would chase off rival dogs and even killed two of the neighbor's dogs who might have ventured into the yard. Protective of Keith, Duke would shield him from any intruders onto the property. This was where Keith got his first insight into the reproductive ways of the world, with Duke attempting to have sex with any female dog he came across. Keith later joked that the dog gave him a "head start about sex."

When Keith did try to make friends, however, things did not proceed in the best of fashions. He was often teased for being taller and more cumbersome than the other children at school. One attempt to befriend a Native American child resulted in Leslie becoming angry and telling Keith to break off any relationship with the boy, as there was simply nothing to be gained from the friendship. A school sports day ended in disaster when a hop, skip, and jump event involved Keith. Rather than running before launching himself forwards, Keith simply stood in one spot, hopped, skipped, and then jumped. The teacher pointed out his efforts as the exact opposite of the desired technique, the other children burst into laughter, and Keith ran home, telling himself that he didn't need anyone else.

His parents attempted to find a friend for Keith, and a boy named Martin would occasionally be welcomed to the home. Martin was a troublesome boy, who would find ways to create mischief and leave Keith saddled with the blame. The clumsy child, too tall for his age, near-sighted and not especially bright, Keith found few ways in which to escape the punishments Martin's behavior brought his way. Subjected to beatings and punishments in front of everybody, one day Martin's actions grew too much for Keith. Keith tracked the boy down and trapped him in the space behind the family's garage. Keith jumped on the youngster, wrapping his hands around Martin's neck. He choked and choked, refusing to let go until Leslie arrived on the scene and pulled him away. By the time Keith relinquished his grip, Martin was unconscious. If his father had not arrived, Keith admits that the boy would likely have become his first victim. Once again, Keith received a beating. This time, he knew he was guilty.

Discussing the event later, Keith Jesperson remembers that this was the first time he was able to envisage himself as two distinct people. The normal, gentle side of his personality stood by and watched as the angrier side took control. This added to the imaginary world into which the boy would often retreat, something he named "Keith's World." In this place, he was able to retreat from the difficulty of everyday life and spend his time with animals, away from antagonists such as his brothers and his classmates.

Keith's relationship with animals was complicated. As well as Duke, whom he loved, and the other family pets, Keith once came across a raven with a broken wing. He picked up the bird, splintered its wing, and made a home for it out of rags. He named the bird Blackie. Arriving home from school one day, Keith discovered that his older brother and a friend had taken the bird and trapped it under an orange milk crate. They hurled their pocket knives at the bird until it died, all while Keith watched. Furious, he ran into his brother's room and threw all of the toy planes out of the window. Leslie was unimpressed, saying Blackie was just a "dumb crow." Keith was punished, Bruce was not.

But animals' deaths were not unfamiliar to Keith. He would help his father out around the land, killing gophers on a regular basis. He would arrive home covered in gopher blood after an enjoyable day's hunting. Leslie could not abide the presence of too many cats on the farm. When kittens were born, they were killed quickly. Keith would help, much to his sisters' disgust. Similarly, he was taught how to deal with garter snakes that were found on the property, taking a hoe and cutting the reptiles in two. But this often wasn't enough. Keith admits that he "enjoyed" watching them struggle as he balanced the blade on their backs, even going as far as to torture the animals with garden tools. For young Keith, it was just one more way of having fun.

Alongside various stories of torturing animals and disagreements with other children, Keith was aware of sex from an early age. As is perhaps inevitable for someone growing up in a rural area, the animals gave some insight for the young boy, providing ideas that were carried over into a relationship with a little girl. When Keith was five, he had his first kiss on the back seat of his mother's car. The two continued their experiments and "practiced sex," which for the children meant kissing, a little bit of inquisitive touching, and showing one another the more private areas of the body. If Gladys had ever discovered her child in such a position, she would likely have been furious.

Sex presented itself in Keith's life in an entirely more dubious fashion when he was playing on a neighbor's farm. While he and some other children entertained themselves, one of the workers offered to teach them about sex. He encouraged the children to undress and did likewise, before encouraging them to touch one another. Keith quickly grew scared and ran away before anything could happen. Later, he would ask one of the boys who had been left behind what had occurred. He was told that the dairy worker had sodomized the youngster, that it had hurt, and that the boy had told his father. The boy's parents encouraged their son to keep quiet, but the worker was never seen again on the farm.

Friendships with the local boys were always fractious. Despite being the same age, in the same class, and living right next door to one boy, Keith managed to provoke nothing but ire in the child. Keith was often bullied by the boy, punched and hit almost every time they met one another. This culminated in another close call when, with the pair swimming at nearby Cultus Lake one summer, the boy took Keith by the head and held him under the surface of the lake, briefly allowed him up to breath, then forced him back down again. This went on for ten minutes, until Keith could see nothing but black. He was saved when a counsellor jumped in the water and pulled him out. But vengeance would be had. When the pair visited a local swimming pool, Keith grabbed the boy by the head and thrust it underwater. Keith was always the bigger, stronger one of the pair, though rarely knew how to use his size advantage. This time, however, he took advantage of his size and held the boy underwater with every intention of letting him die. The boy was only saved when a lifeguard dragged Keith away. It was the second murder attempt of a young life.

As Keith grew older, his interests grew more complicated. After briefly making friends with some boys in the area, he began to learn various techniques for torturing animals. They would attach firecrackers to sparrows, nail crows to a wooden board as throwing knife target practice, or would feed Alka-Seltzer to seagulls, a practice which would make the birds' stomachs burst inside them. But the torture was not limited to birds. Keith and his cohorts would take cats and dogs, nailing them to the same boards and fill them with needles and other sharp objects. Keith still recalls one of his favorite pastimes, which involved crimping together cats' tails using wire, throwing them over either side of a rope, and watching until one clawed the other to death. The boys would sit and laugh. Even after one cat had died, the other would still yelp, howl, and scream until it died of its wounds. The boys found it uproariously funny.

Living in America

At the age of twelve, Keith was informed by his parents that they would be moving to Washington State in the US. Leslie had been approached by an American group who wanted him to design machinery on their hop farm. Despite the fact that Keith had experienced a difficult upbringing in Canada, the thought of moving to the States terrified him. He didn't want to leave Canada. He knew the area. He had a paper route. This didn't matter, of course, and the family was soon leaving Chilliwack for Selah, Washington. They moved into a large home in a middle class neighborhood. But just like back in Canada, Keith was unable to get too close to anyone. While he had been a little bit strange and different in Canada, he was considered downright odd in America.

Keith's sister Jill recalls the effect the move had on her brother, suggesting that it changed him. He began to acquire nicknames, always referring to his large frame. Sloth. Fatty. Hulk. Tiny. But they never seemed to bother Keith that much. The real change Jill remembers was in her older brother's humor, which took a turn towards darker subjects. He would laugh at the disgusting, the morbid. He went out exploring with Duke and had soon tracked out about five miles in every direction from the family home. He was always playing by himself.

One incident saw Keith and the closest thing he had to a friend – a boy named Tom Haggar – caught shoplifting. The pair were paraded around in front of their classmates by the police, taken back to the station, and had their fingerprints taken. When Keith eventually told his parents, he was sent to his room, while Leslie phoned Tom's parents. Leslie was informed that Keith had been the mastermind behind the enterprise, a concept that Leslie found unsurprising. Keith was driven to the store the next day and made to apologize. He was told to clean out the back alley behind the store as a punishment. His father would, for a long time afterward, refer to Keith as his "little thief." Throughout the town, Keith now had a reputation as a corrupting influence. Any friends he had made were now banned from seeing him.

By the time Keith moved into the eighth grade, he was fully ensconced in Keith's World. He lived in his daydreams, without the troublesome friends that he had found so difficult to acquire. Thoughts and ambitions were entertained, especially with the view to becoming a mounted police officer back in Canada, one of the famous Mounties. One slight issue pertaining to this matter was Keith's physical fitness, which was lagging far behind what was required of the Canadian police recruits. An encounter with a distant relative brought the youngster into contact with experiences from the Vietnam War, wherein Keith looked over photos and listened to experiences of soldiers who had killed and tortured the enemies. The ideas brought back memories of Keith's time torturing animals, which he later admitted provided him with sexual pleasure.

In Selah, however, there were fewer targets open to his impulses. Stray dogs and cats were not nearly as abundant as they had been back in Chilliwack. One time, when chasing down a tomcat with his BB gun, Keith managed to corner the animal. It was shot full of pellets until it couldn't move, so the boy moved in with a stone and smashed the cat's paws. He remembers that it took fifty-six BB pellets before the cat finally died.

As he moved into adolescence, however, one of the major problems in Keith's life was left unrequited. The opposite sex presented him with many problems. Often, he would approach girls only to be rejected before he'd even finished his sentence. Always busy at his father's work place, he found himself admiring women from a distance and rarely spending any time in their company. After a few embarrassing fumbles with older girls during a trip to Canada, he decided that he would spend some time researching sex. After looking into various books on the subject, he found himself assuming the role of victim in any potential encounter and mixed the concept of sexual intercourse with rape. When writing about his first sexual encounter, he described the girl who climbed on top of him as having "raped me over and over."

Despite the interactions and experiences, he had meeting girls while away in Canada, getting to know any in Selah seemed an entirely different prospect. In the area, he had acquired the nickname "Igor" and "Ig" for short. The name-calling was led by his older brother Brad, who teased and taunted Keith during the move up to high school, where Brad was already a student. Other students picked on the boy, still big for his age. They asked for loans and to borrow items. They rarely had any intention of returning anything. Keith was happy to yield rather than to fight back and get in trouble once again.

Attempts were made to turn his size into something productive. Noticing that the school athletes all impressed the girls, he tried to take part in the football team. Already six foot, two inches, and over two hundred pounds, it seemed like a natural fit. Keith resented having to play tackle or guard, however, believing these to be "dumb" positions. When the coach encouraged him to "kill" the opposition, he bluntly replied that he would do no such thing. Keith, worried about hurting his teammates in practice, was wary from the outset. When he did get to play in a game against another school, Keith charged into the fray, nearly broke one player's leg, and then smashed two of the quarterback's ribs. Keith was dismissed from the game. The coach was impressed, but Keith was perturbed by the idea of working on a team. The perpetual loner, he quit the team. Wrestling was another brief interest and a more individual sport. But Keith's parents never turned out to watch any of his games. Gladys might arrive for one or two, but never with the enthusiasm shown when any of the other children were participating.

Growing older, Keith Jesperson became more and more exposed to alcohol. With his father already a committed alcoholic, those around him were also beginning to indulge themselves to a greater extent and presented Keith with something of a temptation. Leslie responded to such temptation among his kids by allowing them to drink what they liked as long as they were at home. He sought to remove the glamour and the allure of alcohol and, as Keith remembers, he succeeded. The older brothers would have keg parties at the family home on occasion, events that took on a large level of local notoriety. Keith recalls attending one, getting drunk, and attempting to grope a girl who would later turn out to be his brother's date.

When he turned sixteen, Keith passed his driving test and finally had a means to travel independently further than he could walk. His first car was a brown sedan which he drove until it broke down, and his second car was a Jeep. Gas was always in short supply, and the teenager topped up what he could afford by siphoning fuel out of other people's gas tanks. The freedom of a car allowed Keith to cater to his compulsions. He would be able to drive out into the wilderness with his .22 rifle and shoot at what he found.

By the time Keith was a junior in Selah, his dog Duke was starting to get old. Rather than the boundless companionship of earlier days, Keith now needed to help the dog up into his bed at night, up on to the sofa when they watched TV, and had to care for the dog's arthritic limbs as it moved around the family home. Les Jesperson was never a fan of Duke. The dog, he thought, was stupid, useless for hunting, but Keith loved Duke regardless. One day, he came home from school and was informed by one of the workers on the farm that Duke had died. Distraught, Keith tracked down his father, who played off the death with the suggestion that the dog must have eaten some coyote poison and had grown ill. Les had been forced to shoot him. To Keith, this was essentially murder.

Duke was not the only dog in the Jesperson household, but he was the only one Keith loved. After he died, Keith turned his angry attention to the dogs his father liked better. He would sneer and snarl at them and hit them when they got too close. The other dogs learned not to spend too much time around Keith and would often go running as soon as he entered the room. One of the dogs was so scared that it would urinate whenever Keith came near. Another grew so scared on one occasion that it bolted out into the middle of the road, running away from Keith, whereupon it was hit by a passing car.

Sex still played on Keith's mind. He had matured past his awkward youth and was considered something of a handsome, strapping man. Tall and strong, he was still socially misguided. He found some relief through pleasuring himself, which he found to be easier than the circus around talking to girls. Inevitably, anyone who showed interest in him seemed to want to use him as either a source of money or a means of transport. Outside of the social circle and male comradery he might have expected, he was unable to turn to his peers for advice on interacting with the opposite sex. Asking his parents or brothers seemed out of the question. Thoughts and daydreams began to revolve around rape and kidnapping, of overpowering a smaller girl in order to discover the as-yet-unknown world of sex.

By the time he reached his senior year in high school, the prospect of having a girlfriend had all but evaporated from Keith's mind. His sex life was a solitary affair. That was until he met a girl in the year below, a junior whom he thought to be cute and, shockingly to Keith, seemed to like him back. After a few dates and days out at the local drag races, Keith settled into a pattern with the girl as something of a steady girlfriend.

Wrestling was still an outlet for Keith. As a fully-fledged member of the team, he was technically part of the athletic elite at the high school. There were still ambitions and dreams in the back of his mind revolving around returning to Canada to join the Mounties. In better shape physically, he might even stand a chance of passing their tests. One day, the coach arranged for a rope trial. The students were to climb to the top of the rope as fast as they could. A big teenager, Keith had never managed the feat. Still teased about his size and his clumsiness, such a trial seemed impossible for "Igor." But on this particular occasion, Keith dragged himself all the way to the top. Once he reached the pinnacle, the fastenings began to falter and snapped. Keith fell from twenty-five feet onto the hard floor. There was a sharp pain shooting through the left side of his body. Unable to move, Keith writhed in agony as he was told to get up and walk it off. Assisted, he rose to one foot and limped to the showers.

The coach eventually agreed to call Gladys, and an increasingly dizzy Keith was rushed to the emergency room in an ambulance. After several X-rays and help from his older sister Sharon, who was a nurse, Keith was told he had a nasty sprain but would be up again in a couple of weeks. This wouldn't be the case. A few days later, Keith's left foot swelled up to double its size. He had to rip open a boot to force his foot inside. His girlfriend stopped calling, so he braved the pain and drove to her house. Once there, the girl's mother said that Keith wasn't welcome and no one wanted to see him. Despite the relationship, the mangled foot of Keith Jesperson was too much for the girl. Limping was now common, and any attempt to wrestle was met with opponents deliberately going for his injured foot. All trips to the country to kill animals were put on hold, all potential dates with girls forsaken. Keith cut a larger slit down the side of his boot for his swollen foot and returned to work in his dad's business. Now, he really did fit the "Igor" nickname.

School turned out to be a bust for Keith, who graduated with unimpressive grades. College was out of the question, seemingly, while occasional thoughts of a military career were entertained and rejected. His foot still bothered him, though he took a job pumping gas. Foot trouble continued until he went to see a specialist, whereupon Keith was eventually diagnosed with torn ligaments. This meant needing arch support initially, then three surgeries. For the three months after the first operation, Keith was resigned to crutches. Work turned to more sedate, inside jobs while he recovered, during which time there were considerations of whether or not it would be feasible to sue the school board. He moved in and out of the family home, especially when Leslie Jesperson borrowed Keith's motorbike and drunkenly crashed, landing himself in critical care. Keith was charged with the family business while his father recovered. As well as the accident wounds, Les was told he needed to quit drinking lest the alcohol kill him. Struggling, Les told people that it was for his family that he kicked the habit, though Keith knew better.

Romance was still an issue, while the surgeries and foot issues had put an end to Keith's ambition of joining the Mounties. Aged nineteen, working in the family business, and still not entirely recovered, his life appeared listless and directionless. But a wrong order at a fast food restaurant led to him meeting a seventeen year old named Rose. The pair flirted, dated, and eventually got engaged. Rose's mother didn't trust Keith, while Keith's family constantly reiterated just how lucky he was to have met this girl. For Rose, marriage to Keith seemed like the best way out of a busy household. They were set to marry on her eighteenth birthday, despite Keith's misgivings. On the 2nd of August, 1975, Keith Jesperson married Rose Pernick. Thus, with mixed feelings and an amateur appreciation of romantic relationships, the Happy Face Killer was married and began a new chapter in his life, one that would eventually lead down an ever more twisted road.

Married Life

For the future serial killer, life as a married man was entirely different to what he had experienced before. A job with a lumber company beckoned, but the constant need for surgery on his foot kept Keith close to his parents, working in his father's various workshops when he could. Rose was beginning to discover that life away from her family was not as blissful as she had imagined. The pair moved into a mobile home, which they parked on a part of the Jesperson estate that had been turned into the "Silver Spur Mobile Park." Together with his father, Keith operated the heavy machinery and carried out the work needed to turn a plot of land into a trailer park ready for over a hundred mobile homes. Numbers began to swell as residents moved in. Les was sure to be strict with residents, while Keith took a friendlier approach. Perhaps too friendly, it might have seemed, as his father could recall an instance where a soon-to-be-evicted tenant with a teenage daughter mentioned the possibility of calling the cops, with the charge of statutory rape on her mind. Keith shrugged off the suggestion, but he does remember watching women through the windows of their trailers at night, before returning to his home to fantasize while in bed with his wife about what he had seen.

But the base instincts were never far away. Even when he was busy working at the trailer park, Keith felt the need to return out to the wilderness and find something to kill. With a set of by-laws on the park to guard against strays, Keith one day encountered a cat on the property where he had had trouble before. He picked up the creature and slammed it into the pavement. Picking up the stunned cat, he wrung its neck, and then drove out a few miles to fling it from the window of his car. The tenant was told that the cat had simply run away.

Animals that Keith deemed to be pests were taken out in a variety of ways. While Les has resigned himself to drowning the occasional stray cat in a sack, his son would use anything he had available. Shovels, screwdrivers, sickles, scythes, hammers, or simply his bare hands. He would shoot dogs with his pistol or simply throw them out of the window of a speeding car. A dog rummaging through his garbage was beheaded with a scythe (the blade only managed to cut through half of the neck,) while poisoned meat was used to kill seven cats and kittens in just one night. Other cats were burned alive in an incinerator, or trapped in a barrel with gasoline before Keith threw a match in afterward. Later, he would admit to deriving an almost sexual pleasure from the act of killing.

Eventually, Keith's court case against the school regarding his horrific injury was finally settled. In 1976, he was awarded $33,000 in a settlement. For Keith, this seemed like the chance to finally move back to Chilliwack. Instead, Les managed to convince his son to invest the money in expanding the trailer park. They would be business partners, with Keith and Rose owning ten percent. Rose could even be put in charge of the books. Keith agreed and went about the work of laying concrete for the expansion.

Following the business proposal, Rose began to pressure Keith for children. The idea perturbed Keith, who knew himself to still be attracted to other women, one in particular named Arliss who was a member of his bowling team. After being turned round to the idea by Rose, six months of attempting to conceive bore no results. On checking with a doctor, it was found Keith had a low sperm count. He blamed the stress of his living and working arrangements, especially the influence of his father. Rose, desperate for children, even put the couple on an adoption list.

The dream of the Silver Spur Mobile Home Park did not last. After only two years, money problems forced the family to sell. Spending what money he had from the sale on a series of poor ventures, Keith found that he needed money fast. He took a series of low paying jobs, often all at once. Eventually, he managed to secure a position at a local trucking company. The idea of being an independent truck driver appealed to Keith, and this was his first step along the path. It began with working in the garage, welding, repairing, and performing other tasks. Away from the stress of the trailer park and working sixty hours at his new job, Keith became a father for the first time. Melissa was born in 1979, into a household still experiencing money troubles, but she was well-loved by her parents.

A year later, Jason was born. Keith doted on the children. When they were around their grandfather, Les, Keith was adamant that he should never touch them. Keith never beat his children, and was sure that his father wouldn't either. Keith's beatings and humiliations at his father's hands still festered under the surface of their cordial relationship.

Soon, Keith was driving trucks. His assignments were getting to be longer and longer, with Keith spending more and more time behind the wheel, away from his young family. At this point, he was only present some five or six days every four weeks. This took a toll on the marriage. Arguments began to abound, and tempers frayed. Rose had put on weight during her pregnancy, a fact that Keith was sure to mention. Their libidos were running at different speeds, with Keith's urge to rush to the bedroom on their first meeting not in line with Rose's desires of how to spend what little family time they had.

Even when out driving the truck, Keith was still something of a prisoner to his urges. Sometimes he might start a random fire, or attack a stray cat, even in front of his children. Similarly, old feelings of distance began to creep back into his life as he found it tough to make friends with those in the same business. In Canada, he was viewed as American. In America, he seemed Canadian. So, in 1981, after Keith discovered a new spate of jobs opening up in British Columbia, he moved the family back north of the border. Rose, pregnant once again, was less than enthusiastic. She would follow once Keith was settled in the new home.

Finally, Keith was free. Free from his parents and his father's influence over his life. Free from the rigorous work schedules that locked him down to one place. Even free from his wife and children. Out on the road, he was independent. This was put to the test soon, when an effervescent Keith decided to pull over and help a young girl on the side of the road. She was having trouble with her car. A quick check under the bonnet revealed that it was a simple fix. Delighted, the attractive young girl gave Keith her number and promised to buy him dinner in Spokane. Keith refused the temptation to stray from his martial vows, but he pulled to the side of the road a short while later and masturbated to the image.

It didn't take long for Keith to settle in Canada. He started out by waving flags on site, but was soon driving the coal trucks. In the bottom of the coal pits, the huge trucks that moved the produce weighed up to 170 tons when fully loaded. Driving them around the quarry was dangerous work. If the brakes failed on an incline, the driver was told to drag his truck along the side of the wall in an attempt to slow the vehicles down. This work was great for Keith's long-term goal of cross country trucking adventures. And away from the family, getting to know his new work colleagues, Keith found himself even enjoying his bachelor lifestyle.

But this came to a shuddering halt when Rose and the kids arrived. The family took a two bedroom flat, and Rose made her annoyance at Keith's new misadventures known. Scared he might lose his kids, Keith reeled in his behavior. Jason, Melissa, and the newborn Carrie were very, very important to Keith. But trouble was always just around the corner and, as usual, the relationship between Keith and his father was to blame.

In British Colombia, the real money was in welding. Abandoning his trucking dreams to focus on the large debts he had racked up, Keith retrained as a welder and was soon making good money. But he noticed that everyone around him in the workshop was stealing. Batteries, tools, even engine parts. Everything seemed to go missing, and everyone seemed to be in on the heist. Eventually, Keith was too.

Meanwhile, Les had opened a hardware store back in America. Speaking over the phone, he casually mentioned how nice the leather overalls were that they had in Keith's workshop. Soon, the son was on the lookout for a set in his father's size. A guard posted at the door caught him as he tried to smuggle the clothes out of the shop. Keith was offered a deal: admit the theft and have it all forgotten about in a year. Les advised Keith to deny everything, lest everyone at the company assume he was a thief. Keith, against his better judgement, took his father's advice. He denied everything and was fired. After the good money he had been making in the welding shop, he chose to blame his father once again for his current, precarious predicament.

The next two years were spent looking for a job in Canada. None paid as well as the welding position. Truck driving was back on the cards, but it paid a fraction of the wages. The family moved a hundred miles east to escape any possible rumors about Keith's dismissal. A brief stint as the driver of a huge Peterbilt machine allowed him to control a dream machine, but company layoffs hit after only eight months. A fleeting interest in boxing helped Keith get back into shape, but the cold Alberta weather caused Rose to complain. Soon, news arrived that Gladys had contracted lymph-node cancer. To bring the grandchildren back near their dying grandmother, the whole family moved back to the south. Rose was happy, but Keith was not. It seemed that, though he loved his kids, Keith had fallen out of love with his wife.

With money still tight, the family bought a home. Keith had a trucking job, but nothing to fall back on if he lost it. Les offered to help with the down payment on the mobile home, a move which Keith saw as just another attempt to exert control. But these days, Keith was too busy to argue. He was too busy, still, to indulge his violent fantasies. There were no chances to drive out to the middle of nowhere to dismember a cat or to torture a dog. There was no time to set fires. He had to work.

This meant driving trucks all across the state, and it was something that Keith, finally, liked. At times, he was essentially living in the truck, away from the family. Out on the road, there was no one to criticize or complain to him. In Keith's view, he was the master of his fate, the king of his domain. As an extra benefit, there was always a slew of available women present in the regular truck stop haunts. While he was still adamant about staying "true" to Rose, Keith saw no crime in looking at other women when he was out of town. In every stop, Keith would flirt with the waitresses in the diners and cafes. No longer finding his relationship with Rose sexually gratifying, leaving Keith with masses of stored-up tension in need of release. This meant, at first, bike rides or hikes, attempts to make himself too tired to pursue sex with his wife.

One day, Keith arrived back from a trucking journey to learn that his mother's cancer had grown worse. She died two weeks later, after Keith came to visit her on her deathbed. At the funeral, several people noted that Keith was not showing any real, explicit emotion. When looking back over their fuss, he failed to see the problem. His mother was "just ashes." Within a year, Les would be remarried.

In 1986, Keith faced his worst fear. He lost his trucking job after the boss's son took his place. This made mortgage repayments a problem, and the family soon had to move. Again, Keith was back to juggling part-time jobs, trying to get by on caffeine, sugary drinks, and not enough sleep. At times, he even stole from the bar where he was working as a doorman. Eventually, it got to be too much. Rose accidently overdrew the family bank account, and Keith was furious. Determined not to beat his wife (or his children) as his father might have done, he unleashed his rage on the front door. A big hole was punched through the wood. Rose left for a few hours to allow her husband to cool down. The door was never fixed, existing as a perpetual reminder, Keith thought, to think before writing a check. But it was no good. Eventually, the family declared bankruptcy.

Eventually, Keith found another trucking job. Once again, he was free to travel up and down the state. But his sexual frustration found no release. That was until he chanced upon an encounter with the wife of a friend. After dropping little Jason off to play with the friend's son, the father – Billy – made his excuses and left. As soon as he was gone, the mother – Ginny – began to make advances for Keith. He played them off, worried about Billy finding out. When Billy arrived back home, Keith's confession was met with indifference. The couple were swingers. Confused but interested, Keith had sex with Ginny that night and many time afterward. It was the first time he cheated on Rose, and he only stopped after Billy and Ginny moved away from the area.

From then on, the seal on Keith's promiscuity seemed to have broken. After fantasizing about the women he met while driving his truck, and never skipping an opportunity to assist a damsel in distress on the side of the road, Keith began to pick up a series of mistresses. The divorcee he met in a late-night restaurant. The two young girls who wanted to see inside his truck. Anyone but the prostitutes who frequented the truck stops. They were considered a step too far. Keith liked to assume that his moral compass was still very firmly pointed towards the good, in actions if not in thoughts.

But this wouldn't last long. One night saw Keith and his truck traveling down Highway 97. His lights picked out the shape of a young girl pushing along a bicycle in the middle a storm. Pulling over, he offered her a lift. She was young – possibly around fifteen – and of Native American descent. She reminded Keith of the young girls who had lived near his home in Chilliwack. Already, his fantasies were running wild with ideas. Driving along, he imagined taking her by force. Picking a parking spot, he reached over before he could even completely park the truck. The girl seemed to have predicted such an attack and leaped out of the cabin.

The girl was fifty feet away, and Keith had no hope of catching her. Trying to play off the incident, he returned the girl's bike and sped away as fast as he could. For the next month, he was terrified of being caught. All the possible means of identification flashed through his head – the license plate, the load, his somewhat unique appearance – and he imagined the girl informing her father of the attempted rape. But nothing happened. Keith swore to stick only to girls who wanted to have sex with him. Or his wife.

After a few months of renewed sexual frustration, Keith was back to familiar targets. A cat received a stoning in front of Jason, and Keith drowned a neighbor's dog when he was all alone. He took particular care in the latter, allowing the dog up to breath occasionally to prolong the act. It was a technique he found satisfying in a sexual fashion and one he would use later on. Animals were always under threat from Keith, and his children knew it. He might douse a cat in water and throw it out into the freezing night, or cover a dog in gasoline and throw it a lit match. Even his children's own dog was not safe. After it developed hemorrhoids, Keith took it out into the back yard and smashed the little dog's head. The children cried for days.

Following the incident with the girl who got away – and noting his growing frustrations – Keith decided that he might need to try professional assistance. Out in his truck once again, Keith met Linda, a prostitute. He spent twenty dollars for three hours of Linda's attentions. She was the first of a string of girls as Keith got more and more accustomed to paying for sex. There was a woman in almost every truck stop, dotted along the various routes. When he arrived back home to Rose, he might try to gauge her interest in romantic activity, but she was never able to satisfy his burning urges. One time, Rose asked to come along on one of the trips. The trip was no fun, culminating in her husband pushing her towards a pair of pimps in one truck stop and joking that they could take her. Once they arrived home, Keith immediately went to the irrigation ditch behind the house and drowned a cat. With scratches up his arms, he told the watching children that it had "got in his way." After that, people started to grow worried for Keith's state of mind. In all, it was the beginning of the end of their happy marriage.

It was with the marriage in this state that Keith met Peggy Jones. A waitress in a truck stop who flirted with Keith and eventually went back to his cabin, Peggy was the first woman who Keith met who could keep up with his sexual urges. A few weeks after meeting her, he called her again. Then again. And again. Soon, he was stopping at her home every time he went out on the road. He told Peggy that he wasn't married, and she told him she was going through a divorce. Soon, Keith was spending more time with the new woman than he was with his family. After a short time, Peggy and Keith began to see themselves as a couple and took trips together. The told one another that they were each in love with the other. Peggy advised Keith that he needed to finish his marriage and break away from the father he was always complaining about.

Driving Peggy up to a tavern near his home, Keith went back to the family. Before going to bed, he played with the kids for a few hours. When lying next to Rose, he told her that he wasn't happy, that he wanted a divorce. His wife rolled to one side and went to sleep. No arguments, no disagreements. In the morning, Keith played with the kids again and Rose remained silent. He left to drive his rig south and, when he returned, he found an empty home and a letter informing him that Rose and the kids had gone to live with her mother in Spokane. She wanted everything in the divorce, everything except Keith's bowling ball, his golf clubs, his bicycle, and his clothes. Keith read the letter and sat down and cried.

In the summer of 1988, Keith decided that he might need to turn to his sister Jill for advice. Driving to her place in Seattle, he was involved in a traffic accident and found himself in the hospital. Unable to work, he lost his job. Taking a new position with shorter journeys, Keith discovered that he could smuggle Peggy along for the ride. Despite her waitressing job, she was happy to attend. The manager at her workplace warned Keith against the girl, telling him that she flirted with all of the truckers who came in and very nearly rode off with some of them.

Keith ignored the man. He moved in with Peggy and enjoyed, for the first time, living with a woman who enjoyed sex as much as he did.

But nothing else was quite so rosy. The kids were far away, and keeping up with the child support was proving difficult. Money was in increasingly short supply, and Les wasn't helping, having taken a dislike to Peggy. Keith, always one to take the contrarian view to whatever his father suggested, refused to listen to his father's advice to return to his family. The divorce was finalized on the couple's thirteenth anniversary. Keith would later confess that getting involved with Peggy would prove to be an awful mistake. Losing his family in such a fashion was an even worse mistake.

Life with Peggy quickly lost its sheen. After being together a year, the couple decided that they might benefit from being on the road together. Keith put in the papers to make Peggy his official driving partner. In his fantasy, they could get twice as much work done, and he would be able to have sex as often as he liked. But Keith underwent a sudden change of mind. Whether it was his dad's constant suggestions or guilt about his family, Keith told Peggy to leave and began to make plans to go back to his family. The pair had a goodbye drink just before Keith left. After popping out of the mobile home for a few hours, Keith returned to discover the TV smashed and Peggy passed out on the bed in front of him. He was overcome with his urges.

Removing her shoes and clothes, Keith proceeded to have sex with the sleeping woman. He did so multiple times before leaving to sleep at his dad's house. When he met up with Peggy in the morning, she asked whether they had had sex. Keith admitted they had, but left out the details of the rape. He left to be with his family for the next two and a half weeks. But he couldn't get Peggy out of his head. Despite realizing how much he'd missed his family, Keith couldn't bear to leave behind the sexual gratification that Peggy offered. He chose to return to her and leave his family once again.

The move to make Peggy a co-driver was made official, but Keith soon found that it was less than ideal. Peggy was not a skilled or committed driver. She couldn't work the truck in difficult conditions, resented being given navigational advice, and refused to work the long hours Keith was used to. This meant that he was forced to do a huge majority of the driving, especially in anything resembling tricky conditions. Meanwhile, Peggy would flirt with other truckers over the CB radio. Soon enough, the boss as the trucking company decided that Peggy was a hindrance more than a help and removed her from the rotation.

Keith snuck his girlfriend back into the truck anyway. But he could never rely on her to help with driving. Peggy had no sense of direction and no road smarts. He would take a nap in the bed and, when he woke up, would find that they were parked in a truck stop, miles off course. Peggy would be inside, flirting with the other truckers. When one offered to take her off Keith's hands, he readily agreed. This resulted in Peggy chasing him out into the parking lot, begging forgiveness. They continued this way for a year. Despite all the difficulties presented by the arrangement, Keith was at least happy to be having sex three times a day.

The couple ran into trouble when Keith was laid off from his job. Suffering an injury around the same time, he was unable to work. Now armed with a license, Peggy took to the roads as a trucker. Keith began to hear from his friends that she was perpetually unfaithful and that he would be wise to dump her as quickly as possible.

By the time 1990 rolled around, the pair were nearly finished. When Peggy informed Keith that she was pregnant, his suspicions were suitably riled enough to demand proof. Keith left her at this point, refusing to talk to her until the baby underwent blood tests. Moving in with a retired military veteran with multiple sclerosis and an expert cribbage habit, he took on a position as a care provider. For a while, Keith found himself to be somewhat useful and felt good about what he was doing. This emotion soon turned to pity, however, and Keith began to entertain thoughts about killing the man and putting him out of his misery. Deciding that it was too dangerous to stay around the man lest he be accused of eventual murder, Keith went back to Peggy one final time.

The relationship was more fraught than ever. The couple was living with Peggy's mother, though Keith could go days and weeks without hearing from Peggy. Instead, he would just hear stories about her exploits from fellow truck drivers, about the various liaisons she was having with other men up and down the country.

For the first time in his life, Keith found himself without a job for an extended period of time. He spent his days watching television and going to bars. He began to have ideas, fantasies, and daydreams of a vicious and nasty nature. With the relationship with Peggy heading inevitably towards doom, Keith found himself needing a new outlet for his emotions. His next move would be the final step into the world of mass murder. After a troubled childhood, a difficult adolescence, and a complicated adulthood, Keith Hunter Jesperson would take his first steps towards becoming a serial killer.

Taunja Bennett

Life for Keith Jesperson was complicated. With work harder to come by, any job seemed like the right one, while his home life had been devastated. The wife and kids had moved far away, and the relationship with Peggy was oscillating wildly between furious arguments and wild, lustful reconciliations. To Keith, it felt as though everything that could be going wrong in his life was going wrong. Even the house he was living in with Peggy felt old and haunted, as though he couldn't stay a day longer. He found himself tired, depressed, and with no easy way out.

This had been made especially difficult by the arrival of the Christmas season. Still a dedicated father, Keith had sold the majority of his possessions in order to be able to afford presents for his kids. His truck, his fishing rod, and his childhood toys had all been sold. Amid this, Keith received a phone call while he was staying at Peggy's mother's house. Peggy was out on the road and placed a collect call to Keith to inform him that she had met a new man while trucking and that he was to move out immediately.

Keith was furious. Falling back on old habits, he wandered out into the street. A stray cat was walking by, until Keith cornered it and wrapped his hands around its throat. Choking the life out of the animal relieved some of the anger.

Moving out of the house, Keith began to miss Peggy. Their relationship was far from ideal, but at least it gave a release to some of the sexual tension Keith felt building up inside himself every day. He was still living in Peggy's house while she was away, with her mother and the ghosts of two men who had reportedly hanged themselves in the home half a century ago.

On the morning of the 21st of January, 1990, Keith left the home. He purposefully only took a couple of dollars with him, worried about overspending in his current financial dire straits. As usual, he wandered from place to place, killing time. Visiting a bar, he played some pool for a while (he was very good) and won a bit of money. This cash was taken to a nearby bar, and by 2pm, Keith had started drinking. The establishment was run down and seedy. Playing pool again (and drinking black coffee), Keith noticed a girl on the other side of the room. She was playing pool with a couple of male friends. She was about a foot shorter than Keith, wore her dark her at shoulder length, and looked a little like a slimmer, prettier version of Rose. The girl smiled effortlessly and seemingly without a care in the world.

When the girl noticed that Keith was staring at her from across the bar, she ran right over and gave him a hug. The confused bartender asked why, to which the girl gave no real answer. Asking later, Keith discovered that she was a girl who hung out with many of the bar's less fortunate, run-down customers. Despite her warmth and pleasant character, it was generally accepted that she was far from the brightest girl. Eventually, she asked Keith to join her and her friends in a game of pool and introduced herself as Taunja. Keith took one look at the lack of money on the table. This usually meant one thing. The girl was feigning interest in order to encourage a confused man into buying her beer. Keith left for home.

At home, Keith found little of interest. Television was dull, and there was little on. Everything seemed to be depressing, and he just couldn't shake the image of the girl from the bar out of his mind. His fantasies ran wild thinking about her. Jumping in his truck, he drove back to see if she was still there.

Just as he pulled the truck up in front of the bar, Taunja was walking out. Keith followed her all the way to the parking lot, thinking that he might be able to convince her to get in his car, and that he might be able to seduce her. Even if she wasn't entirely willing, Keith supposed, he might take her anyway. By this point, she was playing on his mind enough that rational thought was moving further and further into the rear-view mirror.

But it seemed the girl remembered him. Walking up to her and starting a conversation, Taunja smiled while she chatted. Keith invited her to have something to eat, after which they might play a little pool somewhere. To his relief, she accepted. Once she hopped in his car, however, he pulled open his empty wallet. Despite the lack of money on him, Keith was certain he had a twenty dollar bill left at home. Would she mind if they went back and collected it?

Arriving at the house belonging to Peggy's mother, Keith invited the girl inside. Again, she agreed, but chose to leave behind a few of her possessions (a purse and a Walkman) in the truck. At this point, Keith considered actually taking the girl to a restaurant. His mind was on fire with the possibilities that lay ahead. The idea of treating her well was compelling, but thoughts about what he had done to the stray cat were also beginning to creep into his mental space. Welcoming her inside, Keith closed the door behind them and stepped into the bedroom while he planned his next move.

Keith, caught up in the moment, wasn't sure what he should do. There were fantasies of kidnapping the girl and keeping her as a sexual slave. There was the idea of taking her to dinner and showing her a good time. Exercising total possession over this attractive young girl was appealing, the opposite of what he had had when he was with Peggy. He could keep her under his control for a few weeks before kicking her out of the house. At the back of his mind, he could recall stories about the serial killer Ted Bundy who had done something similar. Some, he remembered thinking at the time, just had it coming.

But as the two stood in the room, Taunja began to interrupt Keith's thought pattern. She asked about the mattress lying on the floor and above the picture of Jesus hanging on the wall. As he explained to her how he would fall asleep on the mattress while watching TV, Keith was fascinating by how much this girl trusted him. Was it because she had been drinking all day? Keith realized that he had total control of the situation.

Thinking this, he walked up behind the girl and kissed her on the back of the neck. Wriggling free, Taunja ran straight for the door. Keith grabbed her before she could run outside. Asking her whether this meant that sex was totally out of the question and receiving no answer, he picked her up and laid her down on the mattress. To all intents and purposes, with the windows curtained and the door shut, she was trapped. Writhing free once again and running to the door, this started to dawn on the girl. Keith wrestled her back onto the mattress, surprised by her resilient strength. She was trembling. Assuming her to be utterly in terror, Keith was shocked when she kissed him. Hurry up, she whispered.

Keith began to have sex with her, feeling her beginning to accept him slowly. While he raped her, she urged him to hurry up. She wanted to get it over with, but this did not please Keith. As he remembers it, he suddenly saw red. As he lay there with her, he began to bring to mind all of the terrible thoughts he'd had about women during his life. For a short time, she seemed to look exactly like Rose.

Swinging a punch, Keith wanted to knock her out with a single blow. But it wasn't enough. He hit her first in the temple. She was still conscious. Again he hit her, but she just stared back blankly. Keith, a former boxer, couldn't understand why this girl would not just fall down unconscious. In the ring, he had been able to knock down men with one punch. Again and again he hit her in the head. This wasn't like the TV. It reminded him of the cats he would kill, but it felt somehow better. This was the first time in his life he had hit a woman in anger, and it felt good. Twenty times he hit Taunja, smashing her features until she was unrecognizable. But she still wasn't unconscious. Despite her battered face, the girl reached up, pulling at the blankets, calling out for her mother to stop the man from hitting her.

Keith found himself torn. What was he going to do next? Meditating on the idea of hogtying the girl to keep her around for sexual purposes, he began to realize that she was not far from death. He could take her to the hospital, leave her like this, or put her out of her misery. The first option was sure to end in jail. He chose the latter.

With his hands around her throat, Keith Jesperson did not stop choking until his knuckles had turned white. Even when he loosened his grip ever so slightly, she was still breathing. Keith continued. This was much harder than killing cats. The girl urinated herself, struggled, and then finally stopped moving. Keith, at last, got off the body, strolled down to the kitchen and poured himself a cup of black coffee. Sitting at the kitchen table, he mulled over what he should do next.

His first move was to get Taunja dressed again. Blood splatters littered the walls and floor; they had to be cleaned up. Looking at the girl's clothes, Keith wondered whether the metal button on her jeans would hold a fingerprint. He cut it off with a steak knife. He washed and dried his own clothes before putting them back on, before making extra sure that his victim was dead by taking a length of nylon rope and tying it tight around her neck. All the while, he shouted at the ghosts in the house that they now had one more for company. Sitting with the body, Keith was caught between enjoying the domineering sense of power and regretfully wishing he could bring her back to life.

This was abandoned when he realized he would need to get to work to rid himself of the body, set up an alibi, and make sure that he could not be caught in the same way as the criminals on the TV shows he watched, such as Perry Mason. Leaving the body behind, he drove back to the back and began to lay the foundations. Drinking beer and chatting till late in the evening, Keith made sure people saw his solitary exit from the building. Afterward, he drove ten miles out of town to look for a good place to dispose of a body. On the drive home, he made sure he had a full tank of gas and that there were no issues with his headlights that might prompt him being pulled over by the police. He tried to leave nothing to chance, not when he would be transporting a dead girl around.

As he arrived back at the home, he found Taunja still lying there. Feeling woozy while he prepped his exit, he was shocked to hear the phone ring. It was Peggy. They chatted, and it seemed as though Peggy wanted to come home. Staring at the body as he talked, Keith agreed to see her again. As he talked to Peggy, he began to feel sexually stimulated. Staring at the body, he was soon lying next to it, touching the various areas of skin. For years, she would be Keith's favorite fantasy as he remembered the first woman he killed.

By the time he was done, it was after midnight. Rigor mortis had struck the body, and it was difficult to move. Keith dragged her by the rope around her neck. Bundling her into the car, Taunja's head rested against the passenger side window, and it looked as though she was sleeping or drunk. Driving her out into the middle of nowhere, he searched for somewhere to dump the body. New shoes were bought on the way home in case the police could trace the tread of his cycling trainers. As he drove, extra care was taken to stay under the speed limit and not to run any red light. Eventually, a ravine was found about sixty feet from the road. Though he considered covering the body with leaves, Keith was worried he had seen a car approaching and ran away. He drove away quickly, worried that he'd left the girl too exposed.

Taunja's Walkman was thrown onto a road to be run over by traffic, en route to a small truck stop Keith intended to visit. As he sat and drank coffee in the diner, three policemen walked in. Paranoid, Keith seized upon the opportunity to build up his alibi. Thoughts raced back to the girl's purse, which was still in the car. Staying at the truck stop until 8 in the morning, Keith made sure that he was seen by plenty of people. He then drove three miles away and hurled the purse into the center of a blackberry thicket.

Arriving back at the house, he opened a few windows to deal with the smell and cleaned, scraped, and washed the blood from the walls. Sheets and blankets were cleaned, and the floor was vacuumed. Keith even steam-cleaned the carpet. The next few days were spent hastily adding to as many alibis as possible, while worrying about anyone finding out what he'd done. Thoughts of suicide popped across Keith's mind while the girl's face was constantly at the forefront of his thoughts.

Several days later, reports emerged that a biker had found the body. The newspaper seemed to suggest that the police were searching for the two men who had been seen playing pool with Taunja in the bar. Suicidal thoughts were abandoned – it would bring too much shame on the family – but guilty thoughts persisted. Soon these ideas turned to acceptance and then regret that Keith hadn't managed to keep her alive a short while and abused her at his whim. But for now, it seemed as though Keith Jesperson had gotten away with murder.

Claudia

A short time later, Keith read in the paper that two people had been charged with the murder of Taunja Bennett. But rather than her drinking companions, it emerged that a couple Keith described as "barflies" had been arrested instead. The woman had confessed to carrying out the murder with her boyfriend, and this had been enough to convict, especially when the girl had driven the police out to the exact spot where the body was dumped. But as weird as it was, Keith was not going to change anybody's mind. He let the two take the blame for the murder.

Meanwhile Peggy arrived home with her two kids in tow. She went back to waitressing, having abandoned truck driving as too much hard work. Keith was left at home to take care of the kids. The relationship with Peggy was breaking down. Often Keith would wake up in the middle of the night with his hands around her neck. The thoughts of the murdered girl loomed large, and he realized that he would need to get away from the haunted house before he went mad.

Two months after his first murder, Keith moved south. During the drive to Sacramento, thoughts about killing played through his mind. Trying to drive them out, he considered women who he had met during his trucking jobs, considering what they might be up to these days. One in particular, Nancy, occupied his thoughts enough that he decided to pay her a visit. Finding no one at home, he went to a local diner to learn that she had been raped and killed by two men who were now in jail. A shame, Keith thought, as he might have been able to kill her himself.

Back on the road, Keith began to think about the female hitchhikers who were usually trying to pick up a lift at truck stops. A chance encounter with a woman named Jean saw him drive the pair (including Jean's baby) out to a secluded spot. After forcing her into oral sex, Keith's mind ran hot with the idea of murder before he realized he'd have to kill the baby as well. He stepped out of the car and allowed himself to calm down. Jean attempted to run away with the child, but he managed to convince her to allow him to drive her back into town. She agreed, and they set off. Looking back on the incident, Keith was worried. The woman had his name, his destination, and the details of how he'd assaulted her. Chasing the thoughts from his mind, he went back out on to the road.

The incident prompted police interest. Arriving at a hotel, Keith found himself surrounded by cops. He tried to play off the story as a simple misunderstanding, telling the police he regretted having sex with a married woman. If he had wanted to hurt her, he suggested, why would he have let her get away, or why would he have driven her back into town? The cops seemed convinced, but fingerprinted him anyway and told him to check in with a detective back in the town. Keith did exactly this, feeding the detective the same story. Not once did he mention how he had been so sorely tempted to break the woman's neck. The story seemed to be enough, and Keith drove off to attend his new construction job.

The job lasted two months, all spent with the prospect of further recrimination hanging over Keith's head from the police. Once it finished, he headed back to Portland and reconciled with Peggy. But an incident with his and Rose's son, Jason, quickly meant that Keith saw no other option than to move back closer to his original family. With Peggy and her kids in tow, Keith took a trucking job nearer Rose and the kids and hit the road once again, Peggy joining him for the ride. Although it had seemed ideal when viewed through rose-tinted lenses, Keith was soon exhausted and annoyed again. But a stroke of luck saw the couple who had been arrested for Taunja's murder convicted. The woman had changed her plea at the last minute, saying she had just wanted to annoy her boyfriend. However, the process was already too far along. In order to avoid the chance of the death penalty, the couple pleaded guilty and received 15 years to life.

Things didn't continue to be quite so peachy, however. Pulled over for a minor trucking issue, Keith was nearly extradited back to California on charges of sexual assault. When he was being arrested, he told Peggy about how he had killed a girl, though mentioned no names. The charges were eventually reduced, after spending a few nights in the cells, and Keith's trucking company sent him money to catch a bus home. Sitting in one bus stop waiting for a ride, Keith ventured into the toilets. He took out a pen and wrote on the wall. In his piece of graffiti, he confessed to the murder of Taunja Bennett, gave a time and place, mentioned that he had killed and raped the girl, and that he had enjoyed it. The message finished with the proclamation that despite the other people taking the blame, the real killer was still free. He signed the message with a smiley face, summing up the cocky, arrogant attitude he had hoped to convey. Two months later, after nothing had come of the message, Keith did the same in another restroom, this time including the detail about cutting off the button of the girl's jeans. The cops, he thought, must be genuinely too stupid to catch him.

Keith bounced around various jobs but still harbored fantasies about the girl he'd killed. Thoughts of rape led to close calls for a number of women, when Keith abstained at the last minute from pouncing on them in the dark, while he began to solicit prostitutes and, in his own words, "treated them rough." One of these girls fought back and pepper-sprayed him in the face. Despite almost two years passing since his first murder, the thoughts of the second were never far away.

During the hot summer of 1992, these fantasies crept back into his mind. Working on the mechanics of the truck in one stop, Keith was surprised to find a woman introducing herself to him, asking for a ride. She said her name was Claudia, that she wanted a ride to Los Angeles, and that she had been hitching lifts with truckers. To Keith, she wasn't beautiful, but she was "pretty enough." As she was getting into the truck, his mind was already racing with criminal thoughts.

The two spent a short time on the road together before Keith stopped, leaned over, and kissed Claudia. Feeling a lack of returned affection, he sat back to be told that, if he wanted sex, he need only ask. There were set prices for these things. Informing the passenger that he never paid for sex, Keith again pressed against the girl. She still refused, but the moment had taken him, and he instantly starting ripping her clothes off and forcing himself upon her, again and again.

Eventually Keith stopped and drove a little way for lunch. Despite raping her, Claudia didn't run away from Keith as soon as possible. Instead, she asked him for some drugs. When she was informed that he never touched narcotics, she jumped on the CB radio and began to ask any truckers in the area for heroin. Snatching the microphone from her, Keith pressed a twenty dollar bill into her hand. She would not starve in his truck, but he would not tolerate drugs of any kind. Claudia demanded more, threatened to tell a security guard how Keith had forced himself on her. Keith locked the doors.

There was a roll of duct tape hidden beneath his seat, and he grabbed it. Both her arms were taped together in front of her while her ankles received the same treatment. Checking to see if there was anyone else in the parking lot, Keith punched the girl in the side of the neck. She fell unconscious.

Now fully accepting that he was about to murder his second victim, Keith resolved to do a better job of it this time. Taping her to the bed, he decided to rape Claudia again. As he was doing so, a police unit pulled up in the parking lot. They had a dog with them. Parking their car in the shade of Keith's truck, the men went to eat in the diner while the dog cooled down in the car. Starting the truck, Keith pulled out ever so slowly and joined back onto the interstate.

As he was driving along, Claudia was in the back trying to free herself. Unfastened from the bed, she was free of the tape and getting dressed. Braking suddenly, Keith pounced on her and tied the girl down once again. At the next stop, he raped her again. And so he started a lethal game, choking the girl until she was unconscious and then allowing her to breathe again. This happened two, three, four times, again and again and again. When she finally died, Keith pulled to the side of the road, drank an ice tea, and tried to figure out how to dispose of the body.

In the shade of the San Bernardino Mountains, Keith scouted out a deep ravine. He fell asleep, waiting until darkness fell, with only a blanket between him and the dead girl. Waking up around 7 in the evening, the CB radio was alive with truckers talking about a police car parked in front of a truck matching Keith's description. Jumping out, he chatted with the officer and pretended to be concerned about his tires. Satisfied that the cop thought everything was in order, Keith and the corpse pulled out on to the highway and drove some distance.

Over ten miles away, just off Highway 95, Keith pulled over and dragged the corpse into a canyon. Hidden by bushes and taking care to cover the girl with tumbleweed, he was satisfied that she would not be found nearly as quickly. He washed his sleeping bag to rid it of the smell of the dead girl and dried it in the truck's windjammer. To him, Claudia had deserved to die. Having now committed two murders (nearly three) and gotten away with it, Keith was beginning to feel untouchable. The journey was completed as per the schedule, and Keith spent his days thinking about how easy it was to murder.

Cynthia Lyn Rose

Now, Keith had double the murder fantasies. Thoughts of killing both Taunja and Claudia rifled through his mind. Murder and rape became an obsession. But this new lust wasn't matched by his latest driving assignment. The truck itself and the long hours left him feeling tired and despondent when, pulling into a rest area in California a month later, he met a young girl named Cynthia who asked him whether he wanted to party.

Keith fondled a breast beneath the girl's sweatshirt (his method of guarding against potential police sting operations) but declined. She was either in her late twenties or in her early thirties, he couldn't tell. Saying her name was Cynthia, she pressed the matter. But Keith insisted that he was tired. He might be in the mood later, he told the girl, but right now he just wanted to sleep. He shut down the truck, turning off the light to dissuade any further advances. Thoughts on his mind of violent prostitutes in Florida were recalled, when one woman had started killing truckers she picked up in parking lots.

Just as he was lying down to sleep, the passenger door jolted open, and Cynthia jumped in. Keith was furious. Reaching out and grabbing her neck, he dragged her on to the bed and started choking the life out of her. She went limp soon after, and he realized the girl wasn't conscious. Keith Jesperson's third victim was already dead, and all he could feel was regret that he'd missed the chance to play his death games with her. They hadn't even had sex.

Worried that he was being watched, Keith decided that he needed to leave. He drove the truck away fast, driving barefoot. Still driving, the thought occurred to him that Cynthia might wake up, just like Claudia had done. He stopped the truck, and despite all signs pointing toward the girl being dead, he bound and gagged her anyway. Just then, he heard someone breathing. She was still alive.

Content that the bindings would hold her in place, Keith drove on. The aim was to reach the weigh station a few miles away, hoping to provide a convincing alibi of his whereabouts at the time the girl went missing. It was closed when he arrived. Pulling into the parking lot of a nearby café instead, he began to suspect that the cabin was smelling like death. She might have been dead after all.

Once the truck was parked, he jumped into the cabin to check what was happening. Cynthia was a pretty girl. The bed was wet with her urine. There was no indication as to why she had just jumped into his truck. But now here she was. Dead. There was a tree in the corner of the parking lot, one with weeds and garbage at the base. Dumping the body here would keep it hidden for a while. Ripping the duct tape from her wrists, Keith was worried about other truckers arriving. He flung the body onto the garbage, covering her with tumbleweed as a kind of gravestone.

Paranoia was still reigning in his thoughts, and Keith had to drive fast. He needed to get away from the body and the parking lot where Cynthia had last been spotted. During a brief stop, he cleaned the mattress and threw the sheets away. He tried to catch a bit of sleep in the parking lot of a diner. The act of killing itself didn't bother Keith anymore, but the fear of being caught was very real.

108

The next week was spent checking every detail of every parking lot. Wherever Keith stopped, he was worried about police attention. In restaurants, he would eat with his back to the wall, watching all the time. After a few weeks glued to the CB radio in fear, it seemed as though nothing was being said. Keith had gotten away with it once again. By this time, the couple who had been imprisoned for Taunja's murder were serving their third year. Keith was on to his third victim. The fear of repercussions, whether legal or religious, stopped being an issue. Keith Jesperson feared no one.

Laurie Ann Pentland

November, 1992 saw Keith driving up the Pacific coast, heading eventually towards Salem. With a truckload of meat to deliver, his mind was occupied by the thoughts of companionship. Arriving at a truck stop in Wilsonville, he remembered that he had known a prostitute in the area who went by the name of Laurie. To his recollection, the girl was in her early twenties, and despite not being the most beautiful, certainly knew how to show him a good time. The last three stops in Wilsonville had involved a visit from Laurie, though each time she had raised the price she charged. Keith began to wonder about her whereabouts and put out a message on the radio, but it was still early.

An hour later, he heard Laurie's voice calling out over the airwaves. Replying, he told her where to find him. Just as before, he price had gone up five dollars, she informed him upon arrival at the truck. Keith accepted and paid the girl, spending the next hour having sex. As she began to get dressed before leaving to search for another client, Keith got talking to her. She began to insist that Keith owed her an extra forty dollars, having taken up an hour of her time where most men were satisfied with just a quarter of that. The two began to quarrel over the amount, Keith insistent that they'd had a deal. Soon, Laurie was threatening to call the cops. Flatly, Keith informed her that she had no idea about the risk she was taking. Still she argued, insisting on being paid the extra money.

Keith took hold of Laurie and thrust her down on the bed. Taking her throat in his hands, he began to choke her to death. Just before she was completely out of breath, Keith relented. He allowed her to come back to consciousness before choking her again. This was repeated for an hour, with the killer watching and later remembering how Laurie's will to live flickered and eventually died right in front of him. When she closed her eyes for the last time, Keith kept choking until he was sure she had died. Shutting the body up in the cabin, he went into the diner for a cup of coffee.

Drinking his coffee, Keith mulled over what he considered to be the stupidity of the truck stop prostitutes, these women who so willingly put themselves in harm's way. Finished, he walked back to his vehicle and began to grope the body. Inside her pockets was close to $250. Already Keith's thoughts were wandering to how best to dispose of the body. He focused on a little parking lot not far from his final drop off, a place where he could cover her with vines and garbage containers.

The route he took when heading south was determined by which authorities would give him the least bother. While not the most direct course, Keith was at least sure that this would keep him away from cops. By the time he arrived in the parking lot, it was two in the morning. There was not only an abundance of foliage and garbage to hide the body, there was a six-foot fence bordering the property to provide extra cover. The place was empty.

Laurie was dragged out of the cabin by her hair. The body fell to the ground with a dull thud before being dragged to the fence and covered with leaves, junk, and anything else. Satisfied, Keith left the corpse, drove some hundred yards down the road to a nearby Waremart, and slept in the parking lot, ready to deliver the truck's load in the morning.

The next day, Keith's first thoughts were to blame the girl for her own death. If only she hadn't insisted on being paid that little bit extra. Next, he realized that he would have to stop killing soon. One of these days, he was bound to get caught. Murder was almost too easy for him as a trucker. But if he wanted to be sure of stopping, he might have to give up life on the road. Maybe he didn't even know how to stop these murders.

Cindy

It was another four months before Keith Jesperson found himself on the brink of murder. At the time, he was out on a job, driving south on the I-5. It was a cool, rainy evening in March. He made the decision to pull into a diner in California for some refreshment. The police, to this point, were none the wiser about the various killings. There was not even any suggestion that they had been linked at all. Aside from the first murder, which had already seen a conviction, the others were scattered across the country, the bodies dumped where they had been difficult to find. All this time, Keith had continued to crisscross the country, driving wherever he pleased. No one questioned why a trucker might be traveling so far, so frequently. It was almost the perfect cover story, a fact which was incredibly prevalent in Keith's mind. As he arrived at the truck stop, he wiped the rain droplets from his trousers and spotted the thick fog rolling in off the wide ocean. Not wanting to stop long, he decided to leave the engine idling while he stepped inside. This way, the cab would keep its heat for the journey ahead.

Inside was busy. People seemed to have rushed inside to escape the wet and the cold. As ever, Keith was watching his weight, determined to keep any fat from his hefty frame. This meant a diet heavy on Slim Fast, but a craving for fruit meant a change. Despite the crowds, one girl in the truck stop caught his eye. She was wet from the rain, like most of the other clientele, and seemed to just be sitting and staring at her food. Sipping a hot mug of coffee, she seemed to be half starved. To Keith, she seemed like something of a drifter, someone who almost certainly was spending some time on the streets for whatever reason. Her long hair and thick glasses hid a lot of the scarlet complexion from the rest of the world, but Keith had the instinct that she was hoping to score her dinner from someone.

In that instant, Keith Jesperson decided that he would need to have this woman. She reminded him a little of his schoolteachers, of other motherly women who had scolded him. These considerations were pushed out of his mind as he focused on his sudden urges. Thanks to his career as a truck driver, he felt, he was once again presented with the perfect opportunity to exercise his most base desires. Summoning the waitress, he pointed out the sodden girl and told the waitress that anything the girl wanted to eat, he was happy to cover the cost. Don't tell her who bought the food, Keith informed the serving girl, as the last thing he wanted was someone to start following him around hoping for more. In reality, he just hoped that the waitress wouldn't be able to make the connections between the two clients should the police come to call.

The girl ate, and Keith watched her. Looking up at one point, the hungry youngster seemed to offer a thankful glance in Keith's direction, seemingly aware that he was her mysterious benefactor. Motioning her over, she stood up and then sat down again, this time in front of the trucker. And then she talked. Keith let her talk, while she explained her name was Cindy. She tried to pry more information about the man sitting opposite her. Ducking all of the big or personal questions, he let her talk, aware that all the girl probably wanted was a warm, dry bed for the night. Keith was more than happy to oblige.

As time rolled on, conversation turned to where Keith was heading. Revealing that he was heading for Salinas, Cindy begged him to take her along. Drop her in Sacramento, she pleaded, where there was a sister who could offer her somewhere to stay. After Keith played coy, the girl began to beg. This sealed her fate in the killer's eyes. He hated when they begged. All women, Keith thought, seemingly just wanted something from him. He agreed to give her a lift. By the time he had paid for the meals and picked up some orange juice for the trip, the girl was already waiting outside the cabin. Everything she owned was with her, and it wasn't much.

On the road, Keith turned up the heat in the cabin to give her a chance to dry her hair. It also had the side effect of encouraging her to take off her heavy rain coat, allowing him to get a better idea of the body beneath. After the pair stopped in a gas station to use the restroom, Keith could tell that she had spent a little bit longer inside than she needed. Cindy was now wearing makeup, had combed her hair, and had undone the top three buttons on her blouse. They made one more stop and, returning to the cabin, Keith reached over and kissed his passenger. This time, his victim kissed back. Moving back into the bunk, the two had sex for the next few hours.

It was so warm in the cabin, Cindy suggested to Keith as they lay next to one another that they just spend the night there. Keith assured her that they would, though added that she probably wouldn't enjoy herself. Sitting up, the girl asked him what he meant. It meant, Keith revealed, that he was going to kill her. She could only seem to stare back in disbelief. He raped her once more, easily overpowering the smaller victim. Once again, he played his game whereupon he choked the girl until she lost consciousness, allowed her to wake up, and then choked her again. She only lasted five times before she was strangled to death.

By this time, Keith Jesperson was well aware of what he needed to do next. He still thought long and hard about how best to dispose of the body. First, he put Cindy's clothes back on her body and placed her next to the cabin door. Traveling as he was across the country, hiding the body wasn't even that essential. Thanks to the nature of interstate and even intercounty investigations, especially concerning the types of girls who were normally Keith's prey, the threat of investigation was minimal. However, he didn't know this yet. He still spent a good amount of time picking out the right spot, hiding her body, and then covering it in rocks and vegetation. By

111

the time he reached his destination and dropped off the load on the back of the truck, the rain had cleared.

Susanne

In the six months following the murder of the woman known as Cindy, Keith Jesperson avoided killing. By the time 1993 reached the autumn months, however, the feeling and the urge to kill was again creeping up in Keith's mind. At this point, he confessed his actions to a friend, seeking advice on how to stop murdering women. But the friend, after dismissing the subject as a joke, soon didn't want to talk about it anymore. He advised Keith to see a psychologist and ceased to take part in the conversation. Keith lost a potential outlet on his murderous urges.

Fast forward a few months later, and Keith was sitting in a truck stop in Oregon, drinking coffee and watching the world go by. As he sat and watched, a short blonde woman entered the room. The woman sat down in front of Keith, facing away from him in the next booth. Speaking out loud, Keith said that she had a back he would like to rub. The girl laughed and welcomed him over to the table.

She said her name was Julie, Julie Winningham. Struck by Keith's six foot six frame, she wondered where exactly he'd come from. The two spent the next couple of hours chatting and discovered they were very much attuned to one another's sensibilities. Feeling she was a few classes of respectability above most of the women he met in truck stops, Keith invited her along on his trip and promised that there would be no funny business. It was totally down to her, he assured, her choice entirely. She was given free rein to fall in love with him, but it would always be her decision. Julie accepted the invitation, left a little note in her car window assuring any readers that she'd be away for a while and then hopped into the cabin.

Their first stop was Seattle, after which they headed to Yakima. Everywhere they went, people seemed to love Julie. Keith's friends along his regular routes all commented on the short blonde woman he had in tow. The next stop involved hauling potatoes to Irvine, California. Starting Friday night, they had to be there by Sunday morning. Keith decided to drive all night and made it just after midnight on the Saturday. This gave the pair of them a free day, which they spent at a fairground. Keith even bought Julie a necklace and a bracelet. The only bone of contention reared its head when Julie seemed annoyed that her new friend swore off drugs of any type.

Regardless, they spent the night partying together and wound up having sex in Keith's truck, though he confessed that it wasn't the best or most exciting intimate experience he'd ever had. After spending money on jewelry and a night out, he had hoped for a bit more effort on her part. A quick trip to the phone booth to check in with his employers meant that Keith left Julie alone in the truck. By the time he got back, he discovered that she was trying to use the CB radio to try and pick up drugs.

The couple settled into more romantic concerns before Julie asked Keith whether he'd like to marry her. Unknown to the trucker at the time, she was on the lookout for someone to take good care of her, and it seemed as though Keith fit the bill. He agreed, and despite lambasting her for trying to score drugs over the radio, ventured out to buy some marijuana from one of the other drivers at the truck stop. The two spent a few more nights together before Keith drove her back to the place where she had left her car, and the two parted ways.

After that, it became a regular feature of Keith's trips that he would call in and see Julie whenever he passed. She ended up renting a room with his friends, Ginny, and Billy Smith. The arrangement worked for almost twelve months before Keith grew suspicious of both Billy and Julie's intentions. While he suspected his friend of being attracted to his girl, he suspected Julie of simply using him for a ride, for cash, and for drugs. He decided to ditch her after almost a year of dating. In Keith's opinion, she was more in love with marijuana than him.

Just after he dumped Julie, Keith came across an article detailing the case of the two "barflies" who had been convicted of the murder of Taunja Bennett. It annoyed him. The messages he had left scrawled on the restroom walls had failed to have any kind of impact. To rectify this and take back a bit of credit, Keith decided to write a note to the Washington County Courthouse. The note detailed not only where the body had been placed, but the exact wounds, the way she had been tied, where the Walkman and the purse had been thrown away, the buttons cut off from the jeans, and the position she had been left in after he had raped her. Again, he signed the note with a smiley face. In the weeks afterward, there was no mention in the papers. While his instinct told him to leave the matter alone, Keith couldn't help remain curious about what was happening behind the scenes.

In April of 1994, he wrote another note. It had been four years since the first murder. This note contained a first page with the same old Happy Face logo emblazoned across the front. Rather than sending it to the authorities, however, Keith decided that he might get better results by sending it to the press. As well as Taunja, the note explained how he had killed the girl, as well as hinting as to why he might have done it, and that she was not his only victim. This note failed as well, so a follow-up letter was composed and delivered to the same paper. This time, he talked of his latest murder, as well as his life as a long haul trucker. The note informed people of where the body had been left and just how easy it was to get away with all of these killings. There was even a hint that the writer of the note wanted to stop the murders but just didn't know how. Signing off with confirmation that he was the same man who had sent the last letter, he warned the reader to "check over your shoulder."

At the bottom of each communication, whether it was on the wall of a restroom or the blue paper Keith used to send to the newspaper, he always left a signature Happy Face logo. During this period, Keith was desperate to know what was going on inside his own head. He began to read through a lot of magazines and books on the subject of serial killers. On one occasion, on opening a magazine dedicated to the subject, he found an article asking whether there was another serial killer on the loose in Oregon. It was about him. Finally seeing his deeds in print, Keith wrote to the magazine and corrected a few points in their article. He even revealed where they might find another body. But there was never a follow-up piece in the publication.

The library was a great source for books on psychology. One such book, written by a former FBI man, gave the childhood warning signs for a serial killer as three-fold. Typically, they would wet their beds, torture animals, and start fires. To Keith's mind, he filled two out of three categories. Accordingly, he wondered whether setting fires out in the wilderness might satiate the urge to kill. He would start fires and then retreat to a safe distance, from which he could watch as the police and fire brigade struggled to deal with the raging inferno in the dry undergrowth. This worked for a while. Keith thought it might even have saved a few lives. Oregon, Washington, California, Arizona, and Nevada were all victims of his arson attacks at one time or another. It was enough to put off his killing urge for almost a year.

The change came near the end of 1994. Keith Jesperson was driving truckloads of aluminum coils to Florida. After dropping off the delivery, he noticed a blonde woman strolling around a store. She reminded him of Taunja, especially in her slightly Slavic features. The girl was looking for a lift north, and Keith offered up his truck. She gave her name as Susanne.

Susanne was somewhere around thirty years old and carried tarot cards with her. She might have been a fortune-teller, Keith thought. The girl hopped in his truck, and the two were set to drive off. Just before they left, she wondered whether they might stop past Miami along the way to Keith's stop in Georgia. The trucker refused, as it would involve a 400-mile trip out of his way. He refused, but she didn't mind. Susanne just wanted to get out of Florida.

The trip was going according to plan, including stops to eat spaghetti in diners, reloading the truck, and setting off back towards the northwest. Susanne even agreed to sleep in the bunk, provided that they both remain dressed for the entire time. Keith agreed, and they drove until three in the morning, when he had to pull over to sleep. There were a few cop cars out front, and the only parking space was next to the lot's security guard. Keith parked there anyway. He climbed into bed with her, fully clothed, and began to fall asleep. As it seemed, choking, rape, and murder were far from his mind.

But the conditions inside the cabin were hot. The air conditioner was broken, and this caused Keith to wake up in the middle of the night sweating. He needed to open a window, anything to deal with the temperature that was getting close to ninety degrees. Turning on the light inside the truck, he couldn't help but notice the shape of his companion's body as she lay in bed. He couldn't help but take off his clothes and slide in right next to her.

Susanne began to stir, and when she was finally awake and realized what was happening, let out a piercing scream. Keith threw the palm of his hand over her mouth. As she struggled, he desperately tried to think how he might explain this to the security guards or the police. Whatever it was this girl told the police, it seemed that every eventuality ended up in Keith losing his job. Riders were strictly forbidden, rapists even more so.

The girl pleaded to be let go, assuring Keith that she wouldn't tell anyone what had happened. Apologizing, he assured her that she only needed to do as he asked. His first request was that she have sex with him, as though they "were lovers." Susanne saw no way out other than to play along. After a few hours together, she seemed relaxed enough to fall asleep, but Keith was concerned that she might be faking. Becoming aroused again, he lifted her skirt and tried to force his way inside the sleeping girl. Once again, she screamed. This time, he choked her to death.

While the body was still warm, Keith drove away from the truck stop. He hid her body in some bushes along the side of the road. This time, he took the care to tie some lengths of nylon rope around the girl's neck, a calling card should he even need to prove that the murder had been his. Back in the truck, he drove as fast as he could towards the next weigh station, desperate to be noted in the official books as far away from there as possible.

As far as the records went, it seemed like he had never been near the area at all. Once again, Keith Jesperson seemed to have gotten away with murder.

Angela Subrize

A minor accident in January of 1995 meant that Keith was holed up in a hotel in Spokane. After his truck had spontaneously caught fire, he was waiting for a mechanic's report to confirm that he wasn't guilty of error while waiting for his company to give the go-ahead for his next job. While he waited, he sat in the hotel and had a drink. A woman walked into the bar, with long dark hair, pale blue eyes, and a pile of bags. She sat drinking a beer by herself and, soon enough, Keith managed to charm his way into sharing a drink with the girl.

Before she had even checked in, Keith had offered to put her up in his room for the night. She gratefully accepted and said that her name was Angela. Together, they ordered pizza and beer to be sent up to the room. Angela was a strip tease dancer, with a small tattoo of Tweety Bird raising his middle finger to the world. A short talk and a few beers later, the couple spent the night together.

The next day, Keith was awake before his companion. Needing to leave, he placed thirty dollars on the bedside table and a note on how the girl could reach him if she wanted to meet up again. That day, he walked down to the mechanics to find out that he was absolved of guilt for the fire and that his company had a new load ready and waiting to go. A few deliveries later, he checked in with the head office, only to find that a girl named Angela Subrize had been trying to contact him. Keith phoned her and discovered that she was angling for a lift down to Denver. It wasn't on the way, but Keith came to an arrangement whereby he'd pick her up in a few days, and the couple would go together. Angela gave him directions, and the date was set.

They met at Angela's house, and as Keith carried the girl's bags out to his truck, she grabbed hold of his arm and hugged it tight in gratitude. The night they had spent together had pleased Keith, but he still had a long haul of almost 300 miles in the next few hours, so he couldn't think too much about such subjects. They paused to eat at one truck stop and wound up eating alongside a woman named Lady Rose, who ran one of the CB radio stations that truckers turned to for their weather reports. She told Keith that there was snow and ice coming the way he was heading, which would mean a long night ahead with very few miles covered.

The two drove on for the next few days, with Keith driving and Angela sleeping in the back of the cabin. When they pulled to the side of the road, they would find distracting ways of entertaining one another. When they reached Wyoming, Keith overhead his companion arguing in a telephone booth. He had let her use his credit card to make a long distance call, and now it sounded like it wasn't going too well. After speaking with her dad, it seemed that he no longer had any inclination to see her. Instead, she asked Keith whether they could drive to Indiana, where she knew an old boyfriend who might be able to help her out.

By this time, Keith had grown weary of his new passenger. It was clear by this point that she was chiefly interested in him as a means of getting around the country. Now that she had a new man to go to in Indiana, it seemed as though she was someone else's responsibility. They had sex again after Angela got off the phone, but this time – once they were finished – it seemed as though she had started giving orders. Let's go, she told him. Keith didn't take kindly to this sort of instruction. This prompted a long-winded story from Angela about the series of guys who had let her down in the past, culminating in her claim that she believed herself to be pregnant. It was her belief that the baby belonged to the ex-boyfriend in Indiana, though she couldn't be sure. The concept riled Keith, who suggested that she might have even suggested it had been his. He accused Angela of using him as a free ride. They'd both enjoyed themselves, Angela claimed, but now they should get going for Indiana as soon as possible.

With worrying ideas beginning to rise up in his mind, Keith jumped back into the truck with his travel companion and got onto Interstate 80. The roads were thick with snow. While Angela slept in the cabin, Keith's mind ran hot with the ideas of what might happen if the boyfriend in Indiana didn't want to take the girl back. What if he rejected her? What if she claimed the baby belonged to Keith? What if the boyfriend didn't even exist, and she faked the call? Furious, Keith burrowed through the sleeping girl's purse. He found a can of pepper spray and removed it, hiding it where it wouldn't be found.

The weather got worse. They passed a number of jackknifed trucks that were almost wrecked. Visibility fell to just a few feet. There was still two days to go until they reached Indiana, and Keith desperately needed to sleep. They reached a rest area in Nebraska and pulled over. It would take a four- or five-hour lie down until Keith felt up to driving again. But this didn't sit well with Angela. After waking up from the back of the cabin to find that they'd pulled over, she was furious. In a hurry, she wanted to be back on the road instantly and couldn't wait for Keith to sleep. If she wanted to get there quicker, he informed her, she was welcome to get on the radio and beg for a lift.

Angela's mood changed. Instead of anger, she switched into seduction. The pair had sex, though Keith was half asleep. When he finished and rolled over to continue his nap, she went straight back to anger. She wanted to go, and she wanted to go now. Keith didn't care. After he had slept for twenty minutes, she jerked him awake. Angela refused to sit there for one more minute while they were not moving. Turning his back and resuming his sleep, Keith just tried to ignore the girl. This went on for an hour. He'd fall asleep, and just as he was starting to recharge, she'd kick him awake and insist they get back on the road. By this time, the sleepy Keith had already marked her down as a dead girl.

Waking up, Keith started to drive. They drove further through Nebraska until they reached a secluded truck stop with no customers. Stating that he needed to use the restroom, Keith stepped out to make sure that no one was nearby and that there was no traffic passing. There was no one in sight.

Keith climbed back into the cabin and ordered the girl to make the bed. He forced himself upon her, and while she begged him to stop, he pulled out the duct tape. Angela promised to be good, promised to behave. She even started praying for her own safety, her hands clasped in front of her chest, and her words loud enough for Keith to hear. Keith lied to her, saying he'd never hurt her. They had sex again. Afterward, Angela mentioned that she was hungry and asked to stop

116

at a restaurant. Knowing that this was all it took for her to get out and alert the authorities, Keith laughed it off.

Angela reached for her pepper spray. When Keith accused her of doing so, she tried to plead ignorance. Again, he laughed. And so he reached out his hands and began to choke the girl. Four, five times he allowed her to wake up again before he resumed the throttling. After she had finally stopped breathing, Keith slept for five hours.

When he woke up, the first thing Keith did was put Angela's body in a plastic bag. This time was a little bit different than his earlier murders, as people had seen and would be able to remember him spending time with the dead girl. She'd even used his credit card to call up her boyfriend and father. There might even be a police file on her somewhere, possibly with her finger prints already in the records. This wouldn't be someone he could just dump by the side of the road. He would need to make Angela disappear completely.

But first, he needed to eat. Driving to a McDonald's and ordering a meal for two, he sat in the truck and considered his options. Again, he blamed the girl for her own murder, annoyed that she hadn't been up front with him. Again, he fondled the body, just for once last check over what he had done. Once his food was finished, it was time to go to work.

At three in the morning, just ten days after the fire-related accident that had put him up in the hotel, Keith pulled to the side of the road. The body was already starting to take on the rotten smell that was like nothing else in the world. He had grown used to the distinct aroma and knew that it was incriminating. Taking his duct tape, Keith repositioned the girl's hands so that they were stuck out in front of her body. Rigor mortis was already making this a difficult task, so he laid the corpse out along the ground to make it easier. With a length of thick black rope, he fastened the body beneath the truck's trailer. It had just enough give that the body would be able to drag between the wheels, grazing against the tarmac. Fixing her ankles to the underside of the trailer and with her nose almost touching on the road, Keith would be able to grind Angela's face and fingerprints away. She would be unrecognizable.

Next, he waited for a break in the traffic. Putting about three miles between himself and a convoy of truckers, he moved out onto the road. Traveling at around seventy miles an hour, he dragged the body for about twelve miles at top speed before pulling over to check out his handiwork. Looking on the underside of the vehicle, he examined the dead girl. A shoulder was missing, as was a thigh. The chest had been completely smashed, while her intestines, arms, and hands were left strewn somewhere back down the road. The arms were worn away so badly that she only had her shoulders left. To the other truckers on the road, the body pieces must have appeared as just regular road kill.

Dragging the tattered remains out from under the truck and down into a secluded bank, Keith left Angela in the tall grass about fifty feet from the roadside. Trucks were passing, asking whether he needed any help. Keith laughed them off, suggesting that he was just taking a moment to "get rid of [his] coffee." They drove on by. Next, Keith plotted out his route. Phoning into his company and providing a false itinerary, he drove all night to provide himself with a cover story that placed him nowhere near the body. If anyone were to look at the records, Keith Jesperson would apparently have been in an entirely different state.

Julie Ann Winningham

Life after the death of Angela was tough for Keith Jesperson. More than once, he considered suicide. Thoughts of crashing his truck into a concrete barrier were only abandoned after Keith realized how his children might react should the truth about his murders ever come to light. At night, he would steer his truck with the lights off, driving by the light of the full moon. He played pranks on other drivers, slashing fuel lines, puncturing tires, and even chaining two trucks together and watching them try to drive away. It seemed as though, despite the suicidal thoughts, he was having altogether too much fun to die.

That was when Julie Winningham came back into his life. It was a chance encounter in Oregon. Keith ran into his ex-girlfriend while walking out of a restroom in a standard truck stop. He immediately went back into the bathroom, worried that he might not want to talk to her. For all the hassle and annoyance she had brought him, he had a rest day ahead and nothing much to do. Keith decided to spark up a conversation, and the two went for coffee.

Over drinks, they apologized to one another. Keith was certain that she hadn't changed, that she was still a "scammer" but he decided to play along. When she said she was out of cigarettes, he told her that he always kept a special pack of her favorite brand in the truck, just in case he ever ran into her. They were barely in the cabin before she started to kiss him.

The two agreed to go out. First, Julie revealed the hot water she was in. She desperately needed $700 to pay a fine and asked Keith for the money. He played along, hoping that he'd be able to get her into bed and never hand over the actual cash. They went out to a bar, played pool, and got drunk. When they were stumbling back to bed, a drunken Julie proposed. Again, Keith agreed to go along with her, assuming he'd renege on the deal later. His head was already filling up with the old fantasies about trapping a woman and holding her as a sex slave.

They drove up to Julie's mother's house and revealed their engagement plans. They left her shocked mother behind and went back to the truck stop. The two spent the evening together, and by the morning, Keith had fallen back in love with Julie. Murderous thoughts were abandoned, and he was back under her spell.

Calling into his company, Keith found himself with a few days off. Now partnered up with Julie, he had something to do. When he woke her up, she revealed more debts hanging over her head. Car repairs were going to cost her $1000. She had drunkenly crashed the vehicle. A court date had been set and fines for the accident could total a further $1500. If she didn't, then she'd end up in jail. Add in lawyers' bills, and she was having to sell her car in order to make everything work. She asked Keith whether he'd be a witness to the sale and whether he'd sign his name to the contract. The idea worried Keith. What if his signature matched up against the Happy Face letters he had been sending out? If he killed Julie one day, they might be able to match up all the handwriting.

They drove to her friend's house to pay a visit. Keith noticed drugs laid out on the table, and soon enough, Julie was inquiring about buying marijuana. Knowing she had no money to pay for it herself, he started walking back to his truck. In no time, she was chasing him out of the house. Despite his refusal to give her any cash, she whisked his wallet from his pocket and took out two twenty-dollar bills. Fuming, Keith sat in the truck for the next few hours while Julie got high with her friends.

It had been arranged that they would go back out to her mother's house the next day to have dinner. Keith made up some excuse to duck out of the evening. He left and went hiking for a few hours, and by the time he got to the house, Julie and her mother were engaged in a shouting match. They left.

Together over the next week, Keith was eventually reminded of exactly how much Julie used to annoy him. Someone had stolen her car keys. Her own mother had called the police on her. The court date for the drunk-driving case was just around the corner. She didn't have any money. She depended on Keith. She wanted to borrow thirty dollars to get a license to work a temporary job. Keith gave her fifty, but as he fully expected, he got no change. To him, it was "one aggravation after another."

Leaving her with some money at a bar, Keith left to play cribbage. He had fallen asleep by the time Julie made it back to the truck. After they had sex, she sparked up a cigarette, leaned back, and explained just how she and her friends had come to the agreement that it was actually Keith's fault that she had lost her car. He owed her $600 for that. Added to this, she revealed a second drunk-driving offence, so those fines would total more than $2000. She would need that money by the next day. As they were now engaged, she explained, they had to help one another out.

But Keith knew what she was after. This wasn't a marriage of love, but rather one of convenience, He felt she just wanted his money. He didn't have $2000, he informed her, and even if he did, he would never hand it over to her. He didn't like her attitude, and he didn't like being depended on for money. Keith told her as much, but Julie did not react well. She had spent the entire night describing to her friends how often he wanted to have sex with her, and how little she satisfied these urges. If he wasn't going to give her the money, then they would back up her story when she went to the cops and claimed to have been raped.

Angry but remaining calm, Keith warned Julie that she had no idea what she was getting herself into. Julie didn't care. Either she'd get paid, or she'd get the cops. She was already screaming pretty loudly as the pair argued in the back of the truck. Balled up in the corner of the cabin, she just looked like all of the other girls Keith had killed. He lunged for her, surprised to find that she reciprocated his attempts to kiss her. This was all part of the game, Keith thought. After they were done, however, his hands wrapped around her throat and began to cut off her breathing. Her eyes, bulging, seemed to be genuinely shocked.

Choking until Julie passed out, Keith reached for the duct tape, bound her hands behind her back, and tied her ankles together. Her mouth was sealed shut with more tape. Climbing into the driver's seat, he began to steer the truck out onto the road. Julie woke up as they braked hard for a stop sign. Attempting to reach the passenger's seat, she could only flop onto the floor. Falling, her head caught against a corner of the seat, and she cut herself. There was soon blood over the floor. Keith reached down and petted her head. Trying to talk through the duct tape, Julie's words were only muffled noises. She was scared enough that she lost control of her bodily functions. Later, Keith would have to clean the carpet.

When they finally stopped, he picked her up and took her into the back of the cabin. Ripping the tape from her face, Keith announced that they were going to be having a kissing contest. Julie would have to show him just how much her life was worth. And she tried. After they had sex again, Julie plead for her life, explaining that she didn't need the money. She had only been kidding. But it wasn't enough. Bluntly, Keith told Julie Winningham that she was about to die.

Removing the tape from her ankles and closing the curtains, Keith ignored Julie's claims that she felt sick. He tied a shirt around her head as a blindfold and began to touch her body wherever he pleased. Once again, he had sex with her as she pleaded for her life. As she lay on the bed blindfolded, Keith began to recount the stories of his murders. Starting with Taunja Bennett, he rattled off dates and names. He told her how he'd dragged one girl along beneath the truck. And then he started to choke her. Julie woke up and was throttled four times, with Keith even tempted to keep her alive until the next night. But he didn't want to push his luck too far. After he had choked her again, Keith hopped out of the truck and began to urinate against a wheel. As he did so, he spotted a sheriff's car coming along the road. Standing by the wheel of his truck, he waved the officer by as the car carried on past him.

It was nearly dawn. If he waited too long, then it would be too busy to dump the body. But she was still alive. Clambering back inside, Julie was whispering to Keith. She told him that she loved him. She assured him that she would never say anything. He touched her hair, kissed her face, and said that everything would be alright. She would be allowed to prove her love. With his encouragement, they fooled around again. After that, Keith strangled her for the final time.

Keith and the body drove down Highway 14. As it happened, they were near the spot where he had dumped Taunja's body all those years ago. Jumping over a fence at the side of the road, he threw the corpse down a fifteen foot slope and watched as the crumpled Julie lay at the bottom of the ravine. By the time he was back in the truck, he had begun to realize just how many people had seen them together. If the authorities came looking, he'd be a prime suspect. Later on that night, Keith decided to sneak back to the roadside and move the body. But he never bothered. Tired of being a serial killer, he felt that this was the best way to get caught. While he would never hand himself in, he knew that they would be coming for him eventually. This time, he had gone too far.

Capture

Despite Julie's death, Keith tried to keep to his normal schedule. He hauled trucks across the country, stopped occasionally to play cribbage, and even hit on some of the girls in the truck stops. One of the girls received a few of Julie's coats as a present, which he instantly knew was a mistake. Nearly forty now, Keith was worried about his soon-to-expire driving license. Whenever he saw a cop, he didn't know whether he'd be asked about murder, an out-of-date license, or anything else.

Over the coming weeks, he felt paranoid. One night, he almost took a girl back to his truck with murderous deeds on his mind, but they kissed and said good night before she clambered inside. Instead, Keith lay back on his bunk and listened to the CB radio, as truckers and prostitutes arranged to meet one another. The urges were becoming overpowering, and feeling like it was too much, he stepped outside and resolved to go for a walk.

Before he could get both feet on the ground, a voice shouted out from behind. It was the security guard who worked at the truck stop. Fully expecting to hear that he was under arrest, Keith paused with baited breath, but it turned out that the man just wanted to chat.

So Keith tried to get back into his regular life. Several times, he had close run-ins with women, but something always got between him and their murder. They might have had a family, or they changed their mind at the last moment. He took to shoplifting detective magazines, just to see if he could. When he came across fellow truckers who worked for the same company, they seemed to try and avoid him. Everything seemed to be on edge, as though something was wrong.

Keith needed some money to cross into New Mexico. He phoned the company, and they agreed to pay it. When the money arrived, he set off. But when he reached the border, the policeman asked for his full name. This never usually happened. They let him pass through, but it seemed as though someone might be wanting to track him. When arriving at the drop off point, the entire crew worked hard to help him unload the truck. Usually, he was stuck doing it himself.

Phoning in to the company offices, he was told that he would need to check again later for his next job. As he drove into two to kill time, a couple of police patrol cars began to follow. Once he was out of town, they overtook him and drove off into the distance. Ringing the company again, he was told there was something for him tomorrow, but in the meantime, he was not to go anywhere. After three days without a load to haul, it seemed odd that they would delay further. Usually, they couldn't turn the truckers round fast enough. Keith was certain they'd been told what to say by the police. Worried and convinced that running away would only prove his guilt, Keith went to bed.

Waking up in the morning, Keith decided to wash his truck. There wasn't much else to do. As he drove up to the wash station, the little "open" light switched off. A man in a black SUV was watching him from the side of the road. Getting on the radio, he inquired as to whether the facility was open. He was told that it was always ready for business. To Keith, this meant that someone didn't want him washing evidence off the truck. Calling through to his trucking company, he finally got his orders. When he asked what the load was going to be, they didn't have an answer. They always had an answer. Possibly machine parts, they told him.

Keith drove up to the pickup site and parked a good distance away. He watched for any clues, but the fairground seemed deserted. Just as he reached the front gate, the same SUV from earlier pulled up alongside his truck. The man jumped out and told Keith that his load was right in the center of the site, and while he didn't have the keys to the front gate, they just had to drive through a gap at the side of the fence.

As he pulled into the site, he noticed how tight the space was. It had been like threading a needle driving in, and that didn't leave him much room to load. But if he drove in, then Keith believed enough in his own abilities to be able to drive out again. Dismounting from the cabin, he followed the man as they went looking for the load.

Two men stepped out from the shadows. Wearing suits and wielding guns, they ordered Keith to face the wall and spread his legs. They checked him for weapons. After he asked just what the hell was going on, he was informed that he was wanted as part of an "ongoing investigation." This told Keith nothing. Arson. Murder. Rape. He could be wanted for a number of crimes. When he was forced into a patrol car, he was reassured by the New Mexico insignia. He hadn't killed anybody in this state. Sure, he'd set a few wildfires, but that was nothing compared to murder. It was only when the car was a few blocks from the sheriff's office that one of the officers revealed that he was wanted in connection with the death of his fiancé, Julie Winningham. The body had been found a day after the murder. Keith instantly regretted not moving the body. Giving nothing away, Keith feigned disinterest. Julie was into drugs and other such things, he told the officers. They didn't seem convinced.

Arriving at the station, Keith was introduced to cops from Clark County, Washington. This was where the murder had taken place. As a suspect in the death of Julie, they asked Keith for a full confession. He lied. For the next five hours, he was grilled by the police. The longer the quizzing went on, the less evidence Keith was convinced they had. He was photographed, finger printed, and the police took hair and blood samples. DNA, Keith thought, was all over his crime scenes. But without enough evidence, the police turned him free. As the police took away the tarps from the truck and his log book, he figured he might have a few days left of freedom. Keith Jesperson needed to make plans.

Over the coming days, the scale of the problem began to dawn on Keith. There were a lot of witnesses who could attest to him being with Julie at the time of the murder. He considered fleeing to Canada. Still a Canadian citizen, it would at least give him some respite, plus Canada did not have the death penalty. But he couldn't depend on his trucking company to send him up there, as they were in league with the cops. Taking a bus would give the police plenty of time to intercept him, and when he looked through the window, there was a police car stationed outside the diner where he was drinking coffee.

Keith went to the nearest shop. He bought as much pain medicine as he could lay his hands on and retired to the truck, where he knew he had more. Getting undressed and worried that the police car outside would rush in and save his life, Keith debated whether or not he should write a note. But there was no explanation that would make the situation better. He swallowed all the pills as quickly as possible and laid back in the cabin. After an initial feeling like his eyeballs were expanding, he passed out.

It was raining when he woke up, and it was still night. Keith wasn't dead. He crawled to the truck stop restroom, and when he went to climb back into the cabin, someone hit him in the face. Looking around, he realized that he'd tried to get in the wrong truck. Dragging Keith into the offices, the driver deposited him in front of the security guard. Keith could barely speak, yet alone remember his name. He eventually tried to explain the situation, enough that the guard just took his keys and told him to sober up. Suicide was never mentioned.

Back in the truck, Keith took the rest of the pills. He passed out, this time until midday. Waking up again, he realized that this was just another entry in the long list of things Keith Jesperson could never do right. Phoning up his employers, he found that he was now free to get back to work and argued with them about how they had turned the police on him. He hit the road, his mind racing for fresh ideas of how to kill himself. He tried again with sleeping pills but failed and considered wandering up a mountain and allowing himself to die of hypothermia. Instead, he wrote a letter to his brother confessing what he'd done. After that, Keith rang up the detective who'd arrested him and gave a full confession to the murder of Julie Winningham.

Keith Jesperson went to jail to await his trial. He was placed on suicide watch and didn't much like the people he was sharing his cell with. The other inmates didn't like him much either, due to the rape charges they overheard from an officer. Shunned, taunted, and threatened, he was moved to a solitary cell. A few days later, when talking with the cops again, all he could think about was the confession letter he'd sent to his brother and the Happy Face confessions he'd sent to the court houses and the newspapers. They might match up. He'd only confessed to Julie's murder. If they made the connection, he was doomed. While being flown across state lines, he resolved to call his brother at the first opportunity.

He was finally able to call Brad and immediately asked his brother to destroy the letter. But he was told that Les Jesperson, their dad, had already made Brad turn the letter over to the police. Keith was stunned. Les hadn't wanted to be accused of withholding evidence. Keith was visited by his kids. They were rushed away before they could really talk about much. As he was led back to his cells, Keith cried.

But as soon as Keith hit the stage in the court, he was a changed man. He seemed determined to right the wrongs of the court, who had convicted a couple of the murder of Taunja Bennett. He was furious that no one had responded to the confessions he had scrawled on the walls of restrooms. He accused the court of incompetence for their ability to address the Happy Face letters he had sent. It was like a one-an campaign to distract from the actual murders he had committed.

From his cell, Keith seemed happy to confess to more and more murders. At one point, he told his father that the actual figure stretched into three figures. Across the country, convicted killers began to chime up and insist that they had been convicted of Keith's crimes. But the courts refused to entertain such ideas. The only two that stuck around were the pair accused of murdering Taunja, and it took a series of smuggled press releases for the detectives to even consider the idea that the pair might have been falsely convicted. The cops seemed unwilling to overturn the case and even half-heartedly toured Keith around the murder site to try and see if he knew what he was talking about. It took Keith's discussions with journalist Phil Stanford to solve the case. Phil went and found the girl's missing purse following Keith's instructions. It would take another year before the court's overturned their initial decision.

Writing from jail, Keith began to sign letters with a Happy Face. Despite his lawyer's recommendations, he continued to talk to people on the outside and confessed to the crimes. He insisted on his own sanity and even drew diagrams to find the remains of the victims he said he had killed. He even managed to start a website from jail, where he sold a Self-Start Serial Killer Kit, which came with a free inflatable murdered woman.

Eventually, despite the fame Keith was trying to earn himself, the courts ruled against him. He was found guilty of eight counts of murder and sentenced to three consecutive life sentences. Originally serving his time in Oregon, he was transferred in 2009 while police investigated another potential victim of the Happy Face killer. To this day, he is still behind bars and is not likely to ever be released. After spending his life torturing animals, setting fires, and murdering women, Keith Hunter Jesperson is one long haul trucker who is never likely to hit the road ever again.

Conclusion

There are serial killer with higher body counts, and serial killers with more warped and twisted approaches to their crimes. But in Keith Hunter Jesperson, we have a somewhat unique opportunity to trace the lineage, development, methodology, and reasoning of a serial killer. The man himself, nowadays an unabashed self-publicist, is a fascinating figure. The figure who has become known as the Happy Face killer is entirely Keith's own creation. A savvy worker of the media, he knew how to steer the press into making him into something he was not. From the nervous, bullied young boy up to the feared serial killer, there is little in his supposed self-image that deals with the paranoia, the depression, and the resentment that drove Keith to commit murder.

Keith filled a strange niche in 1990s America. Before the rise of tracking technologies, a long haul trucker was essentially off the radar, provided with an excuse to be anywhere and nowhere at the same time. It was almost the perfect career for a serial killer, and it allowed him to remain on the loose for an incredibly long time. But, like many killers, he was eventually caught when his emotions trumped his reasoning. In his final act of murder, Keith Jesperson pushed his crimes too far. Now in jail, having escaped the death sentence, he is keen to chat about his crimes and happy to revel in the identity he has created for himself, the Happy Face killer. If you would like to read more about Keith's case or similar instances of serial killers in America, there is a further reading list at the end of this book.

The Butcher Baker
Robert Christian Hansen

A Hunter of Human Prey

"The best sport in the world," agreed Rainsford.
"For the hunter," amended Whitney. "Not for the jaguar."
"Don't talk rot, Whitney," said Rainsford. "You're a big-game hunter, not a philosopher. Who cares how a jaguar feels?"
"Perhaps the jaguar does," observed Whitney.
"Bah! They've no understanding."
"Even so, I rather think they understand one thing—fear. The fear of pain and the fear of death."
"Nonsense," laughed Rainsford. "This hot weather is making you soft, Whitney. Be a realist. The world is made up of two classes—the hunters and the huntees. Luckily, you and I are hunters. Do you think we've passed that island yet?"
"I can't tell in the dark. I hope so."
—"The Most Dangerous Game" by Richard Connell

Richard Connell wrote his famous short story "The Most Dangerous Game" (also known as "The Hounds of Zaroff") in the early 1920s. By the 1930s it was a movie. The story involved two big game hunters ending up stranded on an island where they intended to hunt jaguars. Instead, they become the prey as a man named Zaroff hunts them with his hounds. A perennial fixture on high school reading lists, the story would take on a macabre new popularity because of a man born over a decade after it was published. Beginning in the early 1970s, Robert Hansen would put his own spin on "The Most Dangerous Game." In his version, women would be sent into the Alaskan wilderness naked and blindfolded and then hunted down like animals.

Raised by strict, religiously overbearing parents, afflicted with a stutter and acne scars, Robert Hansen grew up to become a withdrawn loner. Slowly, a hatred for people, especially women, began to build. He began his life of crime by burning down a city garage used to house school buses. Moving on from there, he became a small-time thief and then discovered the world of prostitution. His anger, though, wasn't satisfied by paying for sex: He would hold working girls at gunpoint, handcuff them, and then rape them. And once he had the wilds of Alaska for his backyard, he turned to murder.

Nevertheless, Robert Hansen was regarded as a polite—if quiet—youth during the early years when he worked in his father's bakery. He ended up purchasing and running a bakery of his own in Alaska. He also became a skilled hunter who collected magnificent trophies of the state's big game. Anchorage residents had no idea what was hiding under the surface. Even after he was arrested, his standing in the community made rape victims reluctant to come forward. Many people just couldn't believe that the man they knew for his fresh donuts and hunting prowess had been killing more than just elk.

The unassuming loner blended in so well that local investigators ended up needing the help of the FBI Behavioral Analysis Unit and the expertise of criminal psychologist John Douglas. Douglas is well known for his book *Mindhunter* and his work on many high profile murder cases. He was able to complete a profile that matched Hansen perfectly, helping investigators sift through the false alibis behind the public persona to find the evil man hiding in plain sight.

Once the profile was complete, it wasn't hard to match it to Hansen. One of his victims, Cindy Paulson, had escaped his clutches only months before and had actually identified him as her rapist. However, Paulson was a prostitute, and Hansen was a respected member of the community, so in a "he said, she said" situation, his word had prevailed—with a little help from a seemingly convincing alibi. But when police got Douglas's profile, Hansen matched. With only the alibi to prevent the evidence from lining up perfectly, they took a harder look at it— and it wasn't long before that alibi fell apart and the truth came out.

Hansen had habitually targeted prostitutes and strippers. He'd gone as far as sending his family away on vacation so he could use his basement as a torture chamber where he held women handcuffed to a pole or hanging from a meat hook, biting, scratching, beating, and raping them. And then he got an airplane. His victims became prey, forced to run naked and afraid through the woods of Alaska as he hunted them down and shot them. Their bodies were buried in shallow graves or dumped along rivers. Hansen took a nightmarish tale and made it a real life scenario for his victims.

Understanding the psychology behind hunting and killing vulnerable people in this manner requires some insight into Hansen's history and how he grew up. Although the great debate of nurture versus nature is still going strong, it's fairly clear that what people live through as they're growing up—and how they adapt to it—has a reflection in their adult lives. Even with the best intentions, overbearing parents can cause an inward dip in a child's self-esteem and self-confidence. Hansen's parents went further than most, instilling a need for normalcy and perfection. They wanted a hard worker. They forced him to write with his right hand instead of his dominant left hand. They pushed him toward certain religious beliefs. Adding that to Hansen's acne issues and severe stuttering problem, he had a difficult time fitting in with kids his age. Puberty was a challenge, and girls weren't very kind. His anger turned inward and grew. Although there's no record of it, it seems entirely possible that he was killing animals and setting fires long before his teen years. And when he did get into hunting, an acceptable form of killing animals, he did so with a passion.

Robert Hansen, dubbed the "Butcher Baker," killed at least 19 women. Taking the crime escalator to the top, Hansen went from petty thief and arsonist to rapist to serial killer over his lifetime, all while maintaining the facade of a shy and gentle family man. He was a baker in Anchorage, Alaska, a husband, and the father to two children. But there are at least 30 women who lived through the horror of being kidnapped, raped, and abused by Hansen—and at least 19 who did not survive their encounters with the hunter at all.

Honing the Hunter

Robert Hansen's career as a baker started in his childhood. Christian Hansen was a Danish immigrant who had his own bakery with his wife, Edna, in Pocahontas, Iowa. On February 15, 1939, Edna gave birth to Robert Christian Hansen, their only child. Christian was a strict family man. He and Edna insisted that Robert work in the family bakery for the majority of the time that he wasn't in school. They also insisted that their left-handed child use his right hand as the dominant hand. Although there is no indication of actual abuse, his parents' controlling tendencies seem to have added a lot of stress to an already anxious child.

Hansen had issues with both a bad stutter and severe acne. He would tell interviewers that his face was "one big pimple" as a teenager and that the forced use of his right hand amplified his stuttering problem. Friends were few and far between, and none were very close to the skinny, shy, awkward child.

As Hansen got older, he experienced even more difficulty with children at school. He was often teased and picked on by the other students. His biggest problem was with the girls. The most attractive girls, to Hansen, were the meanest to him. It was at that time that a slow hatred for females began to bubble up inside of Hansen. The more abuse he received from his fellow classmates, the more withdrawn he became.

When he reached his teen years, Hansen began spending his scant free time out in the woods, hunting. He quickly became a rather adept hunter, and he found peace in the hobby. It was an escape from his life at home with strict, religious, overbearing parents, as well as the hardships he dealt with at school.

In high school, Hansen wasn't much for social activities. He had little money for such things and hardly any friends, and his parents were not fond of recreational events. Hansen did join a few school groups and sports teams so that he would be able to spend less time with his parents at the bakery and more time trying to socialize with students his age. He played basketball, ran track, sang in the school chorus, and was a member of the chess club. He took both driver's education and typing classes. Notwithstanding his attempts to fit in with his fellow classmates, he continued to be shy and withdrawn. His favorite activity was still hunting. Whether he was using a fishing rod, a bow and arrow, or a gun, Hansen preferred the solace of being out in the wilderness killing animals to interacting with other people.

In 1957, Hansen graduated high school and joined the United States Army Reserve. He trained at Fort Dix, New Jersey, and was then sent to Fort Knox, Kentucky. It was there, at age 18, that Hansen met with a prostitute and had his first sexual encounter. It wouldn't be the last, even for his short time at Fort Knox. In 1959, he went back to Iowa as an Army reservist. As a reservist, Hansen had to spend one weekend a month drilling; the remainder of the time, he worked in the family's bakery and volunteered at the Pocahontas County police academy as a drill instructor.

In between the Army, the bakery, and the police academy, Hansen met a local girl. They fell in love and were married in 1960. Six months later, Hansen committed his first crime. Hansen somehow induced a 16-year-old boy to help him set fire to the large Pocahontas County school bus garage. Later, Hansen claimed that he did it because he was angry at how the students and staff had treated him when he was in school. When the teenager went to the authorities and turned himself in, Hansen received a three-year sentence for the arson and his wife filed for divorce. He served 20 months of the sentence before being granted parole. During his incarceration, a psychological evaluation stated that he had an "infantile" personality. Hansen had just taken his first solid step into a lifetime of criminality.

Shortly after his release, Hansen met someone else. Within a short period of time, he was married to his second wife, Darla, who would remain with him until his arrest for murder. The couple moved to Anchorage, Alaska, during the oil boom of the early 1970s. Not only was it a chance for Hansen to start over with his new wife—it was also a place of great opportunity for an avid hunter.

Criminal in the Cold

Alaska not only had a booming economy, it also had a vast wilderness perfect for Hansen's favorite past time, hunting. It didn't take long for him to become proficient at hunting the wild game of the Alaskan forests and mountains. On four different occasions in 1969, 1970, and 1971, he had his trophy kills memorialized in the Pope & Young record books. Hansen's trophy room quickly became flush with monuments of his hunting exploits.

Eventually, though, hunting wild game ceased to satisfy him. Luckily for Hansen, the influx of people into Alaska had brought with it a fair amount of shadier activity. The majority of this activity was run by a Mafia boss from Seattle, Washington, named Frank Colacurio. The area he controlled was referred to as a "tenderloin"—the red light district of Anchorage. There were a multitude of strip clubs such as the Great Alaskan Bush Company, Arctic Fox, Wild Cherry, and Booby Trap. The unnamed dispensaries were the more abhorrent: brothels, magazine stands that sold child pornography and violent sexually explicit material, and drug dens. Crime in the tenderloin was high, featuring assault, robbery, prostitution, and even murder on a not infrequent basis.

Hansen got into the act with petty theft, then began perusing the ladies of the night. For 200 to 300 dollars, Hansen could get any one of these women into his vehicle. It didn't take long for him to move on to raping the women picked up. Most of them never reported the rapes; they did not believe they would be taken seriously, and at any rate it was something of an occupational hazard in their line of work. Even when the news broke years later about what Hansen had done to some of his victims, about the ones who didn't make it, very few of the survivors came forward. An unknown number could not come forward, as they had disappeared from the streets never to be seen again.

Prostitution is illegal in most of the United States for a few reasons. The first is to help prevent the spread of sexually transmitted and drug related diseases. The second is the lack of laws that would enable prostitution to be regulated as a legitimate occupation. Thirdly, prostitution is often associated with other criminal activity; where there is prostitution there are also drugs and often other forms of crime. Of course, the illegal nature of their profession and their proximity to other criminal elements makes prostitutes easy prey. Controllable by drugs and money, disposable in the eyes of sociopaths and solid citizens alike, they are often the target of rape, theft, abuse, and murder.

Many of Hansen's victims who weren't prostitutes were exotic dancers. In 1970s Anchorage, dancing in strip clubs was often a supplementary job for women who were trying to raise children, finish school, or just make enough to get by. In a place with long nights and a burgeoning population of unattached men seeking entertainment, exotic dancing was seen as a decent source of income, without the risk of working the streets or the requirement of sexual interaction. Some strippers also worked as call girls, but the majority did not. For Hansen, however, there was no difference. The strip clubs were mostly in the seedy, shady tenderloin district where reliable witnesses were few and far between. Exotic dancers therefore made easy targets, because it would be very difficult for them to prove that an assault had occurred—or even to get the police to take the complaint seriously. Many of those who disappeared forever did have missing persons reports filed by friends or relatives, but these were not usually a priority for authorities. The high-risk lifestyle was considered a person risk, and police tended to focus on the fact that these women worked in a field that catered to the criminal populace. This fact certainly allowed Hansen to get away with his crimes for longer than he would otherwise have been able.

In November of 1971, a woman pulled up to a stoplight in the Alaskan town of Spenard. She looked over to see Hansen and gave him a polite smile. Hansen lifted a gun and pointed it at her, demanding that she get out of her car and into his. She wisely drove away, and Hansen was arrested. While out on bail prior to the trial, he was arrested again, this time for the kidnapping, rape, and armed assault of an 18-year-old prostitute. Unfortunately for Hansen's future victims, the prostitute failed to show up in court on the day of the trial, and Superior Court Judge James Fitzgerald was forced to drop the charges in that case.

However, Judge Fitzgerald still wanted to keep Hansen off the streets, and he still had the charge of assault with a deadly weapon from the first incident. He later said that he recognized the type of man Hansen was and knew he was a probable repeat offender. The best he could do was to try to slow Hansen down. Unfortunately, he wasn't able to slow him down much. Sentenced to five years, Hansen was jailed in March and paroled in June, when he was moved to a halfway house under psychiatric supervision until November. In Hansen's eventual confession, he told police was already prowling around the red light district searching for his next victim the night he was released. He was the subject of more complaints in 1975, but one by one, the prostitutes dropped the charges. They were afraid that Hansen would go free and follow through on his threats to kill them if they told anyone.

Two women were already missing when Hansen was arrested again in 1977. 17-year-old Megan Emerick had gone missing on July 7, 1973, from Anchorage. Two years later, Mary K. Thill, a 23-year-old housewife, had gone missing from Seward. Hansen was not arrested for these disappearances, however; he had stolen a chainsaw. He was sentenced to another five years in prison. After a psychiatric evaluation, Hansen was diagnosed with behavioral and personality issues, including bipolar disorder. It was ordered that he follow a lithium-based treatment program, but this was never enforced. After one year in jail, Hansen was released back onto the streets.

He quickly resumed his hobby of kidnapping women off those same streets. To make his home available for this dark pastime, he sent his wife and children away for a vacation. Some of the women were raped and released; some went missing. In 1980, Hansen killed a dog belonging to one of his murder victims. He later told investigators that he was afraid that the dog would lead someone to her body.

In that same year, a body was discovered near Eklutna Road. The woman would be dubbed "Eklutna Annie," and is still unidentified to this day. In June, Roxanne Easland, a 24-year-old prostitute, went missing from Anchorage. Joanne Messina's body was discovered in a gravel pit after she disappeared from Seward in July. 41-year-old Lisa Futrell was last seen in Anchorage in September of 1980.

To society, though, Hansen seemed to be doing well. In 1981, Hansen claimed his house had been burglarized and his hunting trophies stolen, resulting in a settlement from his insurance company. He used the money to open a bakery in Anchorage. The insurance company, however, filed a fraud case when it was discovered that the missing trophies were still in Hansen's possession. His excuse was that he had found them in his yard and forgotten to report the fact to the insurance company.

In 1981, two more women went missing from Anchorage: 22-year-old Andrea Altiery and 23-year-old Sherry Morrow. The next year, Hansen bought an airplane, despite his lack of a pilot's license. The Piper Super Cub N3089Z became the key component of his hunting expeditions. Previously, Hansen had picked his victims up and handcuffed them in his vehicle before taking them to nearby rural areas. He now began to fly them out to the Knik River, where he had located a remote sandbar. It was there that he would begin his hunt. The women were stripped, raped, blindfolded, and then released. Hansen would hunt them with his favorite rifle before burying or dumping their bodies and then flying back to Merrill Field, where he kept his plane.

23-year-old Sue Luna was last seen in Anchorage in May of 1982. In September of 1982, the body of Sherry Morrow was found by the Knik River by an off-duty policeman who was out hunting. Paula Goulding, a 31-year-old stripper, went missing in April of 1983. Even as more women began to disappear and bodies began to pile up, Hansen was still maintaining his facade as a baker—and still randomly raping women he picked up in Anchorage's tenderloin district. And then, one of his victims escaped.

The Prey Escapes

Cindy Paulson was a 17-year-old girl who had fallen on hard times. She led a high-risk life working the streets as a prostitute in Anchorage. She had already seen the darker side of human nature up close and personal. And then one day a man picked her up and changed her life forever. It was the worst day of her life—and it was almost the last. She would be one of the lucky ones who survived, but only due to her strength and tenacity.

A sedan stopped to pick up Cindy Paulson on June 13, 1983. Cindy watched the man as they spoke. He was well dressed, but seemed a bit odd, quiet and nervous. Still, there was nothing to indicate that he had any violent tendencies. They discussed what he was looking for and the cost, and he agreed to pay Cindy $200 to perform oral sex. Cindy got into the car.

As soon as she was sitting in the seat, the man changed completely. He pulled out a gun and pointed it at her as he handcuffed her, threatening to kill her if she tried to escape or call any attention to them. He then drove them to his home, where he took Cindy down into the basement. She was forced to strip. He told her that no one would believe her if she tried to escape. He bragged that he was an upstanding citizen whereas cops would see her only as a prostitute and a liar. He also told her he had an alibi already in place. Cindy was already beginning to realize she might not survive the encounter.

Cindy was then tortured and raped repeatedly for hours. Her captor bit her nipples, sexually assaulted her, and then began to use tools, such as a hammer, to rape her. Eventually, he became tired and handcuffed her and chained her neck to a concrete support in the basement. Then he lay down on a nearby couch to take a nap.

When he woke up, he forced Cindy to dress hastily and return to the car. She had to crouch in the back seat as he drove, telling her that he was going to take her to his cabin. Cindy took her shoes and tucked them down into the rear floorboard of the back seat. She would later tell interviewers that she didn't think she would survive the encounter, so she wanted to leave as much evidence as possible to make sure the man wouldn't get away with it.

They arrived at a small airfield. Cindy began scoping out her escape route as he started moving items over to a plane. He un-cuffed her and escorted her to the small aircraft, making her climb inside. However, he didn't secure her as he continued loading guns and supplies into the plane. Cindy saw her chance and took it. She took off, running toward the distant road, 6th Avenue. The man pursued her at first, yelling that he was going to catch her and kill her, but stopped when he saw a truck coming down the road.

36-year-old truck driver Robert Yount saw Cindy, handcuffs dangling from her arm and looking a little worse for wear, and stopped. She climbed in and he took her to the nearby Mush Inn to use a phone. She was trying to call her boyfriend at the Big Timber Motel as Yount left. As he got back on the road, he called the police on his CB radio to report that he had picked up a battered looking woman with no shoes taken her to the Mush Inn. Officer Greg Baker of the Anchorage Police Department went to the Mush Inn, but Cindy was no longer there. The receptionist told him that she had mentioned something about the Big Timber Motel. When he arrived there, Officer Baker found her in Room 110. She was sitting alone, still wearing the handcuffs.

As Officer Baker removed her handcuffs, she told him what had happened to her. She described the kidnapping, the torture she had experienced in the basement of a nice house in a decent suburb, and her abductor's plans to take her to a cabin they could only get to by plane.

The police were incredulous. Some instantly dismissed her story as unbelievable. Others were simply too familiar with the crime in Anchorage, and the criminals. To them, prostitutes were part of the problem. On the other hand, her description of the events and locations was clear and certain, and it was evident that she had suffered some kind of trauma. Officer Baker saw a terrified and beaten woman who was determined to make sure the man who had done this to her would not get away. For this policeman, the crime was too bizarre—and at the same time too strangely familiar—for him to let go.

At the police station, Cindy Paulson filed a formal report, writing down every detail she could remember. The suspect was described as a man in his 40s with reddish hair. Cindy told them about the sedan, the color and style, and that her shoes were in the back seat floorboard. She knew that the house had been in Muldoon. The plane was at Merrill Field, where the trucker had picked her up. After filing her statement, police took her back out to the airfield to see if she could identify the plane the suspect had put her in. Cindy pointed out the blue-and-white Piper Super Cub with the registration identifier N3089Z. She was then taken to the hospital for a physical exam and rape kit. It was confirmed that she had bruising and tearing consistent with sexual assault.

It was easy for police to trace the plane to Hansen. They went to his house and confronted him with Cindy's accusations. Hansen acted surprised and baffled, but readily agreed to cooperate and went down to the police station to make his statement. He was interviewed by an officer from the Anchorage Police Department's Sex Crimes Division, William Dennis. He claimed he had never seen Cindy, and even asked detectives, "You can't rape a prostitute, can you?" He admitted that his family was out of town on a European vacation, but said that his neighbors would give him an alibi—which did check out. His demeanor was calm and confident; in fact, the only suspicious aspect was that he was being accused of very serious crimes and yet was very composed and relaxed. He gave his permission for police to search his house and vehicle.

Investigators did a cursory search of the various locations tied to the alleged crimes. Cindy's descriptions of the interior of the home, car, and plane, as well as her shoes in the car, proved that she had been to all three places at some point. Since Hansen's statement suggested that Cindy was trying to extort him, police began to wonder if he had utilized her services but failed to pay her. Perhaps she was recalling details from that event and applying them to her accusations?

Hansen was known as a meek man and the owner of a well-loved bakery; Cindy was a teenage whore. Cindy had also refused to take a lie detector test. Hansen relied heavily on those facts to help him get out from under police scrutiny, and it worked. After checking Hansen's alibi with his friends John Henning and John Sumrall, Officer Dennis closed the case. Only Officer Greg Baker, the one who'd originally found Cindy at the Big Timber Motel, was still convinced that Hansen was getting away with a crime.

At the time, Anchorage had more than its share of crime—not to mention the increasingly obvious possibility that they had a serial killer on their hands. But police weren't focused on Hansen as being the potential perpetrator. To them, Hansen just didn't seem like the serial killer type. And despite Cindy's statements, her obvious knowledge of Hansen, his home, his vehicle, and his plane, the rape of a prostitute didn't rank high on their list of priorities. Only two members of the Anchorage PD weren't so certain: Officer Baker, and Detective Glenn Flothe, who had been working on the case of the murdered women popping up in the Alaskan wilderness.

Soon, the police would have another name to add to their growing list of potential serial killer victims. On September 9, 1983, the decomposing body of 31-year-old Paula Goulding was found along the banks of the Knik River. Paula had been reported missing over five months before, in April. She had been shot, the same as the others. A .223 caliber bullet was recovered. Most tellingly, Paula's body was found in the same spot that Sherry Morrow's had been almost exactly a year before (minus ten days). With this find, the local police decided that they needed help catching their serial killer. They called in the Federal Bureau of Investigation.

Hunting the Hunter

Alaska had dealt with another serial killer a decade before. Unfortunately, that killer was not discovered until after five women were dead. Aware that the law was closing in, he was on the run before the cops had even finished figuring out who he was. He fled on a motorcycle and ended up killing himself in a high-speed accident. The Anchorage Police Department and the Alaska State Troopers were determined not to have a repeat, but the body count was rising and they still had no idea who their killer was. Detective Flothe called the FBI about his three confirmed victims of a possible serial killer. The FBI assigned the case to Special Agent Roy Hazlewood and criminal psychologist John Douglas.

John Douglas has since become a renowned criminologist. To the general public, he is best known for his 1995 book *Mindhunter*, which describes his work on the Hansen case. Douglas joined the FBI in 1970 after service in the Air Force. In 1976, he moved to the Behavioral Analysis Unit. Together with Robert Ressler, he pioneered the investigative techniques that gave rise to the television term "profiling." Douglas helped solve the 1979-1981 Atlanta Murders when he created a profile that matched the killer Wayne Williams. In both the West Memphis Three and Jon Benet Ramsey cases, Douglas told authorities they had their suspects completely wrong. Jack Crawford in Thomas Harris's *Silence of the Lambs* and Jason Gideon in the television series *Criminal Minds* were both based on John Douglas and the cases he was involved in. Douglas has written 13 non-fiction books and two novels. But what is a criminal psychologist, and is it the same as a profiler?

To understand how important John Douglas's expertise has been to certain cases, including Hansen's, you must understand what a "profiler" is and what it means. In the investigative world, the title "profiler" is not used. Criminal psychologists, behavioral scientists, criminologists, and forensic psychologists are specialists associated with what is referred to as profiling. Much like the fictional Sherlock Holmes, they look at all the clues and evidence, and using deductive reasoning and observation based on probability, they come to a conclusion as to how a crime was committed and who committed it. Everything from weapon to location to victim selection supplies a vast amount of information to a criminal psychologist. The manner in which the crime is carried out, what is and isn't left behind—every detail tells the investigators a bit more about the suspect.

John Douglas's criminal profile for the suspect in the Alaskan murders was very apt. Douglas stated that he was someone who was very insecure. He would have to be normal enough for women to not fear him at first, to go with him. He might have a lisp or stutter and maybe pockmarks or other facial deformities, something that made him self-conscious about his interactions with other people. He would be a loner, someone who normally would not fit into society, but he would have an occupation or position that would help him fit in regardless. He might even have a family. Based on the evidence of charring near some of the bodies, he would have a history of arson. Douglas said the killer was probably a hunter. The victims were all shot with a rifle—the same rifle—and found in the wilderness. Because of his hunting prowess, the murderer would have a trophy room or somewhere else to display his hunting trophies. With that idea in mind, Douglas predicted that his trophy collection would also extend to his victims. Once police got a search warrant, they would be able to find personal belongings of the victims in the killer's house. He would also have more minor crimes on his record, something that started prior to him working up to becoming a killer. The abuse of the victims showed anger and a desire for revenge against women, especially those who worked in the sex industry.

From *Mindhunter: Inside the FBI's Elite Serial Killer Crime Unit*, by John Douglas:

Hansen, I was surmising, regarded prostitutes in much the same way. They were people he could regard as lower and more worthless than himself. And he wouldn't need the gift of gab to get one to come with him. He would pick her up, make her his prisoner, fly her out into the wilderness, strip her naked, let her loose, then hunt her down with a gun or knife.

His MO wouldn't have started this way. He would have started simply by killing the early ones, then using the plane to fly their bodies far away. These were crimes of anger. He would have gotten off on having his victims beg for their lives. Being a hunter, at a certain point it would have occurred to him that he could combine these various activities by flying them out into the wilderness alive, then hunting them down for sport and further sexual gratification. This would have been the ultimate control. And it would have become addictive. He would want to do it again and again.

And this led me to the details of the search warrant. What they wanted from Jim and me was an affidavit they could take to court explaining what profiling was all about, what we would expect to find in the search, and our rationale for being able to say so.

Unlike a common criminal or someone whose gun is an interchangeable tool, Hansen's hunting rifle would be important to him. Therefore, I predicted the rifle would be somewhere in his house, though not in open view. It would be in a crawl space, behind paneling or a false wall, hidden in the attic: someplace like that.

I also predicted our guy would be a "saver," though not entirely for the normal reasons. A lot of sexual killers take souvenirs from their victims and give them to the women in their lives as a sign of dominance and a way of being able to relive the experience. But Hansen couldn't very well put a woman's head on the wall the way he would a big-game animal's, so I thought it likely he would take some other kind of trophy. Since there was no evidence of human mutilation on the bodies, I expected him to have taken jewelry, which he would have given to his wife or daughter, making up a story about where the piece came from. He didn't to appear to have kept the victims' underwear or any other item we could account for, but he might have kept small photographs or something else from a wallet. And from my experience with this type of personality, I thought we might find a journal or list documenting his exploits.

When investigators applied John Douglas's profile to their possible suspects, one man matched all of the criteria. Hansen had pockmarks from severe acne, as well as a stutter. He worked in a bakery. He wasn't well-known, per se, but people in the community were aware of him and he seemed like a "nice, quiet guy" with no outlandish behaviors. He was also an avid hunter; several of the trophies in his trophy room, were even in record books. He had a history of arson, having burned down the bus garage back in Iowa. Hansen also matched the physical description, and his vehicles matched witness descriptions, from several Anchorage rape cases. The icing on the cake was the witness statement of Cindy Paulson, the one who got away. The only problem was that Hansen had an alibi.

Police went back to John Henning and John Sumrall, the neighbors who'd provided that alibi, and informed them that it was a crime to obstruct a federal investigation. The friends had initially assumed that Hansen's need for an alibi had something to do with his insurance fraud case, but now they realized that he was being investigated for more serious crimes. They quickly agreed to recant their statements and admit that Hansen had not been with them during the time that Cindy Paulson said the rape had occurred.

There were still issues with the District Attorney's office and the Anchorage Police Department. Both were hesitant to focus on Hansen as the culprit for the murders. Part of this was because he had been arrested once, for the chainsaw theft, and had been accused of a rape fitting the modus operandi of their serial killer and yet had been set free. If Hansen was the man, they had had the killer in their grasp and then let him go, and that was a difficult pill to swallow. Once the media realized that the authorities had failed to stop Hansen on at least two occasions, they would be in a lot of trouble with the community.

Detective Flothe, though, had been digging deeply into Hansen's past. He was still convinced that Cindy was telling the truth. Among his findings were the arrest for pulling the gun on a woman in traffic and the dropped charges of rape in the early 1970s. With this information, the vanished alibi, and John Douglas's profile, the evidence became too overwhelming to ignore, and the DA's office finally signed off on the warrant.

On October 2, 1983, Anchorage detectives followed Hansen to work. They told him he needed to come down to the station for questioning, and Hansen obeyed without a fuss. While he was being interviewed, two groups of investigators were sent out with warrants, one for his plane and one for his house.

The house was searched from top to bottom. Many weapons were found, most of them typical hunting guns and bows. At first, police were unable to find anything linked to the evidence recovered from the victims' bodies. Then one eagle-eyed officer found a secret wall space in the attic. Inside was a Remington rifle, pieces of jewelry from the victims' bodies, clipped articles from newspapers, a Winchester shotgun, a small single-shot pistol, several driver's licenses and other IDs belonging to the victims, and a .223 Ruger Mini-14 rifle. There was also a map behind his headboard—an aviation map with several red X's marked in the Alaskan wilderness.

Back at the police station, they were finally able to arrest their serial killer. Hansen was charged with insurance fraud, weapons violations, theft, kidnapping, and assault and his bail was set for $500,000. He became increasingly enraged as the charges were announced and the evidence from his home was laid out in front of him. Hansen requested his lawyers, and when they came, police could hear him screaming at them through the walls.

Psychological Analysis

In nature, there is a hierarchy of animal species based upon the predator/prey dynamic. Humans are now at the top of that list, as all of our former predators have become our easy prey thanks to modern firearms. Without a gun, what is a man to a full-grown bear, the man's fingers to the bears claws? With a gun, man is, uniquely in the animal kingdom, every animal's predator.

Animals in the wild hunt for food and to protect themselves by thinning overpopulated areas and removing threats to themselves or their pack. Many people still hunt for food, but many others hunt only for sport. And then there are those who hunt people, to deal with psychological issues or to feed some dark, internal need. Hansen hunted game for sport; he hunted people to satisfy his anger at himself and the people on whom he projected his psychological insecurities.

It seems baffling that someone could look at another person the same way he would look at a wild animal. How does a person hunt another person with no thoughts or feelings about what he is doing? The dark truth is that it is still in our nature, deep and primal, to hunt and kill. It is a part of us that has little to no use nowadays. For the most part, we have learned to deal with those urges, have moved far past those primal feelings and no longer feel the call of killing. Why should we? We don't have to fight for our homes, our food, our mates; we only fight over territory at a national level. There is no need for violence against others. Some, though, cannot dampen those urges.

There is also the fact that people like Hansen don't see other people as belonging to the same species. Such a man craves dominance and control. He doesn't feel for his victims, he doesn't see their tears or fear, and he has no thought that they are beings like him. To him, they are merely disposable things. They are animals to hunt and do with as he pleases. For a man like Hansen, the only thing that would improve hunting humans would be the ability to display his trophies and show the world how strong and powerful he is.

Nature versus nurture is an ongoing debate, but one that is increasingly viewed as incorrect. Current psychological analysis holds that *both* nature and nurture make people who they are. Two people who have lived through a similar situation may deal with the subsequent issues and problems differently based on how they process the experience and how their emotions react. This is explained in the article "Serial Killers: Nature vs. Nurture" on the website of the National Center for Crisis Management American Academy of Experts in Traumatic Stress:

Modern geneticists have pointed out that a nature-nurture dichotomy is clearly untenable, incorrect, and meaningless. The subject has to be discussed in terms of the continuous and complex interactions between an organism and its environment, and the relevant contributions of both sets of variables in determining the behavior of the organism (Athens 12)…

Sociologist Arnold Arluke compared the criminal records of one hundred and fifty three animal abusers with one hundred and fifty three non-animal abusers and what he found in his study is that those who were animal abusers were five times more likely to commit acts of violence such as assault, rape, and murder against others. What was understood from this study is that serial killers in their childhood would resort to killing animals because they felt powerless against their parents who had control over them. Since these children did not have control in the household, they resorted to killing small animals in which they could exert their dominance and power over to do anything that pleased them (Fox 113).

In a study of sixty two male serial killers, Eric Hicky a criminologist found that, forty eight percent of them had been rejected as children by a parent or some other important person in their lives (Fox 113). Though this happens to many children, it certainly represents a turning point for those who become serial killers. Once rejected many of these killers begin to dive into their self-indulgences and are unable to understand how and who they are when going through puberty. "The social experiences which make people dangerous violent criminals are the significant experiences rather than the trivial ones in their lives (Athens 19).

That the truth lies on both sides of the age-old argument has been proven time and time again. Environment can most definitely have a bearing on how a person progresses from a given experience, but one's chemical make-up and physiology is an equally determinative factor. There have been many studies on the brains of killers, covering emotional impulse murderers, spree killers, mass murderers, and serial killers. With the exception of emotional impulse killers (those who murder in the heat of passion, whether anger or fear or some other reactive emotion), between 85-97 percent were deemed likely to have some kind of chemical imbalance or physiological brain defect.

How does this information pertain to Hansen's case? Hansen's parents were strict, religiously overbearing, controlling, and hard on Hansen. However, they were not particularly abusive, and they weren't neglectful. There have been serial killers with both better and worse childhoods, and yet all of them ended up killing. Hansen was not allowed to embrace who he was. He was a lefty forced to use his right hand. He loved sports and athletics, but his parents forced him to focus on family and the family business. Hansen had facial deformities in the form of severe acne and cysts that caused scarring by his late teen years. He wore horn-rimmed glasses, was tall and thin, and wasn't particularly handsome. His parents made him feel embarrassed about the ways in which he was different from others. The strict atmosphere and hard work under his father's thumb caused him to turn inward. His self-confidence and self-esteem dwindled, causing him to be shy and withdrawn.

These reactions, though, were not what made him a killer. They were merely stepping stones that allowed the chemical imbalances from which Hansen suffered to play a larger role in who he was. His parents were not at fault for what he became; they had no way of knowing that their strict upbringing would cause such an explosive reaction. It was merely the beginning. As Hansen grew up and had more interactions with society, his psyche was damaged. Pretty girls made fun of him when he was hitting puberty; just as he began to feel sexual needs, he faced sexual denial and repression. He didn't fit in.

Victims of abuse and rejection, serial killers find comfort in their fantasies and dreams that take them into a realm that only they can control. Psycho killers take their fantasies and make them a reality living their dreams. ("Serial Killers: Nature vs. Nurture")

This caused him to seek other ways to express himself and find a feeling of control over his life. Hunting became that outlet. With hunting, he was the boss. He had control. He decided what lived or died, and he became very good at killing. But using something as primal as death and killing as an outlet for repressed depression and anger created a ticking time bomb within Hansen.

Hansen showed several mental illnesses early on in his criminal career. In a trial transcript from one of his early arrests, his mental state is discussed as an issue with his release and further need for evaluation and treatment:

Although the current offense is Hansen's first for theft, he informed the examining psychiatrists that he had an episodic stealing problem. In 1976, Dr. Parker wrote a second evaluation letter in which he characterizes Hansen's stealing as "probably obsessive" because Hansen "has an inability to resist it and a feeling of being forced." Hansen began therapy with Dr. Robert McManmon who diagnosed Hansen's illness as a bipolar affective disorder which is a variant of a manic-depressive disorder. Dr. McManmon, testifying at Hansen's sentencing hearing, distinguished Hansen's disorder from the classic manic-depressive pattern by the absence of any serious depressive episodes. Hansen's impulses were poorly controlled during the mood and energy upswings of this disorder. During manic episodes sufferers of this disease tend to develop an abnormal preoccupation (mania) toward some activity. Kleptomania, the impulse to steal without economic need, is a manifestation of this illness. Dr. McManmon further testified that Hansen's prior offenses were also likely manifestations of his disorder. The type of behavior indicated by those convictions is "known to occur in this disorder as one of the expressions of the poorly controlled behavior."

Although in 1971 Dr. Parker wrote that it would be difficult to treat Hansen's disorder, the drug lithium has since become acceptable treatment for controlling manic episodes. Lithium checks a patient's manic behavior until he can learn to control himself. Since lithium controls rather than cures, Dr. McManmon stated that complete assurances for Hansen's future behavior were impossible. However, he noted that Hansen had stabilized on lithium, had developed a good rapport with Dr. McManmon, and meaningful therapy had begun so that he "wouldn't anticipate any problems with [Hansen] continuing treatment now." Dr. McManmon believed that the best safeguard against further expression of the illness was continued treatment and it was preferable to have Hansen remain an active member of society. The prognosis was favorable.

The judge himself pointed out Hansen's inability to function in society:

The court, remarking upon the difficulty of the case, described and applied the State v. Chaney, 477 P.2d 441 (Alaska 1970), sentencing criteria. As to rehabilitation potential, Hansen had no trade or educational deficiencies to remedy. His problem was psychiatric. Were rehabilitation the only consideration, the judge stated that he would have granted probation with strict conditions regarding therapy and lithium treatment. Nevertheless, he feared that Hansen was dangerous during manic episodes, and thought that he should be isolated from society. Furthermore, the court believed that the goal of deterrence would only be achieved by a term of incarceration in order to provide Hansen with an "incentive to cooperate" and in recognition of the fact that this offense was Hansen's third felony conviction.

And yet, despite these factors, Hansen not only went back into society unhindered, he quickly stopped taking lithium and receiving treatment for his mental health.

Hansen was diagnosed with an antisocial personality disorder referred to as bipolar disorder. According to the website Psychology Today,

Antisocial personality disorder is characterized by a pattern of disregard for and violation of the rights of others. The diagnosis of antisocial personality disorder is not given to individuals under the age of 18 but is given only if there is a history of some symptoms of conduct disorder before age 15.

The symptoms of antisocial personality disorder can vary in severity. The more egregious, harmful, or dangerous behavior patterns are referred to as sociopathic or psychopathic. There has been much debate as to the distinction between these descriptions. Sociopathy is chiefly characterized as something severely wrong with one's conscience; psychopathy is characterized as a complete lack of conscience regarding others. Some professionals describe people with this constellation of symptoms as "stone cold" to the rights of others. Complications of this disorder include imprisonment, drug abuse, and alcoholism.

People with this illness may seem charming on the surface, but they are likely to be irritable and aggressive as well as irresponsible. They may have numerous somatic complaints and perhaps attempt suicide. Due to their manipulative tendencies, it is difficult to tell whether they are lying or telling the truth.

This term is used as a blanket term for people who suffer from sudden personality splits and changes, impulse control issues, and the inability to feel societally appropriate emotions. Numerous witnesses described Hansen's sudden emotional changes. Cindy Paulson spoke of how he went from a shy and polite man to suddenly turning red, becoming angry, and seeming to almost become someone else. Officers present when the information confirming Hansen's involvement in the murders came in said he seemed to transform. His face turned red, his lips screwed into an angry snarl, and his eyes blazed.

The *Alaska Dispatch* had an article regarding this change:

Rothschild recounted watching Hansen transform into "the monster he was" the day prosecutors sat down with Hansen and laid out the evidence against him. They told Hansen they had seized his map marked with 17 locations, spots that they believed indicated the locations of bodies.

"He was mild-mannered Bob the Baker, and as I'm looking at him, all of sudden he transformed. The hair on the back of his neck stood up and his neck got red, and he was pissed," Rothschild said in a phone interview Thursday.

"I can still see him when he got livid like that," he said.

Hansen asked to speak with his attorneys and went out into another room. "You could hear him screaming at his lawyers," Rothschild said.

Hansen didn't see his victims as human, the attorney said. "In his mind there were good girls and bad girls."

How Hansen saw himself and his victims was one of the more chilling aspects of his confession. In the excerpt below (part of a marathon 12-hour interview), he responds to questions from District Attorney Krumm and Detective Flothe.

KRUMM: Why did you drive out to the road, instead of just going to a hotel or motel in town?

HANSEN: You know if you go to a motel or something with it, it's more or less like a prostitution deal. I'm going and, or I'd—I guess I'm trying to even convince myself maybe I wasn't really buying sex, it was being given to me, in the aspect that I was good enough that it was being given to me. Uh, if I can explain that a little bit better gentlemen. Going back in my life, way back to my high school days and so forth, I was, I guess what you might call very frustrated, upset all the time. I would see my friends and so forth going out on dates and so forth and had a tremendous desire to do the same thing. From the scars and so forth on my face you can probably see, I could see why girls wouldn't want to get close to me and when I'm nervous and upset like this here; if I, I'll try to demonstrate if I can think about exactly what I'm going to say and if I talk slow I can keep myself from stuttering. But at the time during my junior high or high school days I could not control my speech at all. I was always so embarrassed and upset with it from people making fun of me that I hated the word school, I guess this is why I burned down the bus way back in Iowa … I can remember going up and talking to someone, man or woman, classmate or whatever and start to say something and start to stutter so badly that especially in the younger years I would run away crying, run off someplace and hide for a day or so. The worst there was that I was the rebuttal of all the girls around the school and so forth. The jokes. If I could have faced it, I know now if I could have faced it and laughed along with them it would have stopped but I couldn't at the time and it just, it got so it controlled me, I didn't control it. I didn't start to hate all women, as a matter of fact I would venture to say I started to fall in love with every one of them. Every one of them become so precious to me 'cause I wanted their—I wanted their friendship … I wanted them to like me so much. On top of things that have happened, I don't want to, I'm not saying that I hate all women, I don't. Quite to the contrary, if, I guess in my own mind what I'm classifying is a good woman, not a prostitute. I'd do everything in my power, any way, shape or form to do anything for her and to see that no harm ever came to her, but I guess prostitutes are women I'm putting down as lower than myself. I don't know if I'm making sense or not. And you know, when this started to happen I wanted—you know … It happened the first time there, you know, and I went home and I was literally sick to my stomach … Over the years I've gone in many many topless and bottomless bars in town and so forth and never, never touched one of the girls in there in any way, shape, or form until they asked. It's like, it's like it was a game—they had to pitch the ball before I could bat. They had to approach me first saying about I get off at a certain time, we could go out and have a good time, or something like this here. If they don't, we weren't playing the game right. They had to approach me. I've talked to, I suppose I made it a point to try to talk to, every girl in there. Sometimes if I thought there was a possibility that she didn't say it the first time but she might come back and say it again, now I've invited two or three table dances with her and comment to her how nice she looked and everything else and I try to keep it in a joking tone, "Gosh you know, you sure would be some thing, you know, for later on," but that's as far as it would go until she, then she had to make, I guess play out my fantasy. She had to come out and say we could do it but it's going to cost you some money. Then she was no longer—I guess what you might call a decent girl. I didn't look down at the girls dancing, what the hell they're just trying to make a buck.

FLOTHE: But when they propositioned you, then it made things different?

HANSEN: Then, yes.

Most people immediately wonder if a serial killer is a psychopath or a sociopath. The truth is that they aren't always either one, but if anything, Hansen had sociopathic tendencies. Sociopaths can feel emotion; it is just not always what is considered the appropriate emotion for a situation. Hansen, for example, saw his victims as no more than a means to an end, as things rather than people. This is the aspect of his personality that clearly shows sociopathic tendencies.

Hansen was clinically diagnosed with bipolar affective disorder with periods of psychosis. The National Institute of Mental Health explains bipolar disorder as follows:

Bipolar disorder, also known as manic-depressive illness, is a brain disorder that causes unusual shifts in mood, energy, activity levels, and the ability to carry out day-to-day tasks.

There are four basic types of bipolar disorder; all of them involve clear changes in mood, energy, and activity levels. These moods range from periods of extremely "up," elated, and energized behavior (known as manic episodes) to very sad, "down," or hopeless periods (known as depressive episodes). Less severe manic periods are known as hypomanic episodes.

Bipolar I Disorder—defined by manic episodes that last at least 7 days, or by manic symptoms that are so severe that the person needs immediate hospital care. Usually, depressive episodes occur as well, typically lasting at least 2 weeks. Episodes of depression with mixed features (having depression and manic symptoms at the same time) are also possible.

Bipolar II Disorder—defined by a pattern of depressive episodes and hypomanic episodes, but not the full-blown manic episodes described above.

Cyclothymic Disorder (also called cyclothymia)—defined by numerous periods of hypomanic symptoms as well numerous periods of depressive symptoms lasting for at least 2 years (1 year in children and adolescents). However, the symptoms do not meet the diagnostic requirements for a hypomanic episode and a depressive episode.

Other Specified and Unspecified Bipolar and Related Disorders—defined by bipolar disorder symptoms that do not match the three categories listed above.

People with bipolar disorder experience periods of unusually intense emotion, changes in sleep patterns and activity levels, and unusual behaviors. These distinct periods are called "mood episodes." Mood episodes are drastically different from the moods and behaviors that are typical for the person. Extreme changes in energy, activity, and sleep go along with mood episodes.

Sometimes a mood episode includes symptoms of both manic and depressive symptoms. This is called an episode with mixed features. People experiencing an episode with mixed features may feel very sad, empty, or hopeless, while at the same time feeling extremely energized.

Bipolar disorder can be present even when mood swings are less extreme. For example, some people with bipolar disorder experience hypomania, a less severe form of mania. During a hypomanic episode, an individual may feel very good, be highly productive, and function well. The person may not feel that anything is wrong, but family and friends may recognize the mood swings and/or changes in activity levels as possible bipolar disorder. Without proper treatment, people with hypomania may develop severe mania or depression.

Stories of Hansen's life have focused on the stark difference between the face he presented to the community—that of a quiet family man—and the angry murderer whose face was seen only by his victims. What he was like at home, when not killing or putting on a front for other people, is unknown. It is very possible he had periods of depression. Often those who do find solace in the solitude offered by activities like hunting and fishing. Hansen's insecurity and lack of self-confidence bolster the theory that he suffered from depression. He often sent his family away on trips and vacations. One reason for this was that it left him free to hunt and prey on women, but it may also have further enabled his withdrawn personality.

Bipolar disorder is genetic and is a physiologically determinable feature. A chemical imbalance and possible changes to certain aspects of the brain enhance the issues and behavior-causing parts of the human psyche. Although Hansen apparently had no severe trauma in his childhood, he did lack positive reinforcement and love. There was a heavy focus on discipline and physical labor, compounded by his inability to fit in with children his age. His stability declined further in his teen years as his pastime of killing animals and setting fires compensated for the cruel and/or dismissive way his classmates treated him. A study published in the *British Journal of Psychiatry* discusses how such traumas force a negative progression in bipolar-prone children:

Within affective disorder, the relationship between childhood events and psychosis appears to be relatively symptom-specific. It is possible that the pathways leading to psychotic symptoms differ, with delusions and non-hallucinatory symptoms being influenced less by childhood or early environmental experience.

In recent years a number of studies have investigated an association between the presence of psychotic symptoms and a history of childhood trauma. A recent meta-analysis of 36 studies concluded childhood adversity increases the risk of psychosis nearly three-fold. Some authors now propose a causal relationship between these early childhood events and the subsequent development of schizophrenia and this association has influenced key cognitive models of psychosis. One example is the proposal that adverse experiences in childhood will lead to the development of negative schemas of the self and the world (the self as vulnerable and others as dangerous) that facilitate the development of paranoid delusions. Furthermore, Birchwood et al suggest that childhood experience of social adversity leads to the development of negative schemas involving social humiliation and subordination, which in turn may fuel paranoia. Alternatively, it is proposed within biological models of schizophrenia that the experience of abuse creates vulnerability to psychosis through heightened stress reactivity and cortisol dysfunction. In addition, affective dysfunction following childhood trauma is increasingly highlighted as a mechanism through which psychosis develops.

However, this analysis, and much of the literature to date, focuses on non-affective psychosis or data from population-based studies with subclinical psychotic-like experiences. We know that childhood trauma is also associated with a wide number of adverse outcomes, for example depression, suicidal behavior, personality disorder and bipolar disorder. Affective dysfunction is also proposed as a mechanism to explain these associations. For example, Etain et al suggest that a dual role of genetic and environmental influences of socially and morally inappropriate rewards and parental attitudes during childhood induces affective dysregulation in the developing child that precedes the development of bipolar disorder. Thus, given that childhood trauma is proposed as a risk factor for psychosis and affective dysfunction, it is surprising that few studies have investigated the role of childhood trauma in psychotic symptoms as part of an affective disorder to date. In addition, childhood trauma itself encompasses many experiences, but few studies have investigated specific life events in detail. Bentall et al looked at this issue in a large population-based sample and found that sexual abuse was associated only with hallucinations, whereas being brought up in institutional care was associated with 'paranoia'. They proposed the specific associations observed were consistent with current psychological theories about the origins of hallucinations and paranoia. Our study sought to build and expand the current evidence base by exploring the association between a range of adverse childhood events and the presence of psychotic symptoms in a very large, well-characterized sample of patients with bipolar disorder. We hypothesized that for individuals with affective disorder, childhood trauma would show a significant association with psychosis, and in particular with psychotic symptoms coupled with dysregulation of mood (i.e. mood congruent delusions and hallucinations) and with persecutory or abusive content.

Their results focused on the heightened possibility of psychotic episodes, often displayed inwardly as self-harm and suicide or outwardly as violent tendencies. Hansen's psychosis was the latter, an outward expression of primal violence and destruction of the women he hunted and harmed.

At his arson trial, Hansen was initially determined to have psychosis as a byproduct of bipolar disorder and antisocial behavior. The treatment was lithium, a common medication used to help stabilize the chemical balance and therefore the mood of those with bipolar disorder and manic episodes. According to the website of the Virtual Medical Centre,

Lithium has for a long time been the gold standard for mood stabilization. It is effective in both manic and depressive episodes and for long term maintenance therapy. The most common side effects include slight shaking of the hands, thirst, queasiness (usually goes away after some time), headache, tiredness, irregular pulse, loss of appetite, weight gain, bloating and muscle weakness. When a patient is placed on lithium treatment their doctor will do routine blood tests.

Hansen, however, was not monitored after his release and quickly stopped taking his medication. Every time he committed a crime and was caught, the psychological evaluations came to the same conclusion: antisocial personality disorder consisting of bipolar affective disorder with psychosis and manic episodes of violence. He was considered a danger to society, and yet somehow he was always released.

It's hard to say whether Hansen would have followed the criminal path he did if he had been properly treated or even institutionalized. The problem with evaluating some psychiatric disorders is that the person learns how to put on a mask, how to function in society without drawing attention to their darker side. For Hansen, this wasn't entirely the case. He had a multitude of rape victims trying to report him, and he had a criminal past. Instead, there were two other factors that allowed him to continue on for so long. First were the failings of a system that determined him to be a threat and yet refused to incarcerate or institutionalize him. Second was his decision to hunt and prey upon societal outcasts—prostitutes and strippers, women who were down on their luck, living a high-risk lifestyle. Some had a history of drug abuse, many had no family or friends in Anchorage, and most who survived knew that police wouldn't take them seriously or feared that Hansen would come after them if he were arrested.

Hansen was not the stereotypically suave, intelligent, and emotionless serial killer of Hollywood lore. He had a temper, was emotionally unstable, and was even rather sloppy in his work. And yet he was able to murder at least 17 women and rape several dozen more. Regardless of his psychological difficulties, he was well aware that what he was doing was wrong, and yet he persisted. He denied his activities and covered them up. He was clinically sane, but very disturbed.

Those Who Fell Prey

Although Robert Hansen is known for raping and killing prostitutes, some of his victims were ordinary women who simply found themselves outside in one of the "stalking grounds" where he would drive in circles looking for a target. The FBI lists Hansen as having killed 17 women and raped 30. The information is far from certain, though. The red X's that Hansen marked on his aviation map corresponded to the locations of his victims' bodies. A majority of the X's checked out, confirming that Hansen had indeed committed some of the murders in which he was denying guilt. Because most of the locations were in wilderness areas such as parks and forests, however, it would have been easy for wild animals and the elements to remove most, if not all, traces of the victims who weren't found. This, then, is the list of the 17 deceased and 1 escaped victims of Hansen that the FBI has evidence, circumstantial or physical, to confirm. Hansen's modus operandi was very consistent in all cases where the victims were identified, and thus the circumstantial evidence of him hunting in the areas where bodies were not recovered was often convincing enough to the authorities.

Celia "Beth" Van Zanten (17 or 18 years old)
Missing: December 23, 1971
Discovered: December 25, 1971
Location Found: McHugh Creek State Park

Celia Van Zanten, known as Beth, had a difficult home life. She had two brothers and a "foster cousin" by the name of Greg. Her brothers spent most of their time lying around the house, usually high, and her "cousin" liked to frequent bars and clubs and was usually intoxicated. On December 23, 1971, Beth walked to a convenience store and never returned.

On December 25, 1971, Christmas Day, two brothers, Gary and Dennis Lawler, were making a road trip to photograph the winter scenes of Alaska when they stopped at McHugh Creek State Park. The park was a section of wilderness where two ridges intersected with McHugh Creek. Near one of the picnic areas was a waterfall that Dennis wanted to get a bigger angle on for a photograph. In order to capture the scene, he had to climb down a ledge that overlooked the bank of the river. As he prepared to take the perfect shot, his eyes glanced over what looked like a mannequin behind a bush. She was naked from the waist down, lying in the snow at an awkward angle. Dennis returned to his brother Gary and told him what he had seen, and they left to find a phone and call police.

Sergeant Walter Gilmour, an Alaska state trooper, ended up taking the call. At the scene, investigators noted that the woman was young with pale skin and long, light blonde hair. She matched the description of the missing teenager Celia "Beth" Van Zanten. Her body showed signs of sexual molestation, and her chest and torso had been cut up with a knife. Wire had been used to bind her wrists behind her. Taking into consideration the distance from the ledge behind her, the position of her body, and the prevailing temperatures, authorities theorized that she had been running from the parking lot above when she fell off the ledge and proceeded to crawl away. She had eventually frozen to death in the single-digit temperatures. Investigators did find tire marks in the parking lot that suggested someone had circled around several times, but as they searched the scene, it began raining, quickly destroying any usable prints. They did find a silver belt buckle, a black belt, and yellow tissue paper nearby, but nothing else.

Beth's relatives were inebriated when police interviewed them, making their testimony both contradictory and unreliable. Greg had the most suspicious story; he claimed that he had come by before Beth went missing, but her brothers didn't remember seeing him. However, multiple sightings of Greg extremely intoxicated in public (which had resulted in police involvement) during the relevant time period gave him an alibi. Neighborhood witnesses did recall seeing Beth hitchhiking at around 11 PM the night she went missing. No one had seen who picked her up, though, or had any more information.

Then Sergeant Gilmour received information from an informant who had an idea as to what had occurred the night Beth disappeared. Sandra Patterson was an 18-year-old heroin addicted prostitute who also happened to be the daughter of a state trooper. While she was in the Nevada Club parking lot on December 18, a man came up to her with a gun and demanded that she go with him. She told Sergeant Gilmour that he had tied her hands with leather shoelaces and forced her to strip as he drove. He pulled over and attempted to have sex with her on multiple occasions, but she persuaded him not to do so in the car. He eventually took her to a motel out on the Kenai Peninsula. He raped her, but was unable to satisfy himself. Sandra told Sergeant Gilmour that she tried to be as passive as possible. He had hit her once in anger, and she was afraid of what he was going to do to her. Before releasing her, he drove into the woods and warned her that if she told anyone he would kill her.

The culprit was described as mid to late 20s, a bit taller than five and a half feet, skinny, awkward, with dark hair and glasses. In the 70s, criminal records had not generally been computerized; instead, police had what was often referred to as an "asshole book" consisting of mug shots and photographs of known sexual deviants. It included predators, assault suspects, and rape suspects both convicted and not. Sandra Patterson thumbed through the pages and stopped on a photograph of Hansen, absolutely certain that he was the man who had kidnapped her. The incident had occurred while Hansen was awaiting trial for pulling a gun on a woman in traffic. However, Sandra had dropped the charges when she became scared that he wouldn't be convicted and would kill her.

Although Hansen denied involvement in Celia Van Zanten's murder when he was arrested, he did slip up when talking with investigators later. When they mentioned the location where her body had been found, he immediately recalled who it was—but then backtracked, saying that he remembered them trying to pin it on him when he was in trouble for Sandra Patterson's rape. Due to the nature of the crime, the slashed bra strap, the bindings, the partially undressed state, the wilderness location, and the fact that Celia's home was in one of Hansen's stalking areas, authorities were confident that he was responsible for her death. But he was never charged for any crime against Celia Van Zanten.

Megan Emerick (17 years old)
Missing: July 7, 1973
Discovered: Still Missing
Location: Last seen in Seward, Alaska

Megan Emerick was a native of Delta Junction, Alaska. She was an outdoors enthusiast and a student at the Seward Skill Center, later renamed the Alaska Vocational Technical Center. She had no known connection to sex work and simply seems to have been in the wrong place at the wrong time—in her case, leaving a laundromat at her dormitory on July 7, 1973. She had brown hair and hazel eyes and was last seen wearing a long-sleeved shirt with a white checkered pattern under a brown short-sleeve sweater, jeans, and ski boots.

Hansen denied involvement in Megan Emerick's disappearance, claiming that he didn't pick up women in Seward:

Anchorage DA Vic Krumm: "Way back in the early '70s, there were a number of young women from Seward..."

Hansen: "Ah... out of Seward gentlemen, I never had anything... anything to do with any girls out of Seward."

This was later contradicted when he admitted to the kidnapping and murder of Joanne Messina. Megan lived less than 11 minutes from where Joanne Messina was picked up, near a dock where Hansen kept a boat and often visited other fishermen. In September of 2008, two former cellmates of Hansen came forward claiming to have information about some of the women Hansen denied kidnapping and murdering. They said that they had a map with the grave locations of some of the women, and that Megan was one of them, but they refused to hand it over unless unrelated charges against them were dropped. Due to the nature of their crimes and the fact that Hansen had already been jailed for life, authorities declined the deal.

Mary K. Thill (23 years old)
Missing: July 5, 1975
Discovered: Still Missing
Location: Believed to be near Resurrection Bay

Mary Thill was a married woman who asked some friends to give her a ride into town on July 5, 1975. She was last seen at a waterfall near Lowell Point Road between 1:30 and 2:00 PM. Her husband, a worker at Alaska's North Slope, reported her missing when she never came back home. When questioned about her disappearance after his arrest, Hansen told authorities that although he had been in the area at the time she went missing, he was not involved. Mary had light skin, red hair, blue eyes, and wore pink glasses. Her friends said that when they last saw her she was wearing jeans and hiking boots with a gray sweater and an army jacket and carrying a black backpack.

Roxanne Easland (24 years old)
Missing: June 28, 1980
Discovered: Still Missing
Location: 4th Avenue, Anchorage
Also Known As: Roxanne Eastland/Eastlund, Karen Lee Baunsgard, Robin Lee Easland

Roxanne Easland was a well-known prostitute in Anchorage. For two weeks prior to her disappearance, Roxanne had been living with her boyfriend in the Budget Motel on Spenard Road. On June 28, 1980, Roxanne was using the name Karen Lee Baunsgard when she left to meet a client. The meeting was to be in a downtown hotel on 4th Avenue. She was never seen again.

Hansen did admit to kidnapping and murdering Roxanne Easland. Her body, though, was not recovered, even with the use of Hansen's marked aviation map. Her remains may have been disturbed or carried away by wild animals.

"Eklutna Annie" (16 to 25 years old)
Missing: Unknown—possibly Hansen's first murder victim
Discovered: July 21, 1980
Location: Eklutna Road

One of Hansen's unidentified victims, whom he admitted to murdering, was dubbed "Eklutna Annie." Her remains were found by county workers in a shallow grave in a heavily wooded area on Eklutna Lake Road. Her body was badly decomposed and had been severely damaged by wild animals. The evidence at the scene suggested she had been wearing red knee-high high-heeled boots, jeans, a leather jacket and a sleeveless knit top. Gold twisted loop earrings, a copper bangle with turquoise stones, a turquoise-and-shell necklace with a heart pendant, a white-and-brown shell ring, a gold Timex ladies' wristwatch, and a pack of Salem brand matches were also found on her body.

Hansen told police she was a prostitute or topless dancer. He described all his victims this way, but Eklutna Annie's clothing suggests that it was probably true in this case. He also told them he believed she was from a village called Kodiak, but that has not been confirmed, although she was a mixed-race Native American.

Hansen told police he had picked her up and taken her out into the woods in his truck. When she got away from him and ran, he chased her down. Eventually he was able to grab a hold of her hair and pull her back, at which point she pulled a knife from her purse and attempted to defend herself. Hansen said he got the knife away from her, stabbed her in the back and then left her there.

Her remains are currently in the Anchorage Memorial Park under a bronze plaque engraved with "Jane Doe, Died 1980." Authorities believe that she was Hansen's first murder victim.

Joanne (Joanna) Messina (24 years old)
Missing: July 1980
Discovered: July 1980
Location: Near Eklutna Road

As well as an accomplished hunter, Hansen was an avid fisherman. In the 1970s he had a large boat that he kept moored in Seward. He would travel there with his camper and go on fishing trips. "In the spring I would take my boat and pickup and camper and drive to Seward and leave it, then just drive a car back and forth [from Anchorage]," Hansen said in his confession. After his arrest, he told authorities that he had often trolled for victims while walking along the Seward shorefront (although he later denied killing some of the victims he allegedly picked up from the area).

One of the women he noticed was Joanne Messina, who worked at a cannery and as a topless dancer. Some sources say she had previously been a nurse. In July of 1980, Joanne was walking to work at the cannery when Hansen approached her. He tried to get her to go back to his camper, but she refused, not wanting to be late to her job. Hansen said, "I met her and I talked to her and... I had my boat down there and was talking [to] her that I was going to go out, out the next day fishing and so forth, would she like to go along, you know." When she politely declined, Hansen pulled out a gun and forced her to go with him. She was raped and killed out near Eklutna Road. Hansen then left her body in a gravel pit not far from where Eklutna Annie was found.

When Joanne's body was found and the state troopers were called in, they were warned that a large bear had been seen in the area. Arriving on the scene, officers confirmed that the body showed signs of having been gnawed on by a large animal. While they were examining it, the bear returned. They tried to shoo it away so they could recover the evidence, but the bear refused to back down. Since it was a protected species, they couldn't shoot it, even as it began to get hostile. Fortunately, the bear calmed down and left after a while, and the troopers were able to collect the body and what was left of the evidence.

Police initially focused on a different suspect in the murder of Joanne Messina. The man was apprehended and brought in for questioning. He denied murdering Joanne, but he failed the polygraph. Detective Chuck Miller, who was leading the investigation, believed this man was the killer. He was therefore a bit annoyed when Detective Flothe put Joanne Messina on his list of victims of the Alaskan serial killer. Flothe's reasoning was that she was a part-time sex worker, was left near where another victim had been left, was killed in the same manner as other victims, and overall met the MO for his killer. Later, when Hansen was arrested, Joanne Messina was one of the four women he admitted to murdering, and he knew enough about the crime scene and evidence to substantiate this admission.

Lisa Futrell (41 years old)
Missing: September 6, 1980
Discovered: May 9, 1984
Location: South of Old Knik Bridge

There isn't much information on Lisa Futrell, but it is known that she was either a prostitute or a topless dancer. Her body was found south of the Old Knik Bridge and was confirmed as one of Hansen's victims; she was one of the marks on his map.

Sherry Morrow (23 years old)
Missing: November 17, 1981
Discovered: September 12, 1982
Location: Banks of the Knik River

An exotic dancer at the Wild Cherry Bar, Sherry Morrow did what she needed to make money. Unfortunately, that often involved using her body. She had a penchant for fast cash, and that weakness put her directly into harm's way. According to the Wild Cherry's manager, "She was really gullible. She could be talked into anything. When I heard [she'd been killed] I thought, gosh, it was almost inevitable."

On November 17, 1981, Sherry was at a friend's house when she said she was leaving to meet a client at Alice's 210 Cafe. The client, a photographer, had promised her $300 to pose nude for a series of photographs. Her client turned out to be Hansen, who later admitted to kidnapping, raping, and killing Sherry Morrow and explained in detail what he did to her.

When Sherry got into Hansen's car, he immediately handcuffed her and used an Ace bandage to blindfold her. He then forced her into the back seat and made her kneel on the floorboard. Hansen drove out to the Knik River. When he tried to remove her handcuffs, Sherry began to fight back. She kicked and screamed, trying to attack Hansen and get away. Hansen retrieved his semi-automatic rifle from the trunk, then sat down and waited, hoping she would calm down. Sherry charged at Hansen, still screaming and trying to attack him. He told police, "I just pointed the Mini-14 up toward her and pulled the trigger."

Hansen took Sherry's arrowhead necklace before digging a shallow grave. He put both Sherry Morrow and the .223 shell casings into the grave. Hunters found the body almost a year later.

She had three gunshot wounds in her back from a .223 rifle. Although she was fully dressed, there were no bullet holes in her clothing. Investigators believed that she had been raped and was still naked when she was shot, but was then redressed afterward, before she was buried.

"Perhaps it was both naïveté and greed that doomed Sherry Morrow when she left with Hansen in November 1981."—*Anchorage Daily News*

Andrea Altiery (24 years old)
Missing: December 2, 1981
Discovered: Still Missing
Location: Knik River

Andrea Altiery was last seen by her roommate in their apartment. The exotic dancer was leaving to meet a client for either a photography session or a shopping spree at the Boniface Mall (there are two different accounts as to why she was meeting Hansen). Hansen told police what happened after she was in his car.

As with previous victims, Hansen handcuffed her and blindfolded her before driving to a secluded location next to the Knik River railroad bridge. Trying to keep Andrea under control, Hansen told her that he habitually kidnapped and raped women. He said that he'd last done so a week before, in that very spot, and had let her go because she had cooperated. Andrea accordingly did as he asked. He held a gun to her head and forced her to perform oral sex on him while he fondled her.

Eventually, Andrea told Hansen she needed to use the bathroom. Hansen let her get out of the car. He put the pistol on the hood and turned away to urinate. A noise behind him caused him to turn around as Andrea reached for his pistol. He grabbed it before she could and she attacked him, clawing at his face and eyes. Hansen shot her dead. Andrea was wearing a necklace with a fish charm, and Hansen took it, as well as a pearl ring she had. Then he grabbed a bag from his car and filled it with rocks and gravel. He tied the bag around Andrea's neck and pushed both her and the bag into the river. Her body was never found.

Sue Luna (23 years old)
Missing: May 26, 1982
Discovered: April 24, 1984
Location: Knik River

Sue Luna had a rough life before she moved to Alaska. Her husband was abusive and spent many years in prison for murder. Like many at the time, she hoped that she could make some money off of the influx of people moving to Alaska during the oil boom. Working as a topless dancer at the Good Times Bar, and occasionally as a prostitute, Sue didn't realize she had jumped out of the frying pan and into the fire.

Like several other victims, Sue Luna had been promised $300 to do something for a man she was to meet at Alice's 210 Cafe. On May 26, 1982, Sue told her roommate that she was leaving for that appointment. She didn't return, and the roommate and Sue's sister reported her missing four days later.

According to police, Sue Luna was stripped, blindfolded and sent running through the woods near the Knik River. She was shot multiple times in the back before being buried next to a parking lot by the Knik River Bridge, where she was found two years later.

On a website for the friends and families of murder victims, a friend of Sue's left this message:

Sue was a beautiful person, a loving friend with a heart of gold. Her smile could light up a room. Sue could turn your very worst day, into your best, just by being there and talking things out. She had a zest for life, and a deep love for people.

We do not know the exact date of Sue's death. Robert Hansen, Alaska's Serial Killer, took Sue out to the Knik River in Alaska, stripped her, and made her run like an animal while he hunted her down, and eventually killing her. He shot her to death. He did the same to 16 other women. Her death was in 1983. I've never gotten over it, and I never will.

Once in a lifetime, a true friend comes along, that makes your day brighter, and your life better. Sue loved to laugh. She was a clown, always making faces, or imitating Mick Jagger of the Rolling Stones. She would poke her lips out and pretend to be singing "Satisfaction." She would do this until I was literally doubled over with laughter.

I miss her so much, I miss her friendship and love. It has been 17 years since Sue died, and it feels like yesterday in my heart. I have wonderful memories of my friend who made my life so much better, and I will keep them always. I know Sue is in Heaven, looking down on the people she loved and cared for. She will always be remembered.

He killed my friend, but he could never kill my memories of Sue Luna.
Love and miss you Sue
Reva H.

Paula Goulding (31 years old—possibly 21 according to some records)
Missing: April 24, 1983
Discovered: September 2, 1983
Location: Bank of the Knik River

Paula Goulding was a stripper at the Great Alaska Bush Company in Anchorage. The 31-year-old from Kona, Hawaii, had originally moved to Fairbanks and worked as a secretary before relocating to Anchorage to take up dancing. She was rather new to the club scene and had only just transitioned from dancing topless to dancing nude in order to make more money. She met Hansen on her first night of dancing completely nude. He offered her $200 to meet him for a lunch date, telling her to arrive in a cab. On April 24, 1983, Paula's roommate saw her leave their apartment. When she wasn't back after four days, she called and reported her missing.

On September 2 or 3, 1983, Paula Goulding's body was found in a shallow grave near the Knik River, not far from where another body had been found the previous month. Examining the body, investigators came to the conclusion that she had been bound and blindfolded, raped, and had been running for some time before being shot several times in the back with a .223 caliber rifle. She had then been redressed and buried; the shell casings were thrown in with the body. At first investigators did not think that Paula and Sherry Morrow had been murdered by the same person, but the shell casings found with their bodies were later matched.

After his arrest, Hansen admitted to killing Paula Goulding and explained what had happened to her. He said he had taken her at gunpoint to his plane and flown her out to a cabin where he tied her up, blindfolded her, raped her, and tortured her for quite some time. He then released her and opened the cabin door, pushing her out so she would take off running. He grabbed his rifle and went after her, hunting her down and eventually killing her. He then redressed the body and buried it before going back home.

Paula is buried in the Anchorage Memorial Park Cemetery.

Cindy Paulson (17 years old)
Missing: June 13, 1983
Discovered: Escaped
Location: Merrill Field

Cindy Paulson is not Hansen's only surviving rape victim, but she is the only one known to have escaped after he decided to kill her rather than being released. Hansen picked her up on June 13, 1983, then handcuffed her and took her to his home, where he raped and tortured her for hours before chaining her neck to a post in the basement and taking a nap. When he woke, he took Cindy to Merrill Field, where he had his plane. Cindy escaped while he was busy loading supplies into the aircraft.

She was able to flag down a trucker who took her to a nearby motel. Cindy called her boyfriend and went to the motel where he was staying; the trucker called the police. At first, they weren't certain if Cindy was telling the truth. Hansen was questioned and, although her descriptions of his vehicle, home, and plane were spot-on, he was let go when two of his neighbors supplied an alibi. They later recanted when authorities got additional evidence suggesting that Hansen was their killer.

The movie *The Frozen Ground* is based on Cindy Paulson and Detective Glenn Flothe's parts in the investigation into Hansen's crimes. Cindy's report was the reason Detective Flothe became so invested in the case. His dogged response to the attack revealed incidents and police reports from Hansen's past and caused his alibi to be re-evaluated. Unfortunately, as hard as he tried, there were still more deaths before Hansen was finally apprehended and put behind bars.

Malai Larsen (28 years old)
Missing: Unknown
Discovered: April 24, 1984
Location: Near parking lot by the Old Knik Bridge

Not much is known about Malai Larsen other than that her body was found after Hansen admitted to her murder and led authorities to the site.

DeLynn "Sugar" Frey (20 years old)
Missing: April 1983
Discovered: August 25, 1985
Location: Horseshoe Lake or Knik River

DeLynn Frey was a young, blonde prostitute who Hansen flew out to the wilderness in 1983. A native of New Mexico and the mother of a young daughter, she had issues with heroin addiction and ended up taking to the streets in Anchorage, Alaska. Hansen released her nude and blindfolded before shooting her down. He buried her in a shallow grave on a gravel bar either in Horseshoe Lake or the Knik River (sources are unclear). DeLynn was found by a pilot who was out practicing landings on the bar. Even though she was buried with rings her mother recognized, her identity wasn't confirmed until 1990.

Teresa Watson (unknown)
Missing: March 25, 1983
Discovered: April 26, 1984
Location: Scenic Lake on the Kenai Peninsula

Teresa Watson is another victim of whom little is known. However, Hansen admitted to killing her and revealed the location of her body. Teresa was a prostitute who was last seen on March 25, 1983, when she was leaving to meet a client. Hansen said he flew her out to Scenic Lake. After raping and killing her, he tried to bury her, but the ground was still frozen, so he threw her body out of his plane onto the lakeshore. It was discovered a year later, badly damaged by the local wildlife.

Angela Feddern (24 years old)
Missing: February 1983
Discovered: April 26, 1984
Location: Figure Eight Lake in the Susitna Basin

In Fairbanks, Angela Feddern was the mother of a 5-year-old girl; in Anchorage she was a prostitute. Although she was last seen in February of 1983, she wasn't reported missing until May. Her family knew of her shady lifestyle and was used to her disappearing for periods of time. Angela's mother had always feared that her lifestyle would be the end of her; she even told a journalist, "That was the life she chose. Angie just couldn't find it in herself to go out and get a thinking job."

A year after she went missing, Angela's remains were found on the banks of Figure Eight Lake in the Susitna Basin, across from Cook Inlet near Anchorage.

Tamara "Tami" Pederson (20 years old)
Missing: August 1982
Discovered: April 29, 1984
Location: On the banks of the Knik River near Sherry Morrow's body

Tamara Pederson, "Tami," was a stripper at a club in Anchorage. She also worked as a prostitute. In August of 1982, Tami was told she would be paid $200 to model in costumes and naked for a client. She left and was never seen again. Robert Hansen admitted to her murder and helped authorities find her body, which was buried in a shallow grave on the Knik River not far from Sherry Morrow's.

"Horseshoe Harriet" (19-20 years old)
Missing: Unknown
Discovered: April 25, 1984
Location: Horseshoe Lake

Officially labeled as Jane Doe #3 but known to the press as Horseshoe Harriet, this young woman was discovered in skeletal condition on April 25, 1984, in a shallow grave near Horseshoe Lake. As condoms were found with her remains, it was believed that she was a prostitute; however, she didn't match any known missing persons. Damage to her skeleton indicated that she had been stabbed and shot in the back four times each. Investigators concluded that she was another of Hansen's victims who had been running naked through the woods when he hunted her down and killed her.

These are all of Hansen's known and confirmed victims. However, the red X's on his aviation map far outnumbered the murders to which he admitted and the bodies that authorities found. Hansen may have had a cabin somewhere in the Alaskan wilderness, but this has not been confirmed. He did tell investigators that he had a cabin but recanted later on. No cabin was registered in Hansen's name or linked to him during the investigation. However, one structure has become known as the "Butcher Baker Cabin" and has suffered years of vandalism and stigma despite the lack of a confirmed connection to Hansen. The area around this cabin has been dug up multiple times by people trying to find the remains of more victims.

Many of Hansen's victims were prostitutes and/or strippers, and he referred to all of them as such, but it must be noted that this was not true of all of them. At least two just happened to be walking in the wrong place at the wrong time.

The Trial

Upon his initial arrest, Robert Christian Hansen was charged with insurance fraud and theft, assault, several weapons offenses, and kidnapping. Hansen refused to answer questions and requested an attorney. An Anchorage grand jury indicted Hansen for four cases of first-degree assault and kidnapping, five counts of misconduct while using a firearm, second-degree theft, and theft by insurance fraud. Murder charges were delayed until the ballistics information on Hansen's guns was returned. Hansen was taken to jail with a bail of over half a million dollars.

As Hansen continued to deny any involvement in the murders—as well as any guilt in the other charges—forensics technicians were working on matching the evidence to Hansen. Ballistics is a form of forensic science that utilizes tiny details in bullets and expended cartridges to find a match with the suspect's weapon. In this case, the comparison was between the .223 cases recovered near the victims and Hansen's .223 caliber Ruger Mini-14 rifle. There were only four murders that could be tied to the weapon definitively: those of Joanne Messina, Sherry Morrow, Eklutna Annie, and Paula Goulding.

Still, with four ballistic confirmations out of 17 known victims, there was no denying that Hansen was the murderer. On top of the jewelry, aviation map, and Hansen's own history with rape and abduction, the case looked rather solid. An article by Paul Sutherland explained how the police set the stage and quickly acquired the evidence to get Hansen locked up before learning more about his crimes:

At 8am on the 27 October 1983, Hansen was arrested at his bakery and was taken to the Anchorage trooper station. There, Flothe had stage-managed an interview room following pointers from the FBI. Hansen was placed in an interview room that had been carefully set out. There were maps of the Knik River along the walls, pictures of the grave sites, the victims, on the desk. There were files and folders with the names of Hansen's family, friends, and acquaintances on them. He was left to sit in here alone for a while, in an attempt to make him stew, and was watched by Flothe through a two-way mirror. Hansen appeared more intrigued than concerned. A few minutes later Flothe and Sergeant Darryl Galyan entered the room and began an interview with Hansen that was to last 5 hours.

Whilst Hansen was being interviewed, a team of officers was searching his house. Behind wooden paneling, in his trophy room, police found items of cheap jewelry that was later traced back to the dead girls. Police also found a Ruger Mini-14 hunting rifle hidden under floorboards, which was later matched by ballistics as being the weapon that had killed Sherry Morrow and Paula Goulding. The most telling item found was an aviation map of the Anchorage region, which was dotted with 20 drawn on asterisks. Two of these corresponded with sites where bodies had been found, and a third indicated the spot where the body of Joanne Messina, a 24-year-old prostitute, was found in July 1980. Investigators later discovered that she had last been seen with a small, stammering man, with a pockmarked face.

Hansen initially denied any connection with the murders, but when confronted with the wealth of evidence against him, decided to confess. He admitted that the asterisks on the map were grave sites of prostitutes that he had murdered. Hansen claimed that he had not killed every girl he had taken up into the wilderness. He claimed that he only wanted oral sex, and if the girls complied, they were flown home. If they resisted, he would force them to strip at gunpoint, and then make them run. They would usually be given a head start, and then Hansen would stalk them like an animal. Chillingly, he would sometimes allow the victim to think she had escaped, but would then track her down and make her run again. This would continue until the victim was too cold and exhausted to continue running, when the victims would be shot. The redressing, Hansen claimed, was to satisfy his need for control and he likened it to a trophy.

Hansen had his lawyer meet with District Attorney Krumm to make a deal. Hansen agreed to plead guilty to the four murders and tell authorities where the other bodies were if they didn't charge him for the other 13 murders. Knowing that the sentence for four murders would be more than enough to keep Hansen in jail for the rest of his life, the DA agreed.

Hansen ended up showing the police a total of 15 graves from his map. Twelve of these were for murders they had not been aware of, and only 11 contained bodies. There were other markers on his map that they were not able to check for one reason or another, including freezing weather, inaccessible locations, and Hansen's refusal to help.

The search for and retrieval of the bodies of Hansen's victims was an arduous process—at least for the police officers involved. Hansen, however, seemed to enjoy explaining his crimes and what he had done to each victim as they traveled to the sites. He would walk around the crime scenes, almost smiling as he recounted the events.

Although Hansen refused to confirm whether or not he was responsible for many of the disappearances, this is not to say he was uncooperative. He helped detectives uncover where he had buried many of his victims. This was a task Hansen took to with a sickening relish. During a helicopter tour of the gravesites, he would frequently become excited and exhilarated, reliving the murders over and over in his head. Handcuffed, Hansen would plough through chest-high snow drifts and triumphantly point out the grave of one of his victims. Sometimes he would drop to his knees and dig furiously with his bare hands, wild-eyed with a broad grin on his face. By the end of the summer of 1984, 11 bodies had been found, 10 of which were formally identified.

Hansen walked investigators through his "process" as well:

"I pull out the gun—I think the standard speech was, 'Look, you're a professional. You don't get excited, you know there is some risk to what you've been doing. If you do exactly what I tell you, you're not going to get hurt. You're just going to count this off as a bad experience and be a little more careful next time who you are gonna proposition or go out with,' you know. I tried to act as tough as I could, to get them as scared as possible. Give that right away, even before I started talking at all. Reach over, you know, and hold that head back and put a gun in her face and get 'em to feel helpless, scared, right there I'm sure—maybe it's not the same procedure for you—you always try to get control of the situation, so some things don't start going bad, maybe? I've seen some cop shows on TV, I don't know, OK?"

The officers went along with his "show" and gathered as much information as they could. The trial was long, but not as long as it would have been if Hansen had been tried for all 17 murders. When a serial killer is being tried, it's not uncommon for prosecution to be halted before all of the cases have been heard.

One reason is that, after the first few verdicts, the defendant has usually been sentenced to more prison time than he could possibly survive. Further trials would only tie up the courts and cost taxpayers money.

Another reason is the possibility of some or all of the guilty verdicts being overturned. Due to the double jeopardy rule, those cases couldn't be retried; but if prosecutors have kept some murders in reserve, they can file new charges in those to ensure that the killer doesn't escape on a technicality.

The third reason is that a single murder trial can take anywhere from weeks to years, depending on how many loopholes and stays the defense pulls to slow the progress of the case. Multiply that by 17 and the entire process could take a very long time indeed. During this time, the defendant would be held in a less-secure temporary detention facility, increasing escape risk—and he might even die of old age before he ever faced punishment in the penitentiary!

So while Hansen was convicted of just four murders out of the 17 he certainly committed, he was sentenced to 461 years plus life without parole, and prosecutors were more than content with that outcome.

Caging the Hunter

On February 27, 1984, a week after pleading guilty, Robert Hansen went before Superior Court Judge Ralph Moody for sentencing. He had pled to four first-degree murders (Eklutna Annie, Joanna Messina, Paula Goulding, and Sherry Morrow) and unofficially admitted to 13 more. When recounting what he had done, Hansen showed no remorse, fear, sadness, or any emotion other than the odd smile. The judge sentenced him to 461 years plus life without the possibility of parole.

Hansen was first taken to the United States Penitentiary in Lewisburg, Pennsylvania. Part of his agreement was that he be incarcerated in a federal penitentiary rather than a maximum security state prison. Nonetheless, he was moved to the Lemon Creek Correctional Center in Juneau, Alaska, in 1988 and then to the newly-built Spring Creek Correctional Center in Seward, Alaska. He stayed there until he fell ill and was taken to a prison hospital, Alaska Regional Hospital, where he passed away at 1:30 AM on April 21, 2014, at the age of 75.

Several inmates have come forward with information they say Hansen gave them in prison. They claim to know the whereabouts of still-missing victims and about Hansen's involvement in additional murders. However, authorities believe that most of these claims have no basis in fact and are simply attempts to capitalize on the open questions of the Hansen case in exchange for sentence reductions. Furthermore, they have consistently decided not to pursue even potentially valid claims. They have stated that, while they mean no disrespect to the families and victims, they do not see the recovery of bones (if even bones remain by now) as a reason for allowing other criminals to escape their own sentences.

After Hansen's incarceration, the Pope & Young company removed his trophies from their publications. They stated that although his records remained valid, they did not wish to publicize them. Hansen had once stated that hunting the women was like "going after a Dall sheep or a grizzly bear," but this was apparently not an association that Pope & Young wanted to make.

Hansen's wife, Darla, and their two children stayed in Anchorage for a time, but they faced constant scrutiny and harassment. They eventually left Alaska for Arkansas, where they hoped to start life over again in a place where their husband and father was less well known. Darla has only done a handful of interviews.

Alaskan hunters occasionally find bodies in areas that Hansen was known to frequent. These bodies are routinely analyzed to determine if they might belong to one of Hansen's still-missing or unknown victims. There have also been issues with "serial killer tourists" who travel to the scenes where bodies were found. They also dig up areas where bodies were believed to have been dumped but were never discovered. The Big Timber Motel and the privately owned "Butcher Baker Cabin" have suffered from vandals and enthusiasts alike due to Hansen's history.

Several key figures in the investigation had a few choice words, published by the *Alaskan Dispatch*, about the death of Robert Hansen:

"On this day we should only remember his many victims and all of their families and my heart goes out to all of them," wrote Glenn Flothe, retired Alaska State Trooper who was instrumental in Hansen's capture. *"As far as Hansen is concerned, this world is better without him,"* Flothe wrote. *"It's a sad day for me, for their families."*

"He will not be missed," said Frank Rothschild, the assistant district attorney who tried the case, from Hawaii on Thursday afternoon. *"Good riddance to him."*

"He's one of those kind of guys that you kind of hope every breath he takes in his life, there's some pain associated with it, because he caused such pain," Rothschild added. *"When the Hansen case was over… I was ready,"* Rothschild said. *"It was just so heavy to see what this human being was capable of doing."*

Modern Portrayals

Efforts are still being made to identify Horseshoe Harriet and Eklutna Annie. It is also believed that some of Hansen's victims are still unknown. The Alaska State Troopers have information online asking people to help identify the victims and provide any other information regarding the murders and victims of Robert Hansen. Because most of his victims were women down on their luck, drug addicts living on the streets or in rundown apartments and working as prostitutes or strippers, there were often no family members around to claim them. Many of the women were buried in the Anchorage Memorial Cemetery under bronze plaques with their names and dates of birth and death, if known. At the time of Hansen's conviction, one woman held a mass funeral for the victims who had no one come forward to claim them or grieve for them.

There has been a multitude of books, movies, and crime drama episodes based on the Hansen case. The most high profile of them is the movie *The Frozen Ground*, which stars John Cusack as Robert Hansen, Nicholas Cage as Detective Glenn Flothe (renamed Sergeant Jack Holcombe), and Vanessa Hudgens as Cindy Paulson. The movie actually started off as fiction; it was conceived as a more modern twist on the short story "The Most Dangerous Game," the twist being a serial killer who captured people and released them into the wild to hunt them. Then the writer, Scott Walker, learned about Hansen. Here is an excerpt of his interview with Sheila Roberts of Collider:

Scott Walker: I wanted this to be a drama. It has a serial killer in it, which means people call it a serial killer film, but to me it's a drama about this relationship. Why I opened the film the way I did is I wanted the feeling that you are dropped into the middle of this case like it's a bomb going off and then it just ripples. You don't know where the tentacles are going to go and it's going to touch a lot of people and affect them considerably. It's going to wreck lives. I wanted to keep it concise. I didn't want it to be like Zodiac or the stories which have those kinds of [structure]. It could have been thirteen years of titles saying "Six months later and another killing and another body turning up." I just didn't want that. I thought sure, that could tell the story, but that's a documentary as far as I was thinking. I wanted something that was short, intense, and like you were just on the shoulder of these three characters, going into their worlds knowing they're going to collide at some point. It's how and when. That's what you're waiting to find out. It's one of those cases that, to tell it truthfully and honor as many of the facts as I possibly could, Holcombe and Cindy need to meet early on or else there's no story. He doesn't know who the killer is until he meets her. If that happened at the end of Act Two, there are just bodies to be found before then. I wasn't interested in that. There's no relationship going on there. That's just another serial killer film. So, that was the first big decision—that you're going to know very early on who the killer is. And then, it becomes about can he find an overwhelming amount of evidence and how much of it is going to fall away between his fingers in order to get a conviction. And so, that became what the story was about and why I wanted to tell it that way.

Sheila Roberts: How did the finished film compare to what you originally envisioned?

Walker: The script had 275 scenes. I shot 225. That was the reality of when we were two weeks out from starting to shoot. It was like 50 scenes have got to go. And then, I think 30 scenes got cut in the editing to get the time down. The film is about 90 percent of what I envisioned. There are places where it's got more score than I was originally wanting. I always saw it as a drama much more than anything else, and it just has this serial killer element, which means it's getting talked about as a serial killer film. But really, all I mostly was interested in was this relationship. It's a police procedural, but Cindy Paulson is the heart of the film. In the same way as in The Accused, Jody Foster is who the film is about, but some things happen to her, and Kelly McGillis plays what is the backbone of the film. And that's what the police procedural is in this. It's Jack Holcombe's story. He solves the case, but she's the key to it and it's about this relationship between the two of them. I was really pleased that's still in the film, and there are these great moments between the two of them which are based on the reality of when they first met. They didn't go to Skateland [referring to a scene in the film]. They went to Chuck E. Cheese's. She would see moose and bizarre things in the snow.

Roberts: In hindsight, is there anything you wish you had known on the first day of shooting that you discovered later would have been helpful to know?

Walker: I'm sure there is. There are probably hundreds of things I wished I'd known because I knew that on day one. The first shot we did was at 5:00 in the morning, and there was condensed fog and the sun was coming up. It's the shot where John (Cusack) drives down the road. He actually pulls out from behind the school bus, which was intentional imagery of this guy, and pulls into his bakery. I suppose the first learning was that's going to have to be cut because you're never going to be able to have time to use that, and we're just going to have him pulling into the parking lot. All the stuff that I cut out, I don't regret that we went faster to get because I then have the choice. If you don't shoot it, you never have the choice. I was always pushing for more, more, more. We did incredible numbers of set-ups which I didn't realize were incredible until people were saying, "We just did 47 set-ups. That's nuts!" and we were doing that consistently. Literally, every time we did another take, I would remove the cameras and everything because I had to have coverage that I wasn't going to get if I just stayed in the same positions and did takes. That served the film. It was part of the style.

Roberts: What were some of the challenges of writing this and condensing a true story that spans 12 or 13 years into a 2-hour film while also balancing the facts and exploring both sides of the story?

Walker: That is the biggest challenge. The real people were supporting me and helping me with all the information, and I was going after more and more information, and I became overwhelmed with the amount of information that I had. It's the responsibility for whatever ends up in those pages, and if they read it, the worst thing would have been if they go, "This has got nothing to do with what we told you and it's disrespectful." That was the thing, to get the tone right. The only people who I was really concerned about what they thought of the film were the real people. To have feedback from real people that had seen it and they go, "Wow! We're really pleased with the film and think it's terrific. We're really pleased that you were able to stay true to the intent of when we first started talking about what you wanted to do." That's still there. The photos at the end was a big decision.

It was like, "Wow. Is this right or not?" and then going back to the real people and saying, "What do you think because this is about you. I'm just telling your story from another perspective." And then, phoning one of the victim's families and she's saying, "Could you use this photo? That is amazing that my sister will be up there and mentioned because nobody ever mentioned her and she was one of the victims." With stuff like that, you go, "I don't really care what anybody else thinks." I wish I could have tracked down every victim's family but a lot of them didn't use their real names. And a lot of the families don't even know what happened to their daughter. Some of the bodies were never identified so nobody even knows who they are. That's a challenge. But the biggest challenge was how to take 13 years and put it into less than two hours and still have it be true to what happened. You can't tell everything, and you can't have every character, every real person, be in there, because you'd have 30 investigators investigating 30 cases and that would become a mess for an audience to follow.

Walker didn't discuss his decision to rename Detective Glenn Flothe, but he did spend a lot of time with Cindy Paulson learning about her side of the story, her life, and how it all affected her. She has done several interviews about her experience and has moved on with her life, but her encounter with Hansen changed her forever. She lives with the knowledge that he did not intend her to be one of his typical rape victims, free to go after enduring his nightmare. Cindy Paulson saved herself from becoming another red X on an aviation map behind a headboard, and that is something that she will never be able to forget or completely come to terms with. But she has used her story to help share her strength and her hardships.

Most people know about Hansen only because of the movie *The Frozen Ground*, but for many, that is enough to chill them to the bone. Hansen preyed upon people, women who he saw as less than himself. He was a man deranged, mentally ill, and with an uncontrollable need to feel powerful by diminishing other lives. He found pleasure in rape and death. He compared his victims to game, to wild animals. He saw these women, with their difficult and challenging but very human lives, as just another day in the woods.

"Nerve, nerve, nerve!" he panted, as he dashed along. A blue gap showed between the trees dead ahead. Ever nearer drew the hounds. Rainsford forced himself on toward that gap. He reached it. It was the shore of the sea. Across a cove he could see the gloomy gray stone of the chateau. Twenty feet below him the sea rumbled and hissed. Rainsford hesitated. He heard the hounds. Then he leaped far out into the sea… .

When the general and his pack reached the place by the sea, the Cossack stopped. For some minutes he stood regarding the blue-green expanse of water. He shrugged his shoulders. Then be sat down, took a drink of brandy from a silver flask, lit a cigarette, and hummed a bit from Madame Butterfly.

—"The Most Dangerous Game" by Richard Connell

The Timeline

1939—February 15: Robert Christian Hansen is born to Christian and Edna Hansen in Esterville, Iowa.

1949—Hansen begins working for his father in the family bakery. He is dealing with stress brought on by a severe stutter and religiously fundamentalist, overbearing parents who force the left-handed boy to fit in by writing with his right hand.

1951—Stuttering, acne and the awkwardness of puberty decrease Hansen's ability to fit in socially, and he begins to deal with rage and inadequacy issues.

1953—Hansen enters high school. He does not have much of a social life but participates in multiple sports and after-school activities (basketball, pep club, chorus, track, long distance, and long/high jump). He still works in the bakery but has taken up hunting with guns and bows, as well as fishing, as a way to "get the anger out."

1957—Hansen graduates from high school.
—After signing up for the U.S. Army Reserve, he is flown out to basic training in Fort Dix in New Jersey.
—While stationed at Fort Knox, Kentucky, Hansen has his first sexual experience, with a prostitute.

1959—Hansen finishes his first year in the Army Reserve and is moved to "weekend warrior" status in which he trains one weekend a month and two weeks a year. He moves back home to live with his parents and work in the bakery. He also began volunteering at the police academy as a drill instructor.

1960—Hansen meets a young woman in town and marries her a short time later.
—December 7: Hansen decides to let out some of his anger about how he was treated in school. He recruits a teenager (possibly by force) to go with him to the county school bus garage, where they set the building on fire. He is sentenced to three years for the arson.
—December: Hansen's wife files for divorce.

1962—June: Hansen is released after serving 20 months of his sentence. Psychological evaluations state that he has child-like impulses and anger as well as issues with self-esteem and social interactions.

1963—Hansen meets Darla and marries her very shortly afterward.

1967—Robert and Darla Hansen move to Alaska to start over with a new life. Hansen steps up his hunting hobby, stalking bigger game in Alaska's large wilderness areas.

1969—Hansen submits a trophy animal to Pope & Young and garners an entry in the record books.

1970—Hansen secures a second entry into the trophy hunting record books.

1971—Hansen finds himself in the record books again for two more big game trophies.
—November: Hansen pulls a gun on a woman in traffic in Spenard and demands that she get into his car. She flees and Hansen is arrested, but he is immediately released on bail to await trial.
—Hansen is arrested again, this time for kidnapping, rape, and assault with a deadly weapon. The victim, an 18-year-old prostitute, fails to show up in court and the charges are dropped.
—December 23: 17-year-old Celia "Beth" Van Zanten goes missing from Anchorage, Alaska.
—December 25: Beth's body is found at McHugh State Park.

1972—Hansen stands trial for the weapons charge and is sentenced to five years in prison.
—March: Hansen begins serving his sentence and applies for parole.
—June: Hansen is granted parole and moves into a halfway house for psychiatric supervision and reform.
—December: Hansen is released from the halfway house.

1973—July 7: 17-year-old Megan Emerick goes missing in Anchorage.

1975—23-year-old Mary K. Thill goes missing from Seward.
—Hansen is accused of assault and rape by a prostitute who then stops cooperating with police. No charges are brought.

1976—Hansen is caught stealing a chainsaw from Fred Meyer's, a store in Anchorage. Due to his previous felony convictions for arson and weapons violations, he is sentenced to five years in prison.

1978—August: Hansen appeals to the parole board on the grounds that five years was an unduly harsh sentence for the theft of a chainsaw. He is granted parole but told to seek psychiatric treatment; however this condition is never enforced.
—Hansen applies for a pilot's license but is denied because he has a prescription for lithium. This causes him to discontinue the medication.

1980—June 28: 24-year-old Roxanne Easland goes missing in Anchorage.
—July 21: Near Eklutna Road, the badly decomposed body of a young woman later dubbed "Eklutna Annie" is found.
—July: Joanne Messina goes missing from Seward.
—September 6: 41-year-old Lisa Futrell goes missing in Anchorage.
—The body of Joanne Messina is found in a gravel pit near Eklutna Road.

1981—Hansen files a fraudulent claim with his insurance company stating that his house was burglarized, and his valuable hunting trophies were stolen. He receives a sizable payout.
—Hansen uses the money from his insurance settlement to open his own bakery in a mini-mall in Anchorage. He becomes known in the community for his donuts and polite demeanor.
—November 17: 23-year-old Sherry Morrow goes missing from Anchorage.
—December 2: 22-year-old Andrea Altiery goes missing from Anchorage.

1982—Hansen purchases a Piper Super Club prop plane with the registration identifier N3089Z. He uses the plane to get to more secluded regions of the Alaskan wilderness for his legitimate hunting trips. He also uses it, initially, to dump bodies in more rural areas; toward the end of his killing spree he will fly his victims to the desolate forests to "hunt" them.
—May 26: 23-year-old Sue Luna goes missing in Anchorage.
—September 12: While on a hunting trip, an off-duty police officer and some friends find the body of Sherry Morrow along the bank of the Knik River.

1983—April 25: 31-year-old Paula Goulding goes missing from Anchorage.
—June 13: Cindy Paulson is kidnapped, raped, and tortured by Hansen. She escapes and goes to police. Hansen is investigated, but charges are dropped because he is able to provide an alibi. During the investigation, police search his home, car, and plane, finding information that will later prove valuable.
—September 2: Paula Goulding's body is found in a shallow grave near where Sherry Morrow's body was located, confirming to the Alaska State Troopers that they have a serial killer. The FBI is called in to assist with the case. Detective Glenn Flothe uncovers Hansen's incriminating past, and criminal psychologist John Douglas creates a profile of the serial killer.
—October 27: Hansen is brought in for questioning while his plane and house are searched. Authorities find the gun used in the murders, a map marked with red X's indicating the location of bodies, and IDs and jewelry from victims.
—November 3: A grand jury indicts Hansen on charges of first degree assault on a person, second degree theft, insurance fraud, and five counts of misconduct with a deadly weapon.
—November 20: The crime lab finishes its ballistics analysis of the bullets found in the victims and Hansen's .223 Mini-14 rifle and announces a match.

1984—February 18: Hansen enters a plea of guilty in the murders of Paula Goulding, Sherry Monroe, Joanna Messina, and the unidentified body known as Eklutna Annie.
—February 22: Hansen's defense attorney, Fred Dewey, and District Attorney Victor Krumm make a deal that in exchange for his full confession in the four murders for which he has been indicted, Hansen will not be prosecuted for the other killings and will serve his time in a federal prison. Hansen accepts the deal.
—February 27: Hansen is given the maximum sentence of 461 years plus life without the possibility of parole. He is sent to the Lewisburg Federal Penitentiary in Pennsylvania.
—April 24: The body of Sue Luna is found along the Knik River.
—April 24: Malai Larsen's body is found in a parking lot by the Old Knik Bridge at the Knik River.
—April 25: DeLynn Frey's body is found by Horseshoe Lake.
—April 26: Teresa Watson's body is found on the Kenai Peninsula.
—April 26: Angela Feddern's body is found near Figure Eight Lake.
—April 29: Tamara Pederson's body is found a mile and a half from the Old Knik Bridge along the Knik River.

—May 9: Lisa Futrell's body is found south of the Old Knik Bridge by the Knik River.

1988—Hansen is transferred to the Spring Creek Correctional Center in Seward, Alaska, as one of the first inmates in the new prison.

1990—Darla Hansen files for divorce and leaves Alaska because of the harassment and embarrassment. She and her children flee to Arkansas to try to start over.
1995—John Douglas publishes his book *Mindhunter*, which contains details about his part in the investigation of Hansen and the Alaskan serial killings.

1999- An episode of *The FBI Files*, "Hunter's Game," airs about Hansen.

2003—February 21: Police use true crime television shows and other media channels to try to identify Eklutna Annie and the other unknown victims from the jewelry found in Hansen's home.

2007—*Crime Stories* airs an episode documenting the case of the "Butcher Baker."

2010—May 12: An episode of *Criminal Minds*, "Exit Wounds," discusses Hansen.

2012—January 25: *Alaska: Ice Cold Killers* on Investigation Discovery documents the Hansen case with an episode titled "Hunting Humans."
—February 21: The Travel Channel's *Hidden City* episode "Anchorage: Robert Hansen's Most Dangerous Game, the Legend of Blackjack Sturges, Eskimo Hu" airs.
—February 22: The *Law and Order: Special Victims Unit* episode "Hunting Ground" depicts a fictional rendition of Hansen.

2013—The movie *The Frozen Ground* is released. Starring John Cusack as Robert Hansen, Nicholas Cage as Detective Glenn Flothe, and Vanessa Hudgens as Cindy Paulson, it portrays the case from the perspective of Cindy and Detective Flothe.

2014—August 21: Robert Hansen dies in a prison hospital in Alaska at the age of 75.

Upthegrove, Rachel, Christine Chard, Lisa Jones, Katherine Gordon-Smith, Liz Forty, Ian Jones, and Nick Craddock. "Adverse childhood events and psychosis in bipolar affective disorder." *The British Journal of Psychiatry*. March 01, 2015. Accessed August 19, 2017. http://bjp.rcpsych.org/content/206/3/191.

"Watching True Crime Stories." Tapatalk-powered-by. May 3, 2008. Accessed August 15, 2017. https://www.tapatalk.com/groups/watchingrobertpickton88015/robert-Hansen-Alaskan-serial-killer-t1557.html.

Dr. Death
Michael Swago

The Exception to the Rule

Joseph Michael Swango was born on October 21, 1954, the same year that Senator Joseph McCarthy was censured, ending the long reign of political terror that McCarthy had instigated against perceived enemies of the state. This other Joseph coming into this slightly thawing Cold War world wouldn't get too much into politics as he grew older, but he would one day conduct his own personal reign of terror that would leave at least 60 people dead. Just looking at the diabolical end results of Michael Swango's life begs the oft-asked question: Were there any warning signs?

If you are attempting to look for the exact formula that created this killer, you certainly won't find it in the town where he was raised. Michael Swango grew up in the idyllic confines of Quincy, Illinois, a quaint piece of Mid-America that doesn't exactly present itself as a monster factory. It's just one of many nondescript, safely middle-class towns in the American heartland. Michael was the middle of three children born to John and Muriel Swango. His mother Muriel tried to create a nice home for her children, and by all accounts she was a loving parent.

However, the Swango kids would later recall a few odd things about their childhood, such as the fact that their mother never seemed to want to invest in wrapping paper for Christmas presents. She would simply put their gifts in brown paper bags, staple them shut, and shove them under the tree. But no matter how unconventional that may be, would the fact that Swango's mom brown paper bagged Christmas make him a serial killer? Probably not; it didn't make his siblings into any such thing. And odd little idiosyncrasies aside, Muriel did at least try to create a loving home for her kids. That wasn't always easy, since she was often left by herself to do it.

Her husband, John, was rarely ever home. Michael Swango's father was a very busy man, a real mover and shaker in the United States military who served as a career officer all throughout the exceedingly unpopular Vietnam War. Like many soldiers of that era, Michael's dad was deeply affected by the reception he was given upon his return to the States. The war itself was bad enough, but that was to be expected; but John Swango found that how he was treated and perceived by his fellow citizens was even worse.

While the soldiers of World War Two and the Korean War were perceived as heroes and given ticker-tape parades, John Swango and the men he led in Vietnam were less than universally acclaimed. Those who believed what they heard on the evening news about American GIs burning down villages and brutalizing innocent civilians could not see these men as heroes who had sacrificed everything for their country. They were treated with suspicion at worst, and pity at best. Facing such psychological pressure in the early 1970s—a time before PTSD was a household word, a time in which such dysfunction was often incomprehensible to the public—Michael's father began to drown his demons in alcohol.

167

He sunk into an impenetrable void of depression, and as a result young Michael's family soon broke apart in divorce. Michael's father was almost completely out of his life after this, and Michael became even more dependent on his mother, to a degree that some described as "clingy." As Michael progressed through adolescence, it seemed that he wanted to impress Muriel and win her approval more than anything else—and he succeeded admirably.

He became an accomplished musician, learning to play the piano and playing the clarinet in the school band. He managed to attain the position of first chair, and eventually became so good that the band teacher, who also played in a professional symphony orchestra, had him take part in their seasonal tour while he was still a senior in high school.

Nor was music the only area in which Michael excelled. He made A's and B's throughout his high school career, and he became the valedictorian of his graduating class in 1972. Far from the stereotype of an isolated loser who grows up to commit heinous crimes, Michael was a well-adjusted and really popular kid. He seemed to get along well with just about everyone, and no problems with classmates or teachers were ever reported. Due to his popularity and accomplishments both academic and extracurricular, Michael Swango was even elected class president.

The story so far doesn't exactly seem to reflect the origins of a misanthrope and sociopath, does it? No, Michael Swango's youth doesn't fit the profile of such highly depraved characters—but of course, there is always an exception to every rule.

Pursuing Excellence

Shortly after his high school graduation, Swango began attending Millikin University in Decatur, Illinois, just a three-hour drive from his hometown of Quincy. With Swango's grades and SAT scores he could have attended school just about anywhere, but it seems in these early years he wanted to stay close to home. At Millikin, a small liberal arts college, Swango excelled well above and beyond his peers, with his GPA reaching the crystalized perfection of a 4.0. But on a personal level, the formerly positive and chipper Michael Swango began to have his ups and downs.

His world changed somewhere around his sophomore year in college and a messy breakup with his first serious girlfriend. This breakup seems to have hit Swango particularly hard and left a lasting psychological impact on him. Friends say that after the breakup he started to act and dress differently. Previously he had dressed in conservative khakis and polo shirts; now he began to wear all-out military attire. His friends knew that he came from a military family, but Swango wasn't in the military at the time, so they didn't quite know what to make of it.

Remember that Swango was doing this right at the height of the Vietnam War, when many of his peers were burning draft cards and otherwise attempting to stay as far away from the military as possible. For him to sport such pro-military attire was really pretty bizarre in the early 1970s. And then Swango took things a step further and joined the military himself. In a seemingly random, spur-of-the-moment decision, he abruptly left Millikin University after his sophomore year, enlisted with the Marines, and went to basic training for the summer. Was he trying to follow in his father's footsteps?

Perhaps, but at this point he wasn't even in contact with his dad. If he was trying to impress or gain his father's approval, he had no way of even letting him know about it. Nevertheless, Swango seemed to excel in the military; he even obtained the special rank of "sharpshooter" for his prowess with a rifle. Not a lot is known about Swango's service, but according to the public record he made the rounds. He entered into training at the base in St. Louis and was eventually transferred to Camp Lejeune in North Carolina, where he was ultimately given an honorable discharge in 1976.

Swango was not only honorably discharged, he also received a number of medals, including distinctions such as the Meritorious Mast and the Defense Service Medal. Swango never went to war, and his reasons for leaving the service are as unclear as his reasons for enlisting in the first place. But leave it he did, stepping away from active duty in the Marines to pick up his academic career where he had left it behind. He enrolled as a full-time student at Quincy University in his hometown of Quincy, Illinois—and immediately began to stand out like a sore thumb due to his military mannerisms and attire.

It was later discovered that Swango had greatly embellished his military record on his application to Quincy. Despite never having seen combat, he claimed to have received the Bronze Star and a Purple Heart for his service, which were both outright lies. But regardless of the deception, he was once again an ideal student, obtaining a GPA of 3.89, well above most of his classmates. He double majored in biology and chemistry and expressed an interest in attending medical school, and to most he seemed to be on the fast track to doing so.

But in stark contrast to his earlier years, Swango was becoming quite isolated during his time at Quincy University. His only real extracurricular activity was spending late nights in the science lab to conduct chemistry research and experiments. This fascination with chemistry prefigured later years when he was accused of putting together lethal chemical compounds with which to poison his patients. But even more shockingly telling in retrospect was Swango's senior thesis, which discussed the assassination of Georgi Markov.

Markov was a Bulgarian writer and dissident who was exiled in Great Britain. He worked on foreign affairs for the BBC, and was a vocal critic of Communism in general and Bulgaria in particular. It is believed that he was killed by a Soviet-backed Bulgarian agent in London. Georgi was waiting at a bus stop to catch a ride to the BBC station when he felt a sharp pain in his leg. He turned to see a man next to him fumbling with an umbrella. The man simply muttered, "Sorry," and went on his way.

Georgi assumed that this "Umbrella Man" (as the mysterious figure was later called) had simply bumped into him, but when he arrived at the BBC station to begin his shift, it became clear that there was something more to this seemingly random incident. Georgi soon became deathly ill and had to be rushed to the hospital. He would die just a few days later from what was later determined to be a lethal dose of ricin that had been injected into his leg.

This lethal toxin was precisely the kind of chemical that Swango had been experimenting with so intently at the science lab at Quincy, and it would come to prominence in his later crimes as well. Swango graduated from Quincy University in 1979 with an award from the American Chemical Society for academic excellence. If only they knew that Michael Swango's "excellence" would one day be used for murder!

Some Serious Medicine

Swango was accepted into the Southern Illinois University (SIU) School of Medicine that same year and was already attending classes by the fall. The sprawling campus of SIU is situated in the Illinois state capital of Springfield, with further campuses in Edwardsville and Carbondale. Here, Swango once again immersed himself in his studies, and once again he took an incredible amount of interest in courses on pharmacology, toxicology, and pathology. Any course that dealt with chemistry, drugs, disease, and lethal toxins was always on Swango's short list while at SIU.

Swango made it a point to live a rigid lifestyle at SIU. His classmates were often amused—if not slightly disturbed—to find him doing pushups and other military-style exercises outside on campus grounds. He also continued to wear military attire, which continued to set him apart from his more stylish peers. At med school, his study habits also set him apart.

Notes were strictly forbidden during test time, but Swango had developed a way around this. He would begin taking a test and then make an excuse to go out into the hallway and cram his notes on the fly before coming back in to answer the questions. This underhanded method seemed to work for him, and as he aced test after test with this strategy, some of his classmates took notice and began to copy his system. This little loophole for accessing notes eventually became so epidemic that teachers began to call it "Swangoing" and specifically told their students before a test, "There will be no Swangoing."

The next thing that Swango would become famous for during his tenure at SIU was his dissection method. Dissecting a corpse is a rite of passage for all med students, but when the turn came for Swango to dissect a cadaver, the results were so gruesome that the rest of his classmates would never forget it. Instead of a body with clean incisions and organs neatly removed, the corpse was a mangled mess of formaldehyde-preserved flesh. Classmates said it looked like Swango had done his dissecting with a chainsaw rather than a scalpel. It was actually so bad that even Swango had to admit that there was no way he could continue with his handiwork, so when it came time for him to present his findings to the class, he had to rely on pictures from his textbook rather than the desecrated corpse right in front of him.

But despite these oddities, Swango was able to persevere. By his final year of med school, he had chosen neurosurgery as his specialty and was given real-world work in the hospital under residency staff. Most had a distinct disdain for Swango, but he did gain the admiration of one of the neurosurgeons, a man named Dr. Lyle Wacaser. Where others saw bizarre eccentricity, Dr. Wacaser saw a hard-working genius. To most faculty, though, Swango's hard work and dedication to the field seemed to be paying off in a negative way. They began to notice that more patients than usual expired when Swango was administering treatment.

Some of the other med students, perhaps recalling Swango's military background, then crafted what they felt was a fitting nickname for the strange medical intern. They began calling him "Double-O Swango" in reference to the James Bond movies in which "OO" agents were licensed to kill. This was predominantly just the morbid humor of med students and faculty who spent many late nights together and often witnessed tragic events. They never really believed what they were saying; for them it was just a joke. The only trouble was that Michael Swango wasn't laughing. And soon he would show them all just how serious he was.

Swango Gets His License

Michael Swango was in his last year of med school when he received word that his father had passed away. It was shortly after New Year's, in January of 1982, that Muriel placed the phone call that would send her son back to Quincy. At his father's funeral, everyone Swango met was impressed with how far he had come. They saw an ambitious, handsome young man speaking of his life on the fast track to being a neurosurgeon and felt that Swango was hands down the star of the entire family.

But his illustrious future career in medicine was not quite as assured as the relatives at his dad's funeral believed. In fact, in his last month of med school, he was nearly kicked out altogether. It was Swango's cavalier attitude and cocky self-assurance that led to his near dismissal. He had been finishing up one of his last requirements, a mandatory observational course in OB/GYN at the hospital, when it was revealed that he had been fudging all of his H & P (History and Physical) reports. He had been observed going into patients' rooms for less than ten minutes and then coming back with full-length reports that normally took 30 to 45 minutes to complete.

Suspecting something wasn't right, doctors investigated Swango's H & P reports and discovered that they had indeed been completely fabricated. This alone was enough grounds to have Swango expelled, but luck would intervene on his behalf. When a hearing was held to determine what to do with him, there was one dissenting vote in his favor. Without a unanimous decision to dismiss him, he was allowed to go forward and finish med school. Amazingly, even with such a poor track record at SUI, Swango was able to gain a spot for himself at Ohio State University Medical Center in 1983 after sending out a flurry of applications all over the Midwest.

Swango was able to beat out 60 other applicants for this residency, primarily because of how convincing he was in his personal interview. Swango, as odd as some of his mannerisms could be, was usually able to leave a good impression. He always seemed to know just the right things to say, and apparently that was enough to convince the gatekeepers at the Ohio Medical Center to give him a chance. He signed an agreement that would grant him a residency in neurosurgery after a 12-month internship in general surgery starting on the 1st of July, 1983.

Not long after his arrival, many patients under his care began to become gravely ill, and some died. Nursing staff in Rhodes Hall, where Swango was assigned, began to take note of the unusually high amount of "Code Blues" that occurred while he was present. One of these Code Blues was a patient named Ruth Barrick. Ms. Barrick had checked into the hospital on January 17th for head trauma resulting from a fall.

In the immediate aftermath of the fall she had suffered from a fairly serious cerebral hematoma. However, she was quickly stabilized upon arriving at the medical center, and was now in fair condition, seeming to improve every day. Her progress dramatically reversed itself on January 31st, however, after an impromptu bedside visit by Doctor Swango. According to one of the attending nurses that morning, a woman named Deborah Kennedy, she had given

Ruth Barrick her breakfast meal, and found her in good health, communicative, and following instructions well.

It was right in the middle of her checkup with Ruth, around 9:45 in the morning, that Swango appeared and informed the nurse that he needed to check on the patient. Deborah then left the room, allowing Swango space for whatever procedures he needed to carry out. Less than twenty minutes later, she returned to find that her previously healthy patient had turned blue and was barely breathing. The nurse immediately called out a Code Blue, and as medical personnel rushed onto the scene, Swango was one of the first to respond.

With a group effort, the team was able to revive the ailing patient. She was then stabilized and sent to the ICU for recovery. Ruth was once again doing very well when on February 6th a nurse named Anne Ritchie happened to notice that one of her IVs seemed to be malfunctioning. She called for a doctor to come down to help with the equipment, and none other than Swango arrived. The nurse then excused herself and allowed Swango to get to work.

Swango drew the curtains around Ruth's bed shut, obscuring his handiwork, but the Nurse Ritchie periodically peeked in to see if she could be of assistance. At one point she witnessed Swango working on the IV with several unknown syringes. She asked if he needed help, but he was adamant that he didn't, so she stayed out of his way after that. Several more minutes passed before she finally saw Swango leave the patient's room. The nurse then came in to check on the patient and was horrified to find her gasping for air immediately before going into complete cardiac arrest.

Just like Nurse Kennedy before her, Nurse Ritchie frantically called out a Code Blue. This time, however, Swango had stuck around to see the results of his handiwork. He came right back around the corner to witness the frazzled nurse attempting to give the dying patient CPR. Instead of trying to be a hero and lending his help, he just stepped back and cavalierly criticized the nurse's prowess with cardiopulmonary resuscitation.

As he watched her put her mouth on the old woman's in a desperate attempt to breathe life back into her, Swango cruelly remarked, "That is so disgusting." In complete bewilderment at what she was experiencing, the nurse looked away from her dying patient to see Swango staring at her with a satisfied smirk on his face. In disgusted outrage, she screamed at him, "You jerk!" Shortly after this confrontation, the rest of the ER team arrived to try their hand at resuscitation, and Swango slipped away in the chaos.

Unfortunately for Ruth Barrick, she would not survive the swirling medical mayhem Swango had created at her expense. She was pronounced dead a few hours later. The official cause of death was listed as "cardiopulmonary arrest due to cerebrovascular accident." But the two nurses who had personally cared for the patient during her stay at the hospital weren't so sure that what they had witnessed was an accident. They weren't entirely sure what to make of her death, but whatever had happened, they knew that Swango was somehow at fault.

As of yet, no one wanted to consider the possibility that Dr. Swango was purposelessly harming patients. There was, however, some gossip that—perhaps through gross negligence or flat-out incompetence—he was adversely affecting those entrusted to his care.

This suspicion only increased when the head of the nursing staff, Amy Moore, witnessed Swango refusing to administer immediate respiratory aid to a patient who was having obvious difficulty in breathing. Instead, Swango was belligerently insisting that the patient needed to have her heart monitored. The patient's heart was fine, however; it was just her breathing that needed immediate attention. The head nurse actually had to physically intervene, separating Swango from the patient in order to deliver the life-saving treatment she needed for her lungs.

Complaints regarding Swango's odd protocol with patients began to pile up—so many that the hospital was forced to conduct an internal investigation. But since they could not find any direct evidence of wrongdoing, all the investigation accomplished was to officially clear him.

Once he had been cleared, Swango was quietly moved to another section of the hospital, away from the complaining patients and coworkers. The hospital administration hoped that this simple measure might solve the problem, and if that problem had in fact been a matter of misunderstandings and personality conflicts with the staff of Rhodes Hall, it might well have done the trick. But not long after Swango was moved to another wing of the hospital, patients mysteriously began to die there as well.

And soon it was not only patients who were becoming mysteriously ill. Soon, Swango's own troublesome coworkers would suffer from a mysterious illness as well. In one incident, Swango generously offered to buy lunch and came back with a bunch of Kentucky Fried Chicken for his coworkers. The only trouble was that this chicken was laced with poison. As soon as they started eating the food, everyone became violently ill, throwing up and developing dangerously high fevers. Swango, meanwhile, was munching on his own choice pieces of chicken and not having any problem whatsoever.

Even with all of these strange occurrences, there was still no real proof of any wrongdoing on Swango's part. But in light of all the anecdotal claims and rumors surrounding this troubled resident, Ohio Medical Center decided not to bring Swango back to finish his residency. They just wanted to put this unsettling chapter behind them, as quietly as they could. This didn't stop Swango from getting his medical license, however, and the med student who had once been derided as "Double-O Swango, license to kill" now had an official license to practice medicine.

Swango's New Job

Swango received his medical license in September of 1984. After obtaining this prize, he moved back to Quincy to find work. He initially lied to his family about why he had left what had been promising opportunities in Ohio. Swango claimed it was just a matter of his own personal preference; he hadn't been able to get along with the medical staff there, so he had chosen not to return. He conveniently omitted the fact that they had declined to *let* him return. In Quincy, Swango found a new job—even though it was a significant demotion—working as an EMT for an ambulance company based out of a local medical facility called Blessing Hospital.

This job was a 24-hour, round-the-clock kind of gig in which the EMTs were constantly on call. Swango greatly enjoyed the thrill and excitement of suddenly being rushed to the scene of an emergency—a scene that often included horrific trauma and severely wounded victims. And while enthusiasm for emergency rescues is a desirable trait for an EMT, his coworkers soon took notice that Swango was just a little bit too enthusiastic about his job. Mark Krzystofczyk, a fellow SIU graduate who worked with Swango during this stint as an EMT, was particularly disturbed by the unbridled enthusiasm that Swango exhibited when they happened upon a fatality.

The sight of a dead body was bizarrely exhilarating for Swango. He even said as much to Krzystofczyk after one of these deadly run-ins, asking him, "Wasn't that great?" Swango made similarly unsettling idle comments to other colleagues from time to time as they rode in the back of the ambulance. He also produced some startling visual material that caused even more unease. He called it his scrapbook, and it was filled with collections that he had made over the years of newspaper clippings and photos of natural disasters, crime scenes, traffic accidents, and various other forms of gory death and destruction.

Sharing these images with his coworkers during their downtime, Swango discussed his fascination with these events openly and at great length. Working as an EMT puts people on the front lines of disaster on a daily basis and is known to create thick skins and dark humor. But Swango's macabre behavior was too much for even these hardened emergency personnel to stomach. Most of his coworkers were sincerely creeped out, but others just chalked up Swango's antics to eccentricity and that same trademark dark humor that they all displayed—if not with quite as much gusto as Swango did.

Besides his obsession with death and destruction, the other thing that his coworkers truly marveled at when it came to Swango was his seemingly endless energy. During this period in his life he appeared to be going on next to no sleep on a routine basis. While he worked in Quincy he still had a girlfriend back in Columbus, Ohio, a nurse named Rita Dumas whom he had met during his residency at OSU, and it wasn't uncommon for him to work a long shift, drive to Columbus to see her, drive back, sleep for just 30 minutes in a break room, and then begin another long shift. The man seemed naturally manic and full of energetic enthusiasm whether he slept or not. Even when his colleagues were zoning out and falling asleep on the job, he was absolutely wired.

In his mania, he often sought to please his colleagues in any way he could. On September 14th, that avid enthusiasm seemed to manifest itself in a box of donuts that Swango laid out in the lounge that the EMTs frequented. Swango happily announced to his comrades, "I got you guys a bunch of doughnuts." His tired and hungry coworkers appreciated the gesture, but there was only one problem: the donuts were poisoned. About 30 minutes after Swango's colleagues consumed the donuts, they all became violently ill, vomiting uncontrollably and becoming horribly sick. Every single one of these emergency first responders had to go to their own emergency room for treatment.

It was suspected that the donuts were responsible, but suspicion did not immediately fall on Swango. Instead, authorities looked into the conditions at the donut shop. This led to an official County Health Department report detailing suspicions of negligence on the part of the vendor. However, the owner of the bakery was adamant that his shop had had no part in compromising the food, and after a thorough inspection of his facility, no indication of food poisoning (either deliberate or accidental) could be found.

Investigators still failed to point the finger at Swango, though; they decided that the donuts must have been contaminated with some unknown stomach virus, causing everyone to get sick. After getting away with his donut contamination, Swango became even more prolific with the poisoning of his coworkers. He poisoned soft drinks on several separate occasions before handing them off to colleagues. He even poisoned a whole pitcher of tea in the break room. Swango was soon universally suspected of tampering with his coworkers' food and beverages, but the smoking gun didn't come until he rushed off on ambulance duty and left an open duffel bag behind.

Coworkers discovered that this duffel bag had containers of ant poison inside of it. They theorized that Swango had caused the periodic sickness that had ravaged their ranks by slipping doses of this ant poison into their food and drinks. Samples from the spiked tea were then sent off to a forensics lab, and they were found to contain a direct match for the ant poison in Swango's duffel bag. On October 26, 1984, Swango was arrested and charged with aggravated battery by way of poison.

With Swango in custody, police conducted a search of his apartment and found what could only be described as a kind of chemical laboratory filled with several canisters of toxins and drugs that Swango had apparently been experimenting with. There were vials of ricin, arsenic, and other lethal materials strewn all over the apartment, as well as a small cache of firearms including a shotgun and several handguns. He also had some strange reading materials, such as a thick volume on his coffee table entitled *The Book of Ceremonial Magic*, *The Modern Witch's Spell Book*, and even a copy of the mythical (and mostly fabricated) *Necronomicon*.

In the words of Swango's coworkers, "he was a weird guy." But no one had expected him to have such a bizarre interest in the occult. The well-worn pages of these books, however—along with several pieces of notebook paper with handwritten "spells" on them—seemed to indicate much more than a passing fancy with these dark arts. Just who was Michael Swango, anyway? A doctor? A mad scientist? A mass murderer? An aspiring magician? The deeper anyone delved into his strange and twisted life, the more diabolically mind boggling it all became.

It All Comes Crashing Down

Michael Swango's trial for aggravated battery kicked off on April 22, 1985, with Swango's plea of Not Guilty. His attorney already knew him on a personal level; in fact, his legal counsel was his former high school history teacher. Daniel Cook, not too much older than Swango himself, had returned to school and received his law degree in the years after Swango had left Quincy, and he was eager to defend someone he viewed as "one of his best students."

Following Cook's advice, Swango chose to waive his right to a jury trial and leave his fate in the hands of just one person: trial judge Dennis Cashman. Swango had a host of supportive figures on display in the courtroom, with his mother, brothers, and girlfriend all present. But nearly all of his coworkers at the ambulance company showed up as well. These men all testified against Swango, each offering up his own unique perspective on his character and the likelihood that he had indeed poisoned his colleagues.

These eyewitnesses related account after account of just how obsessed Swango was with violence and death. One of his coworkers even recalled an incident in which Swango had made the offhand remark during a shift that he felt it would "be nice to walk into the Emergency Room and start blowing people away." But of course, as damning as some of these remarks might seem, you cannot convict someone for words alone, and Swango's defense attorney was quick to point this out.

Basically admitting that Swango may have had some odd proclivities, Daniel Cook stated that a verdict of guilt "cannot be based upon guesses, hunches, and baseless opinions." In other words, the defense allowed that Swango might very well be an extremely odd guy, but that didn't make him a poisoner. In order to prove he was capable of that, the prosecution would have to establish much more solid evidence than mere anecdotal recollections from late night banter in and around Blessing Hospital's Emergency Room. In order to get a conviction, they had to connect Swango directly to the crime of poisoning itself.

The prosecution sought to do this through the police reports detailing the stockpiled chemicals found in Swango's apartment, and in particular the ant poison that matched the poison found in the tainted tea from the ER's break room. But the defense was ready for this and brought in their own expert witness, a local exterminator named Kevin O'Donnell. O'Donnell had done his own personal investigation of Swango's apartment and reported that he had discovered many "reddish-type" ants infesting the defendant's living quarters.

According to the defense, this proved that the only reason that Swango had such a large amount of ant poison was that he had an equally large number of ants infesting his apartment. But this appeal to the seemingly common-sense assumption that ant poison was used for ants rather than poisoning coworkers fell flat during cross examination. Under oath, O'Donnell had to admit one peculiar fact about Swango's ant infestation: The ants in his apartment were not normally found in the Midwest; they were more likely natives of Florida.

The prosecution was then quick to point out that Swango's mother had recently moved to a part of Florida that was literally crawling with this type of ants—and coincidentally enough, Swango had recently visited his mother's home in Florida. You could imagine that the ants might have hitched a ride with him on his trip back, but the prosecution asserted that Swango had deliberately brought them to Quincy to build a cover story as to why he had ant poison. Of course, if this was the case, one might wonder why he hadn't just gathered local Midwestern ants to infest his apartment. Why go to all the trouble of bringing ants across state lines?

But any rate, this was the prosecution's stance on the matter, and they were sticking to it. And with all voices and opinions aired out for Judge Cashman's consumption, the entire debate was put to rest on May 2nd. Judge Cashman came back the next day with his verdict. Many in the courtroom were shocked when they heard the words, "On count 1, aggravated battery, I find the defendant Michael Swango not guilty." There was an audible gasp among his former coworkers, and there was suddenly a very real fear that Swango had beat the system and would walk out a free man.

The judge wasn't finished yet, however; he had only read his verdict on one of the seven counts of battery that Swango was facing. And for the remaining six counts, Judge Cashman issued a resounding "guilty as charged." Swango didn't have much of a reaction to the verdict; he simply covered his face with one hand in a muted display of shock. His girlfriend, Rita Dumas, had the most poignant reaction in the courtroom, breaking into heart-wrenching sobs for the man she had thought she was going to spend the rest of her life with.

Swango was then seen trying to hand her a Styrofoam cup, and to add even more drama to what was already a circus, a nearby police officer, fearing that Swango was passing her some sort of poisoned beverage, slapped the cup right out of Swango's hands, causing it to fall to the ground. But this cup didn't hold any coffee, tea, or soda, poisoned or otherwise—it just had a piece of paper inside of it, a piece of paper with the words scrawled in Swango's own handwriting, "I love you, Dumas. Hang in there." Graphologists trained to judge handwriting could spend hours determining whether Swango was sincere—and perhaps pondering why he would refer to his girlfriend by her last name in a love letter!

He wrote "I love you, Dumas." Who really calls his beloved by her last name? Some have even remarked that his scrawled handwriting almost made it look like he wrote "I love you, Dumbass," as if it were one last sick joke to fulfill Swango's sadistic urge to play upon the emotions of the young woman who was indeed desperately in love with him. But we can leave all of this petty speculation to the courtroom junkies and amateur criminal psychologists, because there was one person in that courtroom who could interpret Swango's motives better than anyone else: his mother. And her mind was already made up.

As Swango and Cook huddled outside the courtroom to discuss the possibility of an appeal, Swango's mother and brothers stood in attendance. Swango still insisted he was innocent of all charges and requested Muriel to help him pay the cost of his appeal. Muriel was resolute, however, and with arms crossed, looking right at her convicted son, she shook her head and responded, "I don't have the money". She then looked away and added with certainty, "Anyway, I was there. I know you're guilty. The evidence showed you were guilty."

Just one week later, Muriel would second this opinion about her son to the judge who had convicted him. She had called and scheduled a meeting with the judge shortly after the verdict was rendered. During this meeting she unequivocally stated, "I understand why you reached the decision you did, and I have no quarrel with the verdict." But then, in a sad attempt to rationalize her son's actions, she informed Judge Cashman that her son was "a very troubled young man." She went on to explain that he had become very unsettled after she and her husband had divorced, and had been especially affected by the disconnect that his father seemed to have after his return from service in Vietnam.

She also highlighted Swango's own military service as a factor that had led to his personality change. Although he had avoided combat, Swango had changed considerably when he returned from the Marine Corps, and his mother claimed that he had exhibited symptoms that today might be described as PTSD. She stated that he was easily agitated and seemed to never sleep, as if the threat of the nightmares emerging from the darkness of his troubled psyche was enough to enough to keep him awake at all hours of the day and night.

Muriel may have hoped that these insights into her son's frame of mind would cause the judge to extend some leniency on his behalf. But if this was the case, it had hopelessly backfired, because when the judge read out the sentence that he intended to hand down to Michael Swango, it carried the maximum allotment for the charges leveled against him. On August 23, 1985, Swango was given a sentence of five years in prison.

Some Kind of Nut

After serving only two years of his five-year sentence, Michael Swango was granted supervised release from the Illinois prison system on August 21, 1987, with the stipulation that he would be actively monitored on probation for another 12 months. Swango's most loyal subject upon his release was his girlfriend Rita Dumas, who was there to welcome him back with open arms. In the meantime, Rita had come up with a cleverly concocted story to explain away her beloved boyfriend's conviction. She told anyone who would listen that there was a conspiracy afoot: Swango had actually been framed by the then District Coroner, Wayne Johnson, because Swango had been applying for his job.

Rita was convinced that out of fear of losing his position to the "more skilled" Swango, Johnson had engineered to have Swango prosecuted. These wild assertions perhaps tell us more about Rita's character than anything else. Some have said that if she could believe these outrageous claims, she could probably believe anything. Upon his release, Swango and Rita moved to Virginia, where Swango tried his luck with the Virginia state licensing board, applying to have his medical license renewed there. But the board in Virginia did their homework and ultimately refused his request, citing the numerous red flags that had surfaced around his previous conviction.

Unable to find employment in a hospital, Swango cut his losses and got a job as a counselor at a career development center. But it wasn't long after he began work for this facility that his colleagues began to come down with mysterious illnesses. Here too, his colleagues were alarmed when they saw Swango perusing his scrapbook of death and destruction in the break room and other periods of downtime. But the last straw came when it was revealed that Swango had converted a basement room of the center into his own personal living space.

With increasing pressure on him to leave, Swango parted company with the career center in May of 1989.

Shortly after his departure, one of his erstwhile colleagues tipped off the local police department about Swango's strange activities and the spate of unexplained illness that had plagued the career center. The ensuing investigation followed Swango back to Ohio, where Virginia police sought to collaborate with their counterparts in that state in order to find some reason to charge Swango. All of this digging into Swango's activities attracted the attention of the local news media, and a story surfaced in the *Columbus Dispatch* that Swango was under investigation once again.

Nothing resulted from this investigation, but the pressure was enough to prompt Swango to change his name. On January 18, 1990, he had his name officially changed from Joseph Michael Swango to David Jackson Adams. In the meantime, he had also finally married his longtime girlfriend Rita Dumas, on July 8, 1989. With a name change and a new wife, Swango sought to reestablish himself in life. But it wasn't long into his marriage with Rita that cracks began to emerge in the relationship. Swango and Rita Dumas had carried on for years as an unmarried couple just fine, but once they were married and living under the same roof day after day, night after night, the difficulties surfaced.

According to Rita, despite her many years of courtship, she knew almost immediately after the wedding that she had made a terrible mistake. And so, in January of 1991, less than two years after tying the knot, the two were separated and heading towards a finalized divorce. Shortly before his marriage to Rita, Swango had begun work as a lab technician at one of Virginia's premier coal companies, Aticoal Services, where his job was to test coal before it was shipped off to overseas clients. At first Swango appeared to be an ideal employee, and he was a personal favorite of the company's president, William C. Banks.

But shortly after his marriage crumbled, so too did Swango's behavior on the job. And soon enough, his coworkers began to exhibit the same telltale signs of poisoning that had followed Swango's toxic trail wherever he went. After his divorce was finalized in May of 1991, Swango was moving on again. Back in Ohio, he applied for admission to the Ohio Valley Medical Center. All of his applications in Virginia having been rejected, Swango decided it was time to lie his way out of his problems. Drawing upon his previous experience in fabrication, he submitted a completely fraudulent application in which he claimed that his license had been suspended due to a felony battery conviction over a fistfight at a local restaurant.

There was of course no mention of poison, and no mention of all the patients and colleagues who had been left either dead or severely ill by his actions. Swango laid it on thick, and his sob story of being in the wrong place at the wrong time and falling victim to a heavy-handed judge who had it in for him managed to win over his prospective employers. Hospital director Dr. Jeffrey Schultz was soon chomping at the bit to bring Swango on board and "give the young man a second chance."

But Swango had gone a little too far with his deception. He had even meticulously created false legal documents, such as a fake prison discharge sheet and a similarly forged docketing statement. He used these falsified documents to support his claims that he had been imprisoned over a minor fistfight in a restaurant, rather than the premeditated poisoning of his colleagues. In his sheer audacity, he even went so far as to type up a letter from the governor of Virginia stating that the governor had moved to completely restore all of Swango's rights as a citizen. But these very documents led Dr. Schultz to become suspicious that Swango was not quite what he claimed to be.

As his doubts began to build, he reached out to the police in Quincy, Illinois, to find out the truth. The results of these conversations were twofold: Dr. Schultz immediately suspended Swango's application process, and the authorities in Illinois were alerted to the fact that Swango was apparently forging documents, a serious criminal offense. Prosecutors began exploring the possibility of charging Swango with forgery, but by the time they had built a solid case against him, he had already moved on.

Incredibly enough, Swango had applied and been accepted at the University of South Dakota with the same forged documents that Dr. Schultz had uncovered. It was during this same period, in the summer of 1991, that Swango met a young nurse named Kristin Kinney. Kristin was engaged to a local doctor name Jerome Provenzano, but she was immediately enamored by the attention and charm that Swango showered her with. Feeling that he was offering her a lot more than what Dr. Provenzano was offering her, she eventually called off her engagement and began to see Swango full time instead.

When the two grew serious, Kristin's parents wanted to meet the man she was so smitten with, so the two arranged for them to have dinner together. For the most part, her parents were just as impressed with Swango as Kristin was, but there were a few areas of concern. They picked up on the fact that there were about three years of Swango's life that he could not account for: From about 1984 to 1987, he drew a complete blank. It seemed almost like he had amnesia. These were, of course, the years that Swango had been incarcerated for poisoning his coworkers. The other thing that bothered Kristin's parents was the fact that Swango supplied so little information on his own parents and family.

He was the most forthcoming about his father's background, detailing his military career and service in glowing terms. But about his mother he said next to nothing at all. He simply told them that she had grown ill and was living in a nursing home in Missouri. This was in fact true. A part of Muriel had died on the day that her son was convicted, and she had never fully recovered. Shortly after Swango went to prison, she had developed an acute case of Alzheimer's that was deemed bad enough for her to be placed in an assisted living center. Many believe that it was the stress of her son's conviction that sent her over the edge.

Not only that, after Muriel refused to pony up for his appeal, Swango had washed his hands of her completely and had no plans of seeing her ever again. Even though they didn't know the details of the divide, this obvious disconnect with his own family was something that greatly troubled Kristin's parents. But Kristin, who viewed her new man with the tunnel vision of love, could see no wrong. Despite her family's misgivings, the couple was engaged to be married in May of 1992. Kristin's mother expressed their feelings of confused foreboding best when she stated, "This is either the most wonderful thing in the world for Kristin, or he's some kind of nut."

The Truth Comes Out

For Michael Swango, 1992 seemed to be a comeback year. Against all odds he had managed to gain a residency at the University of South Dakota, and he was happily engaged to a beautiful young woman who adored him. They both moved to the state capital, Sioux Falls, and both found jobs at Royal C. Johnson Veterans Memorial Hospital. Kristin worked as a nurse in the intensive care unit while Swango was serving out the first rotation of his new residency at the same facility.

They tried at first to keep their relationship a secret, but the two were seen talking together on multiple occasions, and it soon became clear to Kristin's coworkers that she had a relationship with the new resident doctor. Kristin confided in one of her colleagues at the nursing station that she was indeed engaged to be married to Dr. Swango. Shortly after Kristin's revelation, Swango completed his rotation in the ICU and moved on to other sections of the medical campus. By all accounts, things were going well.

At this point, there were no mysterious illnesses following at Swango's heels, and he actually seemed to be doing a really good job as a doctor. There were no more fabricated five-minute H & P charts; this time he was doing things by the book. Even to an observer privy to Swango's previously tumultuous and questionable history, it would have seemed that Swango was really trying to turn his life around. Those who didn't know his past were immediately convinced that Swango was nothing other than what he claimed to be: a competent and hardworking doctor with no troubling history at all.

Swango may even have convinced himself of this false narrative, because in his increasing hubris, he actually sent in an application to the American Medical Association. It seems rather incredible that Swango wouldn't know that an application to the AMA might raise all of the old red flags he had tried so hard to bury, and in fact he soon realized his error and tried to withdraw his application. But it was too late. Not only the AMA reject him; they immediately contacted the administration at Royal C. Johnson Veterans Memorial Hospital.

It was now the middle of November, 1992, and the administrators at the South Dakota campus were growing increasingly alarmed about what they were hearing about their new doctor. They discovered that not only had he been convicted of poisoning coworkers, he was also suspected of causing the deaths of patients at OSU. This was obviously too much for them to accept, and they determined that Swango would have to go. This revelation occurred right before Thanksgiving, however, and so they decided to wait until after the holiday to let Dr. Swango know what they had found out.

They wanted to keep the matter quiet while they decided exactly what to do. But in an instance of incredible irony, right when they were trying to quietly sweep their findings under the rug, the Discovery Channel aired a documentary about the Swango case on their true crime series *Justice Files*. Several doctors, nurses, and other members of the hospital's medical staff saw this episode and recognized Dr. Swango.

Bear in mind that this was 1992, the year before the September that never ended and long before Google would become a household name. Nowadays a simple Google search will reveal just about everything you want to know about a person, but in 1992 it took a nationally syndicated television program for the folks in faraway Sioux Falls to learn what Dr. Swango had been convicted of in Illinois, and what he was suspected of doing in Ohio. This revelatory episode of *Justice Files* detonated a gigantic gossip bomb at the nurses' station, with everyone running in every direction to proclaim what they had heard about Dr. Swango.

In the aftermath of the explosion, Dr. Anthony Salem, the director of the hospital's medical residency program, quickly moved to cancel Swango's access to the pharmacy and terminate his status as a resident. Dr. Salem then contacted Swango and informed him that he didn't have to report to his next shift. He asked to meet him the next day at around two in the afternoon. Swango showed up to the meeting with a very nervous Kristin in tow and tried to play dumb, acting like he had no idea what all the fuss was about.

Even when Dr. Salem popped a recording of the *Justice Files* episode into the VCR, Swango still acted indignant and incredulous about the whole affair. He claimed to have no knowledge of any investigations begin conducted into his work at Ohio State, and he stuck to his story that his conviction for poisoning his colleagues had been a great miscarriage of justice in which he was completely railroaded by a biased judge and prosecution.

But for Kristin, the video was a revelation. She had had no inkling of any of this dark history until she saw it presented to her in Dr. Salem's office on his videotaped copy of that fateful episode of *Justice Files*. She remained quiet but visibly agitated during the meeting. But whatever she did, the end result of the encounter was going to be the same. Dr. Swango was ordered to tender his resignation by December 4, 1992.

Just a Little Bit of Charm

Following his forced resignation, Swango hired an attorney named Dennis McFarland in January of 1993. This lawyer worked as Swango's counsel during the final suspension hearings held at the end of the month. As the hearings came to a close, McFarland suggested that Swango contact Vern Cook, who was the president of the hospital employees union. McFarland believed that since Swango had occasionally worked at the local VA during his residency, he could be classified as a federal employee, thereby making him eligible for the federal protections that this would provide.

Swango and Cook met in person a handful of times before Cook agreed to take on his case. Over the next few weeks Swango bonded with Cook, who was a fellow former soldier and a Vietnam veteran. The two would spend countless hours together at Cook's house engaging in what they called "strategy sessions." At times they would be up all night and into the early morning hours rifling through legal documents and discussing just how they should handle Swango's case.

While Cook and Swango were deliberating, Kristin was becoming more and more unglued. She wanted to stand by Swango's side, but the increased scrutiny of the media, who now followed Swango's every movement, with photographers literally jumping out of the bushes at them, was making it much harder to do so. And in the cold winter days of early February, she reached a breaking point. It was at this time that she reached out to a former colleague, a fellow nurse named Lynette Mueller, for help. Meeting up with Mueller at a popular local hangout called Champs, Kristin expressed her frustration with the situation, saying point blank, "I need out." She then asked Mueller if she could perhaps live with her and her husband for a while. She also revealed that Swango had been discussing the idea of moving overseas so that he could work somewhere far away from the charges that were being leveled at him.

The fact that Swango was already making such plans is very telling, since he would later make good on just such a strategy. But Kristin never did move in with her friend Mueller. Instead of getting away from it all, she sought to stem her growing anxiety by self-medicating. She began to take Prozac and to drink heavily just to get through the day. In addition to what she was doing to herself through medication and alcohol, she also had a suspicion that Swango was slipping her a little something as well. She began to have strange headaches out of nowhere, and she grew even more apprehensive when she realized that some of the symptoms she was experiencing were the same as those of Swango's previous victims.

Probably due to a combination of all of these things, Kristin felt like she was losing her mind. And on a cold night in late February 1993, when the police found the young woman taking a walk down a busy Sioux Falls street without any clothes on, they too realized that something was very wrong with Kristin Kinney. This incident of walking completely naked in the cold bought her an immediate ticket to the psych ward of Charter Hospital. She remained there for about four days before she was deemed stable enough to be released.

Kristin spent the next few weeks complaining of her headaches and heartache before she finally packed up her things and hopped into her pickup truck to head back to her parents in Virginia. When she got there her aunt offered to put her up in an apartment that she rented out in the town of Portsmouth, just across the Elizabeth River from Norfolk. Kristin's mom and stepfather felt that their prayers had been answered when Kristin came back to Virginia, but less than two weeks later this dream turned into a nightmare when Swango resurfaced as well.

When Kristin's mother answered to her door on April 23, 1993, she was dismayed to see Swango standing arm in arm with her daughter. They were apparently reunited once again. During Swango's brief stay with Kristin in Virginia he once again sent out a rapid-fire burst of applications to hospitals and medical centers for residency, and amazingly he received a response, this time for a psychiatric position at the State University of New York at Stony Brook on Long Island. Swango hoped that a location so far removed from Sioux Falls, North Dakota, would enable him to shed some of the excess baggage of his past.

Swango's application was received and reviewed by Dr. Alan Miller, the director of the resident psychiatry department. Dr. Miller immediately arranged for an in-person interview with Swango on April 27th. Also present were the department chair and one of the faculty members. As the interview began, it seemed to be going exceedingly well. The group was impressed with Swango's easy personality, his obvious intelligence and his graceful charm. But then Swango dropped his bombshell by informing them, "I have to tell you, I've served time in jail. I want you to know that."

Swango then brought up the same old lie he had used in South Dakota: that he had been incarcerated not for poisoning his colleagues, but for his part in a barroom brawl. Swango then pulled out the same bogus legal documents he had shown in South Dakota in order to bolster his claim. Fortunately for Swango, but rather unfortunately for the general public, Miller and his colleagues readily accepted Swango's story. His staff did a cursory check of Swango's references, but the superficial correspondence between the institutions failed to bring up any red flags, and without further ado Swango was accepted into the program on June 1, 1993.

Before he left for New York, on June 20th, Swango and Kristin had dinner with her parents. It was supposed to be a Father's Day celebration for Kristin's stepfather, Al Cooper. But Swango seemed to think it was a congratulatory dinner for him instead, and he treated it as such, going on and on for most of the night about how great it was that he had been accepted in New York. In light of the recent drama surrounding his sudden dismissal from Royal C. Johnson Veterans Memorial Hospital, Al was a little more skeptical about Swango's prospects, however. He asked him, "Michael, after all of these problems, what if they hear about them?"

Absolutely beaming with confidence, Swango was quick to dismiss Al's concern, cheerfully chirping, "What they don't know, they don't know." Swango then left his fiancée and her family behind for what would be his third attempt to finish his residency since he had graduated from med school nearly a decade ago in 1983. Swango was hoping that the third time would be the charm—but in the end his actions would be a little bit less than charming.

The Road to Destruction

Swango officially began his residency at Stony Brook on July 1, 1993, moving into a dormitory that was provided for hospital residents. Swango's first patient at the hospital was a man named Dominic Buffalino. Buffalino was well-known in his community; he was a World War Two veteran and a longtime organizer for the Long Island Republican Party. He had come to the hospital for a mild case of lung congestion. His family believed it was nothing more than a bad cold bug, but at his age they didn't want to take any chances.

Buffalino was in good spirits when he first met the new resident doctor, Michael Swango—or as Swango had introduced himself, Dr. Kirk. Swango, a longtime Star Trek fan, had decided to go by an alias during this residency, perhaps hoping that confusion over his name might just throw investigators off the trail should there be trouble. After meeting the patient, Swango was then introduced to his wife, Teresa, who was very impressed by the doctor's bedside manner. She found him to be very "pleasant and reassuring."

But his reassuring tone would completely flat line on her the very next morning when Swango himself telephoned to coldly deliver the news, "I'm sorry to inform you that your husband is dead." Teresa was instantly beside herself with grief, as if someone had just stabbed her in the heart. Swango, however, playing his strange, warped and sadistic game, seemed like a cat cruelly toying with its captured mouse as he milked the experience for what it was worth. He kept telling Dominic Buffalino's distraught wife, "Stay on the phone. Don't hang up. Talk to me."

When Teresa came to the hospital, accompanied by Dominic's brother Andrew, Swango was there, standing next to the bedside of Theresa's deceased husband. She broke down into tears once again as Swango offered his bizarre explanation of how a patient suffering from pneumonia had spontaneously expired.

Not a whole lot is known about how Swango spent the rest of his first two weeks at Stony Brook; the next significant incident occurred on July 14th, when he called Kristin back in Virginia. It has never been entirely clear what went on during this conversation, but Kristin's next-door neighbor couldn't help hearing the result of it as Kristin's hysterical crying and shouting filtered through the thin walls of the apartment. Shortly after the neighbor heard this disturbance, Kristin placed a call to her mother. She seemed strangely detached and devoid of emotion. Sensing that something was gravely wrong, her mother pleaded with Kristin to come stay with her, but Kristin finally ended the labored and halting conversation by telling her, "No, Mom, I'm fine. I love you."

Kristin's mother knew that she wasn't fine. She was extremely worried, telling her husband, "There's something terribly wrong with Kristin." Her husband didn't quite share her concern, though. Figuring that she was just overreacting, he told her, "She's 27 years old. Give her some space." She tried to take this advice, but then Swango himself called from New York and told her that she should probably check on Kristin because she had sounded pretty upset. Oddly enough, the same mother who had been ready to drop everything to check on her distraught daughter suddenly made a full reversal.

She didn't want to admit to Swango that Kristin had seemed rattled, and so she lied to him, "She's calmed down." Perhaps she suspected that Swango had broken up with Kristin and didn't want to give Swango the satisfaction of knowing that he had broken her daughter's heart. But whatever the case may be, her first intuition was right: Kristin was in fact in dire need of an intervention. Sadly, no one did intervene on her behalf, and the next night her parents received a phone call from the police requesting that they come down to the station in regard to an incident involving their daughter.

They didn't give any details, but shortly after arriving at the police station the couple learned the horrible news. Kristin had been found dead, slumped against a tree. She had apparently taken her own life. Had Kristin committed suicide? Was she capable of such an act? It seemed she was: she left behind extensive journal entries and notes in her own hand that documented her mental decline and her decision to end it all.

One note addressed to her parents read as follows: "I love you both so much. I just didn't want to be here anymore. Just found day to day living a constant struggle with my thoughts. I'd say I'm sorry but I'm not. I feel that sense of peace, 'peace of mind', I've been looking for. It's nice. I'll be seeing you!"

Sadly, these were the last expressions and sentiments that Kristin's family would have from her.

There could be no doubt that she had indeed committed suicide, but the family still couldn't help but wonder if it was the constant psychological pushing and shoving from Swango that had driven her there.

New York, New York

Dr. Swango's next apparent victim during his tenure at Stony Brook was Barron Harris, who checked into the hospital on September 29, 1993. The patient was a 60-year-old man who, aside from the bout of pneumonia that had led to his admission, was a fairly healthy individual. That is, until he was assigned to a certain resident doctor named Michael Swango. Just as was the case with the ill-fated Dominic Buffalino, the Harris family was initially quite impressed with Swango, who seemed to be the epitome of the selfless, caring doctor. Swango appeared to devote all of his time to ensuring that his patients were being cared for properly.

According to Barron's wife, the other doctors always seemed to be in too much of a hurry to engage with family members. Swango, however, took the time to listen to them and assuage their fears and concerns. But her main concern soon became Dr. Swango himself. Just a few days later she found her husband on a respirator and unresponsive, and all Swango would say was the alarming statement, "I hope it's nothing I did". Swango then argued with the grieving wife, coldly challenging her wish to keep her husband alive, by flatly informing her, "He's in a coma, and I know he's not coming out of it. He's already suffered brain damage." He then badgered the poor woman into signing her husband's death warrant in the form of a DNR (Do Not Resuscitate) directive.

While these events were transpiring in New York, back in Virginia, Kristin's still grieving mother had begun corresponding with one of Kristin's former coworkers at the hospital in South Dakota. It was through these exchanges that personnel in South Dakota were tipped off to Swango's latest residency in New York.

When this news reached the dean of the University of South Dakota Medical Center, he in turn alerted the dean of Stony Brook, Jordan Cohen. After hearing all of the disturbing details of Swango's previous history, Cohen immediately notified the department chair, who then sent the word out to the man who had brought Swango to Stony Brook in the first place, Dr. Alan Miller. Dr. Miller arranged an immediate meeting with Swango to question him about the allegations.

Swango, apparently knowing that he was cornered, readily admitted that he had indeed been convicted of poisoning his coworkers. But he adamantly maintained that he was innocent of the charges.

Dr. Miller, however, had had enough of Swango's excuses. He promptly informed him that his residency was going to be suspended. Swango wouldn't let up, though, and like a man obsessed, he found his way to Miller's office once again the next day and began pleading for some form of leniency. While Miller was not prepared to let him stay at Stony Brook, he did offer Swango some advice: "Go somewhere that really needs a doctor, somewhere that's desperate."

Miller was suggesting that Swango make a trip overseas to some impoverished region of the developing world where competent doctors were a scarce resource. Programs such as Doctors Without Borders do indeed exist to let doctors lend a helping hand in far-flung parts of the globe. The doctors who participate in these programs have various reasons for doing so. Some do it so that their student loans will be forgiven, others do it out of a sincere wish to help others, some crave the adventure of the overseas experience—and some hope that the needy host country will overlook some slip-up or negligence that has left them unable to find work in their home country. Dr. Miller was suggesting that Swango fit into this last category and should explore such an avenue as his last chance to get back into medicine.

Shortly after this meeting, the Stony Brook dean, Jordan Cohen, fired off warning letters to every single medical school in the nation. The letters detailed Swango's troubled background and advised them not to consider his applications. Swango had been essentially blacklisted from every hospital in the United States. If he ever wanted to work in medicine again, he basically had no choice but to leave the country to do it.

Swango tried to lay low after leaving Stony Brook, heading south to stay with a friend of his in Atlanta. But it wasn't long before the FBI, which now had an ongoing investigation into his misdeeds, was on his trail. In February of 1994 they tracked him down to Atlanta—and were deeply concerned to find that he had landed a job at a wastewater plant. Fearing that Swango might have the opportunity to poison the water supply, the FBI determined that they had to act. They immediately alerted the waste treatment facility about Swango's past, and he was accordingly dismissed from the company on July 22, 1994.

But despite the diligent investigation, the slow bureaucracy that often plagues the Bureau meant that the FBI didn't get around to issuing a warrant for Michael Swango's arrest until October 27, 1994. It was a little too late. Swango, apparently having taken Dr. Miller's advice to heart, had decided to take his career overseas. He would soon be thousands of miles away in the sunny African republic of Zimbabwe.

The Homicidal Medical Missionary

Michael Swango arrived in Zimbabwe in November of 1994. Even as the FBI's dragnet was closing in on him, he had managed to establish contact with the director of a little-known Zimbabwean hospital called the Mnene Mission through an overseas job agency called Options. This agency's main mission was to fill medical positions in other countries with American doctors. The director, a man named Christopher Zshiri, was at first greatly impressed with Swango's credentials—but the more he witnessed the doctor in the field, the more he realized that he seemed woefully unprepared for even some of the most basic tasks.

Swango attempted to chalk up this lack of general knowledge to the fact that he had previously been practicing in the highly specialized field of neurosurgery and did not have much experience outside of it. In reality, Swango was clumsy in certain areas simply because he had never been able to hold a job long enough to gain the experience that he should have had at this point in his career. But Dr. Zshiri was an easygoing and understanding man, and he simply took Swango's word for it.

He also came up with a way to erase Swango's ineptitude: He instructed him to take a 5-month position as an intern at Mpilo Hospital in nearby Bulawayo, a historic city that is the second largest in Zimbabwe. Ever since the 1980s, Mpilo Hospital has been a major treatment center for AIDS patients. And in late 1994 when Swango arrived, they were in desperate need of extra medical help for the massive influx of those affected by the disease.

It was for this reason—as well as Swango's amiable bedside manner—that Mpilo's superintendent, Dr. Chaibva, was so excited to bring him on board. He was also quite impressed with the seemingly boundless energy that Swango exhibited. Just as he had during his days as an EMT, Swango seemed to be able to work literally round the clock on 24-hour shifts without any sleep. At Mpilo Hospital, Swango put on his best face for the medical staff, and according to most he did a stellar job. There were some who had their doubts, however.

Many wondered why this skilled American doctor would leave the comfort of the United States, where he could make a ton of money, for third-world Zimbabwe, where he made next to nothing. These skeptics were not quite sold on the explanation that Swango generally supplied, which was that he was there for purely altruistic purposes—that he just wanted to make the world a better place. To them, it seemed that there had to be some hidden motive.

One of Swango's most skeptical colleagues was Abdi Mesbah, a doctor on loan from Iran. In fact, Dr. Mesbah may have been a little *too* skeptical; he even went so far as to explain Swango's medical inexpertness by claiming that he was an agent working for the CIA! But most Mpilo staff dismissed this theory as absurd anti-Americanism, and besides Dr. Mesbah and a few other dissenters, the general consensus was that Swango was telling them the truth and simply wanted to be part of a good cause.

Swango's main go-to guy, while he was at Mpilo Hospital, was a 27-year-old staffer named Ian Lorimer. Ian was a welcoming guide who showed Swango the ins and outs of the hospital. The two worked long shifts together, and Ian helped Swango develop the necessary experience in some of the more basic areas of general practice treatment. The two hit it off well together and seemed to be almost the best of friends. The only time that Swango really rubbed Lorimer wrong was when he used excessive profanity. Lorimer and his wife, Cheryl, were both devout Christians; they even headed a bible study group at the Bulawayo Central Presbyterian Church.

Although Swango had been in the habit of unbridled "locker room talk" during his paramedic days, he was able to switch off this more abrasive side of his personality out of respect for Lorimer. He even showed an interest in Christianity, attending Sunday services with Lorimer and his wife. The two continued to be close friends until Swango's time at Mpilo came to a close in May of 1995. It was near the end of his term at this hospital he had grown to enjoy that Swango first expressed some disdain about the job he was going to be doing.

He was leaving a modern hospital in Zimbabwe's second largest city and going back to a low-budget, ill-equipped, substandard facility in the middle of nowhere. Swango quietly told himself that after he finished his contract at the Mnene Mission, he would return to Bulawayo and his friends at Mpilo Hospital. But besides his dissatisfaction, there was another factor in whether or not Swango could successfully finish his term at Mnene Mission: the pesky problem that as soon as he arrived, people started to die.

Killers Can't be Choosers

Swango returned to Mnene Mission with his own diabolical mission ready to launch, and he soon left a string of victims in his wake, all of whom died of mysterious causes.

The first of these mysterious deaths was Rhoda Mahlamvana. This woman dropped dead for seemingly no reason shortly after Swango paid a visit. Swango was right on the scene afterward as well, preparing her death certificate before her body was even cold. Rhoda had come in for relatively minor burns, and how she could suddenly die like that would become an enduring mystery.

The next odd incident involving Dr. Swango was the case of Keneas Mzezewa. Swango approached Keneas while he was slumbering, then woke him up to give him an injection. This injection almost completely paralyzed Keneas, but right before his lungs seized up on him, he managed to hiss out the words, "Dr. Mike gave me an injection!" As fellow staff members looked on, Swango resorted to his old tactic of claiming that the patient was delusional. He adamantly denied the charge and retorted that Keneas was obviously hallucinating and had imagined the whole thing.

But while the word of one person can be easily dismissed, the word of several witnesses is much harder to ignore. And on June 26th, Katazo Shavo, who was recovering from surgery on his leg, had his whole family with him to witness the peculiar "extra treatments" Dr. Swango delivered to his patients.

Swango arrived on the scene to find Katazo's relatives huddled around his bedside. In order to administer his handiwork, he requested that they leave the room. Swango then closed the curtains around the man's bed and got to work. But even though they could no longer see what was happening to their relative, they could hear his screams. They later described his cries as akin to those of a wild animal. Moments later, they saw Dr. Swango rush out of the room without saying a word.

The family quickly reentered Katazo's room and found him still crying out in intense pain. Then he told them with the kind of certainty that only the imminent specter of death can bring, "We won't go home together because I am going to die. The doctor has injected me with something, and I think I am going to die. I won't get home. I am going to die." The family reassured him and left, but when they returned later that evening, they were stopped by a nurse who confirmed what Katazo himself had predicted: He was dead. There was no explanation, no reason; just a family who saw their loved one laughing and smiling one second, and then, after Dr. Swango left his side, dying a horrible death the next.

Dr. Swango was busy, and now apparently really in the swing of things with his murderous routine. The very next day, on June 27th, he found his next victim, a local farmer named Phillimon Chipoko. The whole thing happened right under his wife's nose. It was late at night in the hospital, and Phillimon was already sleeping his bed. Just a few minutes later his wife, Yeudzirai, would be asleep as well, dozing off in the chair next to her husband's bedside. She only drifted back to wakefulness when she heard the door of the room open and saw Dr. Swango go over to her husband and tinker with his IV.
Yeudzirai snapped back to consciousness several minutes later as a nurse shook her awake and asked bluntly, "Did anyone tell you your husband is dead?" The patient had apparently expired with his corpse curled up in bed as if he were still asleep. But this "sleeper" would never wake up again.

As was commonplace with Swango, despite the mounting evidence that something wasn't right, the hospital administrators didn't dare think that their new doctor was the one causing the problems. And if it wasn't for some quick-thinking nurses, Swango would have claimed another victim in July. Virginia Sibanda was in the maternity ward expecting to have a baby at any moment when she crossed paths with the doctor of death himself, Michael Swango. On July 7th, Swango was assigned to evaluate the stage and condition of Virginia's pregnancy. After a cursory examination, he noted that she was dilating and progressing through her labor well and told her that he did not expect any complications.

Swango returned a few hours later and injected a syringe of pink liquid into Virginia's IV. She noted that he seemed to be trying to inject the liquid quickly, before the nurses turned to see what he was doing. It was as if he didn't want anyone to see it—but Virginia saw it, and she wouldn't forget it. Shortly thereafter, she experienced excruciating pain in her abdomen and felt her baby react violently inside of her. She then had a feverish sensation like she was boiling from the inside out.

Virginia screamed for help and asked for the nurses to douse her in cold water because of the unbearable heat she felt. The concerned nurses dutifully fulfilled her request by covering her in cold compresses. As soon as they were able to calm her down enough, they asked about the cause of her distress. Virginia told them that "Dr. Mike" (as many of the patients at the mission called Swango) had injected her with something just before the onset of the unbearable pain that the entire nursing staff had seen her go through.

It is no coincidence that no matter where Swango went to perpetrate his acts, it was usually the nursing staff who caught on to his depredations before anyone else. They were the ones most often on site with the patients. They know who comes and goes, and who does what, better than anyone else. And in Zimbabwe, just like in America, they were the first to realize that something was definitely not right about Dr. Michael Swango.

Swango did have one defender, however, a nurse's aide by the name of Edith Ngwenya. While the others gossiped openly about the possibility of Swango having a sinister agenda, Edith always rejected such claims. She reminded them that someone like Swango had sacrificed much to come to Zimbabwe to help them. He wouldn't come all the way to Zimbabwe just to kill people, right? That would be ridiculous, right? At least, that was young Edith's logic. Not believing that Swango could be capable of such things, she felt that the nurses' complaints against him were based on nothing more than their own petty jealousies and personal resentments.

But even this defender would desert Swango when she too developed a mystery illness and suddenly and inexplicably dropped dead just a few days later. Apparently, Swango had such little control over his murderous compulsions that he couldn't resist killing even when it meant eradicating one of the few people who would have continued to shield him from blame. It appears that Swango was an equal opportunity murderer who struck whenever the opportunity presented itself, killing friend and foe alike.

Swango's Last Chance

It was midsummer under the hot Zimbabwe sun, and the dead bodies had been piling up at the Mnene Mission ever since Dr. Swango's arrival in May. The hospital administration either did not know the full extent of what was happening or was not willing to think the unthinkable when it came to Swango's true character. But on July 20, 1995, an incident occurred that forced them to confront what was happening.

Thirty-five-year-old Margaret Zhou had come into the mission after enduring a nearly full-term miscarriage. Medical staff treated her pain with medication and then worked to remove the fetal remains from her womb. The procedure seemed to have been completed without any complications, yet later that day Margaret was found to be deceased. Incredibly alarmed that a healthy woman who had undergone a routine procedure had died for no apparent reason, mission director Dr. Zshiri began to question the hospital staff about what had happened.

After some digging, he obtained the testimony of a maternity nurse who informed him not of what had happened to Margaret Zhou, but of what she had witnessed with Virginia Sibanda. She explained to Dr. Zshiri that the patient had claimed that "Dr. Mike" had injected her with something. Hearing this story for the first time, Dr. Zshiri immediately went to Virginia's bedside and personally questioned her about what had happened. Still quite shaken up by the event, she recounted what she had experienced in great detail.

Dr. Zshiri was greatly disturbed to hear this account, but he was even more alarmed when shortly thereafter another nurse came forward and relayed the story of Keneas Mzezewa, whom Swango had woken up and given a shot that paralyzed his whole body and nearly took his life. Dr. Zshiri then interviewed this man as well, and after he recounted his horrific tale, Keneas offered up the statement, "I do not understand what happened—but I nearly lost my life." He also informed Dr. Zshiri that he was still terrified of Swango and feared that he might come back to finish him off.

Sensing Keneas's sincerity, Dr. Zshiri began to fear for him as well, and so he had him transferred to the neighboring Mzume Mission Hospital until he could figure out just what was going on with his new American doctor. Deeply concerned Dr. Zshiri contacted the Lutheran church headquarters and spoke with the director, Howard Mpofu. After taking in the disturbing news, the director instructed him to contact Dr. David Dhakama, the superintendent for the whole region and Dr. Zshiri's immediate supervisor, to inform him of what was happening.

Upon hearing the story, Dr. Dhakama didn't waste any time in bringing the police onto the case. The police soon obtained a search warrant for Swango's living quarters. When they got there, they encountered Swango outside speaking with a staff member. Informing him of the warrant, they ordered him to step aside as they searched his room. The first thing they noticed was that Swango's clothes were strewn all over the place. The second was the huge stockpile of pharmaceuticals, syringes, and vials of chemicals that Swango had amassed.

When the police reemerged from Swango's quarters, Dr. Dhakama personally informed Swango that his license to practice medicine in Zimbabwe would be temporarily suspended and all privileges revoked until he was cleared in the investigation. Then, on October 13th, Lutheran Church representative Howard Mpofu arrived at Swango's door and personally handed him a letter announcing his termination from the Mnene Mission.

Probably unsure of where else he could run to, Swango went to the only other place he knew in Zimbabwe, the city of Bulawayo, his old training grounds where he had spent his first five months in the country. There he contacted Ian Lorimer and informed him of his plight (at least from his own warped perspective). Ian, wishing to help his friend, directed him to a human rights lawyer named David Coltart. This attorney had quite an illustrious career at this point, and Ian figured if anyone could help Swango, Coltart could.

Swango met up with Coltart in his downtown law office on August 23, 1995, to discuss his options. Coltart, like so many others, was convinced by Swango's demeanor that he was a sincere individual who had been unfairly treated. Coltart was used to fighting all manner of human rights abuses in the iron-clad dictatorship of Zimbabwe's Robert Mugabe, and he could easily believe that Swango was indeed being subject to some sort of discrimination. Coltart was a champion ready for a righteous cause, but unfortunately, he wouldn't find any such thing in Swango's case.

Swango was more than ready to latch onto the narrative that he had been singled out for unfair treatment as the only American doctor at the clinic. The defense seemed tailor-made to shield himself from his own diabolical indiscretions. As a devout Presbyterian, Swango's friend Ian Lorimer was also quick to accept that Swango had been wronged by the Lutheran Mnene Mission, and he was ready to fight on his friend's behalf as well. Fully championing the cause, he even went to the director of Mpilo Hospital in Bulawayo, Dr. Chaibva, and petitioned him to hire Swango and restore his privileges to practice medicine.

Dr. Chaibva was a cautious administrator, however. He wanted to know why Swango had been suspended from the Mnene Mission in the first place, so he contacted Dr. Zshiri to ask him personally. But when he raised the question of whether he should take Swango on board at Mpilo, all Dr. Zshiri would say was, "If I were you, I would not employ him." And when Dr. Chaibva asked him to explain this cryptic remark, Dr. Zshiri would only tell him, "It's under investigation."

Dr. Zshiri doubtless didn't feel at liberty to discuss the details until the investigation had run its course. But without any other information, Dr. Chaibva figured that the suspension was probably due to a personal dispute that the director did not wish to get into, rather than any medical negligence on Swango's part. And so, despite Dr. Zshiri's warning, Dr. Chaibva took this as his own personal green light to restore Swango's privileges and hire him at Mpilo Hospital. He would end up regretting this decision for the rest of his life.

Swango's reign of terror at Mpilo Hospital began shortly after he was reinstated and began working at the facility. With nowhere else to stay, Swango was actually given a spare room in the hospital itself. With this kind of 24-hour access it was easier than ever for him to administer his lethal injections to patients. It was quite unlike the open-air environment of the Mnene Mission, where he was almost constantly within earshot of or being observed by someone. At Mpilo, Swango could plot his murders at leisure from the privacy of his sleeping quarters, making sure that no one ever heard or saw a thing.
But while there were no longer any witnesses to his crimes, there were still plenty of mysterious deaths. The first of these was a patient who came in for routine hernia treatment and then just up and died in the early morning hours of the next day. Another patient, who had drunk hydrochloric acid in a botched suicide attempt resulting in the severe burning of the tissue in his throat and stomach, died under similarly strange conditions. It can be surmised that Swango decided to help finish what the suicidal patient had started because just a few days later, the patient was dead—not from his injuries, but with the same calling cards as all the other strange deaths that followed Swango around.

These mysterious deaths continued, but in the hustle and bustle of the busy hospital, they were mostly overlooked. Then a reporter from the local newspaper, the *Bulawayo Chronicle*, tracked Swango down to Mpilo Hospital, and Swango was back in the spotlight once again.

Journalists had been asking around with hospital staff for a while, but they usually hit a brick wall of silence. On this particular day, however, a reporter named Foster Dongozi just happened to be in the right place at the right time. He was in the middle of asking the hospital's switchboard operator to page Dr. Swango when Swango himself walked right up behind him and told him, "I'm Dr. Swango. Can I help you?" Surprised to actually bump into Swango in person, Dongozi turned around and said, "My name is Foster Dongozi, and I'm a reporter for the *Chronicle*."

Swango was taken aback by this statement. Looking incredibly nervous and uncomfortable, he began to back away. He lifted an arm as if to defend himself as he managed to choke out, "I can't answer that. Talk to my lawyer!" He then literally ran from the scene, with half the hospital staff staring after him. But instead of going to Swango's lawyer, the reporter went straight to Swango's employer and launched an improvisational interview on an unsuspecting Dr. Chaibva.

He asked whether Swango was actually living at the hospital and if he had indeed been investigated in the deaths of patients. Dr. Chaibva responded that he didn't know on both counts, but Dongozi suspected that he knew a whole lot more than he was telling. To be fair, the only information that Dr. Chaibva was withholding was his knowledge about where Swango lived. When it came to him being linked to the deaths of patients, Dr. Chaibva was just as much in the dark as everyone else. He still figured that Swango's dismissal from the Mnene Mission had been due to a personality conflict.

But now the heat was on, and he had been pushed too far; he had no choice but to launch his own personal investigation. He contacted Zimbabwe's Minister of Health and Child Welfare, Timothy Stamps, who told him everything he knew about why Swango had been expelled from the Mnene Mission, including the unsettling eyewitness accounts of the surviving patients. Dr. Chaibva had now heard enough, and in mid-March of 1996 he ordered Swango to meet him in a Mpilo Hospital conference room, where he promptly informed the expat doctor, "Your services are no longer required here."

Swango's Eviction Notice

On March 31, 1996, Michael Swango paid a visit to the estate of Lynette O'Hare. He had met her daughter Paulette through his bible study meetings with the Lorimers. During a brief discussion with Lynette, Swango was able to muster up enough of the old charm to convince this lady he barely knew to let him lodge with her. Paulette was moving to England, and Lynette figured she could use both the money and the company that Swango's presence would bring, but she didn't quite know what she was getting into.

Swango was currently dating another girl he had met at the Lorimers' bible study sessions, one LeeAnne, and he subsequently introduced her to Lynette. The relationship didn't last, however; LeeAnne broke it off shortly thereafter. After this breakup, Swango's mood changed completely. He went from being relatively pleasant and sociable to hiding in his room for days at a time. Growing increasingly concerned for her house guest, Lynette called up the Lorimers to see if she could get any insight about the situation.

It was during this phone call that Ian Lorimer confirmed that Swango was the same expat doctor Lynette had heard about on the news who was accused of "experimenting" on patients. Ian was quick to inform her, however, that the whole thing was a "put-up job" arranged to frame Swango. Lynette, who believed in many of the conspiracy theories and tales of persecution that were continually floating around Zimbabwe in those years, readily accepted this explanation. She knew that the corrupt government of Zimbabwe was capable of such human rights abuses and worse.

This is perhaps the great irony of a corrupt and draconian dictatorship such as those of Zimbabwe's Robert Mugabe and Iraq's Saddam Hussein. These heavy-handed leaders create

195

a unique problem for themselves through their horrible human rights records, documented corruption, and their own non-existent credibility. When the regime itself is frequently abusing the public trust and persecuting the innocent, when someone like Michael Swango comes along, who really is a threat to the public, and the corrupt dictatorship calls him out as such, the public trust in that government is so lacking that no one believes the truth!

This was the very sweet spot in which Swango found himself under Robert Mugabe's hated regime. What made the story even sweeter to Lynette's ears was the fact that famed human rights lawyer David Coltart was representing Swango as legal counsel. Lynette assumed that if a respected attorney like Coltart believed in Swango enough to represent him, then he must be telling the truth. Figuring that she now understood Swango's plight a little better, she asked Ian to give Swango a call, in the hope that a pep talk from his friend could raise his spirits.

This strategy seemed to have worked. Whatever Ian said to Swango broke him out of his funk, and he came out of his room the next day to join Lynette for breakfast and morning tea. He even apologized for his odd behavior over the last few days and assured her that everything would be alright. Now apparently without a care in the world, Swango sailed through the rest of the spring without incident.

Then, as spring turned to summer, Swango was gratified to meet a new love interest in the person of Joanna Daly, a lifelong resident of Zimbabwe and recent divorcee. The two were introduced by a mutual friend at a dinner in June of 1996. Swango and Joanna hit it off almost immediately and soon were spending all of their time together. Although Daly had three children to care for, it became routine for her to drop her kids off at school, pick up Swango at Lynette's estate, and then drop him back off before she showed up at the school again to bring her children home. This evolved into Swango staying over not just during school hours but at all hours of the day. But the longer Swango stayed, the more ill at ease they all became—literally!

As was all too common in the life of Michael Swango, the longer he was around Joanna and her children, the more illness-prone they became. First, her kids came down with what she thought was the flu or some other viral infection and were plagued with severe vomiting and diarrhea. Then, after one quiet night at home with Swango in which he offered her a simple cup of tea—a kind, caring action from anyone else, but deadly in Swango's book—Joanna too fell horribly ill, vomiting for hours before collapsing in bed and blacking out in exhaustion.

And Joanna's home wasn't the only one to be paid a visit by the poison fairy. From the accounts of Lynette O'Hare, it seems highly likely that she and her two maids were being poisoned as well. Lynette would spend the entire day vomiting sometimes, but she tried to pass it off as a particularly aggressive flu bug. Her maids, though, suspected that Swango was tampering with the food. In fact, they were fairly convinced that he was sneaking into their house, which was situated across from Lynette's main residence, and lacing certain foods with poison.

For example, on one occasion they had bought a brand-new jar of peanut butter. They had never opened the jar's seal. Yet one day they found the seal broken and the surface of the peanut butter looking like someone had pressed something down inside of it. (Such "tamper evident" seals exist to make sure no one has compromised our food and beverages, and this kind of incident just goes to show you why they're necessary!) The maids could clearly see that their peanut butter had been tampered with, so they threw it out lest they come down with some mystery illness from eating it. The women reported their findings to Lynette and were finally able to convince her that something was just not quite right about her house guest.

Soon after the peanut butter incident, the maids began to sleep inside the main house, right next to Lynette's room. This was partially out of their fear of Swango cornering them in their house, and partly out of a desire to protect Lynette by keeping an eye on her. During their nocturnal vigilance, they saw Swango get up in the middle of the night, walk down the hall, and stand in front of Lynette's open door. He just stood there, for no apparent reason. Upon seeing this, one of the maids started making noise, clearing her throat and humming, to let him know they were still awake and paying attention. As soon as Swango heard this, he ran back into his room.

The behavior was so odd that the maids began to seriously fear for their lives. They wondered if Swango was planning on murdering them all in their sleep, and there wasn't a night after this that at least one of them didn't stay awake and keep watch. Living with Swango was proving to be quite a tiresome business, and Lynette O'Hare eventually had enough of his odd and frequently menacing behavior. On August 7, 1996, she told him that he would have to go. She had cooked up an excuse that her son was coming to town and needed to stay in the room Swango was using.

Initially, she gave him two weeks' notice, but the following day she came home to him blasting music on her CD player and her entire house a wreck. She had had enough and ordered Swango to leave that very day, adding that she was going to change the locks and hire a security guard upon his departure. Swango marched out of Lynette's house and—so she hoped—out of her life for good.

But he didn't leave without a parting gift. The next day when Lynette tried to start her car, she discovered that the engine wouldn't even turn over; it would die as soon as she turned the key. She had to have the car towed to a mechanic, and his diagnosis provoked an immediate fury in her veins. A large amount of sugar had been deposited into the gas tank. Michael Swango had left his chemical calling card once again.

Skipping Bail and Skipping Town

After being kicked out of Lynette's house, Swango began to live with his girlfriend Joanna on a full-time basis. His days now consisted mostly of following the latest developments in his case with his lawyer Coltart and lazily lounging around Joanna's house. Then one afternoon his repose was interrupted by a startling phone call from the police. They wanted to interview him in person.

Knowing that they wouldn't take no for an answer, Swango agreed to come in on August 29th. But even as he was setting the date, Swango had no intention of showing up. Under the pretense of wanting to go on a hiking trip to "get away from it all," Swango had Joanna drop him off at the Zimbabwean equivalent of a Greyhound bus station, a Blue Arrow terminal, on August 14th. He said he was going to the Nyanga National Park to walk in the mountainous and rugged terrain of this wilderness reserve in order to clear his mind before he faced the police.

August 29th came and went, and there was still no sign of Swango. Just a few weeks later, however, Swango resurfaced in Zambia with a job at the University Teaching Hospital in Lusaka, the country's capital. After about two months of uneventful employment, Zimbabwe sent out a bulletin notifying all of the countries in southwest Africa of the charges Swango was facing. Once the Zambians learned of Swango's background, they dropped him like a hot potato, officially firing him on November 19, 1996. Once again, he was forced to seek employment elsewhere.

Swango crossed over into neighboring Namibia. He was able to get some minor temporary work there, but he soon opted to head to South Africa, where he figured he would have more opportunity. Here he came into contact with a medical placement company and secured a position at a medical facility in Saudi Arabia. He was scheduled to begin work at the Royal Hospital in Dhahran in March of 1997. But first, he had to get there. With all of the charges he faced, flying was a much more dangerous proposition than traveling over land.

To make matters infinitely more difficult, the Saudi government had a policy that all visas had to be issued in a visitor's country of origin. This meant that Swango would have to go back to the United States and risk capture just to get his Saudi visa. Swango argued that it was ridiculous for him to fly all the way to the U.S. and then fly all the way back when South Africa was so much closer to Saudi Arabia. But the Saudi consulate refused to budge.

Was Michael Swango desperate, or just completely insane? Did he not realize that he would be captured upon setting foot in the United States? It's hard to know for sure what was going through his mind. Perhaps his back was against the wall with nowhere else to go, and he thought that just maybe he might get lucky. It was a gamble, it was a roll of the dice, and he went ahead and played the hand he'd been dealt, hoping that he would win big. But on June 27, 1997, as soon as Swango stepped off his plane at O'Hare International Airport in Chicago, he was detained by immigration officials and his passport was confiscated.

As soon as Swango was in custody, he caved. Threatened with extradition back to Zimbabwe, he agreed to plead guilty to the forgery charges that had long ago been leveled against him.

Swango put in a guilty plea on a charge of defrauding the government in March of 1998. Just a few months later, in July, he was found guilty and sentenced to three-and-a-half years in prison. But if Swango breathed a sigh of relief while he filled up on prison food and got caught up on the latest American soap operas, expecting to be released in just a few years' time, he was sadly mistaken.

Because while Swango was safely locked away, investigators were compiling enough evidence to put him away for a very long time for all of the other accusations against him. Documents were uncovered and bodies were dug up. After examining medical charts and chemical traces from deceased patients, authorities could prove that Swango had deliberately given his patients lethal doses of medication—and in some cases outright poison.

As a result of this mountain of accumulated evidence, on July 11, 2000, just as Swango was on the verge of finishing his three-and-a-half-year sentence for fraud, he was slapped with three counts of murder and several other lesser charges. He was indicted for all these new charges on July 17. At first, Swango followed the same course of action he had when he was charged with poisoning his coworkers in the 1980s: He pled Not Guilty.

But then prosecutors informed him of the stakes. Should the courts come back with guilty verdicts—and even Swango had to admit that the odds were leaning in that direction—he stood a good chance of getting a death sentence in New York and an even better one of being extradited back to Zimbabwe. It's unclear what Swango feared more—dying, or being extradited and imprisoned in a foreign country that had developed a virulent hatred for him—but he cracked under the pressure once again and agreed to plead guilty.

After everything was said and done, Swango was handed three life terms for the three charges of murder. Now in his late 60s, Swango is still locked away in a maximum-security prison in Florence, Colorado. Since his incarceration in 2000, the previously outspoken Swango has made a point of being silent, refusing all requests for interviews or any other inquiry into his life behind bars.

***

Even though he pled guilty to his crimes—or at least the crimes that resulted in indictments—in the world of Michael Swango this is a mere technicality in the chess game that he has always played with the world. Even though he entered a guilty plea, his victims will most likely never get a heartfelt confession of guilt from him. Swango continues to present himself as a victim of unjust persecution and seems determined to continue doing so until the day he dies. It's hard for the rest of the world to understand the darkness that resides in the heart of someone like Swango. We can only hope that there aren't too many more of his disposition out there seeking residencies and doing round-the-clock rotations at our clinics and hospitals.

The Scorecard Killer
Randy Steven Kraft

Randy Steven Kraft, a Southern California man who appeared to be a normal computer programmer, spent his evenings seeking hitchhikers and unsuspecting bar hoppers for sadistic thrills that only he enjoyed. He is Southern California's most prolific serial killer, and possibly the most prolific serial killer in the modern United States. His 'kill list' also known as the scorecard has a total of sixty-five murders on it, but some claim he may have murdered as many as one hundred people – or even more.

His killings began in the early 1970s and continued until he was arrested in 1983. All of his victims were male, most were homosexuals, and all were tortured, mutilated, and sexually assaulted while they were still alive. Some psychologists believe that Kraft was not himself homosexual, but was rather seriously confused about his sexual identity and who he was. Others believe that the physical and sexual abuse he experienced as a youth is what turned him into a killer.

No matter what the reasons may be, Randy Kraft killed many innocent men, and he's currently paying for his heinous crimes on death row in California's San Quentin State Prison.

Unlike most serial killers, especially those on death row, he denies having participated in the deaths of any of his victims. He has denied many requests for interviews, and seems to be trying to keep the spotlight off himself as much as possible. He has never offered an explanation for his killings, nor has he shown any interest in helping investigators clear up any of the unsolved murders on his kill list.

As a result of his stubbornness, the authorities may never know how many men Kraft actually killed. However, considering his many business trips, it's suspected the death toll could be in at least the seventies.

How the Scorecard Killer Operated

December 31, 1975. Three young men were looking for somewhere to get cheap drinks and have a good time. They had been paid at two that afternoon, and after cashing their checks, had promptly headed to a local dive they frequented often. From there they wandered to another bar because they wanted something a little stronger than beer and wine. Mark Hall was one of these three musketeers.

At a place where a shot of bourbon or gin cost the same as a beer, one of their coworkers invited them to a New Year's Eve bash he was having. It was dark by the time they left the bar and rode to the party in the back of a convertible. When they arrived, they continued their drinking binge. They mingled, drank, and drifted away from one another as they started talking with other people.

However, it became clear these three young men weren't going to find what they were really looking for that New Year's Eve, which was pretty much what every unattached young male was looking for – women. Hope was at hand, though. A flyer one of them had picked up at the payroll office promised loads of women at a party in San Juan Capistrano.

By the time they headed down to the other party, it was getting close to midnight. The two of them who survived that night couldn't remember how they got to the final party because they were terribly drunk by this time. Unfortunately, by the time they arrived, the party had been reduced to a few men who were playing poker with each other, which wasn't what the three were looking for. Two out of the three decided to make the best of it and play poker, while Hall decided it wasn't the scene for him.

Hall's friend helped him limp to the living room, where he curled up on one of the sofas to sleep it off. Around midnight, the friend who had helped Hall to the sofa went to the kitchen to find some pots and pans to bang together, an old time New Year's tradition. He went to the living room to wake Mark Hall, but he wasn't there.

They searched the house and the front lawn, but they couldn't find him. They did, however, find that they were missing some cash. Two hundred dollars short and a little sour over the theft, they gave up on looking for their friend and went back to playing poker. They waited until dawn for him to return, but he never did, and he never would.

***

On the same night Mark Hall went missing, Randy Steven Kraft was celebrating New Year's Eve with his family. It had recently been divulged that Randy was gay, so no one was particularly comfortable with him at the party. In fact, it wasn't being held at his place due to this new revelation. He and his roommate seemed normal enough, but there was no need for the family to have to wonder what was happening behind closed doors. Harold Kraft, Randy's father, was still coming to terms with his only son's homosexuality, and his mother – a leader at a local Presbyterian church – was trying to deny it completely.

Randy worked as a computer operator at the time. He ran payroll programs for a business in Orange County and Long Beach and made a mere four dollars an hour. However, there was a huge need for overtime, so it wasn't a shock when he told his sister he'd be a little late to the New Year's Eve party.

He was attempting to get his life back together after having been discharged from the Air Force in 1969. After thirteen years as an aircraft painter, he'd confessed to his superiors that he was a homosexual. It had been a shock for his entire family.

It was difficult finding work at the time. He went through a number of jobs – truck driver, bartender, dispatcher, and teacher's aide. He'd been hoping to follow in his sister's footsteps and become an elementary school teacher, but that didn't work out for him. Finally, he got into computers. Not only was he good at it, but he also loved it.

Taking some night classes at Long Beach State University, Randy mastered the basics quickly. It wasn't unusual for him to work all night on a computer problem. He took his job very seriously and his work ethic gained him the trust of his employers. In fact, after only a few weeks of working at Aztec Aircraft, he was given a key that allowed him to access the building whenever he needed. He was usually the first one to arrive and the last one to leave.

That being the case, no one was surprised that Randy didn't arrive at his family's party until almost ten that evening.

Thirty years old, he was the youngest of four children. He was a neat, clean man with a tight smile and a short mustache. Since he'd settled comfortably into his new lifestyle, there was a relaxed aura about him. He spent a lot of time at the beach, so he was nicely tanned. He didn't look anything like the stereotypical gay man of the time.

He was a hit with his nieces and nephews because, unlike the other adults, he tended to listen to them. When he showed up at the party that evening, he appeared exhausted, but he joined in with the conversations, card games, and feasting like everyone else.

As midnight came around, a bottle of champagne was opened. Some of the Kraft family drank to excess, but Randy wasn't one of them. It was a shock when he took up a glass to toast with everyone else at midnight.

Half an hour after midnight, he left the family's party. At eight the following morning, his sister noticed him sleeping on their parents' couch. He lived about twenty miles away in an affluent neighborhood in Long Beach, but he still had a key to the family home and would let himself in and out whenever he was close by.

His sister noted that he wore the same clothes he'd worn the night before. He was just as neat and tidy as he'd been the night before, curled up on the sofa in a deep sleep. His sister and her daughter snuck to the sofa and turned on the television with the volume low to watch the Tournament of Roses.

Randy didn't wake up right away, but he was awake and ready to play more games by noon. He stayed until the late afternoon before he finally left.

Four off-duty police officers were riding dune buggies close to a ranger station in the Cleveland National Forest when they came across a body.

On Saturday, January 3, 1976, at four in the afternoon, a nude man was discovered in heavy brush on the west side of Bedford Peak, the east end of Santiago Canyon, in the Saddleback Mountains. The location was about thirty miles south of San Juan Capistrano.

The killer had wrapped the body's legs around a small tree and left it slumped against the tree in the fetal position. The victim had long brown hair, a thin mustache, stood five-foot-ten, and weighed around 165 pounds.

The man had died from alcohol and asphyxiation, according to the pathologist. At the time of death, which was somewhere in the early hours of New Year's Day, the body had the equivalent of five six-packs in the bloodstream. That equates to a blood alcohol level of .67, which is seven times the legal definition of intoxication in California. The level in his brain was just a bit less at .59, and there were traces of Valium or diazepam in his system.

If the alcohol had not killed him, the loam and leaves that were packed into his throat had. An autopsy revealed that the soil had been shoved so far down his throat that it reached his lungs. The man had choked to death on dirt.

Before the victim had died, his killer had tortured him. The man had been tied up with his hands and feet bound together, and he'd been stripped of all clothing. A cigarette lighter had been used to burn him on various parts of his body, including his eyes, scrotum, nose, cheeks, and upper lip. A knife had been used to carve grooves in his skin, and some of the cuts went almost to the bone. He'd also been sodomized, and a swizzle stick had been lodged in his urethra all the way to his bladder.

As if that wasn't enough, his genitals had been cut from his body and placed in his anus. More leaves and burned material were also discovered in his rectum. Based on the way the blood had dried, medical examiners came to the conclusion that the man had been alive through most of the torture.

***

Later that week, there was a knock at the front door of Mark Hall's friend's apartment. Both friends who had been out with him that night were currently inside, arguing about the disappearance of the two hundred dollars and Hall himself. Their questions as to where Hall had gone were about to be answered. Two Orange County Sheriff's homicide investigators were standing outside the apartment to question the two friends about the night Hall disappeared.

***

LAPD Sergeant John St. John stood on the steep sides of Santiago Canyon. Mark Hall's remains had long since been shipped back to his family's home state. However, he hadn't been the first one to die in the vicinity. He was somewhere between number thirty and forty, according to Sergeant St. John. Police officers across Southern California had lost count of the number of bodies as they tried to keep each other informed about the latest murder victims discovered. St. John had been picked to head an interagency task force investigating the unsolved murders plaguing this part of the state.

Some of the bodies were discovered off coastal canyons, such as the one Mark Hall had been found in. Most of them were dumped in the desert outside Palm Springs. A few of them popped up in a fisherman's net or were discovered in the surf. The newspaper would print a few paragraphs about them when they were first discovered, but no one seemed to put the dots together and see that there was a regularity to the body count.

The victims didn't have much more in common than the fact that they were all young men. Some of them, like Mark Hall, were party animals with long hair. Then there were the Marines, married men, known homosexuals, and kids still in high school. Some had been shot, strangled, or beaten to death, and some of them had been tortured before they'd been killed. Most had been sodomized, a few hadn't. Some were drugged, some weren't. Some were known to hitchhike, while others were known to be terrified of the prospect.

The entire investigation was wearing on St. John.

He'd driven to Bedford Peak and scoured the same trail the crime lab crew had walked three weeks prior. Three other task force members were with him – his partner, an officer from the Orange County DA's office, and a sergeant from Seal Beach. Half a dozen bodies had been dumped in the area, and the obvious evidence had already been collected. However, St. John and his crew insisted on going down into the canyon to take a look for themselves.

They looked for anything that might provide them with a clue. A bit of fabric or a bit of paper, something that might point them in the right direction. The man they were looking for had been playing a cat and mouse game with them for the past six years.

They found some of Mark Hall's skin where he'd been dragged over the terrain to his final destination. There was also an empty packet of cigarettes, but nothing else at the scene. The killer was careful to leave nothing behind that would point to who he was.

The only other item they found was a shattered bottle of vodka. There was a fingerprint on the bottle that wasn't Mark Hall's, and there was a fingerprint on a piece of glass nearby that also wasn't Mark Hall's. One of the prints was a partial, and once they were readable by a computer, the databases revealed that they didn't belong to anyone who had been booked before.

However, it was something. On June 28, 1976, the prints were entered into the task force logbook to be filed away with all the other evidence they couldn't match to someone yet. But someday, they might help to figure out who Mark Hall's killer was.

The Crimes Begin

Thirteen-year-old Joey Fancher didn't like school, and he didn't like home. His only salvation was his bicycle, which he would get on and ride away from whatever was bothering him. He'd run away from home on multiple occasions, and he grabbed another opportunity to flee in March of 1970. He went to an area commonly referred to as the Boardwalk.

He rode his bike up and down the street a few times before he noticed a man staring at him. To him, the man appeared tall and cool. He had sandy hair, a mustache, and an urbane appearance.

Joey was feeling smug because he'd run away from home and no one could tell him what to do. He asked the man for a cigarette, and the man gave him one. As he spoke to the stranger, he told him about how he'd run away from home, and the reasons why.

The stranger asked Joey if he needed somewhere to stay, and Joey responded with a quick yes. Then the stranger asked him an odd question. Had he ever slept with a woman before? Joey told the man he hadn't, and the man told him he knew just the woman and the apartment where Joey could get a place to stay and a lay.

While they rode up the highway on the man's motorcycle, Joey sat behind the stranger and held tight to his waist. It was a short ride from the Boardwalk to the trendy beaches of Belmont Shore, where young college graduates occupied upscale studio apartments.

The man pulled up to a corner apartment building and led Joey inside. He asked Joey if he'd smoked dope before, and Joey responded with a yes. They shared a joint, and Joey complained he wasn't feeling well. The man disappeared for a moment, saying he had something that would make Joey feel better. When he returned, he gave Joey four red pills that Joey obediently took. A bit later he said he still felt the same, and the man gave him four more.

Joey felt drowsy and out of it, and was unable to move his limbs. That's when his nightmare began. The stranger repeatedly raped him, telling him he would kill him if he moved or made a noise. Then he left the apartment.

What seemed like a lifetime later, two people knocked on the door and asked where Randy was. Joey told them he didn't know, and then he went back inside. He pulled on the rest of his clothes and stumbled down to the sidewalk outside of the apartment, where he sobbed until someone noticed him. He remembered he was helped across the street and was almost hit by a car. He walked to the neighborhood bar, where someone called an ambulance, and then he waited on the bus bench out front.

Joey's stomach was pumped at the hospital. The doctor informed him that if he had taken two more of the red pills, he would have died. He'd been lucky, but he didn't feel so lucky.

When the police showed up, they took him back to the apartment, and one of them interviewed him while the other searched the premises. They found prescription medications that were under a woman's name, as well as other medications that were obviously not for a woman. There was a pamphlet for a gay bar on the coffee table beside the wine glass Joey had used to wash down the pills. There were some snapshots that depicted men and women in various sexual positions. Randy was featured in most of the photos.

Unfortunately, the officers didn't have much. Joey didn't tell them he'd been sexually assaulted, so they had a story of a kid who went to an apartment voluntarily, took prescription medications and drank voluntarily – and the kid had a history of trouble. To make it worse, the police had gone into the apartment without a warrant, so it was almost impossible for them to charge Randy with anything.

When they went back to the station, they filed their reports, and for the following thirteen years, Joey's story was buried.

***

Ortega Highway is a two-lane road that goes from San Juan Capistrano over the Santa Ana Mountains into Riverside County. It was so remote and wild in the sixties and seventies that motorists would sometimes be discovered stiff and lifeless days after having had heart attacks while driving it.

On October 5, 1971, the naked, decomposed body of a man was discovered at the bottom of a ravine off Ortega Highway.

The coroner put the day the man died at around September 20th, but two weeks of decomposition made his exact cause of death difficult to determine. If there had been marks that indicated foul play, the elements had gotten rid of them.

The coroner's report listed 'other conditions' as the cause of death, but his blood alcohol level was 0.36. For the death certificate, the coroner wrote 'alcohol poisoning' as the cause of death.

The police knew they had a body dump almost right away. The easiest way to turn someone into a John Doe was to remove the clothes and all other personal items from the body and toss them out of the car a long way away. Despite this, it didn't take long for the police to identify the body.

Wayne Dukette had not been to his Long Beach apartment for more than two weeks. The thirty-year-old had not been reported missing, but his vehicle was discovered still parked next to the beach bar where he'd last been spotted, and where he worked nights.

Investigators very much doubted that Wayne had left his car behind, stripped naked, and fallen off a mountain highway on his own, no matter how drunk he was. They began an investigation, but there were no leads. They had no evidence of foul play, no witnesses, and no evidence near the body. However, when detectives questioned friends and coworkers, they quickly determined that Wayne Dukette had been a homosexual.

They theorized that his vehicle might have broken down the night he disappeared, or maybe he'd been so intoxicated that he decided he needed someone else to drive him home. His apartment was five miles away from the bar, so walking didn't seem a likely option.

Unfortunately, the trail was two weeks cold by the time his body was discovered, so the odds of finding the person who had removed Wayne's clothing and left him in the ravine were slim to none. On October 8th, he was buried in the Pacific View Memorial Park in Newport Beach without ceremony.

Connecting the Murders

Between 1972 and 1975, there were eleven homicides in the general vicinity of Seal Beach, Long Beach, Irvine, Salton Sea, San Bernardino, and L.A.'s Harbor District. The media had not caught on to the similarities among these killings – a good thing, as the half-dozen police departments handling the cases were not ready for questions from reporters yet. However, the task force wasn't making a lot of progress either, which was bad news.

The FBI began to get involved at this point, sending along some forensic psychologists to Orange County to talk to local law enforcement about possible suspect profiles.

The first body on the victim list was Edward Daniel Moore of Seal Beach. Police had investigated a few friends of his, but to no avail. No evidence or motive could link any of them to his murder, which had occurred on December 23, 1972. Dozens of other leads had been followed in a desperate attempt to figure out who had killed Eddie Moore, and officers thought they were close a few times, but they never found a suspect.

Body dumps of nude young men, maimed and raped, were generally traced back to a lover whose anger and/or ecstasy had gotten out of control. The results were usually ghastly. Eddie Moore's case was no different. He'd been found with a stocking stuffed into his anal cavity and had suffered bite marks around his genital area.

But if it had been a lover who had killed Moore, the investigators couldn't find him. It wasn't long after Moore's body was discovered that corpses began turning up regularly along the roadside. Three unidentified bodies were found dead in Huntington Beach, Wilmington, and Long Beach within six months of Eddie Moore's murder.

***

Randy moved on from his bartending career, and his relationship with his lover, Jeff Graves, started to sour. They had an open relationship, but that was beginning to take its toll on Randy. When Jeff went out with other men, Randy would go driving. And that's when the bodies began to pile up.

Around eleven thirty in the morning on February 6, 1973, the naked body of a John Doe was found next to the Terminal Island Freeway in L.A. He was of average height, thin, bearded, and lying face up in a ditch.

His only clothing was a brown sock that had been jammed into his anus, and the only mark on his body was a maroon ligature ring around his neck. Detectives made a note that the mark was probably the result of being garroted with piano wire.

The John Doe was around eighteen and had been dead between twenty-four and forty-eight hours. Sketches of his face were made, distributed, and printed in the local newspaper. No one came up with a name, but a few people said they had seen him soliciting tricks along the Belmont Shore bluffs.

Fingerprints and the missing persons database came up with nothing either. He was given a name – John Doe 16. Unfortunately, he would never have a different one.

Two months after John Doe 16 was found, at 1:30 in the morning on Easter Sunday, a passing driver reported another body lying in the road on Ellis. Unlike John Doe 16, the body they found was dressed and wore socks on its feet. There were no shoes, though. The man was around eighteen, with long brown hair that came down to his shoulders. He had a tattoo of a cross on his arm. He also had tattoos of a spider, a swastika, and the number 13 tattooed in black on his arms and shoulders.

Judging from the scratches on his body, he'd been tossed from a moving vehicle. The cord marks on his wrists indicated he'd been tied up for the last hour or so of his existence. When the police arrived, the first thing they discovered was a dark red stain on the seat of his pants. The autopsy revealed that his genitals had been cut off around fifteen minutes before he died, and he'd been sodomized. The medical examiner was not certain of the cause of death. His lips were purple and puffy, which indicated suffocation, but the loss of blood could have killed him, too.

He had nothing on him to identify him – no wallet, key chain, or driver's license. His clothes looked like a gas station attendant's, and a flyer went out to the gay community in the area a few weeks later. Police only received a few responses. People had seen him in the amusement park where carnies, hustlers, and petty thieves hung out. However, no one knew who he was. He was given a name – John Doe Huntington Beach.

John Doe 52 met a much worse fate. He may have met it on Easter Sunday, too, but the coroner couldn't be sure. His body was carved up and deposited all around Southern California. His head was discovered in Long Beach, his arms, right leg, and torso in San Pedro, and his left leg behind a bar in Sunset Beach.

By the time most of his body was assembled on the morgue table, two weeks after the discovery of John Doe Huntington Beach, the body parts were so decomposed that it wasn't possible to tell whether he'd been taking drugs or drinking before he died, or where he'd spent his final moments.

The medical examiner could say that he'd been tied up like the others. His eyelids had been removed, he'd been castrated, and he'd been stored in a refrigerator for a while.

His hands were never found.

***

What started off as a permanent and friendly relationship between Randy Kraft and Jeff Graves turned strained as the years went on. Their arguments and their temporary splits became more and more frequent, and Jeff would answer Randy's rages by doing more of what made him upset to begin with, which was finding one-night stands. When he would leave for a night or weekend, Randy would go out driving. He would boast about finding marines in the bars who wanted to come home with him.

Despite the romantic issues Randy had with Jeff, the other areas of his life were going well. He quit his forklift job in 1973 and, with the encouragement of his sister, tried to get a job as a teacher's aide. For some time, Jeff and Randy had teacher positions in common. But around the same time, Randy started dabbling in the computer field.

He found a part-time job as a dispatcher at Aztec Aircraft and worked there for two years. He switched from the phones to the office computers, where he taught himself how to handle scheduling, payroll, and data-processing tasks.

Randy had finally found what he was looking for – computers. His identity crisis after quitting the military seemed to be fading, and he was finally going down a good path in life. He had a real chance at a good career in the data processing industry. He had a steady relationship with an intelligent young man, and he was a positive fixture in the growing gay community in Long Beach.

***

Then along came the body of Ronnie Wiebe, the victim who dispelled the theory that all the other men had been killed by jealous gay lovers. Wiebe was a twenty-year-old from Fullerton, and his body was found in almost the same Seal Beach location where Eddie Moore had been discovered six months prior.

On July 30, 1973, at around 6:20 in the morning, officers were called to the eastbound 405 on-ramp at Seventh Street in regard to a body lying in the ice plant. The victim was dressed, except for his shoes and a sock, which was later found stuffed into his anal cavity. His pants were unbuttoned but zipped, and his penis had been partially exposed. There were ligature marks around his neck, as well as facial trauma. No valuables or identification were found on the body. The coroner determined that Ronnie had been dead for two days, and that he'd been dumped from a moving vehicle. There were teeth marks on Ronnie's genitals and stomach, and he'd been tied to the rafters. The settling blood and the stretch marks on his ankles and wrists showed he'd been suspended from the rafters while his head and chest had hung down.

It also looked like the murder had more than one suspect. It was possible that one man could have carried the 135-pound corpse over his shoulder from an idling car to the ice plant, but it wasn't likely, as corpses are hard to maneuver alone. It was more likely that someone else was involved, too. Most probably, one man had carried the feet and another had grasped Wiebe beneath the arms.

Perhaps the most troubling aspect was that Wiebe was married. He was separated and living with his father, but he was seeing another woman. He was definitely not a homosexual. That took the investigation out of the realm of homosexual men killing other homosexual men. That meant kids who were hitchhiking to the beach, soldiers who were off on the weekends, and young husbands fixing a flat tire alongside the road were all vulnerable to these killers.

The last time someone had seen Wiebe was on Saturday, July 28th, at closing time at the Sportsman Bar in Los Alamitos. It had been a quarter to two when he'd wandered out the door, waving goodbye to everyone before he left. He'd owned a car, but it had a flat tire. When his sister became worried and went looking for him the following day, she found the car still parked at the bar.

The following morning, he turned up dead in the freeway ice plant.

After Ronnie Wiebe, the list continued to grow substantially.

On December 29, 1973, hikers discovered twenty-three-year-old Vincent Cruz Mestas's body at the bottom of a ravine in San Bernardino. Mestas was completely clothed except for his shoes and a single sock that was later found in his rectum like other victims. Someone had shaved his head and face after he was dead, and cut off both of his hands. The killer had wrapped his bloody stubs in plastic sandwich bags. The hands were never recovered. A toothpick or small stick had been jammed into his urethra before he'd died.

It was known that Mestas was bisexual. He had a male roommate, and he had been caught a few times trying to hustle sex at the Belmont Shore bluff. A few days before his body was discovered, he'd told his roommate he was going to the mountains to do a little drawing. He took some drawing pencils and a sketchpad and left. He never returned.

On June 2, 1974, the naked body of Malcolm Eugene Little, who'd just turned twenty, was discovered propped against a mesquite tree on Highway 86. His legs had been spread wide, and his genitals were missing. A branch from a nearby tree had been forced half a foot up his rectum.

He'd been an out-of-work truck driver from Alabama, who'd just arrived by Greyhound the previous week for a visit with his brother. No sooner had he arrived than his girlfriend called from home, complaining about how he'd left her behind. Malcolm explained that he'd only had ten dollars and no return bus ticket, but she was not mollified.

The following morning, his brother dropped him off at Garden Grove and Santa Ana freeway so he could hitchhike back to Alabama. He had on a purple shirt and pants, an army field jacket, and Western boots. The last time his brother saw him, he'd had his right thumb pointing east and a green suitcase beside him.

On June 22, 1974, the naked body of an eighteen-year-old Marine was found off a dead-end Laguna Beach street near a golf course. Roger E. Dickerson's penis and left nipple showed signs of having been chewed, and he had also been sodomized and strangled.

The previous night, he'd been drinking at Bud's Cove Bar with a few friends from Camp Pendleton. He told them he'd found someone who was going to drive him to Los Angeles for the weekend, but left without telling anyone who that someone was.

The autopsy showed there was a good amount of alcohol in his system, but there was something even more interesting. There was Valium in his system, too.

On August 3, 1974, the morning shift employees at a Long Beach harbor oilfield found the fully clothed body of Thomas Paxton Lee halfway down a nine-foot embankment. Thomas was a twenty-five-year-old waiter at the Princess Louise restaurant. His blood alcohol level showed he'd drunk more than a six-pack of beer the previous night, but that wasn't what had killed him. Manual strangulation had.

He was a regular at gay bars in Long Beach, and he was a well-known solicitor of one-night stands. The last time his roommate had seen him alive was closing time at the Diamond Horseshoe on Friday, August 2nd. The following day, he was dead.

On August 12, 1974, the sockless, shoeless body of Gary Wayne Cordova was discovered off an embankment in Orange County. He was twenty-three, and had just moved out of his house in Pasadena and told friends he was going to hitchhike to Oceanside. His cause of death was acute intoxication and an overdose of diazepam.

On November 29, 1974, shortly after four in the afternoon, the Irvine police received a report of a partially nude body near the San Diego Freeway. Except for a white, blood-soaked T-shirt, nineteen-year-old James Dale Reeves was naked, face down between two trees twenty feet off the southern edge of the road. His white Levis, stained at the crotch, were in a heap at the base of one of the trees.

His legs had been spread apart, making a Y, and a four-foot tree branch had been lodged in his rectum.

Reeves, who had still been living with his parents in Long Beach, had taken the family car for a joyride on November 27, Thanksgiving. He drove to a newly formed gay community church where he shared Thanksgiving dinner with the members. He then wound up in a bar called Ripples, where the family car was later discovered abandoned.

A seventeen-year-old high school kid from Long Beach was discovered floating in the surf off Sunset Beach on January 3, 1975, with a wooden surveyor's stake in his rectum. John Leras had alcohol in his system and had been tied up and strangled to death. His body had been dragged through the sand and dumped in the ocean. Two sets of footprints indicated that two people had dragged the body.

John had last been seen alive a day earlier, boarding a bus for the Long Beach skating rink with some roller skates he'd received as a Christmas present slung over his shoulder.

Ten minutes away by car from where Leras was found, another body was discovered two weeks later. On January 17, 1975, construction workers found Craig Victor Jonaites in a vacant lot near the Golden Sails Hotel. Except for his missing shoes and socks, the twenty-one-year-old was completely clothed. In fact, he was wearing two pairs of pants rather than one. The red ring around his neck and blackened tongue protruding from his mouth gave evidence of how he died. A string pulled tight around his trachea had cut off his air supply long enough to strangle him to death.

A police officer wrote up his report on the victims and the similarities among their murders. All of them were men between the ages of seventeen and twenty-five, and they were all Caucasian. All but three of the victims were homosexuals, and with the exception of the one found in Bernardino, all the bodies had been left in locations where they were easily discovered by passing drivers or the police. Four of the victims had socks inserted into their rectums, and two of them were found with tissue plugging their noses.

The investigators believed the stocking-and-tissue technique was intended to keep the victims from purging while they were kept in a room or as they were being transported before they were dumped. Investigators also believed there were two or more perpetrators, because it would have been difficult for one person to have dumped the bodies.

But that was all they had to go on.

Being Investigated

In May 1975, on a Thursday afternoon, three teenagers climbing over the rocks of Bell Gardens discovered something wedged among them. Weeks of decomposition in the salt water and sun had reduced the object to something less than human, but upon closer inspection, the boys discovered it was a skull with rotting strips of flesh still attached. Though the police scoured the surrounding area, they were unable to find a body to go with the head.

Two days later, an x-ray technician was able to identify the body of Keith Crotwell.

Crotwell's friends wasted no time in pointing the finger at a local bar, Ripples, where Crotwell had last been seen. While the homicide detectives opened up their investigation, Crotwell's friends started a block by block search of the area for the black-and-white Mustang they'd seen Crotwell leave in. Five days later, they discovered a vehicle matching that description parked in front of an apartment less than five miles from Ripples.

The following week, the DMV ran the plates for the registered owner and came up with Randy Steven Kraft. The registration gave an address from which Kraft had moved a few months prior, so an investigator quizzed a few mail carriers in the area about the name. One recognized it and directed the officer to Kraft's current address.

Officer Woodward went to ask Randy Kraft about his whereabouts the night Crotwell went missing. When the investigator knocked on the apartment door, Kraft invited him inside. Woodward initially thought that the suspect looked like an average Joe with a mustache, but quickly realized he was a homosexual. His roommate was male, there was a gay magazine on the coffee table, and there was a poster of a gay man on the living room wall.

Randy was gay, but so were half the residents of Belmont Shore in 1975. At this point in time he was a dispatcher and a part-time computer operator, running the accounts receivable programs and payroll at Aztec Aircraft.

When Woodward asked Randy about the evening of March 29 that year, when Crotwell had gone missing, Kraft denied ever meeting Crotwell. The investigator didn't believe Randy was telling the truth, but he wasn't ready to suspect Randy of murder, either.

There was no evidence that Crotwell was gay, but the area around Ripples was well-known for being popular with homosexuals. A likely scenario began to come together for the investigator. The teenager drank too much, found himself propositioned by an older man, and opted for a quick liaison on the marina jetty. In the dark, the drunken boy fell to his death in the water and drowned. The older man panicked, fearing that his homosexuality would be discovered and reported, and so he walked away from the accident.

Woodward wasn't all that confident about his theory, though, so he asked Randy Kraft to come down to the station to do an interview. Kraft said he'd been sick recently and didn't feel up to it, but the officer insisted. Kraft still wouldn't come in immediately, so Woodward walked back to his patrol vehicle and radioed to headquarters to put Kraft under surveillance.

That afternoon, Randy told his roommate he was going to the Long Beach Police Station.

On May 19, 1975, at five in the afternoon, Randy sat down with Officer Woodward and his partner, Detective Bell. After introducing the two men, Woodward started to take notes. One of the first things he took note of was that Randy was less rattled than he'd been that morning, and he'd changed his story. Twenty-seven minutes later, the investigation was over.

There were still plenty of questions, but Randy, displaying a mild-mannered attitude and a confident manner, had offered the investigators a plausible explanation. They told him he was still under suspicion and took his photograph before he left. Woodward asked if it was okay if they also took pictures of Randy's vehicle. He balked at first, but then relented and took them out front to his Mustang.

As Bell snapped some pictures, Woodward took a look inside. On the floor were a plastic prescription vial, a half-smoked pack of cigarettes, and a bottle of Coricidin (a cold and flu medicine). When Kraft was asked about them, he said he'd been sick and that the over the counter and prescription medications were for the flu.

After Randy had left, the officers decided to check out the story he'd told them about his vehicle being stuck the night Keith Crotwell had disappeared. He'd spun a tale about how he'd been riding around with Keith in his car, and they were both drunk. Randy had let Keith drive, but Keith had never driven before and had gotten the vehicle stuck on an embankment. Keith had stayed with the vehicle while Randy went to get his partner, Jeff, to help get the vehicle unstuck. By the time Randy came back with Jeff, Keith had disappeared.

When they got the car unstuck, Keith was still nowhere in sight. The two went to a nearby restaurant to have breakfast and coffee.

About a mile from the freeway Randy had told the investigators he was on, they found a dirt road with ruts deep enough and soil soft enough that they were satisfied his vehicle might have been bogged down. They had already spoken with Jeff, who had corroborated Randy's story.

Still, the investigators thought something was off. How had Keith, a teenager, gotten from southern Orange County to Long Beach Marina in the middle of the night? Why was his head found floating in the ocean without any other body parts? Where was the rest of him?

The conclusion they were being asked to accept was that Keith Crotwell, a strong swimmer, had stumbled into the rocks and rendered himself unconscious. What became of his body was anyone's guess.

They thought there was enough to charge Kraft with killing Crotwell, so they asked for an arrest warrant the following week. However, they were told to drop the case. There was no body and no evidence, so there was no murder.

***

June of 1975 was a bad month for Randy Kraft. Jeff was called in for questioning and a lie detector test. He passed the test, but it didn't make Randy feel much better. The two detectives who'd interviewed him and Jeff didn't strike Randy as being satisfied with his version of the events of the night Keith disappeared. His headaches were coming back, and the indigestion and insomnia that had haunted him since college were acting up again. He took some tests to figure out the root of the issue, and it was discovered that he suffered from hypoglycemia.

To make matters worse, especially since he was a murder suspect and had to be careful with the police, he was charged with lewd conduct following an arrest near Belmont Shore.

The same month, his boss laid him off from the first job he'd had since college, which was also one that he genuinely enjoyed.

As Randy approached thirty, he wanted a more monogamous relationship, but Jeff Graves didn't. The Crotwell business seemed to have pushed Graves over the edge, and Randy, too.

For the final year they were together, Graves and Kraft were nothing but roommates. Jeff began talking to Randy about moving out, and he eventually did at the end of 1975.

Changing Partners

By the beginning of 1976, Randy Kraft was living with another man in an apartment in Laguna Hills.

The summer of 1975 had looked like it was going to be a drag for Randy Kraft. Then he was invited to a party where he met Jeff Seelig, a chubby baker from a well-off Jewish family in Long Beach. Randy was twenty-nine and Jeff was only nineteen, but he told Randy he was twenty-six. Randy was self-sufficient and not particularly ready to settle down again, but if he did, he wanted it to be with someone who was around his own age.

While Jeff said he was twenty-six, he appeared and acted even older. He took over Randy's kitchen, redecorated Randy's apartment, and cleaned up Randy's appearance. Randy relented and told himself that a three-year age difference didn't mean much when Jeff was so mature. Six months later, they were living together. Then, while the two were at a party together, Jeff found himself surrounded by several teenage girls who claimed they had graduated from high school with him the previous June.

The next day, Randy learned that Jeff was only nineteen, and they had the first of the many fights that would characterize the following eight years of their relationship.

When Jeff wasn't cooking at work, he was cooking for Randy. In many respects, he behaved as if he were a traditional working wife. Randy's friends later noted that, under the surface, Jeff was actually very immature about a lot of subjects. After all, he was still a teenager, and they were in their thirties.

Jeff's feelings were easily hurt, and he was naive about things such as politics, culture, sex, and music. Randy was the quiet, strong, wise one in the relationship, while Jeff often flew off the handle and flitted around.

Among other things, Randy instructed Jeff on how to troll the freeway for a threesome, according to court records. Randy was Jeff's mentor in the homosexual world.

For some reason, no bodies were discovered through the spring and summer of 1976. By the end of the year, they began turning up again.

***

Mark Howard Hall was murdered on New Year's Eve, and two more bodies were discovered along Ortega Highway before the year was over – a John Doe discovered on August 22, 1976, and Mark Andrew Orach, twenty, discovered shot and dumped on the same stretch of road on October 6, 1976. Larry Gene Walters died on Halloween in Los Angeles County.

Police began another investigation into the possibility that the same person was committing these murders. Only two things had changed – the victims were becoming younger, and the killer had switched from a steel wire to bullets.

Oliver Peter Molitor was thirteen when he was discovered on Manhattan Beach on March 21, 1976. Kenneth Eugene Buchanan was seventeen when he was found in Inglewood on April 7th. Larry Armendariz was fourteen when he was found in Los Angeles on April 19th. Michael Craig McGhee was thirteen when he was found at Redondo Beach on June 11th.

On August 28th, Wilford Lawrence Faherty's body was discovered on Redondo Beach. He was twenty when he was shot to death.

The bodies were still dumped by the side of the road, but the killers were becoming a bit tidier about it. Rather than tossing the bodies from a vehicle, they were stuffing them into plastic trash bags and leaving them in the desert or in a dumpster. A nineteen-year-old youth turned up in a sack a few miles south of Borrego Hot Springs in September. A month later, Randall Lawrence Moore, sixteen, was found bagged and dropped on Highway 80. A few more bodies were dumped right at the Mexican border.

Sometimes it wasn't until the trash truck came along to empty the dumpster that the bodies were discovered. There's no telling how many runaway children were buried at the bottom of a landfill that year.

At first it looked like the killers were only targeting homosexuals again, but then they grew bolder and began picking up young kids and straight servicemen. None of them had been young enough – or affluent enough – to catch the press's attention, but it was just a matter of time. There were already some reporters looking around, wanting to know how many unsolved homicides had occurred in Southern California in the previous year or two.

David Allen, a twenty-seven-year-old Camp Pendleton Marine, was found on October 9th off a remote road in the Fallbrook area. He too had been shot to death.

***

Paul Fuchs sat down to Sunday dinner with his family on December 10, 1976. He finished his meal quickly and ran out the front door to get a ride with a few friends. He left so fast he forgot his wallet.

He was nineteen, parked cars for money, and planned to be an artist. His parents reported him missing the following week. His mother, Elizabeth, doted on her youngest son, and she told police he would never have left without telling her where he was going. When he left for even a few minutes, he would leave a note saying where he would be and when he would come back.

The desk sergeant was sympathetic to the couple's concerns, but he was firm. Fuchs was listed as a runaway. If something else came up that suggested foul play, then his designation would change. Otherwise, they could assume that he'd run off and joined the Navy or something of the sort.

They checked crew lists for his name for years. Elizabeth would weep daily for her son. Her husband tried to console her, but there was nothing to be done. Their son had left and never come back.

Paul was a drinker. A few weeks before disappearing, he'd been to a bar in San Pedro and had been cited with a misdemeanor for drunkenness. His mother went to court in the hope he'd show up for his scheduled appearance. But he never did.

His parents went through the names in his address book. None of his friends knew where he'd gone the day he vanished. No one knew whose car had stopped outside of their home to pick him up. They checked the bank. There hadn't been any withdrawals from his account.

The police believed that his parents most likely knew, but found it difficult to accept, that their son was homosexual. He'd last been seen at Ripples, a local gay bar in Belmont Shore, but when police showed up there to ask questions, no one had any idea what had become of him.

***

On July 1, 1977, an unlikely pair of murder suspects went to the Riverside County Sheriff's Office and pointed to a wanted poster, saying that they were on it. Thirty-seven-year-old Patrick Kearney looked like he sold life insurance for a living, and his thirty-four-year-old roommate and lover, David Hill, was a tall, well-built high school dropout from Lubbock, Texas. He'd been married for a time, and then he'd joined the Army before he met Kearney and moved with him to California in 1962.

It turned out that Hill knew nothing of his lover's murderous tendencies. Kearney, though, led investigators to the many bodies he'd shot and buried. The police thought they were done with the freeway killings. The task forces assigned to these killings packed up and their members moved on to other things.

Then, on April 16, 1978, at around seven in the morning, the body of a man was discovered on the eastbound on-ramp of the 91 Freeway by an employee of the Martin Luther Hospital in Orange County on his way home from work.

The victim was later identified as Scott Michael Hughes. He'd been eighteen. When he was found, he was fully clothed, but the laces were missing from his shoes. Yellow fibers were discovered on his shirt and pants, and the investigators bagged them as evidence. There was blood on the crotch of his pants and ligature marks on his neck. The coroner put his time of death at around three that morning.

The autopsy revealed he'd been drinking, and he'd taken a dose of Valium before he'd died. The cause of death had been strangulation, but after his death, the killer had slit open his scrotum and removed his left testicle.

Hughes had been a U.S. Marine stationed at Camp Pendleton. He'd been known for drinking, smoking pot, and dropping LSD on occasion. He'd had girlfriends, and had occasionally been known to visit prostitutes.

The last time anyone had seen him alive was at the base barracks at around two in the afternoon the previous Friday. At the time of his death, Kearney had completed his seventh week in San Quentin.

***

At 3:30 in the morning of June 11, 1978, an off-duty Santa Ana fireman saw something in his headlights that was a bit too big to be a dead dog. Even by flashlight, it was obvious that the body had been dumped head first from a car moving very fast. There were cuts and scrapes all over the man. The Irvine police department recognized his shoes as being issued from the prison Roland Young had been in just a few hours before. He wore no belt or jewelry. A single shoelace was missing from his left shoe.

The seat of his pants was soaked in blood, and his right wrist had a red ligature ring. He'd been stabbed four times in the chest, and one of the wounds had pierced his heart.

Someone had given him Valium and beer, according to the toxicology screening, but he'd still been awake enough to feel the knife cut into his scrotum. Both of his testicles and the end of his penis had been removed. A woman who had lived nearby had heard screams that night, and she told the investigators two days later when she read about the body in her local newspaper. She believed that the screams had come from a passenger in a car or van that had gone past her house.

The same day Mrs. Young put her son in the ground, Richard Keith – a lance corporal at Camp Pendleton – hitchhiked to the Los Angeles suburbs to visit his girlfriend.

At eleven in the evening, he told his girlfriend he was hitchhiking back to the base. She let him kiss her goodnight and told him he'd better not hitchhike. But he said he was going to anyway, leaving her upset on the front porch. She walked back inside and slammed the door without looking back to see if he'd found a ride.

Seven hours later, Orange County detective Jim Sidebotham stood over Keith's body in the middle of a two-lane road off Moulton Parkway. Just like with the Young case the previous week, a fireman had been the one to find the body. This time, it had been an off-duty captain.

It was the undertaker who gave Sidebotham and his team the first real lead on the death of the twenty-year-old Marine. The undertaker said he'd been driving by where the body had been dumped at around five in the morning, and there had been a camper parked not too far from there. Unfortunately, that was the only description he could give them, and no one else remembered a camper.

There was a ninety-foot arc of blood and skin on the pavement where Keith's body had bounced and rolled to where it rested in the middle of the road. The body had been pushed out of a moving vehicle that was going at least fifty miles an hour. The investigators wondered how one person could have pushed the body out of the vehicle and still held onto the steering wheel.

The police wanted to believe the camper story. A body bouncing out the back of a camper made more sense than one being pushed out of a car. Everything else about Keith's murder was too familiar. He was naked, had no identification, was dumped from a moving vehicle, had ligature marks on his wrists and neck, and had been drinking and taking Valium. The lab also came back with a few new twists, though. He'd had an overdose of flurazepam, a drug used to

219

treat insomnia, too. In addition, salt water found in his throat indicated he'd been drowned in salt water before, or at the same time, he was stabbed.

***

Keith Klingbeil was a Navy brat whose family moved across the country while he grew up. He was no stranger to hitchhiking. He kissed his girlfriend goodbye before he left Everett, Washington, and hitchhiked as far as Sacramento before he disappeared. An officer had written him a citation for hitchhiking, and that was the last anyone saw of him.

Two days after Independence Day, Keith's body was found lying in a northbound lane of Interstate 5 six hundred miles south of Sacramento near Mission Viejo in Orange County. He was still alive, but he was quickly dying from an overdose of Tylenol and beer. It was 3:30 in the morning when the paramedics found him. There were enough signs of life to warrant a rush to the hospital, but by the time sheriff's deputies arrived, he'd succumbed to the overdose.

A matchbook from a Long Beach business was found in a pocket of his Levi's, and a ligature mark was around his neck. One lace was missing from his left hiking boot.

Just beneath the black skull and crossbones he'd etched on his chest himself was the sear mark of an automobile cigarette lighter.

***

An unprecedented number of task force members showed up at the 1978 year-end meeting about the freeway killer or killers. It was twelve days before Christmas.

Perhaps the most disturbing body they had found was Michael Inderbeiten, a twenty-one-year-old Long Beach truck driver who'd been dumped into morning rush-hour traffic and found on November 18th.

His hand and eyelids had been burnt with a cigarette lighter, and he'd been emasculated. His body had been dumped not twenty feet from where the Seal Beach Police found one of the first victims back in 1972 – Eddie Moore.

One of the task force members spoke about both investigative procedures and the escalating tactics on the part of their killer. He emphasized the need to share as much information as they could – leads, questionable homicides, suspects, and anything else that might trace back to another jurisdiction. He had a notebook of possible suspects, more than a dozen, along with mug shots and criminal histories. There would be more in the following months.

But at the end of the last meeting of the year, they were no closer to their answer than they had been at the first meeting.

Bodies Keep Piling Up

1979 was a record year for cadavers discovered on or near Southern California highways. The bodies of more than a dozen young men ranging from thirteen to twenty-four years old were found. They had been tossed from moving cars like they were trash.

Thomas Lundgren was picked up before eleven in the morning on May 28th in Reseda and discovered two and a half hours later a hundred feet off Mulholland Drive in Agoura, around fifteen miles away. He'd been strangled and stabbed, his throat had been cut, and the back of his head had been caved in. He wore a T-shirt, shoes, and socks, but his underwear and cutoff jeans were in the weeds nearby. His severed genitals were found near the jeans. He had only been thirteen.

**

On June 16, 1979, a slow-moving vehicle dumped a body on the on-ramp of the 405 Freeway at Irvine Center Drive. It was a thirty-minute car ride from Silverado Canyon. The body, clad only in boxer shorts, was still warm when the Irvine police arrived on the scene. It was ten at night, and there were plenty of people standing around, but no one could describe the vehicle that had dumped the corpse. The best guess they had was it was a van.

The man had not been dead long. Blood was still dripping from his nostrils, and his nose was red. He had two loose teeth and scrapes on his sides and arms where he'd hit the pavement. There were marks around his neck and on one of his wrists. His left nipple had been burned with a car cigarette lighter. He'd died from alcohol and drugs, mixed to a lethal level. There were only a few beers in his system, but the combination of the beer and Tylenol, decongestant, antihistamine, and appetite suppressants had killed him.

There were tire marks on his back and shorts. Someone had backed over him after they tossed him out the car door.

Nine days before, Donald Harold Crisel had just celebrated his twentieth birthday. A Marine, he'd been transferred to the helicopter base in Tustin after spending more than a year in Okinawa. Friends in the Corps knew him to be a bit of a bad boy. He smoked pot, drank like a fish, and propositioned Japanese waitresses with his last dollars. However, he was not a homosexual.

A few friends from his base had seen him weaving toward a restaurant across the street from the main gate at about two in the morning, probably to get some coffee and sober up so he could get back to the barracks and sleep the rest of it off.

Twenty hours later, he was dead, lying crumpled on the pavement near the San Diego and Santa Ana freeway junction.

**

Marcus Grabs had found a ride around ten at night on August 5th from Pacific Coast Highway in Newport Beach. The vehicle that picked him up took him a few miles south of the Ventura Freeway near the L.A. County line. He'd been strangled, stabbed, and sodomized when a rancher discovered his body at 6:30 in the morning the following day. His clothes had been tossed into an open field. He'd been just seventeen.

Donald Hayden was walking in Hollywood at one in the morning on August 27th. Ten hours later, construction workers found his body in a trash bin. He'd been sodomized and strangled. His wrists had ligature marks on them as if he'd been handcuffed, and both his testicles and neck had knife wounds. He was fifteen.

David Murillo got a ride south on Highway 101 shortly after noon on September 9th. Three days later, he was found off the highway. The back of his head had been crushed, and his neck had been ligatured. He had handcuff marks on his wrists, sodomy marks in his anus, and rope marks on his ankles. He'd been seventeen.

The protectors of youth – teachers, youth group counselors, and high school principals – began to sound the anti-hitchhiking alarm. Before the year was over, the killer had a name – the Freeway Killer – and headlines in the Southern California newspapers had warnings for teenagers about the risks of hitchhiking.

In the gay bars of Long Beach and Hollywood, fliers about dead John Does were being handed out so frequently the bartenders had the format down by heart.

***

If they were upset by the frequency of the killings, Randy and Jeff Seelig didn't let on. They always went out together, were never out at night alone, and were careful. They were way beyond their hitchhiking days, so they weren't worried. Jeff was a partner at Grandma's Sugar Plums in Belmont Shore, which was doing amazing business in specialty candies and pastries. Kraft went to four months of Erhard Seminars Training sessions and became an 'EST' convert.

His supervisor at Jay-El Products, where he spent a few months setting up computer programs on a freelance basis, wrote that he had an even disposition, was knowledgeable about programming and systems and was always available, neat, thorough, and quick. She couldn't say anything bad about him.

He was a data-processing consultant who was proficient in System/32, System/34, and IBM System/3. By then, he was good enough to find regular freelance work setting up small business systems, and he earned a good living at it.

It was good enough to purchase a house. On July 30, 1979, Jeff and Randy moved into a bungalow with a red tile roof on Roswell Avenue in Long Beach. It was close enough that he and Jeff could drive down to Ripples whenever they wanted.

***

William Bonin was arrested on June 11, 1980. The boy he'd picked up a few hours earlier said the sex they were having was consensual, and that the handcuffs had been Bonin's idea, but the boy wasn't upset about them. What he didn't know was that Bonin had a habit of taking kids' t-shirts, twisting them around a tire iron, and squeezing their necks until they were lifeless. Then he would dump their bodies. This kid was lucky.

Police had caught another one of their Freeway Killers. Perhaps it was the last one, but they were skeptical. While Bonin's victims, young teenage boys, and a few young men, were all homosexuals, the MO didn't match that of the killer who was throwing bodies out of a moving vehicle.

It only took a few hours after his arrest for the investigators, who were tracking the deaths as far back as Marine Edward Daniel Moore – Eddie Moore – to prove that Bonin was a Freeway Killer, but not the Freeway Killer they were looking for.

**

In the summer of 1980, Randy Kraft had finally arrived.

He was a young professional. He and Jeff were homeowners in a modestly upscale neighborhood. Jeff did well at Grandma's Sugar Plums. Randy was a suit-and-tie-wearing troubleshooter for Lear Siegler Industries. He was an on-the-payroll data-processing expert who had his own subordinates, business account, and travel allowance. He made plans to enroll in Southern California University's M.B.A. program the following year so he could climb even higher in the company.

He traded in his Mustang for a Toyota Celica, became active in gay politics, and used his new assertiveness skills to overcome his inhibitions about his homosexuality and get the message out to neighbors and friends to vote against the anti-gay Proposition 6, which aimed to keep homosexuals out of government jobs in California.

His father had developed hypertension, and his mother was now studying astrology, so he tried to stay away from home as much as possible. He went back when it was a birthday or a major holiday, but otherwise spent most of his time with Jeff's family. They treated Randy as if he were Jeff's husband, just like they treated Jeff's older sister's husband.

Randy continued to visit his older sister as much as he could. She was still teaching, and her new husband was an accountant. They had honeymooned in Hawaii, and Randy had made a mental note that he wanted to take Jeff there someday, but they had pending plans for traveling to Europe.

Randy's job satisfied his personal urge to travel. He went mostly to the Bay Area, but in 1980, he took his first out of state trip, which was to Oregon. It was while he was in Oregon that news of the Freeway Killer's capture was reported, and Jeff relayed the information to Randy to keep him informed.

Some time after William Bonin was arrested, a gay activist group offered fifty thousand dollars for any information that led to the arrest of the Freeway Killer. A supermarket chain had pledged thirty thousand to the fund.

Randy's interest in the Bonin case was casual. He was a thousand miles away from the frenzy that had hit Southern California. The remote location and friendly people of Oregon provided a natural peace for Randy.

In the summer of 1980, his only concern was to set up computers. The capture of the Freeway Killer was the last thing he had to worry about.

***

Two days after Labor Day, some children were playing in the morning at the end of Paseo Sombra in a new housing development close to the El Toro Marine Air Base. They discovered a dark green trash bag discarded in the gutter containing something that smelled putrid. In fact, it smelled so bad they had to breathe through their mouths to get near the bag. If they'd been old enough to recognize the smell of death, they might not have gotten any closer.

When they looked inside, what they saw was a lot worse than what they'd smelled. There was a terror in their screams as they ran home to tell their mothers of the kneeling remains of a man, encased in plastic and folded up into a ball as if he were a newborn.

Pathologists saw something even more horrible. There were flesh and bones, a cracked and purple face, and decomposition so bad the coroner was not able to give a definitive time of death.

Robert Wyatt Loggins, Jr. had been tied up and bunched up in the trash bag for at least three to four days, possibly a week. It was impossible to know what had killed him. The skin was too rancid to determine how long he'd been deceased.

The last people who'd seen him alive remembered how bad he wanted to go out and party. Until Friday, August 22nd, he'd spent the best part of his time in Southern California restricted to Barracks 134, Marine Corps Air Station, Santa Ana. He'd been nineteen years old when he'd died.

He was violent when he drank, and he liked to drink a lot, according to his fellow Marines. That's why he'd been restricted to base in the first place. He'd had a drunken brawl at the Miramar Naval Station in San Diego at the start of the summer season.

After a few weeks of not being able to go out and have a drink, he gathered his friends and bought a bottle of Southern Comfort. They drove out to Laguna Canyon Road to celebrate that fine Friday evening. They drove around for a time before they found themselves at a liquor store across the street from the Huntington Beach pier. They believed they were studs on the prowl and thought they might come across some women who were willing to party with them that night.

However, their primary mission – Loggins's, anyway – was to get good and drunk to make up for the weeks he'd been sober on the base. The other Marines weren't able to keep up with him, and they had to be back at the base for duty the next day. By midnight, when they were ready to depart, Loggins was heavily intoxicated.

When they began to get ready to go, Loggins decided to stay put. Both his friends knew it was hopeless to try to get him to leave. He usually swore at them, swung his arms at them, and raved his displeasure with the world. Tonight, however, he wasn't angry. He was just determined to spend his night on the beach.

His friends left him heading south, down the Pacific Coast Highway, to look for a place to sleep it off. They never knew whether he found it.

On the morgue table, about a week and a half later, the coroner unfolded Loggins's body as best he could. He discovered a sock next to the anus and a cord around Wyatt's neck. His blood alcohol level was 0.25, but the fact that his body had been baking in the sun for days could have caused the test to register a higher amount of alcohol than Wyatt had actually drunk. Nevertheless, it was likely that what he'd drunk, mixed with an antihistamine, had killed him. On the death certificate, the examiner wrote out the cause of death to be an acute intoxication of chlorpheniramine, ethanol, and diphenhydramine. Only one patch of skin appeared to be intact. It happened to be where a small red devil was tattooed on Loggins's shoulder.

The coroner's office officially labeled his death an accident. It wasn't refiled as a homicide until three years later.

***

Michael Cluck was a strapping young boy with a strong handshake, blond hair, and a shy smile that disarmed most people he met. While he seemed passive and deferential to his peers, he was headstrong when it came to his parents. He was a high school dropout, and he was looking for somewhere to get a good start in life. He found it when his good friend, another Kentwood High dropout, called him from Bakersfield in Southern California. Scott had gone to the oil fields to work for his uncle. He had some big money stories to tell Mike.

Mike twice told his father that he was going to work in the oil fields, and twice his father talked him out of it. The third time, his father relented, and Mike got going. His father handed him a wad of cash to help him get to where he was headed while his mother cried over the loss of her son.

His father wasn't worried about the trip. Mike was big enough to take care of himself. He was more worried about what might happen to Mike when he got to Bakersfield and discovered that Standard Oil didn't just hand out twenty-dollar-an-hour jobs to every dropout with a nice smile and a strong pair of shoulders.

However, his father knew something about being a seventeen-year-old boy and having big dreams. He knew that he'd tried twice to talk some sense into his son when it clearly wasn't a logical issue. When he was a young man in the Navy, he himself had bummed around California, sticking out his thumb to get a ride between Long Beach and San Diego.

That was why he reached into his back pocket and pulled out some money. Mike took it, gave both his parents a hug, and told them not to worry about him. That was the last they would ever see of him.

His body was found the following morning, on April 10, 1981, outside the Short Mountain Landfill on Peebles Road, right off the I-5 highway near Goshen, Oregon. He was naked from the hips down, and his t-shirt had been pulled up to his armpits to reveal his chest. Blood, still warm, had coagulated in a pool around his head, which had been bashed in with a heavy instrument.

There was blood all over his body, face, and clothes. His rectum was torn and bleeding, and there were fingernail marks on his groin and thighs.

His resting place was a ditch around five hundred feet off the highway. The grass was green and high, almost a foot tall in some areas. It was waving in the breeze when the Lane County Sheriff's vehicles showed up shortly after eight in the morning. A crime scene photographer took some close-ups of Mike from all angles. There was an empty pack of Marlboros near his body, a knife that had bloodstains on it, and some white pills were strewn about nearby. They discovered more pills in Mike Cluck's jacket. They also found a Washington State driver's permit issued to a Michael Duane Cluck.

The autopsy revealed a.09 blood alcohol level and a large dose of antihistamines, flurazepam, and codeine.

His murder was shocking to the local law enforcement officers just because of the sheer savagery. The killer had gone into a frenzy when he'd killed Mike. He'd kicked, hit, and bashed in Mike's head after he was dead.

However, Oregon had witnessed its share of murders. His death was disturbing, but it wasn't anything that hadn't been seen before.

Continuing the Murders Spree in Oregon

The final week of July of 1981 was hot and dry in L.A. In the afternoon, a breeze might waft off the ocean, but it didn't bring the temperature down. Instead, it caught the stench of the Vernon slaughterhouse right at sunset and settled over the central city.

The mostly Hispanic residents along the 1400 block of Bellevue Avenue in the Echo Park section of L.A. thought that was what they smelled at first. However, it became worse over the next few days, and by the time it was strong enough to make them physically ill when they went outside, it seemed too close to blame on the slaughterhouse.

The LAPD Rampart Division sent a request to CalTrans to see if a dog had died in the weeds near the Hollywood Freeway. Maybe that was what the numerous phone calls about the horrific smell were about. A cleanup crew found something deceased, but it wasn't a dog. Buried beneath the leaves and dirt in a landscaped area near the off-ramp, they found a thirty-eight-pound body wearing a single Nike tennis shoe, jeans, underwear, green-and-white socks, and a black Derby jacket over a blue t-shirt.

The body was that of a thirteen-year-old boy from Pittsburg, California, far to the north. He'd been visiting his relatives in Echo Park a few weeks before. Now, while the crew held their breath and got closer to take a look, they saw that his body had been reduced to a skeleton with a bit of decomposed skin stretched over the little remaining flesh.

His name was Raymond Davis. His mother confirmed it was him when the police brought her the clothes. It looked like he'd been strangled with his own shoelaces, judging from the string that was tightly knotted and wrapped five times around his neck. Similar string had been wrapped around his wrist bones, behind his back.

The boy had disappeared after going into the neighborhood to find his dog.

When the detectives arrived, the traffic had already started to build up. Curious onlookers were slowing down on the highway to see what the police activity was all about. Most rolled their windows back up once they caught the odor.

While the police spread out and looked for clues, one officer yelled out loud for the others to move to a spot about forty feet south of the boy's body.

The second body was also bound with shoelaces. It had been strangled, but with some stereo speaker wire rather than a cord. This body weighed eighty-one pounds and wore Levi's and a green-and-white scarf. It was put into the van along with Raymond Davis's remains and taken to the LAPD Forensics Science Lab for testing and identification.

This body remained John Doe 270 for a couple of days until a mother showed up at the county morgue. She'd been to relatives, the police, neighbors, a priest, and a psychic in an attempt to find out where her sixteen-year-old son was. When the two detectives laid out the clothes, she knew that her son – Robert Avila – had finally been found.

On August 20, 1981, Christopher R. Williams, seventeen years old, was discovered lying off a road in the San Bernardino Mountains. He was clothed except for his shoes, underwear, and socks. His nostrils were stuffed with paper, and the cause of his death was pneumonia due to aspiration. He'd choked to death on his own mucus.

He might have been able to move his limbs and pull the paper out, but he'd been drugged to the point that his legs, arms, hands, and feet were useless. His body was filled with phenobarbital and benzodiazepines, which had a paralytic effect in that quantity.

There might have been more made of his death, but he was the kind of victim the cops like to refer to as misdemeanor murders. He was a prostitute working the bus stops of Hollywood, offering his hand, mouth, or ass in exchange for a few dollars or a place to stay that night. The police were not callous enough to write him off completely, and the case remained open. However, the newspaper didn't publish even a short paragraph about his death, and the leads were pretty much nonexistent. People had seen him out soliciting tricks, but he did that every night. No one paid attention to whether he'd been picked up or by whom.

There wasn't much to go on when prostitutes wound up dead. Unfortunately for them, they were the perfect victims. Someone would drive up and wave some money, and they would get in the vehicle. There would be no connection between them and the killer to trace. Their families might not know they were prostitutes, or might know and not care what happened to them. Once the killer was finished, the body was usually far from the scene of the crime, with little or no evidence that could be traced back to a suspect.

There was no murder weapon, fingerprints, leads, suspects, or media outrage for Christopher Williams; therefore, there was no investigation.

***

Twenty-six-year-old Brian Whitcher did not like homosexuals. He did a lot of boasting, but most of it didn't come to fruition due to his constant need for a drink. He liked to haunt Burnside Avenue in southwest Portland, where his boasts weren't worth a can of malt liquor at a dive bar or a night's stay in one of the seedy hotels.

Burnside was Portland's beer neighborhood, and that's where Brian could be found most of the time. He preferred Rotten Robert's and Terrible Terry's when it came to local bars. Earl Davis, a friend of Brian's, remembered him mentioning he was going to Rotten Robert's the night he disappeared. Earl was a retired Army cook in his sixties who'd seen his fair share of downtime in Portland bars. He'd met Brian at a health club where they worked together for a short time a few years ago. Their relationship was closer to father/son rather than friends, and Earl would take Brian in as an occasional roommate despite his drug addiction. Earl was a drinking man, but he didn't like drugs much.

When he answered the phone after ten that night he could hear Brian shouting into his ear, asking him how he was. There was a steady thrum of rock music in the background. He asked Brian where he was.

Brian told him he was at a house, not at a bar, and that Earl should come over.

Earl told Brian he wasn't interested, but Brian had handed the phone over to someone else who came on the line to give directions to the place. Earl remembered almost hanging up halfway through the call, but he waited long enough to talk to Brian again. However, all he said was that he wanted the five dollars Earl owed him. Earl hung up. He'd had enough of his almost-son's nonsense for the night.

Earl only half-remembered that phone conversation when Clackamas County Sheriff's investigators showed up at his door a month later with the news that Brian had been murdered. It seemed Brian had wound up dead the day before Thanksgiving on Canby Hubbard Highway close to the I-5 south of Portland.

Earl wasn't sure if the police suspected him or not, but he didn't have a thing to hide from them. Brian was a bum in many ways, but Earl considered him a friend. The week Brian disappeared, Earl had given him eighty-five dollars to have his teeth fixed. He'd also literally given Brian the shirt off his back. It was a warm, long-sleeved brown sweater to keep him from being cold during his nighttime bar-hopping.

The investigators told Earl they'd found Brian lying in a pool of his own blood with the sweater pulled up to expose his chest. He had no socks, shoes, jacket, or long-sleeved shirt on. They figured someone had robbed him and dumped the body from a moving vehicle. Brian didn't have identification on him, and it had taken them some time to figure out who he was. He might have been hustling homosexuals, planning to roll them for a bit of beer money, but the police weren't too keen on the idea.

The toxicology report showed that he had a deadly combination of Valium and alcohol in his system. However, the coroner put his cause of death as asphyxiation.

Earl told the police that Brian wasn't a bad kid. He was originally from California, and he'd once worked for his father at his print shop in Portland. He chased women a lot when he wasn't drunk, especially near Rotten Robert's, but he'd never had a girlfriend. His family lived in southeast Portland, but he stayed away from them most of the time.

Most of his friends were the down-on-their-luck sort, just like Brian himself. He had a tendency to go out drinking with almost anyone. He wasn't too particular about the company he kept as long as they paid for their own drinks, Earl told the police.

There was one guy Earl remembered. He was a sloppy guy in his early thirties with blond hair and blue jeans. He was most likely five-foot-eight or nine, and he talked a lot. Brian knew him from the Locker Room bar on Burnside at Broadway.

The guy was always putting his hand on Brian's shoulder to ask him for a cigarette, and Brian always told him he didn't have one. So the guy would look at Brian and say maybe Earl had one. Earl hadn't liked the looks of the guy from the moment he saw him. In fact, he was pretty sure it was the guy he spoke with on the phone the night Brian was murdered. The guy who gave Earl directions to the party Brian said he was at.

He had an unfriendly tone and a medium-to-high – but mature – masculine voice that was easily understood. That was about all he could tell the police about the guy. He had no idea where to find him.

***

Parallel to Interstate 5, just outside the Oregon town of Hubbard, is a road called Boone's Ferry. Back in the seventies and eighties, people tossed their trash onto this road from the windows of their vehicles. Some of this trash was a gold mine for local Boy Scout troops and anyone else who wanted to make a few dollars collecting soda cans and trading them in for the refund.

Between Thanksgiving and Christmas daytime temperatures were in the forties, and it rained almost every day. With the cold, wet weather, the can harvesters tended to lighten up. Only the hardiest – or most desperate – went searching through the mud, grass, and bushes for that little bit of extra money.

Late in the morning, just a week before Christmas in 1982, one of these rugged, impecunious souls was picking through the wet weeds and bushes along Boone's Ferry Road when he found a body belonging to Anthony Jose Silveira.

The body was completely nude, but the really weird thing was that it was lying face down in the weeds with a red plastic object sticking out from between the buttocks. The aluminum can collector didn't inspect the scene any further. He dropped his bag of recyclables and ran to the closest pay phone to call the police.

The Marian County Sheriff's Office arrived on the scene a little before noon. Sergeant Will Hingston took a closer look at the red plastic object poking out from Silveira's rectum. It was an adult-sized toothbrush that had been rammed five inches up the victim's anus – which had recently accommodated something much larger. The anus of a deceased person relaxes, but not so much that it opens up to more than an inch in diameter. Before Silveira was sodomized with a toothbrush, something closer to the size of a table leg had been shoved inside his colon.

He'd been there long enough for a few crows and field mice to partake of his corpse. Something a little bigger had gnawed off his toes. Despite having seen plenty of dead bodies in his dozen years on the police force, Hingston still wasn't able to look at this one without feeling a bit sick. There was no way to guess how long the man had been there, lying like garbage in the weeds.

He'd been there for quite some time, though. There was no doubt about that. With the weather acting as a natural refrigerator, the twenty-nine-year-old carpenter could have been there until spring before someone smelled him. By then, most of his flesh would have been ingested by scavengers.

Lyla Silveira was still able to identify her husband, though. She helped the sergeant with times and dates, too. The body had been there for between one and two weeks if Mrs. Silveira's memory was right.

230

On December 3rd, a Friday, the young husband had a few beers after finishing work at a construction site some distance from his home. He didn't have a car. He told his drinking buddies he was going to hitchhike back to Eagle Point, the next county over, and then do his regular weekend stint with the National Guard. He never arrived home.

He was a pushover and a big drinker, the police learned from Lyla and his coworkers. He didn't bash gay people, but he wasn't a homosexual himself. He and Lyla had two children, and if she was worried about the possibility of him sleeping around, it wasn't with other men.

However, everyone Hingston spoke with said that when Tony was loaded, he was pliable. One of the things that showed up in his lab results was Valium along with the alcohol. In fact, his blood alcohol level was .23. There was also semen in his rectum, along with the toothbrush.

Circling his neck was a thin, one-inch wide mark that was still visible two weeks after he'd been strangled to death.

His wife was worried from the moment he disappeared. He did go on binges, but he never stayed away long, and he was responsible enough to always make his monthly reserve training weekends. It took her some time to calm down after the police showed up asking for a description of what he'd last been wearing.

It was nothing special. He was wearing his old jeans and work shoes, along with a T-shirt. The only thing she was able to remember that was distinctive was his National Guard coat, which was an old green fatigue jacket with his last name stenciled on the top of the right-hand breast pocket.

***

On Wednesday, December 8th, Randy was in Michigan, but he wouldn't be there for long. Before eight in the morning, he was ready to meet with another LSI computer troubleshooter, Ronnie Titgen, at the checkout desk of the Amway Grand Hotel to share a rental car to the Lear Siegler corporate headquarters in downtown Grand Rapids. They'd just wrapped up a training seminar, but they both needed to go through an annual performance review with immediate supervisors before they headed back west.

Ronnie Titgen was a little amazed by Randy. He'd been to all the sessions during the three-day conference, put together a presentation on computer management techniques at the last Tuesday afternoon session, and proceeded to out-drink everyone, closing down bars long after the other guys had gone to bed. The last thing Titgen remembered was Randy standing by the bar in Tootsie Van Kelly's, where he was listening to one of the locals talk and purchasing another round.

It was morning, and Titgen figured he'd find Kraft still hung over in his room, but he was wrong. When Ronnie rode the elevator up to Kraft's room on the eleventh floor of their hotel, Randy met him at the door looking as fresh as ever. He told Titgen he'd already checked out and said he'd meet him in front of the hotel. Their rental vehicle was parked in the garage across the street.

231

Understandably, Ronnie Titgen was a little flummoxed, but he didn't show it. It took him about fifteen minutes to check out, and then he waited in the cool morning air for another fifteen minutes, wondering what had become of Randy. Around eight thirty in the morning, just as Ronnie was going to go up to check Randy's room again, Randy pulled the rental car up to the curb and got out to help Ronnie put his luggage in the trunk. Ronnie looked Randy over for any signs of fatigue, but Randy looked as alert as ever. They made it to the corporate headquarters with time to spare, heard their performance reviews, and were back on the road to the Grand Rapids airport by ten that morning.

At the terminal, the two of them shook hands and parted company. Ronnie was flying back to L.A., but Randy had some unfinished business in Portland. Before noon, they were both on their respective flights and heading west.

Meanwhile, back at the Amway Grand Plaza, security guard Ron Ortega was making his usual rounds on the eleventh floor when he discovered a green military-style jacket laid out on a couch near the elevators. He admired it momentarily, thought about trying it on, and then did his duty and took it to lost and found.

Around the same time, about a dozen feet away, Kimberley Ann Kinney, a member of the hotel's housekeeping staff, was letting herself into Room 1169. The first thing she noticed was that the guest, who had checked out, had left a set of keys on the nightstand. They looked like truck keys. She wrote him off as another absentminded guest who would remember where he left them and return later on in the day to retrieve them. She took the keys to lost and found immediately.

Lost and found had everything, from shoes and wigs to whole suitcases. There were a lot of watches, wallets, and purses. People would leave their pets behind sometimes. Lost and found was where it all ended up at the Amway Grand. Unless they had left money, credit cards, or some form of identification, most people didn't bother to come back to get their stuff. That's why the room resembled a huge garage sale. It was loaded with all the items no one cared enough about to bother coming back for. About the only thing security or housekeeping had not found abandoned in a corridor or forgotten in a guest room was a dead body.

Connecting the Oregon Murders

Detective Lieutenant Jack Christiansen was designated as the liaison officer between the Kent County Sheriff's Office and the Schoenborn family. He had to go out to their farm on Thursday morning after two dead young men were discovered.

A power company meter reader had found them arranged neatly on the ground next to the Plainfield Township water tower. The nude one was lying on his back with his legs spread out in a V shape. The clothed victim was also lying on his back, perpendicular to the nude man.

The police identified the nude corpse as Christopher Schoenborn, twenty. The shorter, still clothed man was Dennis Patrick Alt, twenty-four. They were both frozen and covered in an inch of snow that had fallen not too long before they were discovered.

There was something strange about the scene. From a distance, it looked like Alt had been carefully aligned at a right angle to Schoenborn to create the base of a triangle. Schoenborn's legs created the two sides of the triangle, and one of his bare feet was resting on Alt's abdomen. It was a geometrically grisly scene.

A ballpoint pen had been lodged in Schoenborn's penis and penetrated into his bladder. It belonged to the Amway Grand Hotel. The only blood at the scene was from his urethra. It took some time for the Kent County Sheriff's deputies to figure out who the man was, because there was nothing to identify him with, not even a scar or tattoo. It was just an athletic looking corpse with no distinguishing marks. However, there was a ligature mark on his neck.

Alt had a sweater that had been pulled up to expose his chest. His pants were unzipped and his genitals exposed. He wore socks, but he didn't have on any shoes.

Lieutenant Christiansen kept the gruesome details imprinted in his memory. He didn't tell the victim's parents how their son had been found. He knew they knew, though, and the disgusting vision stayed with him when he tried to be sympathetic and businesslike during his visit with them. Nevertheless, he tried to make the interview as pragmatic and sensible as possible under the circumstances, keeping detailed notes in a little notebook.

Chris had last been seen wearing a yellow velour western-style shirt, size sixteen-and-a-half with thirty-three-inch sleeves. They told the investigator that Chris had been wearing a blue t-shirt with 'Adidas' printed across the chest. Christiansen's notebook cataloged the rest of the clothes Chris had been seeing wearing the Tuesday night he disappeared – a pair of Levi's blue jeans, blue men's bikini-style underwear, and a tan-and-maroon ski jacket. The Schoenborns told Christiansen that there was a nametag on the inner left front panel of the jacket with Chris's name written in ink.

Christiansen's notes also reflected the fact that Chris had been wearing a pair of black work boots that had nine-inch tops and heavy cleated soles. The boots were in new condition.

The parents advised the investigator that their son carried a brown fold-over style wallet with identification, photos, and papers in his name; these included his Michigan state driver's license, a Social Security card, and another identification card. When he left their home, he'd most likely had around twenty dollars on him.

The keys to his Chevrolet pickup truck should have been in his possession as well. They had not been found after his disappearance.

When he was finished with Chris's parents, Christiansen excused himself, maintaining his dour but sympathetic manner. He hadn't mentioned that their son's blood alcohol level was .16, and his cousin's was .14, or that both of them had taken Valium with their beer, which had effectively put them into a comatose state while the killer tormented them.

The killer had sadistically tortured them before they died. Not only had he killed them and dumped their bodies, he had degraded and debauched them with imagination and glee. The white Amway Grand pen stuck in Chris's penis was a grotesque signature.

The department, led by homicide detective Sergeant Larry French, spent the following week retracing the last hours of the two young men's lives, interviewing all who had come in contact with them at the hotel. Every lead failed. As each week passed into the next, the case grew colder.

It didn't take long for the investigators to realize that their suspect was most likely a seasoned killer from somewhere far removed from Grand Rapids. Homicide detectives put out a telex message on the crime to other agencies and other states before the year was up. Then they kept their fingers crossed and hoped.

***

Jim Reed of the Oregon State Police began putting the pieces of the puzzle together around the same time Salem, Oregon, homicide sergeant Will Hingston did.

They realized that the killings were happening sporadically, with a varied assortment of victims scattered over a large distance, and they figured the killer had to be someone who was out of state. Perhaps he was from California, but they were looking at suspects in other states, too. One guy they were really focused on was from Colorado. They'd gotten that lead from a telex message sent by the Lane County Sheriff down in Eugene.

If there was any doubt there was a pattern to the Oregon killings, it was dispelled by mid-December. Even the press started to catch on when Silveira's body was found. The Eugene Register-Guard and Portland papers printed maps showing the location of the bodies that had been discovered near freeways during the previous three years, and stories speculating on the possibility of a serial killer began to circulate.

By December 9, two days and a week before a can collector discovered Anthony Silveira's body off Boone's Ferry Road in Marion County, the police and press had another victim to add to the list.

The Clackamas County Sheriff's Department received the call for this body. Around six in the morning, a man who was driving to work spotted Lance Trenton Taggs's body in the weeds off

Airport Road near Wilsonville. Just two weeks before, Brian Whitcher's body had been discovered on the side of a road that ran parallel to Airport Road, a fact that didn't escape the media or the homicide detectives.

Wearing a t-shirt and sweatshirt imprinted with 'Hawaii' and 'Local Motion', nineteen-year-old Taggs was discovered barefoot, with alcohol in his system and Valium in his bloodstream. However, he'd died from choking to death on a sock that had been stuffed down his throat. His pants had been unzipped, and one of his pockets had been turned inside out. He wasn't carrying any identification.

Taggs had lived with his grandparents on Koauka Loop in Honolulu until September. He saw himself as a beach bum and a martial arts buff, and he was not especially pleased about moving back to the mainland to live with his mother. But he'd been arrested for smoking pot in Hawaii, and his grandparents found him to be a little too much to handle. He was unambitious, immature, and plagued with a learning disability that made him not particularly suited for college. The arrest was the last straw for them. Afterward, his grandparents sent him home to live with his mother.

Her home was in the Portland suburb of Tigard, where surfboards and sun were pretty unfamiliar to the locals. It didn't take long for the constant rain and gray skies to get to Taggs. He told his mother he couldn't live there and he certainly wasn't going to work there. Almost as soon as he landed, he was on the phone with a cousin who lived in L.A., looking for a way to get back to what he loved, surfing.

On December 8, 1982, he left his mother's home and began hitchhiking down I-5 with a tote bag carrying all the beach essentials he needed – tank tops, baggy shorts, sandals, and shirts that said 'Hawaii' on them. He threw a pair of homemade nunchakus in his bag, which was part of his Bruce Lee act.

However, he never made it past Wilsonville, which was ten miles south of his mother's front door. Sometime on the night of December 9, he caught a ride with the same killer the Oregon State Police believed had been picking up, drugging, and killing hitchhikers for the past three years.

It was possible the murderer was a homegrown nutcase – Oregon had its fair share of those – but the pattern was more likely that of someone who was passing through from time to time, either as a tourist or on business. This person would commit a murder and then be were gone for months at a time. For a while, the homicide investigators of Clackamas, Marion, and Lane counties banded together to share information on the murders. They suspected that perhaps a crazy trucker was involved. It made sense that the victims, who were all young male hitchhikers, could have gotten into the truck cab of a friendly diesel driver who offered them a beer or two and a few pills.

However, the telex messages the Oregon counties began receiving from out of state started to give them another idea. The first ones were from Orange County in Southern California, where alcohol and drugs were showing up in the blood of strangulation victims who'd been dumped alongside the freeway, having been molested before meeting their demise. When Oregon investigators saw the similarities, they phoned the name on the teletype, Sergeant James Sidebotham of the Orange County Sheriff's Department.

They learned that there weren't clear-cut clues or any solid suspects, but the killings had been going on for quite some time in Orange County – over ten years. That didn't put the Oregon police any closer to finding the killer, but at least they had more ideas than they did before. Maybe the guy they were searching for was a Southern Californian who had the opportunity and the inclination to export his murders to other states from time to time.

Two investigators came up with a plan to check with every hotel, airline, and rental car agency in the Portland and Eugene areas with regard to the times the six bodies were dumped. It would be time-consuming, though, and could take up to a year to complete.

However, if the same name turned up enough times on the rental car slips or the motel registration ledgers, and that name could be traced back to someone who was from Southern California, then maybe they would finally have a suspect.

***

On January 26, 1983, Southern California experienced its worst rainstorm in years. The Pacific Ocean was so terrifyingly angry as it beat down on the one-hundred-year-old Seal Beach Pier that the frenzied waves washed the pilings up onto the beach.

Around eleven in the morning the next day, a workman with the California Department of Transportation saw a mannequin in the ice plant off the shoulder of the 605 Freeway on-ramp. When he inspected the mannequin more closely, he saw that it was wearing a black shirt and pants, and the hair had been plastered down by the rain. He noticed that the skin was very gray and the eyes were shut. There were no shoes on the feet and no belt around the waist. When he knelt down beside the mannequin, he realized he was looking at a body instead.

The body did not have any identification. The coroner said the man had died around one in the morning of January 27th, and he'd had a couple of drinks mixed with Valium before meeting his end. However, it was the strangulation and crushing blows to the right side of his forehead that had killed him. There were rope burns on his wrists, too. The autopsy revealed that he'd been sodomized before his death.

Initially designated 'John Doe Seal Beach', he was identified as Eric Herbert Church a week after the discovery.

***

About an hour from Sacramento, twenty-four-year-old Mikeal Laine was last seen getting onto a southbound Greyhound around the same time of year Eric Church caught his last bus ride to the West Coast.

He left Modesto, California, after telling his mother he was traveling 150 miles to Bakersfield to find a job. He had a drug problem, and the whole town was aware of it. The cops had arrested him for possession once already, and Modesto, the inspiration for George Lucas's classic comedy American Graffiti, was still small enough that word got around pretty quick.

He couldn't get a job driving a bus, cooking at a local diner, or even pushing a broom anywhere in the city. He needed work, and he wouldn't find it at home. Unfortunately, he didn't find it in Bakersfield, either. He kept right on traveling down the road, using his thumb to take him to Orange County.

However, his mother didn't know that when she went to the police the following week to get a handle on what had happened to her son. She had kissed him and waved him goodbye as the bus pulled out of the depot, and she never heard from him again.

Another year passed before San Diego County Sheriff's deputies found Mikeal Laine's skeleton on a remote mountain hillside by the town of Ramona. As in the Eric Church case, there were no shoes and no belt. In fact, there was nothing to indicate the body had been clothed at all when it had been tossed out of a moving vehicle. The remains were so old it was impossible to tell how he'd died.

But by then, the police had a pretty good idea of who had killed him.

The End of the Road

Donald Batchelder, an off-duty LAPD officer, was heading to work when his headlights illuminated a body in the road. It was Saturday, February 12, 1983, at around 5:20 in the morning, when it was still dark out.

He started to get out of the vehicle when he saw the shoeless right foot twitch. Figuring some kid had gotten so drunk he'd passed out on the pavement, he climbed back into his car, backed off the off-ramp and pulled into a service station to call for a patrol unit.

When they arrived just three minutes later on the westbound on-ramp of the Garden Grove Freeway at Euclid Avenue, they found no pulse, even though the body was warm to the touch. The boy was completely naked.

When they flipped him over, they were horrified. It wasn't a drunken teenager. There was a gaping hole where his genitals had been, and the gash was still dripping blood. When the paramedics got to the scene, they pronounced him dead.

The body didn't have any identification. Judging by the skid marks, it had been pushed out of a moving vehicle. A trail of hair, skin, and blood marked the asphalt where he'd bounced and rolled before coming to a stop at the side of the road. There was a single diamond stud in his left earlobe.

There were no missing person reports on a thin, white male around five-foot-nine and blond. He was tagged with a John Doe number and autopsied before being brought to the county

237

morgue. The most intriguing thing the coroner found was the contents of his stomach. He had ingested aspirin, diazepam, and a drug known as propranolol that was used to treat heart trouble and hypertension. In addition, he'd eaten grapes and potato skins. He'd also been drinking, maybe a six pack or two.

One other detail had already become familiar to area police. There was a red ring, around the width of a pencil, around the boy's neck. The booze, drugs, and mutilation hadn't helped him much, but it was the strangulation that had killed him. On an off-ramp of the 605 Freeway near Long Beach, two weeks earlier, they'd seen the same thing on the body of a twenty-one-year-old hitchhiker from Connecticut.

This type of killing had seemed to lapse with the close of the 1970s. Since William George Bonin had been arrested in 1980, the occasional body of a derelict or gay prostitute had been found near a roadway, but none of them so viciously mutilated or blatantly disposed of on a freeway as the last few. Recent teletypes from Oregon – and as far away as Michigan – implied that the predator who had been stalking Southern California roadways for a decade was finally moving on to other areas – assuming he was still on the loose and hadn't been Bill Bonin.

However, this last ghastly discovery seemed to end the speculation that the killer had been apprehended.
The first task at hand was to identify the John Doe, and the best way to do that was to get a handbill printed up for immediate distribution throughout the gay community. The police had a lot of experience with this by now. Time was of the essence in a murder investigation. The trail would grow cold quickly, and any witnesses, leads, or evidence might vanish completely if they didn't find out who the victim was and start interviewing his family and friends as soon as possible.

It was entirely possible the victim wasn't gay, of course – the kid from Connecticut wasn't – but chances were good he was. For some years, the Freeway Killer task force had been convinced that the suspect they were looking for was active in some way within the growing gay community.

A transvestite recognized the image on the handbill and immediately called the Garden Grove Police Department.

Franco had known the victim as Coco, a gay prostitute who liked to pick up men at the DOK Bar in the Garden Grove area where Franco worked cleaning the restrooms. Around Christmas, Franco met the kid outside the bar looking for money in exchange for some friendly interaction.

They saw one another a total of four times. Their second date was at Rumor Has It, which was another gay bar. The last few times they met, at a hotel and Franco's apartment, they'd had sex. Franco expected the worst of Coco, but it never happened. He hadn't hurt or hit him. Then he kind of faded away, out of his life forever. There were no addresses, names, or phone numbers exchanged. The quick, hurried encounters between two strangers were characteristic of many of the sexual liaisons in the gay community at the time.

Franco had given Coco a single token of his affection during their time together. It was a single diamond stud earring that he wore in his left earlobe. It was the same earring he'd spotted right away in the picture on the flyer.

That didn't help the police much, though. Coco could have been anyone. The only real lead Franco could give them was that the boy said he lived somewhere near Knott's Berry Farm at Buena Park. One Geoffrey Alan Nelson lived in the same neighborhood, and a year later, Franco would state that Coco and Geoff Nelson were one and the same person.

Sunday afternoon, February 13th, when the flyers were being distributed to places like Rumor Has It and DOK, another clue to the identity of the dead man with the diamond stud in his earlobe was being collected on a mountainside forty miles away.

Shortly after three in the afternoon, a ranger from Mount Baldy Village pulled over on Glendora Ridge Road to take in the view. In a ravine about fifteen feet down the embankment off the west side of the highway, he saw what he thought was someone lying precariously in a dead tree branch at the edge of a cliff. When the ranger called out to the man, he didn't move. If he'd fallen, he would have tumbled another thousand feet down the mountainside.

An hour later, L.A. County Sheriff's deputies carefully pulled the body up the hillside. He was wearing an orange-and-white nylon windbreaker, a long-sleeved t-shirt with a palm tree on the chest, and black denim jeans with the top button and fly undone. His underwear had been rolled down past his genitals, so they were hanging out of his pants. He had a tattoo on his right arm, abrasions next to his right ear and under his right eye, and a short mustache. His identification and wallet were nowhere to be found, and he was lightly coated from head to foot in beach sand.

Whoever had taken him to the beach had sodomized him, according to the lab results. He had been tied up and strangled with a small cord after he'd taken a sizeable dose of propranolol, diazepam, and beer. He'd also ingested grapes and potato skins.

His cause of death was asphyxia due to the compression of his neck.

***

Shortly after one in the morning on Saturday, May 14, 1983, two California Highway Patrol officers pulled over a 1979 Toyota Celica in the southern Orange County community of Mission Viejo. The remote stretch of highway, known as Interstate 5, where Sergeant Michael Howard and Officer Michael Sterling made the routine traffic stop, runs parallel to the Atcheson, Santa Fe, and Topeka railroad around fifty miles south of L.A.

Sterling believed they were going to arrest their second drunk driver of the evening. That was pretty routine for the Saturday morning graveyard shift. The cops called it the 'deuce' shift, which was a reference to Section 502 of the California penal code – driving under the influence. Seven in the evening on Friday to four in the morning on Saturday is prime time for drunk drivers, as any law enforcement officer will attest to.

239

Sergeant Howard and Officer Sterling had been following the Toyota in the far right-hand lane for a few minutes, watching it weave northward, on and off the freeway shoulder. When the driver made an illegal lane change, they switched on their lights. The Celica slowed down from forty-five to around thirty miles an hour, and the driver steadied his steering, but he wasn't pulling over. Sterling flashed the high beams and shone a spotlight into the vehicle.

The driver reached into the back seat to get a dark jacket which he proceeded to toss onto the passenger seat. When Sterling went onto the public address system and ordered the car to pull over, the driver pulled off the road and parked next to a guard rail on the freeway shoulder.

Randy Steven Kraft, a wiry, thin, middleweight man with a prominent chin, sandy blond hair, mustache, and dark brown eyes got out of the Toyota Celica. He walked quickly back toward the CHP black-and-white vehicle. Sterling, a veteran of close to five thousand drunk-driving arrests in the three years he'd been working the highways of Orange County, knew that drivers didn't normally do this unless they had something to hide.

To him, it signaled that the driver had an open container in his vehicle, probably a beer.

Randy did have a beer in his car, as it turned out. In fact, he had a whole cooler packed with ice and Moosehead lager. As he got out of the vehicle, he dumped a half-empty bottle on the pavement before walking back to the patrol car. However, the broken beer bottle was the least of the evidence Howard and Sterling would find in the Celica.

Sterling recalls doing a field sobriety test on Kraft. He asked him to put his finger to his nose and walk a straight line. Sterling noticed that the fly on Kraft's pants was open except for the top button.

The thirty-eight-year-old computer analyst admitted he'd had three or four drinks, but told Sterling he was definitely sober. At that point, Sterling saw him as just another guy who thought he could toss back a few at the bar and still drive home safely.

He wasn't drunk, but he was under the influence, according to Sterling.

As Sterling went through the routine of cuffing Kraft and letting him know he was under arrest, Howard walked up to the passenger side of the Toyota and saw that Randy was not traveling alone. He tapped on the glass to get the passenger's attention.

There was no response.

Howard banged on the window a bit harder and shouted at the passenger. There was still no response. There was no way he was going to get one, but he didn't know that at the time.

A twenty-five-year-old Indiana farm boy who had joined the Marines, that's who Terry Lee Gambrel was. He was stationed at nearby El Toro Marine Air Base, but he was slumped in the seat with a black jacket draped over his lap. He looked like he was sleeping.

While he kept rapping on the window, Howard yelled to Sterling that there was a passenger in the vehicle. Sterling asked Kraft where his friend lived. Kraft responded that he didn't know. He was a hitchhiker he'd picked up a few miles back. Normally, the highway patrolmen gave a sober passenger the opportunity to drive the car home, so the arrested driver wouldn't need to pay the impound fees in addition to bail and fines.

In this case, though, it seemed likely to Howard that the Marine corporal was as drunk as Kraft, if not drunker. When he tried opening the passenger side door, he found it was locked. He went around to the driver's side of the vehicle.

What he saw indicated that he was most likely right about Gambrel's intoxication. A few empty Moosehead bottles and pill vials littered the floorboards. Resting on Randy's seat was a folded five-inch buck knife.

Howard let out a weary sigh of disgust. Gambrel was so drunk he'd actually passed out. However, the veteran officer recoiled when he touched the clammy, cold flesh of the young Marine's forearm. It was pretty obvious that he wasn't drunk; he was dead.

Setting the pill vials and knife on the roof, Howard reached across the motionless Marine and unlocked the passenger side door. He walked around to check Gambrel's pulse and pupils for any signs of life.

There was no real loss of color in his face, but his arms were a waxy yellow.

Howard lifted the man's jacket.

His fly was open and pulled up tight around his scrotum so that his penis and testicles were in an obscene upright position. His lap was wet because his bladder had relaxed and released as he'd died.

His hands were bound with the laces from his shoes. There were fresh pink ligature marks deep in his wrists. His shoes had been removed from his feet and carefully tucked underneath the front seat.

There were marks on his neck, which had been made by the tightening and loosening of his own belt.

He wasn't breathing.

Howard went back to the patrol vehicle, where Sterling had buckled his benign, handcuffed suspect into the back seat. The sergeant nervously asked his partner to go up and check the passenger for a pulse while Howard waited in the vehicle with Kraft.

He'd been dead for just a little while, but he was definitely dead.

Sterling was the same age and build as the six-foot corpse sitting in the passenger seat of Randy Kraft's Toyota.

His regular partner had been on leave, and they wouldn't allow anyone to drive on patrol alone at night. That's how Howard and Sterling had wound up being in the vehicle together. If Sterling's regular partner had been with him, he probably wouldn't have been on that stretch of road at that particular time, and Kraft wouldn't have been caught.

Just like Howard, Sterling knew within a few seconds of touching Gambrel's limp, clammy wrist that he was dead.

He'd been transferred to the southern Orange County precinct four or five months earlier. He remembered a sergeant at the orientation briefing telling him about how dead bodies were being found on the freeways at night and how there was a killer on the loose.

Indeed, the bodies had been showing up on off-ramps and near hilltops in the brush for more than ten years. Most of them were bodies of hitchhiking young men.

At first, Sterling didn't connect that with what he saw now. He just thought it was weird – until the paramedics turned up and started talking about it. Then he wondered if they could have actually caught the guy responsible for all of those murders. Then everything snowballed.

They called in for the paramedics at 1:17 in the morning and waited in the patrol car with Kraft. It took only four minutes for the firemen and paramedics to arrive. The two officers were silent and grim, realizing they might have someone a lot more menacing than just a drunk driver in the back seat of their patrol car. Kraft was just as silent.

Randy Kraft did ask how his 'friend' was, though, which pointed to the other passenger in the Toyota Celica being more than just a hitchhiker he'd just picked up. That just made things even more perplexing.

When the paramedics hooked Gambrel up to the electrocardiogram monitor, the line reflected the total absence of a heartbeat. They decided to work on him anyway.

One of the paramedics, Dan Deslauriers, stuck his head into the back of the patrol car to ask Kraft what Gambrel could have taken to go into full cardiac arrest. Kraft volunteered he'd given the Marine some of his Ativan.

In the meantime, Steve Werth, Deslauriers's partner, was furiously trying to pump the life back into Gambrel's body. Jerry Flores, a paramedic intern, later said the two CHP officers tried to prevent them from treating Gambrel. He was dead, and they didn't want to disturb the evidence.

He wasn't breathing and didn't have a pulse, but his color, body temperature, and moistness were still within the normal range. The paramedics insisted on pulling him out of the Toyota. They put an EOA tube down his throat. EOA's, esophageal orbitrator airways, have little balloons on the tip that are blown up once inserted, which keeps the patient from vomiting and getting it into their lungs.

After intravenous drug treatment and cardiopulmonary resuscitation, Gambrel's heart had some faint electrical activity.

With a doctor instructing them via a radio what drugs and dosages to use, the paramedics gave Gambrel all the life-saving treatments they could. They gave him sodium bicarbonate to neutralize the acid in his blood, dextrose to boost his blood sugar, Narcan to counteract the drugs he'd taken, calcium fluoride to balance his electrolytes, dopamine and epinephrine to boost his blood pressure, and atropine to stimulate his heart.

They used electric shock paddles to stimulate his heart back into a regular heartbeat. His body rose off the pavement every time the rush of electricity ran through him.

His pupils stayed in a death stare the entire time.

At 1:35 in the morning they put him into the ambulance and rushed to the Saddleback Community Hospital. The paramedics were pumping his chest throughout the entire ten-minute ride. The officers followed close behind with Randy sitting quietly in the back seat. When they arrived, Sterling stayed in the vehicle with Kraft.

Sterling had to remain with him for a while by himself. There was no one else around, and Kraft was handcuffed in the back seat. Sterling had his service revolver with him, but he was still nervous. He knew that Kraft could be the guy who'd been killing for over ten years.

At 2:19 in the morning, the on-duty emergency room physician examined Terry Gambrel for vital signs. In less than five minutes, he declared Terry deceased.

Identifying the Victims

Kraft's Toyota Celica was impounded for investigation, and while investigators suspected they would find a good amount of evidence, they could have had no idea how much. The floor mat on the driver's side of the vehicle hid a treasure trove of evidence beneath it. White, one of the investigators, lifted it up and discovered an envelope filled with forty-seven photographs of young men. Some of them were nude, while others were clothed. Some of them were dead or appeared that way.

One image was of a young man who was naked and draped over a couch upholstered in a distinctive floral pattern. He appeared to be either dead or stoned. His eyes were glazed over as they stared at the camera, and his mouth hung open.

Others looked like they could be sleeping. They were around the same weight and height as Kraft and had distinct military haircuts.

There were even more shocking things to be found in the car, though. The seat Gambrel had been sitting on was soaked with blood. It wasn't Gambrel's, because he didn't have any open wounds.

By the time investigators got to the trunk, there was both dread and expectation. They were prepared for the worst, and they weren't disappointed.

They found a briefcase with a wood-grained binder harboring a tablet that had sixty-one neatly printed notations. At first glance, the list didn't make much sense. It began with words like 'stable', 'angel', 'hari-kari', and 'EDM'.

When they showed the list to Sidebotham, though, he had a pretty good idea of what it was. Every entry was a meticulously coded memory trigger for a murder that had been committed. Sometimes, more than one number was used, such as '2 in 1 hitch'. The investigators concluded that what they had in their hands was a two-column list of murder victims that dated back years. The list added up to a total of sixty-five victims if they included the murders where there were two victims. If Sidebotham was correct, it would make Kraft the most prolific serial killer in modern times.

It also opened up an investigator's nightmare. Matching the photos of the bodies to the list and identifying the victims became Sidebotham's full-time job for years. Several of the cryptic entries never had a body matched to them.

Sidebotham left all the microscope work and fingerprint dusting to the experts over the following weeks while he went back to his office. He got on the phone with prosecutor Bryan Brown and Judge Beacom to begin the process of prosecuting Randy Steven Kraft.

Sidebotham wasn't one to show emotion or excitement, but he had a tough time keeping his emotions in check during the formal interview that took place. A sort of low-key competition to find the real freeway killer had been going on among Southern California investigators for quite some time. Bryan Brown, who was in the process of convicting William Bonin on four counts of murder in Orange County at the time Kraft was arrested, was as aware as Sidebotham that Bonin had been awarded the title of Freeway Killer under false assumptions.

The real killer had always been out there, operating under the police officers' noses. He tweaked his MO from time to time and had even taunted them by leaving a naked, emasculated body right in the middle of the freeway off-ramp.

Now it appeared that the cat and mouse game was over. Sidebotham described the forty-seven photo collection he discovered in Kraft's vehicle to Judge Beacom, including a picture he was sure depicted Eric Church, and another flash photo that was Rodger DeVaul, Jr., wearing his nylon windbreaker, which was orange with brown shoulders, and a white undershirt. It was the same windbreaker his grandmother had given him a short time before he was found dead on the Euclid on-ramp of the Garden Grove Freeway.

***

After his second phone session with Judge Beacom, Sidebotham found himself on his way to Long Beach. At 5:30 in the afternoon, he pulled up to 824 Roswell Avenue with a search warrant in his hands. He announced himself and knocked on the door, but there was no one home except for Kraft's dog, Max. As police barricades went up around the home, Sidebotham let himself inside, followed by a small army of law enforcement officers. There were two Orange County Sheriff's forensic experts, several investigators from the L.A. County Sheriff's Office, four Sheriff's detectives, and officers from the Seal Beach, Garden Grove Police, and Long Beach Police Departments.

Jeff Seelig returned from a chocolate convention, demanding to know what was happening, but he was kept outside the barricades.

Inside, investigators were tearing the house to shreds, which Jeff would later complain about. Part of the den wall was removed, and a pair of couches with the distinctive floral pattern was hauled out the front door to the Sheriff's van later on that week. The wall was stained with blood, and the couches matched the one in the photo taken from Kraft's vehicle, depicting a dead, nude young man.

In the bathroom, a brown shaving kit with the name Mike Cluck was discovered.

In the garage, they found a maroon-and-tan jacket that had belonged to Chris Schoenborn, the twenty-year-old farmer from Grand Rapids, Michigan. Loose threads in the lining marked the place where a label bearing his name had been sewn.

The horrifying tidbits of evidence began to pile up. A camera that once belonged to Michael Sean O'Fallon, a dead Colorado youth, was found. A Norelco shaver with two floating heads, still in the dark gray carrying case with the red felt lining, was found. It had been given to Eric Church before he'd taken the bus across the United States. A tote bag with the word 'Hawaii' was found with a pair of Japanese nunchakus, once the property of Lance Taggs from Oregon.

By the time investigators had left the modest single-story home on Roswell Avenue at 2:05 the following morning, they had enough clothing, rugs, and furniture to fill the moving van and enough apprehension about what they had stumbled upon to fill their nightmares for lifetimes.

But that was only the beginning.

***

The list itself was not particularly surprising.

It took up the top half of a single sheet torn from a yellow legal pad, and the carefully block-printed words were innocuous. There were thirty names or phrases on the far left side of the page and thirty-one on the right. A smear of something inky and dark that had spilled on the paper decorated the center of the page. The sheet of paper could have been a checklist for a scavenger hunt or an encoded list of things to do.

Kraft explained it as just being a list of nicknames he'd given to his friends in the gay community. Phil Crabtree was 'Airplane Hill', and another acquaintance was 'Jail Out'. However, Sergeant Sidebotham and prosecutor Bryan Brown believed that the evidence from Kraft's trunk was far more sinister than a catalog of friends.

Early on in the court process, Brown started referring to the sheet as a scorecard. Every entry, he would later tell jurors, represented a victim, or two, of the most prolific serial killer in the modern history of the United States. Beginning with the cryptic 'Stable' and ending with the equally mysterious 'What You Got', the list was put under seal by the prosecution nearly as

245

soon as it was discovered, for fear that it might lead to charges of foul play from Kraft's defense lawyer. Indeed, linking the entries to anything as horrific as serial murder appeared to be complete speculation upon initial examination.

However, investigators continued to look at the list.

For one thing, there were seven entries that started with the word 'Portland'.

- Portland
- Portland Denver
- Portland Hawaii
- Portland Blood
- Portland Reserve
- Portland Eck
- Portland Head

It didn't take long for the Oregon State homicide investigators to match the entries with six unsolved murders of young hitchhikers along Interstate 5 south of Portland, starting with Michael O'Fallon, who was Portland Denver, in the summer of 1980. The one-word entry, 'Portland', was apparently just a heading. No murder was ever linked to it.

Following the Portland entries was GR2, one of the four notations on the list that contained the number 2. Dennis Alt and Chris Schoenborn, two young men from Grand Rapids, Michigan, died the same night in December 1982, shortly after they had shared a drink with Kraft at the bar of the Amway Grand Hotel.

From there, the mix and match game started to become as baffling as an acrostic puzzle, albeit considerably more morbid. The task became one of locating a body or a missing person who fit the description of one of Kraft's photographed victims and looking for a setting, characteristic, or keyword that linked him with the list of dead men.

Six years after Kraft was arrested, detectives had pieced together only around two-thirds of this puzzle. Of the sixty-one entries, detectives managed to match forty-one to murders of young men who had been killed between 1971 and 1983. Two of the entries, '2 in 1 Beach' and 'GR2', represented occasions when Kraft had murdered two victims at once, according to the prosecution.

Twenty entries on the list still remained a mystery. They were still showing up on the screen of the Compaq computer in the Randy Kraft inventory room on the ground floor of the Orange County Courthouse seven years after he was arrested. Every entry was followed by the phrase 'Name unconnected to any unsolved murder.'

Two of these entries have the disturbing number 2 in them, '2 in 1 MKV to PL' and '2 in 1 Hitch'.

Two of Kraft's last victims, Eric Church and Terry Lee Gambrel, were never entered on the list. He hadn't found the time to jot them down before the officers pulled him over on the freeway.

The alarming box score of identified and still unmatched names on the list added up to a frightening total if the investigators were right. By the time he was caught, Randy had been responsible for sixty-seven murders over a twelve-and-a-half year period.

Texas drifter Henry Lee Lucas claimed responsibility for more than two hundred killings following his arrest four months after Kraft, but that figure was pared down to less than sixty, and maybe as few as just two, by investigators who discounted his confession as too exaggerated. More notorious killers, such as John Wayne Gacy and Jack the Ripper, were connected to far fewer killings. London's lust-murderer's reputation rested on the slaughter of just five prostitutes, while Gacy had buried the bodies of thirty-three young men beneath his home.

Randy outpaced them all. If his scorecard was accurate, not since Giles de Rais, who was executed in the fifteenth century after being found guilty of murdering several hundred young boys for sexual pleasure, had a single serial killer been responsible for so many thrill murders.

***

As one member of the team of investigators was on the phone with Terry Gambrel's family and fiancée, a pair of L.A. County Sheriff's deputies took on the job of interviewing the second suspect in the case. He was a chocolate candy maker, a little chubby, and shared the home on Roswell Avenue with Randy Kraft.

The house had been searched the previous evening, and six camera-toting, fingerprint-dusting detectives had discovered two-foot-long dildos, a jar of petroleum jelly, and a container of Crisco in the nightstand next to the bed Kraft and Seelig shared. Sidebotham, Doug Storm, and all the rest of the team were curious as to how someone who was so intimate with Kraft couldn't have known about his night prowler activities.

Jeffry Alan Seelig began by telling the police officers that he and Randy were both gay and had lived together since Seelig graduated from high school in 1975. He said he was into sadomasochism, but Randy wasn't.

Jeff Seelig related to the officers that he and Randy Kraft would sometimes pick up hitchhikers on the freeway and bring them home for sex. However, whenever they had an argument, Randy would drive the highways alone, sometimes going as far south as San Diego and bringing back hitchhikers to the house.

For the past two-and-a-half months, Randy had not been able to have sex with him, Seelig admitted. It was partly because of that reason they were both seeing a couples counselor. Jeff confirmed that Randy had frequently traveled to places such as Grand Rapids, Portland, and Washington State while he was employed with Lear Siegler. He confirmed that Randy carried a supply of tranquilizers in his vehicle, including meprobamate, Equanol, and drugs that were used to treat anxiety disorders and high blood pressure.

Following his interview with the deputies, Jeff got on the phone to call the counselor, Sandra Hare, who recorded notes of the late afternoon conversation.

She wrote that Jeff was hysterical and afraid. Randy had been stopped on a 502, and there had been a half-dead body in the vehicle. Jeff told her he loved Randy so much that he could hardly stand it, and that he couldn't stand not having him close by. He told her that Randy was a good person and then wondered why this had happened to him (Jeff).

Jeff asked her to call Dr. McArthur, Randy's physician, and then asked her to pray for Randy.

For the first few weeks after Randy's arrest, Seelig was an active suspect in the case. At one point during the first seven days, Orange County Sheriff Brad Gates publically confirmed to reporters that his department believed that Seelig could be guilty of the crimes because they didn't think that Randy could have committed them by himself.

But as more and more acquaintances and friends were interviewed, that belief started to change, and an even more amazing possibility started to arise. Perhaps Seelig had lived with Randy for more than eight years, at three different addresses, and never known about his lover's secret life.

Years later, after he'd broken off communication with Randy, Seelig described himself as the "only living victim" of the Freeway Killer.

***

Both circumstantial and DNA evidence caused numerous investigators to believe that not all of the murders Randy Kraft committed were committed alone. The prosecution believed that certain facts could only be explained if Kraft had had an accomplice in several of the murders.

First and foremost, he would have had a hard time dumping a 200-pound corpse from a moving vehicle alone without being noticed and without compromising his driving. Abrasions and debris found at some of the crime scenes indicated that the bodies had been dumped from a vehicle moving more than fifty miles an hour.

In addition, footprints in the sand close to where John Leras's body was discovered at Sunset Beach in 1975 indicated that two people had carried the corpse to where it was dumped. Semen samples found on Eric Church's body were inconsistent with Randy Kraft's DNA. Finally, the photographs of the victims found in his vehicle had to have been processed somewhere. Kraft did not have a darkroom or equipment able to do this at his residence or where he worked. But there wasn't a photo developer around that admitted to having printed Kraft's morbid images.

During the trial, prosecutors confessed confidentially that they hadn't charged Kraft in a few of the murders they were certain he'd committed because the facts pointed to more than one suspect. While DNA evidence found on the body of Eric Church wasn't compatible with Kraft, investigators found photographs that depicted Church in Kraft's vehicle, and they found his razor in Kraft's home.

One person suspected of helping Kraft was Jeff Graves, Randy's first live-in boyfriend. The prosecution believed Graves might have assisted Randy in several of the murders. Graves, who had lived with Randy between 1971 and 1976, was questioned about the Crotwell abduction and murder in 1975 when he verified part of Kraft's statement to the police. When he was questioned further about the incident and Kraft's arrest in 1983, he denied responsibility.

He died of AIDS on July 27, 1987. At the time he died, the police were gearing up to question him again about the murders.

Conclusion

Randy's trial was the longest and most expensive in Orange County history at the time. It lasted thirteen months and cost ten million dollars, but the appeals process dragged on for even longer. Even though Kraft was arrested in 1983, he did not face trial until 1988. In 1989, he was convicted of sixteen counts of murder, one count of sodomy, and another count of emasculation. At the writing of this book, he has been on death row for twenty-eight years. His initial appeal claimed that California's gas chamber violated his religious rights under the First Amendment by forcing him to actively participate in his own killing. This was quickly rejected, but he then turned to other legal tricks to delay his death.

In 1992, he sued Dennis McDougal and Warner Books for publishing *Angel of Darkness*, a study of his case that he claimed smeared his good name. He claimed the book portrayed him as a sick and twisted man, and thereby scuttled his prospects of future employment. He sought $62 million in damages, but the lawsuit was dismissed as being frivolous in June of 1994. However, it still cost McDougal and Warner around fifty thousand dollars in legal fees.

The authorities were more concerned about the unidentified names from the scorecard they had found in Randy's trunk, and with the prospect of identifying his accomplices. The Huntington Beach John Doe victim was positively identified in 1995 as Kevin Clark Bailey, an eighteen-year-old drifter, but twenty-two of the victims on the death list still remain unknown.

McDougal, the author of *Angel of Darkness*, believes he has shone light on a bit of the mystery of Kraft. In an article published in Beach Magazine in January of 2000, he recounted an interview with a man named Bob Jackson, who apparently confessed to murdering two victims with Kraft. He claimed that one was in Wyoming in 1975, and the other was in Wisconsin in 1976. He said he joined Kraft in several of the California murders after 1977. Kraft had nicknamed him Twiggy. Jackson thought one of the notations on Kraft's list referred to a joint homicide.

More disturbing yet, Jackson told McDougal that the list included only Kraft's more memorable killings and that the total body count was closer to a hundred. McDougal reported Jackson's claims to the Orange County Sheriff's Department and provided them with the recordings of the interviews.

The detectives questioned Jackson and persuaded him to enter a mental institution, but no charges were ever filed. The authorities in Wyoming and Colorado were not able to confirm the killings of the two nameless drifters almost thirty years prior.

Meanwhile, Randy Kraft spends his time playing bridge with other inmates on death row. His regular partners have included Lawrence Bittaker (known as Pliers), Douglas Clark (the Sunset Strip Slayer), and – somewhat ironically – William Bonin, the other Freeway Killer. Together, they are convicted of forty-one murders, and if the police are correct, the true tally of their killings is closer to a hundred dead, with Kraft being responsible for around sixty percent of that total.

Bonin was executed on February 23, 1996, but the others are still alive. Randy's death sentence was upheld by the California Supreme Court on August 11, 2000, yet he's still breathing. Unfortunately, the victims' families have to breathe in that air, too, and they're not happy about his continued survival.

Considering the pain and turmoil he put them through, who could blame them?

Kraft is being held at San Quentin State Prison on death row, where he will remain until his final days. As of the writing of this book, he is seventy-two years old. The home he shared with Jeff Seelig still exists at 824 Roswell Avenue in Long Beach California.

The Beast of Birkenshaw
Peter Manuel

Peter Manuel was Scotland's first serial killer and certainly the country's most notorious mass murderer. But he was so much more than that. As well as the horrific nature of his murders, which killed men, women, and children, he possessed a constant arrogance and a swift intelligence that often allowed him to operate right underneath the noses of the local law enforcement. Always happy to embarrass the police in Glasgow and the surrounding area, he waged a lifelong battle of wits that ended with him being hanged.

But the legend of Peter Manuel lives on. He had a penchant not only for violent killings but for having the audacity to represent himself in court. Sometimes this was successful, and sometimes it was not. Each time, however, he was noted for his deft ability to outmaneuver the best police officers Glasgow had to offer. When he eventually faced his last court hearing, it was described in the tabloids as the Trial of the Century. In this book, we will attempt to look into the history of the killer and the reasons he might have had for carrying out his horrific retinue of crimes.

Throughout the various chapters of this book, we will meet the friends, the family members, and the enemies of Peter Thomas Anthony Manuel, the man described as having the names of the saints, but the heart of Satan himself. We will examine Peter's worst crimes while exploring the background that made him into the man he was. We will even look at his obsession with outsmarting the authorities. If you would like to learn more about the life of Peter Manuel, this is the book for you.

Early Life

Our story begins in 1927. In the Misericordia Hospital in Manhattan, a baby named Peter Thomas Anthony Manuel was welcomed into the world. His father, Samuel, was a welder from Lanarkshire who had traveled to the United States when work in Scotland grew hard to find. To Samuel, this move was the chance to improve the quality of life for his family, buying into the American dream that so many others shared. To his son, this would one day be a talking point – his American upbringing being something to brag about in dingy Scottish bars.

But Peter was not an only son. His elder brother, James, was left behind when the family changed country in 1925. He would stay with relatives in Scotland and would travel over when the family was settled and he was a little bit older. Once arriving in the United States, Samuel found it tough to find the welding jobs he coveted, but he managed to turn his hand to a variety of other ventures anyway. He bounced around a few states, eventually arriving in Detroit and working in a factory that made car bodies. Living there with his pregnant wife, there was no way for Samuel to predict the Wall Street Crash that would plunge the country into one of the worst depressions in recorded history.

The Great Depression not only plunged much of the country into crushing poverty, but it also gave rise to the legends of American gangsters who grew so famous over the ensuing decades. Peter, in particular, would liken himself to the mobsters, hoping some of their notoriety would rub off on him. Despite the extreme conditions brought about by the economic situation, both Samuel and Bridget (his wife and Peter's mother) were determined to stay. They remained in the country for a further five years, only traveling back to Scotland in 1932, when Samuel fell very ill. In this condition, they may as well be poor in Scotland as in America. On arriving back in their homeland, James and Peter met for the first time. A few years later, they would be joined by a little sister named Teresa, who was born in 1934.

Like many people who grow up to become serial killers and mass murderers, Peter's time at school was not a pleasant one. Prone to ill-discipline, there was an apparent determination to set himself apart from his classmates. The disruptions in class could amount to pranks such as drawing pornographic images, intentionally hoping to attract the adoration of his classmates and the fury of the authorities. He was sent to a Roman Catholic school on Park Street, Motherwell, but he was known to both skip school and start fights.

It might have been the last thing on Samuel's mind, however, as work was still hard to find. Desperate for a job, he took the family south of the Scottish border to Coventry in England. This would be the place where Peter got his first taste of criminality. Having been sent to an approved school, Peter managed to escape as many as eleven times, eventually stealing to keep himself afloat. His schooling was occasional, but he was not a poor student. A bright boy, Peter was a committed letter-writer and loved the chance to show off his talents. His extra-legal activities, however, landed him in trouble with the authorities. Spending some time in prison as a teenager allowed him to work on his education in a confined environment, catching up on the schooling he had missed. Even at this early stage, the letter that we have that Peter wrote from prison show a man confident in his own intelligence and happy to show off his vocabulary, sometimes to a fault. Incarceration perhaps gave Peter a misguided view of his own intelligence. Smarter than the average prisoner, he would later extrapolate this and assume it made him smarter than the wider population.

Peter's school records are hard to find. At his trial many years later, he would claim that he attended the King Henry VIII Grammar School with a scholarship. However, the bombs dropped on Coventry during World War II destroyed the records, so there's no way of verifying the fact. It could well just be a lie perpetuated by Peter Manuel in an effort to back up his intellectual credentials. However, what we do know is that any education he did have was interrupted after he was arrested for breaking and entering. One reason he gave for his constant hijinks was a language barrier. Uprooted from America and then Scotland, his mother recalls one day when he came home to inform her that he couldn't understand a word said to him by those in Coventry. True or not, Peter's childhood was tough.

It grew more difficult during the later years of World War II, however, when Peter recalled that he was involved in an accident. According to his version of events, he took a blow to the head during an air raid, struck by a piece of steel after a bomb was dropped on a nearby building. He spent the next few hours unconscious and could not recall what happened to him over the next week. However, there is another version of this story, given out by the boy's mother. According to her version of events – as she was told by Peter – the story involved an electric shock at the place where Peter happened to be working. As well as harming Peter, three of his colleagues were killed in the incident. Peter required artificial respiration but managed to pull through. His feet and hands were both badly burned, and it added to the memory problems that he had already experienced. There is a story about how he once managed to drive a truck to Preston from Blackpool without being aware of his actions at all, or the time when he went to watch a boxing match but couldn't recall what he did that night or for the next few days. These injuries and memory blackspots seem to have blighted Peter's early adult life.

Trying to discover Peter's early life is also difficult. He was not only prone to embellishment and straight out lies, he also managed to keep much of his upbringing hidden. However, we do have some evidence to corroborate claims thanks to his frequent interactions with the authorities. Claiming to be mad, he was examined by a psychiatrist. The doctor found a large scar on the right side of his forehead, as well as the remnants of burn marks across his hands, or at least, surgical marks that might be likely caused by doctors' efforts to relieve a septic condition brought about by an electric shock. Taking this information, we can establish that Peter both had a troubled childhood and one in which he was occasionally prone to serious injury. When examining the way in which he himself recollected and altered these events, we can understand more about his relaxed attitude towards the truth.

While Peter was in prison, the rest of his family decided to move once again. Returning to Scotland, they were concerned about the frequent bombing of Coventry, where one raid had left their home destroyed. Moving to Uddington near Glasgow, they were joined a few months later by the recently released Peter. By this time, Peter had grown into an experienced and talented burglar. After serving time in a young offenders' institute, his parents hoped that he had put his criminal past behind him. There have been suggestions by some biographers that the parents felt responsible, to the point that Peter's own father was afraid of his son.

Whatever the truth about the matter, Peter didn't last long in Scotland. In a matter of months, he was back in England, taking any job he could find. Staying in Blackpool, the pleasant weather meant that he would often sleep on the beach. Some days he was a street photographer, other days he worked at the amusement park. Sometimes, he was involved with a secret gambling school. All of his earning were spent on cigars, brandy, and girls. He was known to carry a silver dollar in his pocket, flipping it often. Building a reputation as something of a show off, he was known to the police. They knew of his hair-trigger temper, backed up by dreams of being an American gangster, just like the ones in the mob films he loved. One such incident left Peter badly beaten after he tried to relentlessly flirt with the girlfriend of an actual gang member. The incident infuriated Peter, and he returned to the gang badly drunk and having acquired a gun. People managed to talk him down and relieve him of the firearm. A short time later, arrested again for breaking into a house, Peter managed to get away from the courts with a "not guilty" verdict. Altogether, these incidents were giving the young man a feeling of invincibility.

For a while, Peter moved between Scotland and England. His nefarious activities to the south of the border would land him in trouble, and then he would lie low for a while by moving back in with Samuel and Bridget. After a string of housebreakings in various parts of Glasgow, the police noticed that the perpetrator followed the same routine, clambering up drainpipes before gaining entry. Fingerprints were left at each scene, as found by Detective Constable William Muncie.

Muncie was called to a number of burglaries in quick succession and discovered various objects that might contain fingerprints. He had them all checked and cataloged. Then, on the 17th of February, 1946, he met Peter Manuel. The teenager had been strolling down a street near one of the burgled houses Muncie was investigating, and when questioned, was more than happy to reveal his full name. After being accused of entering the home in question, Peter was adamant that he had only been watching the property and that another person had been responsible for entering illegally. When performing a search, the policeman discovered a gold watch in Peter's pocket.

When investigating further, it seemed as though Peter had been using the home as a base of operations. He would steal from other homes and return the items to his base. The watch was just a small part of the stolen loot kept in the home. Furthermore, it seemed as though Peter had been sleeping in the property, regardless of the fact that it was occupied by the owner. He had set up a small bed with blankets and pillows in a corner of the home, hiding his stash behind a sliding panel. The confidence and the nerve to pull such a scheme astonished the police. There was, they suspected, an element of thrill-chasing involved. This was especially true on the occasion when he had hidden behind the sliding panel during a police search of the home. Happy to think about himself as the master criminal, Peter Manuel was arrogantly evading the law.

This finally came to an end in March of 1946, when a court appearance ended with a twelve-month sentence. At the time, Peter was nineteen years old. The prison evaluation gives us some details about his body shape, with his height pegged at five feet four inches and his chest measurement recorded as 33.5 inches. The decision to plead guilty is a great insight into the psychological state of the teenager, with some having suggested that the relatively lenient sentence came as a relief and meant that Peter could be assured the authorities were not looking into his more troublesome crimes. Indeed, this came to a head when – after having the considerable sum of £60 paid by his father for bail – Peter was implicated in a number of sex crimes.

The bail paid by Peter's father, Samuel, was no small amount. It was a reflection of the extent to which he was indulged by his parents and a demonstration of the way in which punishment seemed to evade him. But the burglaries were not the only crimes that he had committed. During the month of March, three different attacks on three different women seemed to pass by without resolution. In the days of no DNA evidence, the police were stumped. Even now, we might not know whether there were more attacks by Manuel at the time, but the three incidents in question all occurred in one place: Mount Vernon, near Glasgow.

The First Attacks

The first of these attacks came when a woman was walking with her three-year-old child down a path without lighting. She was walking slowly, watching where she stepped and where her child was, without the light to help her. Little did she know, Peter Manuel was crouched in the darkness. Already a skilled burglar, and demonstrably willing to act without any regard for morality, his actions clearly show that he had little regard for the child that walked alongside the woman. He was acting on impulse, acting out his urges.

As she walked along the path, Peter leaped out from the darkness. As she fought back, they tussled together before rolling down a hill, crashing into a fence at the base that was topped with barbed wire. Back on the path, the three-year-old was left behind, listening to the screams from the darkness. And just as suddenly as he had started, Peter stopped. Whether he had grown scared or had been spooked by something, we do not know. Leaving his attack, Peter ran up onto the path and left mother and child behind him. But just as she thought she might have escaped his attention, Peter had a second change of heart. He burst back into the darkness and began to kick the poor woman. As her child stood by, he lashed out with his foot, driving her into the ground. And then, just as before, he ran off into the night.

For investigators and those who reviewed the case in hindsight many years later, the attack seemed to be a test. It was a chance for Peter Manuel to investigate just how far he could go in his attacks without being caught. Already an arrogant and confident man, unafraid of the law, he was testing the water, building on his criminal career and moving into sexual violence. Just as much a test of his methods, it was a test of his will. The teenager was discovering whether he had the ability to assault a woman in such a manner. Despite several moments where it appeared he might be fleeing the scene, it seemed as though he had no compunctions with regards to attacking a member of the opposite sex. Regardless of this speculation, this footpath would be a familiar hunting ground for Peter.

Despite the violence of the attack, the woman recovered enough to give a description to the police. The details of the suspect were enough to point police towards Peter, who was already known to them through his burglaries. Added to the description, there were small black hairs found at the scene, similar to those Peter himself possessed. But just as the clues were beginning to point the police towards their suspect, Peter vanished. For four days, he disappeared from public view.

On the first night of his disappearance, a young nurse was walking home from an evening shift at a hospital. She walked along a path roughly six miles from the site of the previous attack. It was a public walkway, demonstrating the few worries Peter held with regards to being seen by others. As the nurse walked along, she saw a shadowy figure leaning up against a fence. He was right where she was about to walk. She would inevitably have to stroll right past him. If she wanted to get home, there were few options. To Peter, it was clear that this was a prime opportunity. With no one around, he prepared to lunge at the nurse. But by the time he reached her, she had time to prepare. Without much in the way of a plan, he simply ran at her, providing her with enough time to drop her bag and brace herself. Peter struck her, hitting her in the face, slapping his hand across her mouth and the two rolled along the floor. As they writhed, Peter's attack pushed them into the undergrowth at the side of the road. His hand slipped just enough that the nurse let out a scream.

The scream was enough to attract the attention of a passing motorcyclist. The noisy bike must have alerted Peter before he could finish his sexual assault. Picking up on the sound, he scrambled away into the night. Once again, his desperate attack had failed to pay off. Thus far, Peter had left two women in his wake. Already a dedicated criminal by this point, his efforts to add rapist to his list of crimes had thus far failed. Each time, the police had been given a vague description of the attacker, close enough that they might link Peter Manuel to the attacks. But he wasn't finished.

Less than twenty-four hours later, Peter struck again. This time, a 26-year-old woman was stepping off a bus and walking home along Fallside Road. At her house, her husband was waiting for her to arrive. He knew she was sick, his wife having suffered from tuberculosis and having undergone a hysterectomy just three weeks previously. Just as before, the location seemed quiet enough, but it was still a public path. The desperation on behalf of Peter Manuel was apparent; he was unwilling to wait and was driven by criminal lust. This is perhaps why the attack occurred just a mile away from his home.

Peter first appeared to the woman at the bus stop where she had alighted. It was a few minutes into her walk that she realized that someone was following her. Looking over her shoulder, she noticed that very same young man who had been lurking near the bus stop. Just as she noticed his presence, Peter seized his opportunity. He landed the first punch after running straight towards her. There was little in the way of complexity about his attacks. Knocking her to the ground, Peter slid his hand over her mouth. His voice growled into her ear. Peter demanded that she be quiet, aware of how screams had ruined his last attack. But she refused to go quietly. A bite of Peter's hand infuriated him, so the attacker reached out and slammed the woman's head into the ground. Again, he demanded silence. This time, she spoke up just enough to plead for mercy. If money was what he wanted, then he was free to take it.

But money was no concern for Peter Manuel. Remembering how he had been foiled the previous evening, Peter picked the woman up and dragged her from the path, hurling her over a fence and onto the raised embankment near a railway line. All the time, he growled in her ear, insisting on complete silence. It wasn't enough, however, and she still screamed for her life. This time, there was no passing motorcyclist. Furious, Peter explained what would happen if the screams continued. He would simply take his boot to her face. And so her voice dropped, explaining that she had just been discharged from a hospital. With hindsight, it was probably this vulnerability only added further drive to Peter's attack.

Already, the woman's false teeth had been smashed and knocked from her mouth. Peter continued to throw his victim to the ground, ripping away her clothes. Then, with that same absolute anger, he raped her. Snatching her scarf, he wrapped it around her eyes. Once he was done, he ran away from his blindfolded victim and vanished back into the Glasgow night. The woman he left behind was frail and wounded. She dragged herself to the road and caught the attention of a passing pedestrian. She recovered enough to report the crime, providing the police with a description of her attacker. It matched the descriptions given by the other two women.

The police responded by organizing a lineup or identity parade. These events were different from today in Glasgow of the mid-20th Century. Unlike today, there was no anonymity for the victim. Instead, they were forced to walk down the line of suspects and tap the relevant man on the shoulder. To identify her rapist, for example, this woman was required to confront and even touch the attacker just a day later. When the woman from the first attack walked along the line, she fainted. The second victim was able to provide a positive identification, while the final victim failed. But it seemed as though Peter Manuel, already sentenced to jail, felt that he wouldn't face prosecution for these crimes while in custody. But, for whatever reason, the investigators felt that there was only enough evidence to try Peter for the third attack. At the trial, a confident Peter elected to defend himself.

Peter Manuel appeared in court charged with raping his third victim. At the time the trial began, he was already serving his twelve-month sentence. Representing himself seemed to endear Peter to certain members of the court, no doubt swelling his already considerable ego. He reiterated his innocence but to no avail. Aged nineteen, he received an eight-year sentence to be completed at the end of his current incarceration. By the time he was set to be released, he would be almost thirty.

In and Out of Prison

Sent to Peterhead Prison with the other sex offenders, life behind bars would prove entirely different for the somewhat mollycoddled, boastful teen. His youthful appearance made him seem younger than nineteen, which prevented many of the more violent convicts from applying the usual treatments given to sex offenders thrown into jail. Inside Peterhead, Manuel seemed to behave well. Suddenly surrounded by a swathe of criminals more skilled and notorious than himself, Peter turned to a more scholarly lifestyle. Always proud of his overly florid writing style, he helped others with their literal endeavors. Occasionally, he even wrote stories and began to sketch. But his braggadocio was never far away and was perhaps best exhibited in his commitment to opining on law-related matters at every opportunity. In addition, his lies spread around the prison, perhaps the most outlandish of which was that he had won a boxing award when fighting in America. With stories such as these, he began to cultivate a gangster image.

Part of this was due to his – as Peter saw it – American heritage. Despite the fact that he had only been a child when living across the Atlantic, he worked to cultivate an American accent. Depending on the context, his particular vocal tics could be emphasized or abandoned to suit. His father, he lied, was a now-deceased mobster who went by the nickname Old Sparky. There were even some suggestions that Peter had been involved with intelligence agencies in both of his homelands. All were examples of his pathological approach to lying. Fights with guards and inmates – though never driving his reputation too far in either direction – did at least give Peter some degree of notoriety, the same notoriety that he craved. Associates from the facility remember his fascination with gangster films, with the exploits of John Dillinger, Al Capone, and Baby Face Nelson. He could quote their lives endlessly and clearly tried to model himself in their image. Some members of the staff accused him of possessing a persecution complex, while other inmates were impressed by the amount of fight that seemed to be bundled up in so small a package.

Peter Manuel was only behind bars for six years. Released in the spring of 1952, he found that he had got time off from his sentence, a reward for good behavior. By the time he had reasserted himself in society some months later, he was 26. Still measuring five feet four inches, he had nevertheless packed on a great deal of muscle while behind bars. Strong and with a stout frame, he relied on his father once again, who replied by getting Peter a job working with the Gas Board, though this only lasted a short while. Sometimes, he worked for the Board, sometimes he worked for the railway, and other times he didn't work at all.

Now in his twenties, Peter prided himself on his presentation. Well-dressed and a decent piano player, he enjoyed presenting himself as being well-mannered. One of his affectations was to wear gloves for the majority of the time. Associates can remember him sitting in pubs and bars, speaking about crimes in the newspaper with a self-determined level of expertise. To his audience, Peter seemed intent to insinuate that he was in some way involved with a complex criminal web that they simply could not comprehend. While robberies and hold-ups were common fodder for his feigned expertise, they did notice that he would fall strangely quiet when the subject of murder was raised in the bar.

Possessing a number of ambitions, Peter purchased a typewriter and began to tell all who would listen about how he would become a journalist. He worked his way back into the criminal world, though this time as a police informant and confidant. It seemed that he even wanted the authorities themselves to acknowledge just how wise and clever he was. This process started with a trip to visit Detective Superintendent James Hendry, to whom Peter complained about the police officers who had appeared at his trial in 1946.

In positions such as these, Peter was able to wax lyrical on one of his favorite subjects: the law. Having spent time in prison, he had fashioned himself as something of an expert on all sorts of legal matters. Despite possessing no official qualifications, Peter was more than happy to offer an opinion on any legal matter, including police investigations and prosecutions. Viewing his time in Peterhead Prison as something of a university stint, Peter's offer to the police was a quid pro quo arrangement. Thinking himself important, he would offer up what he knew about murders in the area in exchange for unspecified favors. Every time he offered up a piece of information, desperate to impress the police officers, further investigations determined that the insights were baseless and, ultimately, worthless. Many of these exchanges would take the form of letters. Remembering Peter Manuel as being fairly shy and bashful in person, one police officer remembered the notes that Peter would pass along to the authorities. They were often written with easily deciphered code words (escaped prisoners, for example, might be "sleeping birds") and spoke in an aloof, knowing manner. They might start with the announcement "Dear Friend?" and continue to take an abrasive, joking tone. One letter delivered in December finished with a postscript which wished a "Merry Christmas" to the police, though admitted that "honesty compels" him to admit to not being too concerned if this festive season was their last.

That isn't to say that Peter entirely turned his back on the criminal lifestyle, however. For example, he spent some time working with a railway company, and it should come as no surprise, convinced a number of friends to help him steal from the parked rail cars. As his friends emptied the trains, Peter would stand in his railway uniform and keep guard, watching out for any nearby policemen. Occasionally, however, Peter's desperate attempts for criminal approval would blow up in his face. While trying to impress a safecracker, he told the man stories about the safe in the railway offices. After assuring the man that it would be a simple job and a good payday, the pair broke in. It was then that the safecracker realized that Peter had been lying. There was little hope of carrying the safe away to crack it at a secure location: it weighed half a ton.

Meeting Anne

In spite of this strange existence, there was a slight reprieve for Peter Manuel. In 1954, he fell in love. Many mass murderers have their lives marked by an inability to form long-lasting bonds, especially those of the romantic variety. In the summer of that year, Peter would find himself tested to such a degree. Anna O'Hara was a bus conductor working in Glasgow. Peter met her three times before asking her out on a date. and she could see no reason not to accept. Knowing nothing of his criminal past, he seemed to her to be fairly quiet, entirely respectful, and perfectly normal. She was a pretty girl, ideally suited to Peter's fascination with looking the part everywhere he went. With his commitment to dressing well, he could escort Anna around the city as another part of his wardrobe. Speaking to friends, he would sometimes tell them that he was either engaged or on the verge of proposing, proud of the relationship. To those around Peter, he seemed something of a changed man, genuinely invested in his bond with Anna.

But everything wasn't quite as it appeared. Despite informing friends of his upcoming nuptials, Peter had neglected to ask Anna anything about marriage. Anna presented to Peter Manuel perhaps the last time at which he could have settled down and enjoyed a normal life. Putting his past behind him, a charm offensive ensured that Anna never pried too far into the criminal activity that had dominated his early life. The effectiveness of Peter's charismatic approach can be read in the reactions of Anna's family. At first, he seemed to be the model son-in-law. The first Christmas, the family got together to exchange gifts and have a fun, festive time. Whenever Peter visited the home, he would bring boxes of chocolates for both Anna and her mother. Eloquent, considerate, and seemingly serious, he was well liked by the O'Hara family. A typical Lanarkshire relationship, the couple went dancing, enjoyed walks, and ventured out to the movies. Fancying himself as something of a crooner, Peter would perform Nat King Cole songs for his paramour.

Being with Anna offered Peter another means of tapping into his American heritage. The films they saw in the cinema – High Noon, On The Waterfront, and The Big Heat – were Hollywood productions centered on the tough guy image. They were cool, essentially, and Peter played up his association with the cinematic characters. Casting himself as the tough guy taking on a world of bad guys, Peter Manuel was his own artistic director. In Anna, he had a captive and willing audience.

Eventually, they actually did get engaged. Despite telling people for months that the couple was already betrothed, Peter asked the question in May of 1955, setting the wedding day for the end of July that very same year. The entire courtship was marked by good behavior on Peter's part. When he was with Anna, he was a far cry from the criminal, amoral youth he had once been. Still prone to boastfulness and the occasional bout of pathological lying, he had at least curbed many of his more violent activities. This part of his character had been pushed down into the depths of his psyche, but there were still times when Peter might indulge his old habits. This was particularly true of the time he spent drinking in an establishment named the Woodend Hotel.

Found in Mossend, the bar had a reputation for being a hangout for many of the area's seedier characters. Peter had friends in the Woodend Hotel, and it was to them that he revealed the hidden nature of his relationship. One of the best examples is the engagement ring he had bought for Anna. When the couple had been shopping for the exact right piece of jewelry, they had come across the perfect ring. At the time, Anna had noted that it was simply too expensive. There was no chance they would be able to afford it. Peter insisted. But before Anna had the chance to actually wear the ring for real, Peter snuck out to buy a cheap imitation. He switched the two, leaving his fiancée with the replica while he returned the authentic ring for the full price. Later, he laughed over the incident with his friends in the bar, happy to reveal his enterprising, amoral approach to life.

But that isn't to say that Anna was not happy. It has been noted with some mass murderers that their home life can be entirely different from their secret, murderous activities. The Yorkshire Ripper, for example, had a wife and family who had little reason to suspect that Peter Sutcliffe might be brutally killing prostitutes on a regular basis. In Peter Manuel's company, Anna seemed safe enough. She was treated well when stepping out into the town with her husband-to-be. But there was still the question of just how she would deal with the truth about Peter's past – his jail sentences and the crimes he had committed.

The reveal was something of a surprise. One day, entirely out of the blue, Anna received an anonymous letter that detailed the crimes her fiancé had committed. The contents of the letter were very specific, noting that Peter had been born in America and moved to Britain. But beyond that, it began to move into the more spurious tales. As well as his crimes, it informed Anna that Peter had been sent to Russia as part of a government Secret Service operation, suggesting that his real father – which was not Samuel – had been executed in an electric chair.

The effect was strange. As well as accurate information about what Peter had done in the past (backing up rumors of his criminality that were present in the community), there was a distinct lack of truth and many outright lies concerning certain sections of Peter Manuel's life. As such, some people believe that the letter was sent by Peter himself. Anna burned the letter but told her fiancée about what it had said. Peter seemed to laugh off the accusations, claiming to know who would have sent such a ridiculous prank.

Aware of the rumors that had been circulating, Peter might have assumed that the letter would be a good way in which he could muddy the waters of his past. By including outrageous claims right next to the true accusations, he could create doubt in Anna's mind. Coupled with that, Peter's noted proclivity towards exaggerating the truth meant that he certainly had the imagination that might be required to work up such a story. It might have been a way in which he could temper the blow of Anna finding out about his past, or imbuing her with the belief that the rumors and accusations were simply an extension of the letter's ridiculous claims. However, neither the letter nor Peter's past were the reason why Anna O'Hara failed to marry Peter Manuel.

Over the course of their relationship, there had always been one sticking point. The issue was both simple and complex: religion. Or, to put it more accurately, the absence of religion. Though both families were nominally Catholic, Peter had long since lapsed. Religion was simply not a major part of his life, while Anna's family truly believed in the importance of traditional ceremonies such as Nuptial Mass. Peter being able to take the Communion at such a ceremony was very important and, it seemed, an impossibility. He would have needed to attend confession with a priest and to admit to his sins. Rather than pretend to do so, Peter refused. Though fully prepared to tell huge lies in almost every single aspect of his existence, this was one issue where Peter simply held his ground and refused. Whether this meant that he held religion in a high or low regard, it is hard to tell. Despite his sins, he might have been reluctant to lie to (or about) a priest, or simply held the view that he wanted in no way to be a part of such religious activities. It might even have been that he was already looking for a way to escape the upcoming wedding. Whatever the reason, the outcome was inevitable. The wedding was called off.

Peter resumed his charm offensive, sending presents to the family. But every attempt failed. By now, Anna had reached her decision, and the marriage was doomed before it had even begun. Following the breakup of the engagement, Peter was a notably changed man. He was spotted back in the Woodend Hotel, drinking by himself. Whereas he had previously reveled in showing off Anna around town, he was now drinking alone. Sitting unshaven in his railway uniform, he was a far cry from the clean-cut young man who had bragged his way around town. Still stealing from the rail yards, fellow thieves noted the bitterness that had appeared in his voice. Stay away from women, Peter advised his cohorts, they'll only get you hanged.

The date of the wedding did not pass by without incident. As was written in Peter's diary at the time, the 30th of July was set aside for his marriage to Anna. This would be the diary entry policemen read when Peter Manuel was to be arrested for the abduction and the indecent assault of a woman. The date of the crime was the same as the abandoned wedding.

The Wedding Day

On the night in question, Peter Manuel was sitting alone in his house. Having had enough of brooding over his failings, he suddenly leaped up and decided to leave the home. Before he left, he snatched up a knife from the kitchen. Just as he was standing in his doorway, 29-year-old Mary McLachlan was walking past. Peter waited until she was beyond his door and then set out after her. Her house was just a few doors away.

But before she could reach the front door, she heard a voice in her ear. Keep quiet, Peter growled, and keep walking. Mary attempted to scare her attacker away. Her husband, she insisted, was following on just behind her. But she couldn't fool Peter, who knew that she was all alone. Leading her away from the street and over a fence, Peter took his victim through to a field near the home of a man named John Buchannan. A shopkeeper who lived next door to his store in a caravan, John was at home that night. While climbing over the barbed wire around the field, Mary cut herself several times, shouting out in pain.

Hushing Mary, Peter told her that if she was to scream again, then he would use the knife to cut off her head. His voice was enough to convey the full gravity of the situation. Mary's head was full of panic. At that moment, she fully expected to be raped and then murdered. It was too much, and she broke down into tears, pleading for her life. Peter was unimpressed. He punched her firmly across the jaw, hard enough to leave her lip bleeding. But elsewhere, in the caravan, John Buchanan had heard the scream.

Hearing the struggle, John had fetched someone to run to the police and set out to investigate the matter himself. Gathering neighbors around him, he set off into the field with a torch. Moments later, a pair of passing policeman responded to the summons. As they began to search the area, there was another young couple trying to find some privacy. When questioned, they revealed that they too had heard the screams. The police and the neighbors carried on their search.

In the field, Peter kept the kitchen knife tight against Mary's throat. One sound might be enough to prompt him to drag it hard and deep across her jugular. But Peter could see the torches searching around him. He could hear the people talking as they moved through the field. Weighing up his chances, Peter soon realized that he had little hope of escaping from this unscathed. If he was going to be caught, murder might not be the easiest charge to wriggle free from. But just as these thoughts were running through his head, the approaching search party stopped. It must have been a random sound, they figured. One by one, the search dwindled in numbers. The police and the neighbors returned to their homes and their duties. Still huddled down close to the ground, Peter kept the knife perched on Mary's throat.

The entire scenario excited him. The thrill of the attack and of almost being caught simply added to the exhilaration of the attack. Together, they lay in the field for almost an hour, knife always in position. As the search party retreated into the darkness, Mary's hopes went with them. Even more excited, Peter began to whisper what he was going to do. He snarled the twisted fantasies into Mary's ear. Groping her, kissing her, forcing himself onto her, Peter took great pleasure in the assault. All the while, Mary sobbed and pleaded for her life.
And then, all of a sudden, Peter stopped. To Mary, it had seemed that the suggestion she might have a child back at home had struck a nerve. It hadn't – Peter had shown himself more than willing to attack a woman in front of her child already – but he ceased anyway. Peter's hands withdrew from her body as he lay back in the field, seemingly satisfied. For Mary, however, the terror had not abated. Even if the sexual assault had stopped, the threat of murder seemed to be very real. She lay in silence, frightened of tempting her attacker into using the knife.

They lay in the field for more than an hour. Peter, satiated, lay with knife in hand. Mary, terrified, lay next to him. On the night of his abandoned marriage, Peter Manuel now found himself in a twisted parody of the marital bed. But rather than cutting off her head, Peter began to talk. Steadily seizing the initiative, Mary began to encourage the conversation. While her attacker was talking, he seemed less likely to want to murder her. As such, she was forced to lie down in the field and listen to the truth as told by Peter Manuel. That is to say, some version of the truth.

Peter mentioned his failed engagement, suggesting that the horror of the situation had caused him to become suicidal. He had considered throwing himself in the River Clyde, but remembered at the last moment that he could swim. Having gotten drunk during the evening, he walked home and happened to see Mary walking down the street. She bore a striking resemblance to his former fiancé, so Peter was faced with little choice but to take out his anger on the passing woman. Had Mary been blonde, Peter informed her, she would likely have made it home safely. Nothing was his fault, it seemed, it was all just an unfortunate circumstance.

After this, he began to pry into Mary's life. He asked her about her name and her job. She responded with false answers, worried that Peter might track her down should she manage to escape. Her answers were slightly twisted versions of the truth, and one such answer prompted Peter to suggest that they might even share a bus to work together each morning. As he lit a cigarette and the light fell across his face, Mary realized that she recognized the man. Even if she didn't know his name, her attacker did indeed share her same bus every morning. To her horror, Peter picked up the knife once again and began to play with it.

As the blade playfully moved through the air, Peter Manuel seemed to be contemplating his actions. Still scared stiff, Mary lay next to him. But just as her fears grew stronger and stronger, Peter took a firm grip of the knife and threw it into the undergrowth. Growing in confidence, Mary tentatively asked whether she might be allowed to go home. To her surprise, Peter even offered to walk her to the front door. As they strolled across the field, Peter asked whether Mary would report him. If she did intend to inform the police, Peter would need to accompany her to the station as he had never done this kind of thing before, he lied. Mary dismissed his concerns, assuring her attacker that she would forget about it. They walked together a short while before heading in separate directions. On reaching her house, Mary broke down in her family's arms. She told them what had happened, and none of the family slept well that night. Little did she know that she would be the last of Peter Manuel's victims to escape with her life.

After a horrid night, Mary resolved to go to the police. She still had no real information about her attacker other than the fact that he lived nearby and that they occasionally shared the same bus. Added to this, she knew his face. But despite the lack of information, a quick trip on the bus with a police officer lead her to Samuel – Peter's father – and then to Peter himself. A quick search of the field in which the attack had occurred turned up the knife (with fingerprints), and Mary was able to pick Peter out of an identity parade. Standing accused of the crime, Peter was shut up inside Barlinnie Prison to await trial.

A Trip to Court

Peter did not admit to the crime. He instead provided an alibi, suggesting that he had spent the night in a certain pub, had met a woman, and then had spent the night with her. This had actually happened, though not on the date in question. The woman, when asked to confirm the alibi, ratified the information, though she told the police it had taken place a week earlier. To add to Peter's problems, the police were able to find traces of Mary's blood on his clothes. It was looking like an open-and-shut case, but once again Peter wrote to the court and elected to defend himself without the need for a lawyer.

This commitment to defending himself meant that – as could happen in the 1950s Glasgow courthouses – the attacker involved in a sexual crime could replicate the thrill of the incident while interviewing the victim on the stand. Taking pleasure in having Mary recollect the events, Peter continued to deny any involvement and even managed to drag a confession to some minor errors from officers involved in the case. One of the accusations – that he had committed perjury –was impossible, he suggested, since he had given the information on the day of his arrest, rather than being under oath. Peter gave an impassioned performance, acting out his cinematic lawyer fantasies in the courtroom. The jury even began to side with him.

Taking advantage of a courtroom custom allowed to those who defended themselves, Peter concocted a story that allowed him to account for all of the facts without implicating himself. To avoid self-defending persons from being bullied by professional and trained lawyers, Peter attempted to convey his story to the courtroom without officially placing himself under oath. Allowed to talk at length, he used various moments to deliver statements to the jury, feeding them his complete alibi. But at no point did he take to the stand and allow the lawyers to question this version of events. This kept Peter from committing perjury, while preventing his accusers of being able to deconstruct his alibi.

According to Peter's new version of events, he and Mary were known to one another. They had been courting for a while but had recently had a falling out. Having met earlier on the night in question, they had quarreled, and Peter had punched her in the face, causing the bloodied lip. At the time, he had apologized and the couple had reconciled. Together, according to Peter's version of events, the couple then went to check a number of rabbit traps he had laid, a journey that caused Mary to get scratched and cut by the barbed wire. The knife had been thrown into the undergrowth when Peter wished to alert his dog's attention to an on-coming train. It was, he argued, simply a misunderstanding.

Because of the way in which Peter conspired to deliver his version of events, there was no chance to question the other witnesses about this story. In modern times, this loophole has been firmly closed, but in the Glaswegian court of the 1950s, it allowed Peter the chance to outwit his prosecutors in what should have been an open-and-shut case. There was not even a charge of perjury that they could level against Peter, as he had delivered his evidence while not technically under oath. When the jury returned from their deliberations, the majority found him "not guilty."

Understandably, Mary was aghast. Inconsolable, she was now faced with the world thinking her a liar, as well as being confronted with the idea that she had actually been dating the man who sexually assaulted her. To her, it seemed as though she was now the one on trial, with Peter Manuel somehow having managed to make it so that he appeared to be the victim in this situation. She was shunned by some members of the community in which Peter was a known figure, and labeled as a troublemaker. Meanwhile, Peter's courtroom antics ended in cheering and celebrations among his friends and family. He had even managed to demonstrate his own intelligence in front of a captive audience. This time, his bragging, audacity, and arrogance had paid off. Reveling in the attention for the moment, there was clearly an even darker undercurrent to his appearance at the court. Next time he attacked someone, it would be far easier to ensure they would never be able to talk to the police at all.

Anne Kneilands

The story of Scotland's first serial killer starts – for some people – with the death of Anne Kneilands. To this point, Peter Manuel had been an immoral, criminal, and mostly unspectacular pest. His sexual assaults and robberies were certainly terrible actions, but he gave the impression to the police of a man desperate to believe his own mythology. Similarly, those in the criminal underworld noted Peter as a pathological liar and knew not to take him too seriously. Though he had a reputation, it was perhaps not the exact image that Peter spent years to impart in everyone's minds. While he saw himself as a smooth talking, cinematic anti-hero, other saw him as a little thief who liked to tell big stories. As happy as he had been to tell everyone about certain aspects of his criminal undertakings, the moment when his crimes became an intrinsic part of Scottish history were kept far quieter by Peter Manuel.

On the 4th of January, 1956, there were reports in Scotland of a daring robbery. Thieves had snatched a safe containing £1,000 and had driven away into the night. The frantic search for their whereabouts led to the scrambling of a mountain rescue team, but no one managed to recover the money, and the search was called off that night. It was exactly the kind of heist that Peter Manuel would typically delight in recalling to anyone who would listen. Possessing little in the way of facts, he would tell people in bars exactly how it had been done, hinting toward some greater level of knowledge that left people wondering whether he might have been involved. But when Peter returned to work the next day, he had few stories to share. He did have cuts and scratches on his face, though his co-workers put this down to nothing more than Peter being Peter.

The news the next day was dominated by stories of the robbery. This meant that the discovery of a body on the East Kilbride golf course was somewhat overlooked. Eventually known as the "5th-Tee Murder," it quickly became clear that this was not just a brutal murder, but that there had been a sexual element to the attack. The victim, Anne Kneilands, had been missing for a number of days. Last seen on the 2nd of January, her friends and family had no idea where she had been. At just seventeen years old, she was still very much a teenager. Standing at five feet and ten inches, she had fair hair and was one of six children. She worked as a machinist at a factory in Howard Street.

According to the reports from her family, she was eagerly anticipating the holiday period. Anne had arranged to meet a man, whom she had met at a dance in the previous week on Monday the 2nd of January. Her sister Alice, who had also attended the dance, could describe the man to the police though knew little about him. To the police, this man was to be considered the number one suspect. Anne had told Alice about her upcoming date, mentioning that the man was Private Andrew Murnin, part of the parachute regiment home for Christmas. The pair had agreed to meet at a bus station the next Monday, traveling into Glasgow together on the 18:15 bus. Anne even confessed her doubts to Alice as to whether the man would turn up, assuring her that she would come straight home is he didn't show.

Having stayed home the entire weekend, Anne left her house just after 17:20. She walked straight to the bus stop but was disappointed to discover that her date didn't turn up. Hanging around in case he was late, Anne eventually gave up and strolled to her friends' home nearby. After spending time with the Simpson family, she left at around 18:40 to catch the bus back home. She never mentioned the failed date to her friends, meaning that the police had assumed she simply went out with the young man afterward or at least went dancing elsewhere. Spending some time trying to question anyone who might have been out dancing that night, the police discovered that she would likely not have been able to afford a night out, having only taken four pence in her purse. Obviously, she had expected her date to cover her costs.

Indeed, Anne's parents had not been too concerned about their daughter until the 4th of January. It was not unusual for her to stay with a friend, so they only began to grow worried a couple of days later. Just a few hours later, they were struck by the news that her body had been discovered. Anne had been brutally murdered, and her body had been dumped on a golf course.

So detectives were left with the possibility of chasing down Andrew Murnin. The soldier, when questioned, was quickly cleared of any involvement. He had a watertight alibi, having spent the night in question with friends and family who could back up his story. Trying to piece together the last hours of Anne's life became increasingly difficult. Left with no further leads, the police were running out of ideas.

The scene of the murder had been horrific. Discovered by a dog walker who enjoyed the pastime of collecting lost golf balls, Anne was found with her skull smashed to pieces. The fragments had been scattered around but there were some clues to what had occurred. Based on the crime scene, the detectives were able to ascertain that Anne had been walking along before a smaller, more powerful man had approached her from behind. Realizing the attacker's intentions, Anne had run down a steep slope and attempted to climb up the other side. In doing so, she had left behind a shoe. It was a dancing shoe. In the dark, she had then run straight into a barbed wire fence. They caused a number of deep cuts, while the struggle meant that she lost her other shoe. Slowed down, the attacker was catching up. Writhing free, the bare-footed Anne ran for several hundred yards across a muddy field. She left footprints in the ground. She would not make it to the other side.

For the police, there was little doubt as to the exact location of the murder. The ground at this spot was covered in blood and bone, though the body itself had been dragged a short distance. To the police, this meant that the killer had either spent some time down near the body before moving it or had returned to the scene of the crime afterward in the hope of moving it to a more secluded area. The victim's underwear and tights had been ripped away, though there was no evidence that Anne had been interfered with sexually, as the police as the time put it. There was nothing to indicate what murder weapon had been used, and Anne's possessions had been spread out over a 300-yard area.

The police were seemingly stumped. One of their best leads came on the 4th of January when thirteen-year-old Elizabeth Simpson – part of the family who Anne had visited - was shoveling ashes at the rear of her farmhouse. In doing so, she came across a handbag filled with metal spools. It was identified as the handbag Anne owned. At this stage, it was unclear just why the attacker had thrown the bag into the Simpson's garden. Perhaps he had tried to implicate them in the death or arouse suspicion among the police. He might have been following Anne from the moment she left their house or had simply happened across the property by chance. Whatever the reason, the police were left with little in the way of clues.

266

However, they had a list of usual suspects and – somewhere in the middle – was Peter Manuel. Perhaps not enough attention was paid to Manuel, however, as not only did he have scratches all over his face, but also he was working near the golf course as part of his time with the Gas Board. Indeed, the man who had discovered the body had briefly paused when running for help to tell some workmen about the find, men who were working on the same project as Peter. The police were eventually drawn back to the site a few days later when one of the staff reported their boots had been stolen from a locker and returned again a few days after that to follow up on the murder inquiry. Occasionally, Peter would be on site when they arrived and showed no problems with piping up and chatting to the officers. He gave false accounts to the police of chasing an unshaven man on the day in question. It was entirely fiction.

This – along with other investigations – continued for some time. Ten days later, Detective Superintendent Hendry appeared on the site with the expressed intention of talking to Peter. Meanwhile, other officers were sent to his parents' home simultaneously for another branch of questioning. What they found was a well-prepared story. On the night of the 2nd, both Peter and his parents maintained, he had stayed in all evening. It had been less than three months since Peter had theatrically defended himself in court, and during this time, the police had become familiar with the clothes he wore. As such, when they searched his room, they noticed that one particular blazer was missing. According to Peter, he had lent it to a friend. Rather than have the police bother said friend, Peter did not give a name. He told this story in front of his father, who willfully lied and corroborated the information. The clothes in question were never seen again. Despite the growing evidence and suspicion around Peter Manuel, the police never acted. To the murderer, it must have seemed like he had escaped punishment once again.

The Criminal Underworld

The killing of Anne Kneilands in January of 1956 seemed to imbue Peter with the idea that he was now a fully paid-up member of the Glasgow criminal underworld. While the majority of real gangsters despised his loose lips, petty theft, and proclivity for sexual assault, Peter saw himself as a gangster. While most people returned to their lives in the wake of the murder, Peter knew that he was at the center of the police suspicions. To him, it seemed as though this cat and mouse game with the police would impress his fellow criminals. Despite the attention paid to him by the authorities, Peter must have thought this to be the perfect moment to cement his status among the criminal fraternity.

Together with an acquaintance, Peter hatched a plan to rob a canteen near Blantyre. Not quite on the level of the safe robbery which had taken place just before the murder of Anne Kneilands, it was more in line with the petty theft that Peter normally practiced. He must have misjudged the trust placed in him by the people he talked to in bars, as when he arrived at the canteen, he found the police ready and waiting for him. Waiting for the two men to attempt to break in, the police moved in and arrested the pair. Despite the seeming ease of the job, Peter still proved elusive. When his partner was taken, Peter managed to escape and flee into the night.

But this time, the police had an advantage. During his escape, Peter's clothes had caught on a piece of wiring and ripped. The investigators recovered the material, drove to Peter's home, and simply waited for their suspect to arrive back at the house in his torn clothing. This time, the evidence was enough to provide a conviction, and Peter was in court the very next day. A date was set for his full trial, and the inevitable custodial sentence while, in the meantime, he was allowed to walk free. Once again, bail was paid, and Peter was allowed back on the streets with insidious intent.

Despite the stack of evidence that had begun to pile up in the police headquarters regarding Peter Manuel, he was proving to be an impossible suspect to catch. It was fairly common knowledge among the authorities that Peter was the one behind Anne's murder as well as a string of other crimes committed throughout the area. Whenever there was a minor burglary, he would be near the top of the list of suspects. But, somehow, he always managed to escape their grasp.

The Watt Family

One of the major crimes of Peter Manuel's serial killer history was defined by the fact that he was, for so long, not the chief suspect. As we shall see, the murders of Marion Watt, Vivienne Watt, and Margaret Brown were followed by a convoluted and misinformed investigative process that left Peter feeling smugger than ever before. His arch enemies, the police, seemed to have derailed off down a tangent while he stood by and watched. To make matters worse, they came close to hanging the wrong man entirely. Few things would likely have pleased Peter more than to see the police grow so convinced in their suspicions that it would lead them to the wrong person, allowing him to demonstrate his titanic intellect once again.

It was eleven days after the triple murder that the police arrested William Watt. William was the husband, father, and brother-in-law to Marion Watt, Vivienne Watt, and Margaret Brown respectively. Two months before, the family had moved to South Glasgow, just around the edges of what might be considered by the police to be "Manuel territory." To the family, the move was a chance to climb up a rung of the social ladder, with a nicer home in a more aspirational area. Marion was recovering from a recent heart operation, while her daughter Vivienne was sixteen years old and increasingly independent. To help Marion with the final stages of the recovery, mother and daughter decided to go on a short holiday together, and when they returned, it would be William's turn for a short break on his own. William relished the chance and already knew where he would be going: the Cairnbaan Hotel near the Crinan Canal. It was an ideal fishing spot, one he'd visited before, and he could take the family Labrador, Queenie, with him. As well as his fishing equipment, he would take his shotgun as well, just in case there was a chance for further sport. A former police reservist, he was considered by his peers to be a respectable man, certainly, one few people would be worried about owning a gun.

On the return of his wife and daughter, William drove out to the hotel on the 9th of September, 1956. It was a ninety-mile trip driving around Loch Lomondside, a route that could be done in just over two hours, as proved by the police. Upon arrival at the hotel, William met up with some old friends and shared a drink or two in the hotel bar, which was run by a couple of his friends.

He was known to the regulars and seemed to be acting in an entirely normal fashion. A week later, on the 16th of September, he filled up his car with seven gallons of petrol and had the engine checked by a local mechanic. Cars in the 1950s were not as reliable as today, and driving along rural Scottish roads meant it often paid to be sure your vehicle was in the best possible condition. William felt there might be an issue with the engine, as well as the occasionally flickering headlights. He arranged for the mechanic to give the car a full check-up the following day. That night, he phoned home just as he had done every few days. He spoke to Marion at around 22:30, who informed him that her sister – Margaret – had come to stay the night. The two talked about whether William would extend his holidays for an additional week. It was, Marion, informed him, William's decision.

Most of our information about what happened next comes from Deanna Valente, a neighbor, and friend of Vivienne. Deanna told the police that Marion and her sister sat in the front room listening to records on that night. As Deanna recalled, Vivienne spoke to her father on the phone and told her friend about how angry he had made her. William had forgotten to give his daughter her pocket money but had promised to give her double the next week. When Deanna left the house later that evening, it would be the last time anyone would see the three women alive.

Meanwhile, William had stayed up late into the night. The police came to be very reliant on the facts that they felt they could prove. They knew that he had been drinking with a man named Mr. Leitch, the owner of the hotel, until 00:30, and had let his dog out before retiring to bed. According to witnesses, William had said that he planned to wake up early in the morning to go fishing. To accomplish this, he had borrowed an alarm clock from the hotel and had set it to ring at 06:00. Though he claimed to have disabled the alarm at some point, the police found that it was still set. Either it had been ignored, William was mistaken, or he was lying. The next time anyone saw him was just after 08:00 in the morning. A waitress from the hotel spotted him wiping away the frost from the windscreen of his car. Their conversation seemed to indicate that he had awakened an hour after he intended but was still determined to drive to the fishing spot to check it out before he would return to the hotel for his breakfast in an hour's time. This was as much as the police could verify.

As the news of the murders broke, however, there was a series of calamitous events. The first of these involved a journalist, who called Margaret's husband at his workplace. Though the journalist tried to pry information from Mr. Brown, he avoided mentioning why he was calling and simply contrived to arouse the man's suspicions. After a visit home, another call from the journalist, and then a call to the police, Mr. Brown discovered the news of his wife's murder in an incredibly roundabout fashion. It is thought that the very same journalist called through to the Cairnbaan Hotel later that morning and claimed to be a business associate of William Watt. When he couldn't remember Watt's first name, the hotel owner hung up the phone.

Just ten minutes later, William's brother John phoned the hotel as well. He spoke to one of the owners and delivered the terrible news. A taxi was sent to collect William from his fishing spot, and when he arrived back at the hotel, he struggled to deal with what he had been told. After placing a call to gather more information, William broke down into tears. Gathering himself together, he changed, packed, and prepared to travel back home. Still distraught, he asked a local man to drive him. Just outside Glasgow, they met up with the police, who drove him the rest of the way. Attempting to put on a brave face, William spent the first leg of the journey preparing himself. This resulted in a weak smile being offered to the police officer who collected him, a fact that eventually worked against him. The policeman took the smile as a guilty gesture, having expected to meet a thoroughly broken man.

This forced smile was the beginning of an arduous period in William's life. With the initial seeds of suspicion sewn, police began to put together a hypothetical itinerary of how he might have accomplished the murders. One fact that worked against him was his extramarital affairs. William had been unfaithful a number of times and police suspected that his murderous actions might have been an extension of this. According to their theory, he had snuck out of the hotel at close to 01:00, driven back home at high speed with the dog in the car, smashed the glass window in the front door, broken into his house to establish a false trail, executed all three women, and then sped back to the hotel as quickly as possible. This four hour round trip (with time allotted for the murders) would have him back at the hotel just in time to meet the staff member in the morning.

But there were a number of small facts working against this. First, he had been seen wiping frost off his windshield in the morning, suggesting that the car had been parked all night. Second, the borrowed alarm clock went off at 18:00 the next day, suggesting that it had been mistakenly set. Thirdly, and perhaps mostly importantly, there was little reason for William to want his family dead. Aside from a string of affairs, there was little reason for the man to want to kill all three women.

Nevertheless, the police endeavored to prove that it would have been possible for him to make the trip. There were even suggestions that he had a secret stash of fuel cans hidden along the route to prevent the petrol levels in the car from changing. Divers began to search through the Crinan Canal near the family home for a murder weapon. They found nothing. In fact, the gun was hidden in an entirely different stretch of the canal some ninety miles away, thrown in by the real murderer. But the weight of opinion began to amount against him. Both the police and the public established him as the number one suspect. Somewhere, Peter Manuel must have been laughing to himself. Once again, he had gotten away with murder.

But what exactly had Peter Manuel done that evening, and what had compelled him to murder three women, tripling his body count in one fell swoop? To find out more, we have to travel down the street to another home. Margaret and Mary Martin were retired sisters who departed on holiday on the 15th of September. As was his style, Peter broke into the home in order to search for anything of value. To get in, he smashed a piece of glass in the front door and once inside, managed to go through every inch of the house. Not only did he search the entire contents, but he lay on the bed in his boots, burned a carpet with a cigarette, poured soup all over the floor, and took a pair of nylon tights from the bedroom to wear over his hands. It was a typical Peter Manuel break-in, the theft marred by the strange behavior once in the home.

In another typically Manuel move, Peter then used this burgled home as a base of operations. He planned to rob houses in the same area and return the loot to the Martin's house. To accomplish this, he had made sure to arm himself. Taking a .38 revolver from his home (legally owned and registered), he had been bragging to friends and fellow drinkers in pubs about how he was now armed and dangerous. According to testimonies later given to the police, he had been discussing how he had used the pistol to ensure it was working. Already armed when he carried out the first burglary, the Martin sisters were lucky that they were not home.

The Watt family were not nearly as fortunate. Leaving number 18 (the Martin's house), Peter went across the road to number 5 (the Watt household). It was the early hours of the 17th of September, and by now, everyone had gone to bed. Just as before, Peter smashed the glass in the front door and gained entry. Moving through the home, he arrived at the bedroom to find Mrs. Watt asleep next to her sister. He shot Marion Watt in the head, which instantly roused the sister. Clambering to her feet, Peter shot the other woman twice. There was a small amount of interference with both women's night clothes, though Peter seems to have saved himself for what was awaiting him in the next bedroom.

Peter arrived in Vivienne's room afterward. Unlike the other two women, she seems not to have been killed right away. There appeared to have been a struggle in her room, which involved the sixteen-year-old taking a forceful blow to the face. After this, it was likely that the murderer tied the girl's hands behind her back, ripping away the black pajamas that she had been wearing. A number of buttons were littered across the floor. Various items of clothing wear found scattered and torn the next day, though it's not clear whether Peter removed the clothes before or after the girl's death. Eventually, however, he executed her with the pistol, leaving three bodies in his wake. Before leaving the home, he covered each corpse with a bedsheet.

This time, there seemed to be nothing taken from the household. There was a cigarette that had burned through the carpet, but it took a number of hours for anyone to grow suspicious. The day before, Marion Watt had ordered a wake-up call from the phone company. It had rung three times after 07:00, though no one had answered. Peter might even have still been in the house at the time. It was 08:45 the next day when a cleaner arrived at the house. Unable to get in and seemingly unable to wake anyone up, she was soon joined by a postman. Together, they managed to gain entry into the house and discovered the horror that lay before them. Hearing snores from Vivienne's room, the postman had assumed it was the dog. Actually, it turned out to be the last sounds Vivienne Watt would ever make. She died a short time later.

The discovery of the burgled house over the road was inevitable after the police were called. To the credit of the authorities, they noticed the hallmarks of Peter Manuel in every aspect of the operation. To gather more information, they obtained a warrant to investigate the .38 revolver owned by Manuel and went to his house. There, they found him in his typically combative fashion. He refused to answer any questions, while his father floated around making claims of harassment and threatened to place a call to the local Member of Parliament. With little else to go on, the police couldn't bring in Peter for questioning and couldn't find the gun in question.

On the 2nd of October, 1956, Peter Manuel began his jail sentence. By that point, he must have considered himself very clever indeed. Seemingly protected behind bars, he was now out of sight while the investigation focused on William Watt. Once again, he had outsmarted the police force.

Meetings

Peter Manuel spent the next thirteen months of his life confined to the Barlinnie Prison in Glasgow. Just because he was locked up, however, that did not mean he couldn't resume his favorite pastime of trying to outsmart the police. Taking a notable interest in the killing of the Watt family, he reached out to Laurence Dowdall. Dowdall was a lawyer who would eventually become a legend in the Glasgow legal system. In years to come, those thrown into jail would be heard to demand the authorities "bring me Dowdall!" He had a reputation as a fiercely intelligent and skilled legal practitioner, and it was he who received a letter from Peter Manuel, in which Peter asked that he assist in appealing against his current conviction. As a bargaining chip, he offered up information regarding a recently required client of Dowdall, whom he described as an "all-round athlete." The client was none other than William Watt, who had competed one time in the Highland Games.

Such a move was classically Manuel. It demonstrated his position of power, suggesting an in-depth knowledge and awareness that would only be available to one who was a key part of the Glasgow criminal underworld. On listening to what Peter had to say, Dowdall advised that he take the information about William Watt to the police. Peter had told Dowdall that he knew who had committed the murders (technically true) and that it was not William Watt. He offered no further information, however. Speaking later, the lawyer recalled Peter's disapproving attitude toward the police.

Peter's relationship with William Watt was certainly odd. After meeting with Dowdall during his prison sentence, he made it clear that he was willing to taunt the man who had just had his family murdered. Suggesting that he knew the perpetrator, but happy to see William take the fall, the matter came to a head when Peter rediscovered his freedom.

Released on the 30th of November, 1957, Peter Manuel was back on the streets of Glasgow with a purpose. Intending to announce his arrival back on the criminal scene, he immediately took to his old routine of house breaking. This time, when entering the homes, he would even cook himself a meal. In addition to this, one of the first things Peter did was visit a number of newspaper offices. He would talk to any journalist who would listen about the Watt killings, though none appear to have taken his information seriously. Watt had been released shortly after his arrest, and nearly a year later, Dowdall suggested that the three of them – the lawyer, the falsely accused, and the secret murderer – sit down to dinner together.

Dowdall requested that Watt allow him half an hour before the meal to talk to Manuel. When arriving at the restaurant, he found Peter was already seated and was casually reading a newspaper. He had been out of jail for three days by this point, though his demeanor gave nothing away. Well-dressed, he spoke to the lawyer in a calm, reasonable, and assured manner. When Watt arrived thirty minutes later, he was anything but. Threatening to tear Peter "to pieces," Watt clearly suspected him of involvement in the murders. Dowdall worked to calm the man down, however, and the three had dinner. Despite the lingering threat of violence, the meal seemed to clear the air between the two men.

Initially, Peter had assured the lawyer of knowledge about the murder. Taking on the role of a consulting criminal, he had told the story of an unnamed man who had requested that Peter assist with a break-in. Informing Peter that there was a great deal of money in the house and only women there to guard it, Peter had refused on principle. He would never condone such cowardly behavior. The day after the murders, Peter had met the man again and this time described him as being in "a hell of a state." Carrying a revolver and asked Peter to get rid of the weapon on his behalf. Peter had thrown it into the river. To back up the story, Peter offered a detailed description of two rings reported stolen by the Martin sisters, which he had said had been dropped down a drain.

Suspecting Peter Manuel's motives, Dowdall spoke to someone in the police who knew about the man. Learning of Peter's character, he decided to indulge his ego, attempting to gather more information and so met with him a number of times. Offering up doubt during a return visit, he managed to get Peter to deliver a detailed description of the Watt's house, a description that had apparently come from the anonymous assassin. Suggesting that this and other snippets of information could have come from the newspapers, Peter desperately tried to demonstrate his knowledge by describing how his mysterious gunman had smashed the glass in the window, how he had shot the first two women, and finally how he had knocked out, tied up, and executed the youngest victim. None of this information had been given out to the press and no one – not even the police – had noticed that the killer had stopped to eat something in the kitchen, a classic Peter Manuel trait.

Dowdall continued to stroke Peter's ego, encouraging him to offer up more and more information. Peter seemed to be enjoying himself, happy to talk at length about his encyclopedic knowledge of the criminal world. And then, just as Peter was beginning to revel in the process, Dowdall ceased his visits. Just as he had expected, Peter made the next move, desperate to continue. A letter was sent to the lawyer, in which it was clear that Peter was desperate to be seen as an intellectual match for Dowdall, yearning for acceptance and acknowledgment. Agreeing to meet again, this time Dowdall had Peter draw a picture of the revolver as he had seen it, a sketch that would form a key part of Peter's eventual trial.

During this time, Peter had not forgotten to carry on with one of his favorite past times – taunting the police. One of his best-loved boasts was that he could get the police to dig up his parents' garden whenever he pleased. He did this again, when talking about the lanyards he had thrown away from the pistol. When they found nothing, Peter delighted in his ability to feed the police false information and send them on a fool's errand.

It was after his release from the prison that Peter was able to turn his winding-up tactics to William Watt himself. After the two managed to clear the air at the restaurant, they met several times in the following weeks. Watt had spent a grand total of 66 days in jail before being cleared of the murders, and in addition to losing his family, he was clearly stung by this criminal who claimed to know what had really happened. During the course of these meetings, Peter expanded on the story he had given Dowdall. The perpetrator, he claimed, was a man named Charles Tallis. Working with two other criminals, Tallis had been the one who broke into the Martin house and had used it to case the home of one of Watt's neighbors (Deanna Valente's home), whom they were convinced possessed a safe containing between £5,000 and £10,000. When the criminals had seen Deanna inside the Watt home that night, they had mistaken the addresses. The whole thing was a tragic misunderstanding, Peter Manuel explained to William Watt.

Watt now demonstrated an amazing amount of self-control. He listened as Peter discussed the crime at length, seemingly pleased to have an especially captive audience. Peter described the home in great detail, supposedly as Tallis had described it to him. One of his accusations related to an earlier robbery, and he went off on a tangent about the gun involved having been used in said burglary. The house had been empty, but a quarrel among the thieves had resulted in the gun being fired into a mattress. Previously, the police had not connected the robbery to the Watt murders (or indeed, to Peter Manuel), but Peter wondered aloud whether being able to trace the bullet from that mattress to the ones used in the Watt murders might exonerate William. William Watt listened quietly, and just as Dowdall had done before him, allowed Peter enough rope to metaphorically hang himself.

To Peter, however, it seemed as though there was pleasure to be had from such a dangerous enterprise. Recalling the way in which he had killed three people to Glasgow's best lawyer and to the family member of the deceased was, to him, a thrill ride. He was careening down the line between the excitement of reliving his crime and the pleasure he took from outsmarting people. Just as the thrill of being caught had excited him so much when he lay next to Mary McLachlan with a knife to her throat, the ecstasy derived from the authorities' fruitless attempts to catch him. As Peter danced around both men, Watt and Dowdall were prepared to play the long game if it meant a conviction. But away from their dalliances and the investigations being conducted by the police, Peter Manuel was playing a far deadlier game.

A Real Killing?

Peter Manuel's fifth victim was killed on Sunday the 8th of December 1957. Sydney John Dunn was a taxi driver, who was working in the early hours of that morning. It was wet and windy when he collected a passenger who needed to travel to Edmondbyers, a small village in County Durham. As 36-year-old man, he was the owner of a taxi company that he operated with his family. Variously described as a hard worker and a sober man, he had spent the war with the Royal Air Force. A romantic interest waited for him in Gateshead, a widow who he would go and see most Saturdays. This week, they had arranged to meet on Sunday evening rather than Saturday. But he would never arrive. The last time a confirmed sighting took place, he was parting ways with a fellow driver as they drove in separate directions.

What happened next is almost entirely speculation. From various witness reports of middling quality, we know that Sydney's car was spotted a number of times throughout Sunday. The first of these came at 08:00, followed up by numerous other accounts as the roads got busier and the light got better. Some even reported seeing a scarf and a cap lying next to the vehicle. To most people, it was safe to assume that the car had just been abandoned and was of no real concern. Some people had even assumed it belonged to people on a picnic. Given the weather conditions, this was a far-fetched idea. Amazingly, no one stopped to investigate the car until a member of the local police force pulled over on his bicycle and decided to have a look.

The taxi had pulled over at a right angle to the main road. On closer inspection, it was clear that both the exterior and interior lights had been smashed, while both front doors were left wide open. When looking inside the vehicle, the officer discovered blood on the steering wheel and assumed that there might have been an accident, with the victim getting hurt in the process. With the weather bad and the light fading, searching for an injured person would prove difficult. Cycling two miles to the nearest town, he checked in to see if there were any reports of an accident or an injury circulating. Even when he checked with the hospitals, there was nothing to report. By this time, it was clear that something had to be done, so a search team was put together.

It didn't take long to find the body. After just 15 minutes of searching, a police dog sniffed out the body of Sydney Dunn. Dumped in a cloister of heather some 150 yards away from the actual car, it was clearly not an accident. He had been dragged there, seemingly by his coat that was now pulled up and over his head. Found nearby, the man's wallet still contained some money. Other items were found scattered between the car, the victim, and the road, though none gave away much information. Judging by the reports in the Durham County Advertiser from the next day, the authorities were baffled by the case. At one point, they even issued a statement saying that foul play might not be suspected. The man's neck injuries, they reckoned, might have been caused by a regular accident. It was just an hour before this statement was withdrawn.

A plea was issued for the passenger from the early hours to come forward. A few days later, the real cause of death was revealed. A post mortem had asserted that Sydney had died of a gunshot to the head. As far as they could tell, the police believe the bullet was fired from either a .32 or .38 caliber "very worn" firearm of British origin. It had likely been fired from just twelve inches away. Piecing together the crime scene, it seemed as though the killer had been sitting in the front passenger seat when he pulled the trigger. After shooting the man in the head, the killer had then taken the time to slice open the taxi driver's throat in an unnecessary burst of violence.

The police investigation brought forth no leads. Thorough searches of the local moors and door-to-door inquiries turned up no relevant information, while the quest to find the murder weapon was floundering. The search became especially difficult when snow started to fall on the areas in question, while one contemporary newspaper reports a police man falling into a "bog-hole," bringing a farcical element to the investigation. No one came forward from the villages nearby to recollect a man on the side of the road seeking a lift, much less one covered in blood. Given the weather at the time of the murder, trying to walk from the car to the nearest built-up area would have been very difficult indeed. Serious questions were asked, though they were left unanswered, as to why the killer had simply not driven off in his victim's car.

Up until Peter Manuel's conviction in Scotland, the English police were left without a real suspect. However, in the days following his final conviction, a jury of coroners gathered together and were able to deliver a verdict on who they felt had killed the taxi driver. In their opinion, Peter Manuel was unquestionably at fault. Charged with capital murder, though unable to answer for his crimes, they determined that he was the guilty party in absentia.

When providing evidence, and without an account from Peter himself to confirm the facts, they presented the following information. One of the taxi drivers who had been working the same shift as Sydney was able to confirm Peter Manuel as being the last passenger to be picked up on that night. When involved in an identity parade, he correctly selected the killer from a lineup, having talked to him on the night. When examining Peter's clothing, the investigators discovered traces of grass that were similar to those found around Edmondbyers Common. A button that had been found inside the abandoned taxi matched one of the missing buttons from one of Peter's jackets. Similarly, two red fibers that were found wrapped around the button were similar to a jumper owner by Peter, as was a yellow thread that matched one of Peter's suits and was also wrapped around the button.

To back this up, Peter Manuel had been around Newcastle at the time of the killing. British Electricity Repairs Limited confirmed that they had offered him a job interview on the Friday before the attack, just a week after he had been released from prison. With traces of evidence and confirmation that Peter had been in the area, the police lacked only one thing: a motive. Most of Peter's earlier crimes were distinguishable by their close proximity to his Glasgow home. After breaking the law, he would invariably return to his parents' house, whereupon he could be assured of an alibi.

This, however, seemed like a random act. While the press had run wild with ideas that the killer might be a fully trained commando with a sinister motive, or an Irish person who had recently crossed into Newcastle looking for work, strongly implying that he might be a member of the IRA. This contradicted the evidence given by fellow taxi drivers, however, and is indicative of the way in which the press resorted to guesswork in the wake of the murder. Trying to piece together motivations for Peter Manuel's actions was always a perilous pastime. Often, some of his worst crimes simply came from a curiosity as to whether he could get away with it.

Looking back now, the general assumption is that this was a crime of opportunity. Peter Manuel, recently released from prison and finding himself armed and far away from home, had stayed in Newcastle for the weekend and killed Sydney Dunn in the early hours of Sunday morning. There had been some suggestion that Peter might have been cross that the driver was taking him to Edmondbyers rather than Edinburgh, but this is entirely speculation. It is just as likely that the murder was simply a spur-of-the-moment act, purely because Peter could do it.

But that is not to say that the evidence is overwhelming. We have seen already how skilled Peter was at escaping repercussions for his actions, and it was not a normal criminal trial that convicted him. Not held to the same standard of proof as a regular court, the coroner's jury was able to supply a conviction based on circumstantial evidence. Not present to defend himself, the killer found his list of victims grow by one.

It is commonly accepted that Peter Manuel murdered Sydney Dunn. We know for a fact that he was in Newcastle at the time and that his identity was confirmed by other taxi drivers. In addition we know that he was certainly capable of this kind of act. The evidence of the grass is difficult to credit, being as it came five weeks after the crime, while the clothes that were taken away for testing were hurled in the back of a van before being transported south. As such, there remains a huge air of mystery around the killing. It bears many of the hallmarks of Peter Manuel's other murders, but there remains a great many unanswered questions. Why would he kill in such a remote location? Why would he want to go to Edmondbyers? What did Sydney Dunn do to anger Peter so badly? Added to this, Peter was determined that he had not been involved. Typically happy to brag, he was adamant that he had not been involved in the murder. Even Peter's mother, talking about her son's murders at a later date, singled out the death of Sydney Dunn as being the only one which she thought he might not have carried out.

As it stands, it might be that Peter Manuel didn't kill Sydney Dunn. To the common observer, Peter Manuel's list of crimes is abhorrent, but it might be the case that it is simply one entry too long. While Peter was certainly indulging his violent side during this period, this particular murder leaves too many open questions to leave the blame entirely at his door. But as we will discover, one potential innocent verdict does nothing to redeem his guilt.

Another Suspect Case

Around the same time, and far closer to Peter Manuel's home, another murder victim was causing consternation. The story of Isabelle Cooke begins – in regards to this case – on Christmas Day, 1957. Peter had been out of jail for 25 days by this point, had visited Newcastle for a job interview, had held numerous meetings with William Watt and Laurence Dowdall, and had never forgotten his criminal inclinations. So on Christmas Day, when the Reverend Alexander Houston returned home with his wife to find their home burgled, Peter was an obvious choice of suspect. The crime had many familiar hallmarks of his work, in much the same way that the killing of Sydney Dunn did not.

Both front and back doors had been forced open and a window had been broken. Once inside, the thief had taken a pair of gloves, a sock, a camera, and a couple of pounds from the collection box that the vicar kept for missionaries in far-off lands. None of the stolen items was too valuable. Mostly, they held sentimental value, like the gloves that had been a gift from family friends who lived around the corner on Carrick Drive. Within eleven days, the Reverend Houston's attentions were diverted when he found himself speaking in front of his congregation and appealing for more information about a girl who had gone missing from Carrick Drive.

The family who lived on Carrick Drive (very close to the glove-giving neighbors) were the Cookes. Mr. and Mrs. Cooke had four children, one girl and three younger boys. Isabelle was seventeen and attended Hamilton Academy. Their home was in a cul-de-sac, only a few hundred yards from the footpath where Peter Manuel had tried to rape the mother who was with her child. Now, twelve years later, he was returning to the scene of one of his sexual assaults.

The parents of the household had departed their home in the 28th of December at around 16:00. They left Isabelle to look after her brothers in the company of their maternal grandmother. They returned four hours later, by which time Isabelle had left the house to go and visit her boyfriend, or so they believed. Most Saturdays, their daughter would travel up to Bellshill to go dancing. This week, just as most weeks, she had left the home at 18:45 to meet her boyfriend, Douglas Bryden. According to Douglas, she never showed up. After waiting 45 minutes for Isabelle, he assumed she might have gone straight to the dance, and he left to find her. But she would never arrive.

A witness who lived nearby, Elsie Gardner, reported a young girl who walked out of the family home and fell straight into the arms of her attacker. According to the report, Elsie had been in her garden in the early evening when she had heard a sudden noise that sounded like a women receiving a very serious fright. Her dog heard it too, responding with a bark, running straight to the gate and raising hell. After the dog had calmed down and stopped its barking, there were no other noises to be heard. It might well have been that Isabelle was already dead.

The Cooke family soon realized something was wrong. They had to undergo the same horrible vacuum of information that had plagued the Kneilands family years earlier. But unlike in the previous case, there was no body right away. Isabelle simply went missing. That was why the Reverend was pleading for information from his pulpit. The disappearance of Isabelle Cooke summoned a huge amount of community spirit as people desperately searched for the girl, acting in the hope that she might still be alive. But Reverend Houston would again be drafted into the process, being asked by the police to break the news to the family when a body was found in the early hours on the 16th of January, 1958.

On the day of the disappearance, Isabelle's absence was already causing worry in the family. Retiring to bed at near midnight, the parents noticed that their daughter was not yet home. This was highly irregular. Ill thoughts plagued Mr. Cooke to the extent that he took a torch and began searching outside, along the very path where Isabelle had passed by hours earlier. However, his search was in vain.

Unluckily, the Cookes' phone was not working. This thought offered up a crumb of comfort, the parents reasoning that the girl might have tried to call home to tell them that she was staying at a friend's house. By the time morning rolled around, they had run out of options. Going to the police, they reported their daughter missing. They waited the entire day until late in the afternoon, a policeman arrived bearing bad news. Isabelle's bag had been found, as had items of her clothing. The horrified parents confirmed that each piece belonged to their daughter, each item further cementing their growing dread that they would never see their little girl alive again.

Items of clothing had been found in the River Calder. It was searched. More items were found near a train track. Every train that had passed through the area was searched in case the killer had dumped the body on a passing locomotive carriage. Hundreds of people were recruited to help in the search. Some of the buttons to her coat had been laid at the entrance to a mineshaft. It was searched, but it was found to be empty. It seemed the killer was delighting in leading the police on a merry trip that ended in nothing. Wherever the body was to be found, the killer had clearly spent a great deal of effort hiding it after the murder. Two graves were found, one of which was empty. The real burial site seemed to follow a trail of clothing, leading the police eventually to the girl's corpse.

To Peter Manuel, this must have all seemed part of a fantastic game. Between Mary McLachlan, Anne Kneilands, and Isabelle Cooke, the three women had fallen prey to his whims, while he had escaped unpunished. The control he was exerting over the police was seen in the muttering to an associate, when the pair watched the police searching through the River Calder. Even at that point, Peter laughed under his breath that they were following a red herring. This kind of trust being placed in his criminal associates was misplaced, however. Despite his beliefs, there were few people in the Glasgow criminal fraternity who were impressed with his crimes against women. They regarded his actions as cowardly, a key insight into why Manuel was never welcomed into the underworld. These confessions of sexual assaults would eventually prove to be part of Peter's undoing, to the regret of none of his associates.

With the murder of Isabelle Cooke still unsolved, Peter Manuel was not pausing to revel in the incompetence of his investigators. At this point, he had barely been out of prison for four weeks, but he had clearly demonstrated little problem with returning right away to his criminal lifestyle. Now a serial murderer, Peter was leaving a trail of enemies. William Watt was increasingly suspicious and was gathering evidence during their encounters. Laurence Dowdall was acting as a go-between for the police and these investigations. The authorities themselves were well aware of Peter's reputation and resented his cockiness and the number of times he had managed to weasel his way out of a more serious conviction. The families of the victims were desperate for some resolution to the criminal spree, not only the Cooke family, but also those who had seen the guilty Peter Manuel already walking free. Finally, the fellow Glaswegian criminals were close to the end of their collective tether. One such criminal, Joe Brannan, was beginning to reveal to the police the extent of Peter's boasts to his drinking buddies. Unimpressed by the cowardly, sexual nature of the crimes, Brannan and the rest of the criminal underworld were prepared to break their policy of not communicating with the police. When it came to Peter Manuel, they were better off without him. But now getting a taste for murder, Peter was far from finished.

The Smart Family

Almost half of the murders carried out by Peter Manuel came in a three week burst. Recently released from prison, he has been accused of killing Sydney Dunn, Isabelle Brown, and three other people. If all of these murders could be attributed to him, then it painted the portrait of a man who had dabbled around the edges of psychopathy for a long time before eventually taking the plunge. There were various motives, from sexual gratification to material reward to simply satisfying his own indulgences. What marked Peter Manuel apart from other killers was that he seemed to have no qualms with abandoning his morals at the drop of a hat. A curious killer, he was content to simply murder and stay one step ahead of the authorities. Always wanting to prove his own intelligence, a cat and mouse game with the police resulted from his hideous crimes. By the end of his criminal career, we can see signs that the actions were beginning to pile up, a murderous acceleration that meant that the police were struggling to keep up with number of bodies Peter was leaving in his wake. Indeed, the culmination of his motivations and his violent tendencies can be seen in the fate of the Smart family.

Peter Smart and his family lived near Peter Manuel in Uddingston. Their bungalow had been built in 1954 and was home to mother, father, and son. The three-person family depended on Peter Smart's position as the owner of a civil engineering firm to get by. On New Year's Eve, 1957, he was paid his monthly wage and made a visit to the bank in order to settle up some debts at work. This would be his last action before taking a short holiday until the 6th of January, a well-deserved rest period after a busy year. Together with the family, he could go and visit family and friends in other parts of Scotland.

In light of the holiday, the office closed early. It was New Year's Eve, and so Peter Smart decided that picking up a bottle or two of whisky might be a good idea ahead of the evening's celebrations. Picking up a couple of bottles from a pub in Uddingston, the landlord could remember the man mentioning his plan to drive up to the Scottish Borders to visit family. Such a trip would require an early start, so Mr. Smart left the pub at 22:00 and made his way home.

Back at the bungalow, Doris Smart had been chatting to the neighbors. They had popped round for some brief celebrations but had left well before the bells rang in the New Year. Like many people in those days, the lights in the household were left on. This was a New Year's tradition, showing a willingness to receive guests and well-wishers on the special night. Neighbors recollected that the lights in the Smart household were switched off at around 02:30 that morning, likely after they had stayed up to toast one another. The young son, Michael, would likely have been sent to bed much earlier.

Switching off the lights in the home would be the last thing anyone noticed about the Smart household. They would be murdered that night, but their bodies not discovered for almost a week. It was the 6th of January before it became clear that something was wrong. Between the family and friends whom they were set to visit, each one had assumed the Smarts were visiting someone else. A series of assumptions, miscommunications, and frugal use of the telephone meant that the Smarts' bodies lay in their home for six days.

Even the neighbors had struggled to notice the lack of activity around the home. One neighbor, a Mr. Jackman, had noticed that the family's garage door had been left open. Assuming them to be away on holiday, he went across on the 1st of January and closed it. The postman and the dustman could both recall the curtains being drawn at one point, then open a few hours later. One of Michael's young friends had even come to call on the house, looking through the windows to no avail. When he had arrived, all the curtains were once again closed. There was clearly someone moving around in the home, but it could not have been any member of the Smart family.

The real worry began when Mr. Smart failed to show up for work. On the 6th of January, he was expected back in the office, and his failure to do so began to unravel the truth behind the entire story. Co-workers were further perturbed when the police phoned up to ask why Peter Smart's company car was parked in a notoriously shady part of Glasgow, seemingly abandoned. A few of them ventured to his home and tried to find their colleague, but the building seemed secure enough. They joined up with the police and chatted to the neighbors, all eventually agreeing that the circumstances were strange enough to warrant breaking into the house.

When the door was forced open, the police found the house still strewn with the Christmas decorations. It was all in order, seemingly, until one sergeant decided to venture upstairs and check the bedrooms. On doing so, he found the bodies of all three family members lying in their beds. Each person had been shot in the head. The beds were soaked with blood, and the rooms were filled with the stench of death and decay.

The news of the murders spread. Adding these to the death of Isabelle Cooke caused near panic among locals. People ran out and bought chains and locks for their homes, terrified that they might be the next victim of the serial killer. The police already had their hands full with one mysterious murder, and now they had three more. As they scrambled to make sense of the horrific deaths, Peter Manuel carried on with his life. In the intervening days between the murder of the Smart family and the time they had been discovered, he seemed to have been returning again and again to the crime scene. He was the one opening and closing the curtains, turning the lights on and off. He may even had fed the family cat. As the local police investigations reached a frenzied state, it must have pleased Peter to note just how much consternation and panic he had caused.

Peter's Evening

While New Year's Eve proved tragic for the Smart family, the Manuel family seemed to enjoy a far better night. The family was gathered together, all apart from Teresa Manuel. Working as a nurse, she was spending the night on duty. That's not to say she didn't hear from her family while they were celebrating. Receiving a phone call, she listened as Peter began to merrily sing. He ran through a number of classic numbers, including "Come Back to Sorrento," which he could sing in the original Italian. The contrast between the jubilance of the Manuel family's celebrations and the stark horror that would soon hit the Smart household was striking. As people began to see in the New Year, there was little indication of what was to come.

Indeed, while Peter Manuel was serenading his sister on a phone line, the Smart family was quietly wishing a Happy New Year to one another. For the cynical observer, it might seem that Peter was doing his best to establish an alibi, ensuring that as many people as possible heard from him on the night he would commit one of his worst crimes.

Such revelry might not have been expected from Peter Manuel in the lead up to the 31st of December. By all accounts, he was flat broke. Having only been released from prison a short while and not yet in full time employment (at least, employment of a legal nature) he was relying on government subsidies to get by. Even these were not very much. That evening, however, he was out with his family. Drinking with his father Samuel and his brother James meant that their trip to the pub was mostly financed by Peter's family members. Added to this, his mother had been so happy that he had attended confession in the local church that she gave him five shillings. The religious visit itself sparked an ominous discussion in the pub about just how strict a priest's vow of confidentiality could be. When Samuel paid for a round of drinks at the bar, Peter pocketed the change and informed his father than it was £1 that he owed him.

Later into the evening, Peter ran into his associate Joe Brannan. Brannan had even seen Peter pocket the change from his father's round, mentally noting what this might say about the current state of Peter's finances. Eventually, the Manuel family made their way back to the house and began to retire, one by one, to bed. Samuel had to work the next day, as per usual, so his wife made him a big bowl of porridge before the pair went upstairs. They left behind the two sons, Peter and James, washing the dishes in the kitchen and clearing up the mess that had been left behind. To Peter's mother, this was a sign that Peter had turned around his criminal ways. This benevolent act was enough to confirm to her that he was a changed man. She had no idea about the true extent of his crimes.

Peter Manuel was in a strange position for a serial killer. Still living at home at the age of 31, he was performing household chores and having a social evening. But the truth was that he was biding his time. He must have been plotting his evening for a while, as he made sure to be the last one awake. When James eventually moved upstairs, he assumed Peter would fall asleep on the fold-out bed that had been set up for his use. James could recall leaving for bed at six in the morning, while Samuel would wake up an hour later to get ready for work. This left Peter with an hour in which to slip out of the house.

According to the witness testimony given by Samuel, Peter was fast asleep on the fold-out bed when he came downstairs. Given Samuel's history of covering up for all of his son's misdeeds and providing dubious alibis at every opportunity, there should be no real reason why the account should be taken as being entirely true. However, the police nevertheless endeavored to prove that a single hour was all that Peter needed to get out of the house, walk a short distance to the Smarts' home, break in, kill the family, and then venture back to his bed. Peter Manuel's home was just fifteen minutes away, less than a mile. An informal recreation of the events by the police demonstrated that it was entirely possible to have traveles from one house to the other, and further evidence began to mount up.

On the morning of the 1st of January, John Buchannan opened his store. He was the storekeeper who lived in the caravan near Peter's home, and the man who had heard screams during the assault of Mary McLachlan. According to John, his very first customer that day was Peter Manuel, who strode into the store at around 10:00. According to the shopkeeper, the man was in high spirits and seemed to be well-groomed. Chatting in a friendly fashion and purchasing a packet of cigarettes, he seemed to be buoyant and cheered.

After this, Peter went to the home of Joe Brannan. The pair began to drink once again, going to a bar in Mossend. According to Brannan, Peter's economic situation had changed overnight. Whereas the previous evening he had been stone-broke and borrowing money from his father, this morning he was more than happy to flash his cash around the bar. At one point, he accidently almost paid for a round of drinks with £5 instead of a £1 note. When this error was pointed out by the bar staff, Peter joked about the mix up and bought the employees a round of drink as a reward. In a strange turn of events, Peter Manuel was now out rewarding people for their honesty.

But his generosity did not end there. Peter bought drinks for all members of Joe Brannan's family, and even thought to give the children a florin each. When it was suggested later that Peter had been spotted on a bus coming back from Glasgow center on that morning, Peter explained the situation to Brannan as a trip to the Gordon Club in order to collect money related to the Watt murders. As ever with Peter's tall tales, he kept specific details scant but was more than happy to allude to some greater criminal conspiracy of which he was clearly heavily involved.

Peter's indulgence did not stop when he parted ways with Joe Brannan that day. He met up with his family once again, and the Manuels resumed their celebrations. Attending a family party at which he sang a few of his favorite songs, Peter reportedly spent more than £10 on drinks and cigarettes. He even paid for a taxi to take his parents home when they decided that they had seen enough. When the party seemed to be in danger of ending, Peter paid for everyone to get entry into a nearby dance being hosted by a local miners' club just around the corner. According to later investigations, at this point Peter had just over two shillings in his bank account, hardly the savings of a man who seemed to be intent on splashing his cash.

Returning to the testimony of John Buchannan, it seems likely that these high spirits were caused by a recent financial windfall. Such a windfall must have come between the early hours of the morning and his visit to the shop. While he might only have had a few hours' sleep, the amount he managed to steal from the Smart household – added to the excitement and thrill of the murders – could well have been enough to propel Peter Manuel through the day without much rest.

For Mr. and Mrs. Manuel, the chance to see their son home from prison and in such a good mood must have been a relief. The idea of him being so kind and generous with his immediate family, his cousins, and his friends looked like the turning over of a new leaf. At last, it seemed as though the family was finally together. But over the next few days, they began to notice that Peter was slipping out of the house at odd hours. Rather than ask where he was going, they seemed more than happy just to have him home.

As well as the visits back and forth to the Smart family home, Peter Manuel's audacity took perhaps the biggest risk yet on the 2nd of January. On that morning, a police constable named Robert Smith left his home and began to walk to work. That day, he was to be involved in the search for the body of Isabelle Cooke. All day, he would be searching the River Calder for any trace of her remains, clothes, or possessions. As he walked alongside the road, a car pulled up alongside him, and the driver was kind enough to offer him a lift. The two were apparently heading in the same direction, and the policeman was more than happy to take advantage of the ride on the cold and depressing morning. As they drove the two and a half miles to the site of the search, they chatted about the murders.

Later on, the same car would be found abandoned in one of the more questionable areas of Glasgow. It had belonged to Peter Smart, who had been found murdered along with the rest of his family. Robert Smith would be asked to take part in a lineup, picking out the man who had offered him a lift on that fateful morning. He picked the man with ease. It was Peter Manuel.

Investigating a Murderer

After Peter Manuel's complicated history with the Scottish legal system, it should come as no surprise to see that the authorities elected to take a slow and steady approach to finally convicting their chief suspect. Peter had previously managed to get away on a technicality, had eluded official prosecution, and had gained a reputation as someone who had bettered the police on numerous occasions in the past. It was something he seemed to enjoy. In the wake of the murders of Isabelle Cooke and the Smart family, as it became clearer and clearer that Peter Manuel was their chief suspect, the police knew they had to get their suspect carefully. So how could they catch the man who had so successfully eluded them to this point?

Joe Brannan had been in communication with the police for some time. While it was normally unheard of for members of the criminal fraternity to divulge information to the police, an exception seemed to be made in the case of Peter Manuel. It was an open secret among members of the underworld that repercussions typically reserved for snitches would not be applied in this instance. Peter's brand of sexual, boastful criminality was deemed both cowardly and bad for business. Accordingly, Joe Brannan had already passed some information along to the police that had kept them in touch with Peter Manuel following his release from prison. News of his financial boon from the start of the year seemed to be of particular interest.

One of the cornerstones of the investigation into Peter Manuel used information from the Commercial Bank of Scotland. This was the institution Peter Smart had visited on the 31st of December, whereupon he had withdrawn £35. The notes handed over to him by the teller were from a brand new set that had been opened that day. This meant that there was a record of the serial numbers on the notes, and being as they had been given out in order, Mr. Smart's withdrawal could be traced. It also meant that 35 £1 notes now possessed a direct link to the murdered man. Finding a person who might have been spending them would tie them to the theft that had taken place from the dead family's home.

By the time Peter Smart had paid off a number of expenses, he had £25 in his wallet when he reached home. The expenses that he had paid allowed the police to check the serial number of the notes he had used, just to confirm their theory. They matched. Knowing through Joe Brannan that Peter Manuel had been suddenly flush with cash, they began to track the notes that he had used to pay his bar bills the day after the murder. As they looked into the matter, they found these notes could be traced back to Mr. Smart's withdrawal on New Year's Eve.

At this point, a strategic decision was made. The police now had enough evidence to tie Peter Manuel to the murders of three people, but they wanted to be absolutely sure they could achieve a conviction. Peter had bettered them in the past, so there could be no chance that this could happen again. They assumed Peter had a good idea of what they might do in mind, and if they acted against his expectations, they might be able to force the killer into making a mistake.

However, there was the legitimate concern that Peter might kill again. In the six weeks since his release from jail, he had been involved in at least four murders. Allowing him to roam free was out of the question. As such, a twenty man task force was put together and given the instruction to watch his every move. Peter was to be considered a particularly dangerous suspect, so they were to take extra precautions when tracking him down. Should any team fail to report back within a 15-minute window, senior members of the team would be alerted right away. Members of the police force began to check the windows and doors of their homes before entering, worried that the suspect might have forced his way inside and be lying in wait.

But there was not only the police response to the murders to think about. Without all of the background information that the authorities possessed, members of the public were scared into a panic. Just as during the war years, there was an effort among families to evacuate their children from the area, with parents fearful that their children might suffer the same fate as ten-year-old Michael Smart, murdered in his bed with his National Health Service glasses still perched on the table. Daughters, especially, were considered at risk. People from all over Glasgow and Lanarkshire were swept up in the terror of the serial killer on the loose. To try and offer some sort of protection, a number of men formed vigilante packs and roamed the streets at night. They escorted women home, arming themselves with household objects such as kitchen knives. Sales of security items in the area went through the roof.

According to the reports from Joe Brannan, Peter Manuel was beginning to worry. The cautious approach the police were taking was causing him to grow concerned. Usually, when he was a suspect, he could predict their actions with amazing accuracy. This time, however, they were not doing as he had expected. To him, it appeared as though they were doing nothing at all. Brannan told the police that Peter was clearly on edge and had suggested they travel down to London for a short while. With a family to think about, Brannan had a natural reason to decline the offer. But the police drew encouragement from the fact that fleeing the city had even crossed Peter's mind.

This continued for almost a week. Selecting their time carefully, the police amassed their evidence and obtained a warrant to search the Manuel home. Arriving at 06:45, they caught Samuel as he was heading out to work. As could be expected of Peter's father, Samuel quickly abandoned his job to stay at home and lambast the police for harassing his poor son. The usual threats followed, that Samuel would contact the local Members of Parliament and inform them of yet another instance of false accusations levelled against his son. Just like his father, James was also preparing to go to work when he found himself caught up in the police raid. Peter, however, just carried on sleeping as the authorities burst into the home.

When he woke up, his first instinct was to demand a look at the search warrant. When this was produced, he resorted to shouting and swearing, challenging the police. This was just what they had expected. Finally, the tables had turned. Now, the investigators were able to predict what Peter would do, rather than the other way around. In another predictable move, Peter's mother reacted by making him a cup of tea. The police allowed him the chance to drink it before he left, as well as allowing him the chance to select his clothes for the day. Peter selected a red tie. It would be the last time he walked out of the family home.

Rather surprisingly, the search of Peter's home returned a number of clues. The police found both the camera and the gloves that had been taken from the Houstons' home. As these items were recovered from the Manuel household, the other members of the family were gradually faced with the growing realization that Peter might not have changed his ways at all. In fact, he might have been capable of far greater evil than they had ever imagined.

The first to acknowledge Peter's guilt was his sister, Teresa. She told the police that the camera had been a Christmas present from Peter. Predictably, Samuel stuck to the story of his son's innocence. According to him, the distinctive sheepskin gloves were actually a present from Christmas, though he could not remember who had given the gift. They might have even originated from one of the family's distant American relatives. Possession of stolen goods was, quite obviously, a crime. It carried with it an assumption that the current holder of the items in question was complicit in the theft. When the items were identified by Reverend Houston, the police had confirmation of Peter Manuel's criminality from a fantastically authoritative source. Despite Peter's previous efforts in charming a jury, it would be hard to offer up his own truth over a man of God.

The police went as far as to take Samuel down to their station in Bellshill. He was eventually charged with being involved in the theft of the items from the Houston home. His possession of the items in question deliberately weighed up against the insistent protection of his own son. It was unlikely that the police actually believed him guilty. Samuel had an impeccably clean record, apart from when it came to protecting Peter, but the police used these charges to try and convince Samuel to break down in his constant efforts to provide alibis and excuses for Peter's behavior. Since he had not had a chance to tally his version of events with what Peter told him, the police hoped that their lack of a coherent story would only condemn Peter further.

Writing in his memoirs many years later, then-Detective Chief Superintendent William Muncie recalled how he had been involved with Peter Manuel at various stages of his criminal career. Muncie had arrested him for breaking into a house, had questioned him on murder charges, and would be directly involved in the court's final judgement. His insight revealed what a delicate stage of investigation the police had arrived at. By charging Samuel with the crimes, the police had hoped to spark an interest in Peter. Whereas Samuel had always defended Peter, now it was times for the roles to be reversed.

The police got exactly what they wanted. When told that his father was being charged, Peter Manuel confessed to the murders. Peter's long-time protection against police investigations – the alibis supplied by his father – were now the very tool that was used to extract a confession. In a man who had frequently displayed a distinct lack of emotion, the move by the police managed to play on the familial sympathies of a serial killer. It had the desired effect. Finally, the long-suffering police had managed to outmaneuver the elusive Peter Manuel.

Convicting a Killer

Such was the nature of Peter Manuel's crimes that his trial was a sensation. There had been nothing like it seen in Scotland ever before. The idea of a serial killer was relatively new to the world and something that locals could more readily expect to find down south in London or on the other side of the Atlantic. People, including members of the police force, were horrified that one man could carry out such beastly acts. With everyone so convinced that Peter must be punished for what he did – coupled with the suspect's proclivity for courtroom drama – the trial and conviction of Peter Manuel are just as interesting as his criminal career.

First though, the police needed to be sure they had enough evidence. One of their first actions was to send the father and the son to different cells in different buildings. This would stop the two comparing and collaborating on their stories. To ascertain that it was Peter who had been using the marked money stolen from the Smart home, the police organized a number of identity line-ups. These involved people selecting the suspect from a line-up when asked who had bought a certain product at a certain time. In the majority of cases, these purchases were alcohol related. In almost every instance, the witnesses selected Peter Manuel as the man who had spent the stolen money.

Oddly, Peter's confidence still grew. Despite the confessions that he had given to the police, he elected to fire all of his solicitors and represent himself. This could probably have been an easy move to predict, with the criminal keen to demonstrate how easy it was to bamboozle and confuse the investigators. Another familiar Peter tactic was employed when he announced the existence of a man named Samuel "Dandy" McKay. According to Peter, McKay was a drinking buddy from the Gordon Club and was the real criminal behind the crime. McKay had paid Peter to give him a guided tour of the area around Sheepburn Road, the police were told, so he must have been planning a hold-up and needed the knowledge of someone who knew the area well.

Just as on many occasions previous, Peter tried to assert an intimate knowledge of the Glaswegian criminal circuit and hoped to demonstrate the extent of this awareness to the authorities. Criminals, he insisted, depended on the advice and intellect Peter possessed. By giving up these names, Peter was suggesting that he was, in fact, doing the police a favor. They shouldn't arrest him, they should thank him.

This willingness to name names was just another example of how different Peter was from those who were the true criminal masterminds in the area. While the actual criminals would refrain from ever discussing such matters with a police officer, Peter had no qualms about dropping names, information, and secrets whenever he wanted to feel powerful and smug. Despite the fact that the majority of this information was invented, the willingness to chat to the police was only exhibited by actual criminals when they were willing to give up Peter himself.

This time, things were different. The police were sure they had a good case on their hands and that they wanted to be sure to pursue every available lead. Added to this, McKay was actually a real person and known to the officers of the law. Hoping to prove Peter's story false, they went to McKay himself and questioned him. The accused man was furious. This was exactly what police wanted. In a somewhat startling move, they allowed the angry McKay to face down Peter and inform him just how ridiculous the accusations had been.

Added to the knowledge that his father was still incarcerated, this confrontation with McKay demonstrated to Peter that this time, he was one step behind the police. Used to having the upper hand in such circumstances, Peter found himself at odds. The police exacerbated this and encouraged his confusion. They deliberately gave him no information regarding his father, allowing Peter's over-active imagination to come up with his own versions of what was happening to Samuel in jail. When Peter asked, he was told that his father was being held in Barlinnie Prison and would be charged with housebreaking. Peter, who had been locked up in the dank, horrible prison himself, was horrified by the thought.

It was on the 15th of January, a short time after midnight, when Peter Manuel asked to see Robert McNeill, one of the inspectors on the case. A few hours later, when this request was granted, Peter informed the authorities that if he were allowed to see his parents, then he would assist the police and "clear up" a number of unsolved crimes that had taken place in Lanarkshire. Once he was able to talk to his parent, Peter promised that he would even take the officers to the location where Isabelle Cooke had been buried.

But the police at the time were taking things very carefully. They wanted to be sure that Peter's tactics of not hiring a lawyer and attempting to catch them out on a technicality were impossible. This was a correct assumption, as when the trial arrived, Peter attempted to manipulate his story. However, the police managed to get hold of a letter, written on the 15th of January, in which Peter Manuel outlined what he was prepared to offer. Even as he sat in a police cell, Peter was still phrasing his words to appear as though it was he who was doing the police a favor. There was some confusion when all of a sudden, Peter decided to write a second letter, one that outlined a different set of feelings. This time, the letter was more specific. It promised to give information regarding the murder of Anne Kneilands, the Watt family, Isabelle Cooke, and the Smart family if Samuel was released and Peter was allowed to see both parents.

But was this another tactic? Even though the second letter promised to outline Peter's role in the homicides, there were still suspicions that it was all part of some elaborate game. It was noted that the letters had different signatures, and the police were worried that Peter would use this information to cry foul in court. Even at the most basic level, it seemed like a power play and an attempt to exert some control over the situation. The inspectors decided that they would keep Peter defensive, and so they played it cool. They informed the suspect that they would discuss the matter with the prosecutor before making any promises.

Now desperate, Peter found himself giving up more information about the murder of the Smart family to try and make the police take up his offer. Despite being warned by the police not to simply give himself up without the advice of a lawyer, it is claimed that Peter admitted to breaking into the Smart house. Once inside, he stole the money from a wallet. Then, he shot Mr. Smart, followed by Mrs. Smart, and finally he executed Michael Smart as the youngster lay in bed. On the final killing, Peter admitted that he had thought that Michael was an adult. Following the triple murder, Peter helped himself to biscuits from the kitchen. He stole some more money and the keys to the car. He remembered giving a lift to the policeman Robert Smith and then admitted to throwing the gun into the River Clyde. After the confession, the police agreed to let Peter see his parents.

What followed was an awkward meeting between mother, father, and son. Sitting in a police cell, Peter found it remarkably hard to reveal the true nature of his crimes to his parents. They had always supported him, to the point where they had helped him escape punishment for quite serious crimes. They were devastated as one by one, Peter spoke about killing people. After the meeting, Samuel was returned to prison while Bridget was driven home in a police car. She was shocked by the confession, having always had a slight hope that her son would one day put his violent past behind him and turn back to religion. Now, she knew that would never happen. A short time later, Samuel was released. Despite the physical freedom he and his wife enjoyed, they were now locked into the knowledge of the true nature of their son. Peter Manuel was a killer, and now the whole world knew.

Trial of the Century

Peter Manuel was tried for murder. At the time, Scotland had seen nothing like it. After all of the panic that his killings had caused throughout the region, the government was determined to see Peter fully punished for his crimes. In Scotland of the 1950s, this included the death sentence. With the prosecutors, the public, and even some of Peter's associates all happy to see him hang, the trial was seemingly an open-and-shut case. But this was Peter Manuel. There were few things he enjoyed in life more than the chance to get up in front of everyone and show off just how clever he was. If that included making the police look silly, then all the better. If that meant risking his life to do so, then Peter would remain committed to his ideals. A showman to the last, he of course elected to represent himself.

The trial began on the 12th of May, 1958. Peter had barely been out of jail for six months when he stood accused of far greater crimes. The trial was so momentous that people had queued through the night to be able to take a seat in the gallery. There were sixty seats available to the public, and nobody wanted to miss the show. The "lucky sixty" were moved into the courtroom at 10:10 with the police having to turn everyone else away.

The interest from the public was matched (if not surpassed) by the interest from the press. For reporters, sixty-eight seats had been made available, and there was a clamor for the special passes that allowed the members of the press to gain entry into the court. They came from across Scotland, England, and even abroad. There was even a television crew stationed outside, still a novelty in the 1950s.

The man tasked with overseeing this circus was Lord Cameron. Judges in those days received something approaching reverential treatment in the press. Despite a long and storied career in the army and as a lawyer, this was the first criminal case that Lord Cameron had presided over. Indeed, all the legal teams involved quickly became notorious in the press. The prosecution and the judge were both regular features on the front page, but trying to figure out Peter's legal team was a far more complicated issue. To put it simply, Peter had been happy enough to try and dismiss his own lawyers, but there were a series of court-appointed advisors who stuck around for the more complex parts of Peter's defense.

Despite the impression that he had given when placed under arrest, it was no great shock to anyone when Peter Manuel decided to reject the charges. While the prosecution set about confirming the truth, Peter began to construct an elaborate web of stories that placed him near to the murders but not exactly guilty. Launching a full charm offensive on the jury and hoping to impress the judge, Peter was faced with eight murder charges but sought to outline just how they had been carried out by other people.

In order to prove these ideas, Peter brought forward a series of witnesses. Possibly the most important to his version of the story was William Watt. He had been meeting with Watt and Dowdall in the weeks between his release and his arrest, and he clearly felt that he had a good hold over Watt's psyche. It was Peter's allegation that William Watt had in fact murdered the three women. But while Watt had been released from custody due to scant evidence, Peter set about trying to convince the jury (or at least place doubt in their minds) that it had been William Watt, not Peter Manuel, who was responsible for the three murders. Peter's plan was slightly set back when it was revealed that William Watt had been in a car accident some days before the current trial. Appearing in the court on a stretcher, it was much harder for Peter to paint his version of the truth when the man he supposed to be a brutal murderer was laying injured on a stretcher having been helped into court.

Nevertheless, there was a feeling among those present that Peter managed to build a somewhat plausible case against William Watt. According to Lord Cameron, Peter handled the situation "with a skill" he considered "quite remarkable," despite his lack of legal experience. Added to his accusations against William Watt, Peter attempted to claim that it had been Mr. Smart who was guilty of the murder of the Smart family. In Peter's version of events, the man had killed his wife and child before turning the gun on himself. He had even suggested that he only went into the house because he was a long-time friend of Peter Smart's and had been given a set of keys by the man himself. It was much more difficult to convince the gathered masses about this, however, especially when he did not have a suspect in the court to badger and berate.

But despite Peter's best (and somewhat admirable) efforts to defend himself, his attempts fell short. When the jury returned from their deliberation, they found Peter Manuel guilty of the murders of Margaret Brown, Marion Watt, Vivienne Watt, Isabelle Cooke, Doris Smart, Peter Smart, and Michael Smart. Peter's version of the truth had failed to convince the jury. His one reprieve that that they considered the evidence against him concerning the murder of Anne Kneilands to be too little. Of that murder, he was not found guilty. Similarly, the killing of Sydney Dunn would be deliberated a few weeks hence and by a different court. It was not considered a part of the so-called Trial of the Century. In all, Peter was found guilty of seven murders.

As a result of the seriousness of Peter Manuel's crimes, he was given the death sentence. This was to take place on the 11th of July, 1958. There had been an appeal against the verdict, and Peter's mother had tried to have the sentence reduced, but both to no avail. At the time, there was a growing argument for the abolition of capital punishment, and it was thought to be gaining ground in Great Britain at the time. As such, Peter Manuel was one of the last people to be hanged for criminal offences in Scotland (though he was not the last, as some mistakenly believe.) The man who was set to carry out the sentence was Harry Allen, a 47-year-old man from Manchester who was ably assisted by his son, a 23-year-old named Brian. In all, Allen executed twenty-nine people and he was one of the top executioners in Britain at the time. One acquiescence made to Peter was to have rubber silencers fitted to the trap door of the gallows. Due to the proximity of Peter's cell to the execution location, this was thought to prevent the sound of other men being hanged from reaching his cell.

According to newspaper results from the time of the execution, Peter chose to wear a black blazer and a set of flannels for the occasion. His march to the gallows was calm enough, having been awakened at 06:00 and allowed to eat a final breakfast with a glass of whisky. He shook hands with the governor of the prison before having his wrists shackled behind his back. He bid farewell to the staff he had gotten to know during his stay. They had chatted about sports and played cards while Peter bided his time. It is said that there was a solemn atmosphere around the cell block, despite the lack of warmth many of the other prisoners felt towards Peter.

Despite the somber feel to the gathering on that morning, there was a slightly strange atmosphere. A radio somewhere was playing "Tea For Two," a throwaway song that happened to be catchy and popular enough at the time. According to some reports, Peter Manuel's last words instructed the guards to "turn up the radio" and he promised to "go quietly." Peter then walked the twelve paces from the cell to the site of the execution. A white hood was placed over his head, and the noose was slipped around his neck. There was little ceremony and hardly any pause. Seconds later, the trap door slammed open, and the short, sharp drop broke the neck of Scotland's most famous serial killer.

* * *

The case of Peter Manuel is different from other serial killers. Many men and women were more violent, reached higher body counts, or were notorious in other ways. But Peter Manuel always thought of himself as different. Convinced of his own intelligence and able to scrape through most of his life unscathed thanks to a mix of good fortune, quick thinking, and administrative errors, Peter managed to act carry out many of his crimes with the local police under no illusions about his guilt.

Similarly, there should surely be questions asked as to just how much he was indulged by certain family members. His father's penchant for providing an alibi whenever needed and his mother's inability to see the full scope of his criminal nature meant that he was often mollycoddled. There are not many serial killers who can say they operated out of their parents' homes.

But in the end, Peter Manuel fascinates us for many reasons. The wickedness of his actions, his utter belief in his own ability, and the arrogance that often meant that he got away with his crimes present us with a type of person who is utterly apart from society. Though perhaps not as twisted as many of the more violent and gruesome members of the pantheon of serial killers, Peter holds his own special place. He was a distinct and singular example of a mass murderer, which is why his crimes are just as interesting today as when they were committed.

The Horrific Crimes of
Gilles De Rais Revisited

La Roche-Bernard, France, September 1438

Peronne Loessart knew that she should feel honored, both for herself and on her young son's behalf. But she was still in a state of unease bordering on fear.

The Baron de Rais and his entourage were in her town, stopping at the hotel of Jean Colin, which was in the immediate neighborhood of Madame Loessart's home. One of the Baron's men, a man named Poitou, had spied her ten-year-old son and approached her about engaging the boy as his page.

Young Loessart often drew such attention. He was an uncommonly beautiful child, with golden hair and expressive blue eyes. But this was the first time that he had come to the notice of a potential patron.

Poitou, whose real name was Étienne Corrillaut, went to Madame Loessart and offered her four pounds for the boy's services, with an added bonus of one hundred *sous* for a new dress. He also promised to continue the child's education at a prestigious institution.

Although distressed at the thought of being parted from her son, Madame Loessart finally agreed. She knew that he had limited opportunities for advancement in La Roche-Bernard. Poitou also gave her his word that the boy would be well provided for.

She believed it. Gilles de Rais was the Marshal of France, a great man who had helped Jeanne d'Arc bring about the victory at Orléans. A regal escort preceded him wherever he went and trumpeters announced his presence at each destination. His ostentatious display of wealth and pageantry turned heads and inspired both awe and adoration. Now her son would have the chance to benefit from such glory.

A pony was purchased from the hotel owner for the boy to ride, and the Baron's entourage left for his castle at Machecoul the following day. There was probably a tearful goodbye, accompanied by promises to send messages and see each other soon.

Despite the excellent opportunity she appeared to be giving her son, Madame Loessart remained anxious. Perhaps separation anxiety was taking hold. Maybe the rumors that had been circulating lately now seemed more plausible. Whatever the reason, she suddenly ran after the departing party.

One of the Baron's servants intercepted the distraught woman and held her back, reminding her that a bargain had been struck. Gilles de Rais did not respond to her pleas. Instead, he spoke to the servant restraining her.

"He (the child) is well chosen. He is as beautiful as an angel."

Finally Madame Loessart calmed down, and the Baron's party resumed its journey.
Two years passed. The Baron's servants passed through the village once during that time, although young Loessart was not with them. On demanding news of her son, the men informed her that the boy was either at Tiffauges or Pouzauges. The truth was that he was long dead.

******

If the Loessart boy's fate was typical (at least according to later testimony), he was taken to one of Gilles de Rais' castles, given a perfumed bath, and dressed in better clothes than he had ever worn. That evening, after a sumptuous meal and plenty of hippocras[27], his keepers brought him to an upstairs room that only Rais and his inner circle had access to. There his keepers bluntly informed him of what lay ahead. The boy's shock and fear served as an aphrodisiac for Rais, exciting him into violence the way that the smell of blood inspires a predator.

Étienne Corrillaut, alias Poitou, was a self-confessed accomplice in many of the murders. He later testified that his master started many of these "sessions" by hanging his victims from a hook to keep them from crying out and then masturbating upon the child's belly or thighs. He would then take the boy down, comfort him, and insist he was only "playing". But what followed next was far from playful. After the games ended, Rais either killed the child himself or designated the task to his cousin Gilles de Sillé, Poitou, or another manservant named Henriet Griert.

This alleged period of rampage and murder coincided with a serious decline in Gilles de Rais' personal fortune. After his military service concluded, he sank money into a series of extravagances: the construction of an opulent chapel (called, ironically, the Chapel of the Holy Innocents) and a theatrical spectacle titled *Le Mistère du Siège d'Orléans*, which featured over 600 costumes and unlimited food and drink for the audience. Alarmed, his family persuaded King Charles VII to intervene, resulting in a royal edict that forbade Rais from selling any more property.[28]

Desperate to restore his fortune, he embraced alchemy and invoked demons to intervene, an arrangement that author Joris-Karl Huysmans called "the chemical coitus." In 1439, he engaged Italian former cleric François Prelati to summon a demon named Barron, who could produce gold.

Prelati fed him stories about Barron wanting sacrifices before providing assistance. The Italian later swore to a panel of judges that Rais offered the hearts, eyes, and sexual organs of his small victims to appease the demon. Predictably, there was no result.

Strangely, despite the murders, rapes, and desecrations he had allegedly committed, Gilles de Rais considered himself a devout Catholic. Huysmans commented, "He carried his zeal for prayer in the territory of blasphemy." When frightened, he would cross himself or entreat God.

---

[27] A spice-laden heated wine, which was consumed as a stimulant
[28] Benedetti, Jean. *Gilles de Rais*, p.135

During his last moments, he continued to believe that he and his accomplices were destined for heaven.

******

Gilles de Rais is purportedly history's most infamous sexual serial murderer. He was accused of the mutilation, rape, and murder of more than 150 boys and girls, although it was rumored for years afterward that the final victim count could have been as high as 800. The record for his trial is one of the best-documented cases of serial murder during the Middle Ages.

Before his alleged deeds were discovered, Gilles de Rais enjoyed both prestige and power. He became Marshal of France at the age of 24, owned large estates, and basked in the glow of an illustrious military career, having been one of France's most active generals in the Hundred Years War. But an extravagant and wasteful lifestyle led him to financial ruin, and his declared lust for innocent blood led him to the gallows.

Legend claimed that whenever he needed fresh victims, Rais would send his most trusted servants out to the villages and countryside to find beautiful children and bring them back. He preferred boys, but settled for girls when no alternative existed. These servants said that once the children were in the castle, a night of lusty mayhem began that ended in murder.

This was an era when there was practically no limit to the power of French feudal lords like Gilles de Rais. He and his contemporaries could theoretically torture or kill subordinates on a whim, without fear of intervention by the King. In what has to be a classic example of power-obsessed hypocrisy, the Catholic Church tolerated such abuses as long as heresy did not creep into the picture, as heresy was a direct threat to the Church's own power. When Catholic authorities heard rumors that the Baron was practicing black magic to influence his declining fortunes, they moved in.

At his trial, Rais reacted to threats of torture and excommunication by making a full confession and corroborating the stories of his co-conspirators. He and his attendants "inflicted various types and manners of torment," he said. Afterward, he disposed of his victims by strangling them, smashing their heads in with a blunt instrument, or hanging them from a hook in his room. As their lives ebbed away, he would "commit the sodomitic vice on them," and keep going even after they died. If the child were especially handsome, he would decapitate them and keep the head for a while afterward, lavishing it with kisses.

Hearing such testimony, the anguish of Peronne Loessart and the mothers of his other victims must have been unspeakable. They had long hesitated to speak out against a nobleman, knowing that their words – and their lives – would be valueless compared to his. Now, shielded – and, some would say, coached – by the Catholic Church, they banded together to bring him down.

After the ecclesiastical court condemned him and his servants, Poitou and Henriet, to death, Rais made a request to die first, so that he might serve as an example to his co-conspirators. It was granted, and later writers like Georges Bataille held this up as an example of the Baron's amoral exhibitionism. Rais had been obsessed with pageantry and spectacle, and Bataille claimed that the thought of everyone being able to watch his hanging, burning body allowed

Gilles de Rais to exit the earthly plane with the same sense of violent theater that accompanied his existence.

******

Centuries later, the question persists, like a blemish on French history that refuses to go away.

Did he do it?

Did Gilles de Rais really massacre hundreds of children undetected before the Church and the citizenry joined forces to stop and punish him?

Aleister Crowley delivered a series of lectures on Gilles de Rais and his alleged crimes at Oxford University in 1930. Crowley believed that the murders were exaggerations at best and outright fabrications at worst. His position was that Gilles de Rais had been targeted and victimized by the Catholic Church.

"He was accused of the same crimes as Joan of Arc by the same people who accused her, and that he was condemned by them to the same penalty," he argued.

The real problem of Gilles de Rais amounts, accordingly, to this. Here we have a person who, in almost every respect, was the male equivalent of Joan of Arc. Both of them have gone down in history. But history is somewhat curious. I am still inclined to think that "there ain't no such animal." In the time of Shakespeare, Joan of Arc was accepted in England as a symbol for everything vile. He makes her out not only as a sorceress, but a charlatan and hypocrite; and on top of that a coward, a liar, and a common slut. I suspect that they began to whitewash her when they decided that she was a virgin, that is a sexually deranged, or at least incomplete, animal, but the idea has always got people going, as any student of religion knows. Anyway, her stock went up to the point of canonization. Gilles de Rais, on the other hand, is equally a household work for monstrous vices and crimes. So much so, that his is even confused with the fabulous figure of Bluebeard, of whom, even were he real, we know nothing much beyond that he reacted in the most manly way to the problem of domestic infelicity.

Others have pointed out that the Duke of Brittany, who brought forth charges for the secular proceedings that accompanied the ecclesiastical ones, received title to the Baron's lands after his conviction. When the Duke started dividing the properties among his own nobles before the verdict was even announced, there were mutterings that the French state framed Rais to seize his assets.

The debate remains, but the general consensus is that Gilles de Rais was a dedicated hedonist whose destructive habits consumed his wealth, destroyed his heroic legacy, and ended scores of lives. As Jason DeBoer wrote in his essay *Blood, Fuck, God: The Prodigal Crimes of Gilles de Rais*, "These medieval crimes still resonate today as hideous, self-negating acts, as the strange gestures of a nobleman and hero transformed by his own ruinous desires into a wastrel and murderer."[29]

---

[29] http://www.absintheliteraryreview.com/archives/fierce9.htm

"Gilles de Rais" by Éloi Firmin Féron -
Agence photo de la Réunion des musées nationaux RMN
Licensed under Public Domain via Commons

Childhood

Gilles de Rais was born in September or October 1404 to Guy II de Montmorency-Laval and Marie de Craon in the family castle at Champtocé-sur-Loire, around 12 miles west of Angers. His baptism was attended by members of the nobility from the surrounding regions, each one bearing a candle. Given the baby's ancestral connection to some of the most illustrious houses in medieval France, this sign of respect and honor was expected.

His father, Guy II de Montmorency-Laval, knight and Lord of Blaison and Chemillé, was descended from the Montmorencys, who were the first Barons of France. Marie de Craon, his mother, was a direct descendant of King Robert II (972-1031). (Ironically, history has credited Robert with restoring the imperial Roman custom of burning heretics at the stake, legitimizing the mode of the execution imposed on Gilles and his associates four hundred years later.[30]) Marie de Craon also claimed kinship to the opulent houses of Machecoul and Rais, ensuring that Gilles and his younger brother René stood to inherit immense wealth.

Like most unions among thirteenth century French nobility, the marriage of Gilles de Rais' parents had been politically motivated. It was also the result of more greed, hatred, and intrigue than a modern soap opera.

******

In 1371, the last Baron of Rais, Chabot V, died without an heir, passing the ancient house to his sister Jeanne, who was also known as "Jeanne la Sage (Sensible)." She too was childless, and in casting about for a successor, decided on her younger cousin Guy II de Montmorency-Laval.

There was a problem, however: Guy's grandmother, "Crazy" Jeanne (Jeanne la Folle) of Rais, had been disinherited after marrying for love, and the decree blocked the rights of her descendants to the Barony of Rais.

With her customary shrewdness, Jeanne la Sage got around that obstacle by offering to adopt her cousin and legally include him in her family line. There was only one condition: Guy II de Montmorency-Laval had to renounce the title and arms of Laval and assume those of the house of Rais. On September 23, 1401, he agreed, and the adoption was formalized.

The family harmony was short-lived. For some reason, Jeanne and her new heir soon had an irreparable argument. She canceled their arrangement and chose another successor, Catherine de Machecoul, who was also a distant cousin. Madame de Machecoul was a widow with a son, Jean de Craon, who now stood to become Baron of Rais under the new arrangement.

Furious, Guy initiated a lawsuit before the Parliament of Paris. The bitter legal battle went on for years. Both sides finally reached a compromise: if Guy married Jean de Craon's daughter, Marie, the barony of Rais would be his. He agreed, and the wedding was duly celebrated on February 5, 1404. Two years after the couple's first child, Gilles, was born, Jeanne la Sage died, and Guy II de Montmorency-Laval officially became the Baron de Rais.

---

[30] MacCulloch, Diarmaid. *A History of Christianity*. Penguin Books, 2010, p. 396

*****

Seal of Guy de Rais

Gilles was a child of above-average intelligence. He spoke Latin fluently, which was a sign of breeding and high station in medieval France, and was a voracious reader. As a grown man, with his dark hair, pale skin, and lithe but powerful form, he cut a figure that contemporaries described as "angelic."

For an individual who was exposed as a sadist in his twenties, Gilles had a relatively benign childhood. He was spoiled and entitled, as were most children of the nobility during that era, but there was no evidence of abnormal behavior during his boyhood, and he committed no known battlefield cruelties during his campaigns against the English during the revival of the Hundred Years War. Had the case been otherwise, it would have been recalled and remarked upon after the child murders came to light.

Eminent crime historian Colin Wilson compared Gilles de Rais to mass murderers like Vlad III, Prince of Wallachia (also known as Vlad the Impaler) and Ivan IV Vasilyevich, more commonly known as Ivan the Terrible. Both men were infamous for their juvenile cruelty: Vlad was especially brutal after the Turks took him prisoner during his teenage years, and Ivan was a bully and sadist who delighted in tormenting anyone too weak to fight back. Gilles does not appear to have experienced any similar traumas or personality disorders that foreshadowed a serial killer.

Wilson wrote, "Gilles' attacks of sadism seem to have descended on him like an epileptic fit." The Baron's purported latent sadism does defy explanation because his early years contained no warning signs. Even H.G. Wells, who commented on his crimes in a book called *Crux Ansata*, ultimately pronounced him "unanalyzable." Yet when he was accused of multiple murders, his judges – and history – have accepted his guilt completely.

Blood Feuds

On September 28, 1415, Guy II de Montmorency-Laval died in what has been described as a "gory hunting accident."[31] His death made his oldest son Gilles the Baron de Rais and heir to one of France's most magnificent fortunes. Rais was the senior barony of Brittany, bordered by Loire on the north, on the west by the Atlantic Ocean, and Lac de Grandlieu and Poitou to the east and south respectively. From his father and grandfather, he would also inherit lands and lordships in Anjou and the surrounding regions.

The fate of Marie de Craon is less certain. According to some accounts, she died shortly before her husband. Other sources claim that soon after the death of her husband she married again, this time to Charles d'Estouteville, Lord of Villebon. In either case, she disappeared from her sons' lives, and their guardianship passed to her father, Jean de Craon.

Craon, who might have inherited the barony himself had Guy II de Montmorency-Laval not agreed to marry his only daughter, was getting on in years. At his trial, Gilles would say that his grandfather was overly indulgent, letting both of his young wards get away with outrageous behavior. Free of boundaries, Gilles became accustomed to getting what he wanted when he wanted it, leading to impatience with delayed gratification and a lack of regard for others.

Although Jean de Craon may not have supervised his grandsons closely, he tirelessly schemed for the advancement of Gilles in particular. On October 25, 1415 Craon's only son, Amaury, was killed at the Battle of Agincourt, which was a disastrous defeat for France. Now Gilles stood to inherit the vast Craon wealth too.

In 1416, Craon arranged a future match between the twelve-year-old boy and four-year-old Jeanne Paynel, one of the wealthiest heiresses in Normandy. The two were betrothed in January 1417, but the plan fell through when Jeanne died after a brief illness. Next, Craon proposed a union between Gilles and Béatrice de Rohan, the niece to the Duke of Brittany, but she died too.

Although child mortality was high in medieval France, the deaths of Jeanne and Béatrice helped form the basis of the claim that Gilles de Rais was the original Bluebeard, the villain in Charles Perrault's famous French folktale. The story chronicles a depraved and violent nobleman who murders one wife after another, a spree that has no resemblance to Rais' alleged crimes except the high victim count.

Craon called a temporary halt to the matchmaking. By 1420, war was on the horizon in their region of France, and his grandson was provided with a different opportunity to honor the family name.

******

The Breton War of Succession, which raged from 1341 until 1364, had been a struggle between the Montforts of Brittany and the Counts of Blois for control of the Duchy of Brittany. The

---

[31] Villalon, L. J. Andrew. *The Hundred Years War (Part III): Further Considerations*, p.146

slaughter levels were horrific: when Charles of Blois overran the city of Quimper in May 1344, an estimated 1400 to 2000 civilians were massacred. Breton and Norman prisoners were sent to Paris where they were executed for treason.

The Montforts prevailed, and a diplomatic treaty was signed, but in the years following the war, the defeated Blois faction continued to plot their comeback. Finally, in February 1420, Olivier de Blois, Count of Penthièvre, reopened the conflict by kidnapping Jean V, the ruling Duke of Brittany.

Jean de Craon and sixteen-year-old Gilles took the side of the kidnapped Duke and the House of Montfort. The Count of Penthièvre sent bands of thugs into the Craon and Rais territories, where they spread terror. Coming from a family of medieval knights, and trained as a soldier after he entered his teens, Gilles fought back with a fierceness that belied his youth. He killed some of the assailants and put the others on the run, exhilarated by the raw violence of combat. Rais also helped his grandfather secure the release of Jean V.

The grateful Duke of Brittany compensated them both for the losses inflicted by enemy marauders and granted them portions of land seized from the Penthièvres. He also gave them an annuity of one hundred pounds.[32]

Fortified by new wealth, Gilles and his grandfather returned their attention to his matrimonial situation, which was yet another way to increase the family fortune. The young Rais set his eyes on – and some said took by force – the beautiful and wealthy Catherine de Thouars of Brittany, heiress of La Vendée and Poitou.

******

Other than the fact that she was the daughter of Milet de Thouars, Lord of Pouzauges and Tiffauges, and Béatrice de Montjean and had vast holdings in Poitou, which adjoined the Barony of Rais, little is known about Catherine at this time. She and Gilles were first cousins, which required a marriage union to be approved by the Church beforehand. Her father also opposed the idea of a match, insisting that they were too closely related.
Catherine's parents later claimed that Gilles de Rais abducted their daughter and forced her to marry him, which is unlikely given the fact that she remained with him willingly afterward and supported his later schemes against her own family. Milet de Thouars attempted to have the marriage dissolved on the grounds of consanguinity, but died of a fever before he could succeed.

Gilles and his grandfather greedily took possession of Catherine's lands and estates, as well as the Thouars-owned fortresses at Tiffauges and Pouzauges. That same year, Jean de Craon's wife died, and he married Anne de Sillé, Catherine's widowed grandmother, further strengthening the ties between the two families. Her grandson, Gilles de Sillé, would one day be an enthusiastic participant in the child murders.

---

[32] Approximately eight million dollars in 2015.

Béatrice de Montjean was unable to fight back until the following year when she married Jacques Meschin de la Roche-Airault, a knight who had been chamberlain in the Dauphin's[33] court. When papal authorities in Rome formally approved the marriage of Gilles and Catherine, Meschin approached the couple and demanded the return of certain seized lands, saying they were part of his wife's dowry instead.

It was a serious mistake on his part. In 1423, Gilles and Jean de Craon kidnapped Béatrice de Montjean and her younger sister and imprisoned them at Champtocé, one of Craon's holdings. They told her that unless she renounced her claim to Tiffauges and Pouzauges, allowing Gilles to own them through Catherine, she would be sewn in a sack and thrown in the river. The same message was conveyed to her husband, Jacques Meschin. To compound the threat, Jean de Craon abducted three of Meschin's men, including his brother Gilles Meschin, and threw them into a deep pit.

Craon's wife, Anne de Sillé, (who was also Béatrice de Montjean's mother) persuaded him to eventually release Béatrice, but Meschin had to pay a ransom to recover his brother and the other two men from the pit. Gilles Meschin died soon afterward from his injuries.
Desperate and terrorized, Jacques de Meschin brought the matter before the royal parliament. For whatever reason, the kidnapping of Béatrice and death of Gilles Meschin were not addressed during the proceedings: the sole focus was on the lands that Gilles de Rais had seized and which Meschin insisted were part of his wife's dowry. A settlement was reached that restored some of Béatrice de Montjean's property to her, but when Adam de Cambrai, President of France's Parliament, came to Gilles and Catherine de Rais' fortress at Pouzauges to see the settlement signed, Jean de Craon and Gilles had him brutally assaulted.

This bold act of defiance resulted in a heavy fine being levied against Craon and Rais, but they ignored it. Royal influence had been seriously weakened by the Agincourt defeat in 1415, so like most feudal lords who knew that the monarchy relied on them for military support, they did what they wanted and got away with it. In 1443, three years after Gilles died, both fines remained unpaid.

******

In 1425, after Gilles de Rais had attained his majority and assumed administration of his lands, he was formally presented at the court of the Dauphin (the future King Charles VII). His good looks and ability to assume courtly manners when it suited him earned royal attention and favor. From 1427 to 1435, Rais was a commander in the Royal Army, distinguishing himself by displaying bravery on the battlefield when the Hundred Years War sprang back to life. One of his more notable accomplishments was the capture of the English captain Blackburn at the battle for the Château of Lude.

It was probably during his time at court (and away from his wife) that Gilles began to indulge his homosexuality. His favorite books included the works of Suetonius, which detailed the sexual excesses and depravities of the Roman emperors. He admitted at his trial that these stories fueled his fantasies and inspired a taste for the forbidden.

---

[33] In France's royal hierarchy, a Dauphin was the heir to the throne

His marital relationship ebbed accordingly. Gilles and Catherine's only child, Marie, was born in 1429. Afterward, the couple was rarely together, but like most men of power, Gilles did not lack for sexual companionship. In 1427 he engaged ten-year-old Étienne Corrillaut as a page. Master and servant were uncommonly – some said unnaturally – close. Corrillaut, who went by the nickname Poitou, became Gilles' valet once old enough to do so. In addition to being his master's lover, he would actively recruit child victims and help kill them afterward.

Years later, Poitou told the ecclesiastical tribunal that his master assaulted him and threatened to kill him with a dagger not long after he entered the latter's service, but he was spared because of his good looks. This testimony, which supported the prosecutor's contention that the murders started in 1426, may or may not have been the result of torture, but it certainly came in handy when Jean de Malestroit, Bishop of Nantes, wanted to portray one of France's greatest war heroes as a degenerate by asserting that she knowingly acted as the consort of a sodomite and murderer.

Her name was Jeanne d'Arc.

Killer Precedents

Although the alleged crimes of Gilles de Rais were shocking enough to be remembered centuries later, he was not history's first mass murderer. While relatively uncommon, serial killing has been a phenomenon since the beginning of time.

One of the earliest recorded instances of multiple murder took place around 331 BC in Ancient Rome. Several Roman men who also happened to be members of the Senate suddenly fell ill with plague-like symptoms and died. They were assumed to be victims of an epidemic until a servant woman came to the aedile, which was responsible for maintaining public order, and revealed that they were actually victims of foul play.

Upon being granted immunity, the girl said that a "conspiracy of matrons" was behind the deaths, which were due to poison. She volunteered to show the officials where the concoctions were being made and led the men to a house where a number of women were found brewing poisons. These mixtures were brought into the Forum, along with twenty married women who had been implicated.

Two of these women, Cornelia and Sergia, insisted that the mixtures were medicinal, and intended to combat the epidemic. The informer servant challenged them to drink the concoctions and prove her wrong in front of everyone. The two noblewomen, after conferring with their accused co-conspirators, finally agreed. Moments after drinking the potion, they perished.

The attendants of the accused women were promptly arrested. These frightened slaves informed against even more matrons, of whom 170 were later found guilty and executed.[34]

---

[34] DONNE, William Mowbray. *C. Sallustii Crispi Catilina Et Bellum Jugurthinum ... With Notes by W.M. Donne*, p.133

Roman authorities, anxious to downplay the idea that women could cunningly band together to take down their masters, dismissed the murders as acts of madness rather than criminal intelligence.

******

Nearly 400 years later, the canonical first solo serial killer appeared. This new "fiend" was also female, and she operated in Rome.

Locusta was born in Gaul, one of the outer Roman provinces (now France). During her youth in the countryside, she acquired an in-depth knowledge of herbs and plants, namely which ones healed and which ones could kill.

When she arrived in Rome, Locusta soon saw that ambitious, greedy people were everywhere. Some of them wanted their political rivals and rich relatives dead so badly that they were willing to pay for a discreet, accomplished murder. Locusta cashed in on these malevolent intentions by becoming a professional poisoner.

After her first successful assassinations, her reputation spread and she was rarely lacking for clients. Although arrested often for her activities, Locusta's influential customers always came to her aid and secured her release.

In 54 AD, the Empress Agrippina, wife of Emperor Claudius, secretly summoned the celebrated poisoner. She wanted Nero, her son from an earlier marriage, to become Emperor, and to realize that ambition, Claudius had to die. Locusta obliged by arranging for the 64-year-old Emperor to eat poisoned mushrooms, clearing Nero's path to the top.
Almost.

Claudius's other son, Britannicus, challenged Nero's right to become Emperor and laid claim to the throne. The worried new Emperor secured Locusta's release from prison where she had been sent for poisoning another victim and even set her up in a large estate where students were sent to learn the art of murder. She reciprocated by poisoning Britannicus' wine.

Business boomed thereafter. Things were good for Locusta until Nero committed suicide. In 69 AD, his successor, Emperor Galba, held the murderess accountable for all the lives she had taken. After being chained and led through the streets of Rome, she was put to death on January 8.

If legend is to be believed, Locusta's execution was brutal even by Ancient Roman standards. After being raped by a specially trained giraffe, she was ripped apart by wild animals while a cheering public looked on. Historians later challenged this allegation, but January 8 was also the Agonalia festival, and bestiality was a routine entertainment at these events. Although horrible to contemplate, Rome's most notorious murderer could actually have died this way.

******

Although the twentieth-century media made a huge deal over the possibility that Prince Albert Victor, the Duke of Clarence, could have been Jack the Ripper, a serial killer of royal blood was not new. From 144-116 BC in Imperial China, a rogue prince murdered over a hundred civilians.

Liu Pengli was the Prince of Jidong during the reign of his uncle, Emperor Jing. The black sheep of an otherwise illustrious family, he assembled groups of violent slaves and set forth at night on murdering, raping, and robbing expeditions. Jidong residents lived in fear of him, locking themselves in their homes at night and refraining from going out after dark.

By the time the authorities stopped the mayhem, Pengli had killed or ordered the killing of over a hundred people. The Chinese court recommended his execution, but the Emperor recoiled from the thought of putting a prince to death, and instead reduced him to a common Chinese subject and exiled him to Shangyong in modern Zhushan County, Hubei Province. If he continued to kill as a commoner, details of the murders were not preserved for posterity.

******

The next serial murder of note was also of noble blood, so by the time Gilles de Rais faced his judges, rogue nobility was not a unique phenomenon.

Queen Anula of Anuradhapura Kingdom (Sri Lanka) could have been remembered for more praiseworthy accomplishments. She was the first woman in the country's history to wield genuine power and authority. During her reign (50-47 BC), she was Asia's first female head of state. But these milestones could not whitewash the fact that she was an evil woman who killed for both pleasure and gain.[35]

Anula's husband, King Chora Naga (63-51 BC), had the unenviable distinction of being her first victim. She poisoned him so that her lover, Siva, could become king while she remained the actual power behind the throne. But before Siva could be crowned, a Sinhalese claimant named Kuda Tissa, the son of Chora Naga's predecessor, moved in. Anula swallowed her resentment and married him, but after a year and four months Tissa mysteriously died of fever-like symptoms. Siva now became king with no opposition.

Anula soon tired of Siva. Perhaps he stopped taking direction from her, or maybe she felt that her new paramour, a Tamil named Vatuka, would be a more malleable monarch. Whatever the reason, fourteen months later, King Siva fell ill with severe stomach pains. He gasped for breath, vomited blood, and complained that his stomach burned. After he died, poisoning may have been suspected, but no one apparently connected the deed to Anula, who must have thrilled with accomplishment after Vatuka was crowned king.

The Tamil monarch lasted just over a year. Then he too, died under mysterious circumstances and a Purohita Brahmin advisor named Neeliya came to power. Anula, who had been sleeping with him for months, remained at his side as queen for the six months that he occupied the throne. Then he joined the growing ranks of murdered kings.

[35] http://unknownmisandry.blogspot.ca/2011/09/anula-of-anuradhapura-sri-lankan-black.html

Anula went through two more royal lovers, Vdsukifor and Bela Tissa. Then she decided that she could do a better job than any of her previous masters and ruled the country herself for four months.

Perhaps the thought of an autonomous queen alarmed the authorities more than the years of regicide. Kutakanna Tissa, brother of the murdered Kuda Tissa, deposed Anula and had her arrested. She was supposedly executed by immolation (burning), either on a funeral pyre or within the palace where she had committed her crimes.

******

Queen Anula's ashes had been cool for over five hundred years when the next serial killer of note appeared. Zu Shenatir, a nobleman residing in fifth century El-Yemen, had an insatiable lust for young men and boys. He would entice them into his palace, rape them repeatedly, and then toss them to their deaths out of upper-level windows. It was one of his victims, not the authorities, who stopped him: a youth named Zerash fought back and succeeded in stabbing him to death.

******

Prior to the trial and execution of Gilles de Rais, Europe's last serial killer was Alice Kyteler, otherwise known as the "witch of Kilkenny." She came from a wealthy and powerful family, and had influential enemies as well as friends.

Alice's first husband was a moneylender named William Outlawe (Utlagh). He died not too long after marrying her. So did two more husbands, which aroused local suspicions even during an era of rampant disease and high mortality rates.

When her last husband, John Le Poer fell gravely ill and Alice set herself up as the sole beneficiary of his estate, gossip escalated into outright accusation. Doctors were unable to determine what was causing Le Poer to burn inside and waste away, and with his children from a previous marriage robbed of their inheritance, he began doubting his wife's integrity.

According to legend, Le Poer and his grown children traveles to Alice Kyteler's home by the sea and found items that smacked of witchcraft. The catalogue of items varies from one version of the story to the next, but they include candles made from human fat, infant body parts, communion wafers with satanic images, and powders that presumably did the unthinkable.

The Le Poers crated everything and brought the evidence to Richard Ledrede, the Bishop of Ossory. Fears of witchcraft, while not yet as rampant as they would later become, was in the early stages of becoming an Irish obsession. The Catholic Church controlled the country, so Alice was potentially in serious trouble.

Knowing that she had powerful friends (her brother-in-law was the Lord Chancellor of Ireland, and the treasurer was a close friend of her son William), Alice pounced when Bishop Ledrede came to her castle to investigate her for witchcraft. She had him imprisoned in the ancient structure, an act that outraged the church hierarchy. The Dean of St. Patrick's cathedral in

Dublin demanded the bishop's release, but Alice stood firm and didn't release her prisoner until 17 days had passed.

Humiliated and furious, Bishop Ledrede enthusiastically led the prosecution against Alice Kyteler. The proceedings represented one of Europe's earliest trials for witchcraft. Alice escaped punishment by fleeing to the home of her brother-in-law, Roger Utlagh, the Lord Chancellor of Ireland. Her servant wasn't so lucky. After confessing under torture that her mistress was a witch who slept with demons, Petronella de Meath was flogged and then burned at the stake on November 3, 1324.

What happened to Alice afterward is not known. By some accounts, she traveled to England and spent the rest of her days there, living to be an old woman. One hundred years later, Gilles de Rais would defy the Catholic Church and suffer a far different fate.

The Maid of Orleans

In 1429, Gilles de Rais was at court when a seventeen-year-old peasant girl named Jeanne, who came from the village of Domrémy, demanded to see the Dauphin. She declared that she had been sent by God to defeat the English, who were now laying siege to Orléans. Although Charles thought she was mad, he was willing to try anything that could bring about a French victory. He ordered Gilles to accompany "the Maid" to face the English forces at Orléans.

Gilles was happy to comply. He found the girl alluring, with her close-cropped hair, boyish figure, and stubborn sense of purpose that rivaled his own.

Jeanne d'Arc (*Library of Congress*)

Jeanne d'Arc, otherwise known as "the Maid of Orléans," was born in 1412 in Domrémy, France, to tenant farmer Jacques d'Arc and his wife Isabelle. At the time of Jeanne's birth, France was still in the throes of yet another conflict in the Hundred Years' War, turning the country's northern regions into a lawless and bloody battleground. In 1415, when she was three, King Henry V of England invaded northern France, shattered the French forces, and won the support of the Burgundians.[36]

The hostilities calmed somewhat with the Treaty of Troyes in 1420, which allowed Henry V to take the French throne as regent for the insane French King Charles VI. The arrangement was that the English king would inherit the throne after Charles died, but both men ended up dying in 1422 and leaving Henry's infant son as king of both countries. French supporters of Charles's son, the future Charles VII, eagerly seized an opportunity to restore a French monarch to the throne.

Around this time, Jeanne began to have mystical visions of St. Michael and St. Catherine proclaiming her as the savior of France and urging her to seek an audience with the Dauphin, Charles. In May, 1428, she cut her hair, dressed in men's clothes, and traveled to Chinon, the

---

[36] The Burgundians were a French political party that formed in the latter half of the Hundred Years' War. Staunchly pro-English, they were opposed by the Armagnacs.

site of the Dauphin's court, where the doubtful but desperate Charles sent her to Orléans to face the English.

Rais was with Jeanne during the battles that raged between May 4 and 7, 1429, when the French troops seized control of the English fortifications. Jeanne was wounded but recovered quickly enough to return to the battlefront and lead a final assault. By mid-June, the English had been successfully routed, and the French people were rejoicing at the thought of their autonomy returning.

After the victory at Orléans, Charles and his procession entered Reims, where he was crowned Charles VII on July 18, 1429. Jeanne was with him, occupying a prominent place at the ceremonies. So was Gilles de Rais.

Rais emerged from the battle at Orléans with nearly as much glory as Jeanne herself. Charles VII made him a Marshal of France, and he was one of four knights who fetched the Holy Ampulla from the Abbey of Saint-Remy to Notre-Dame de Reims for the consecration of Charles VII. He was also awarded the right to add a border of the royal arms, the fleur-de-lys on a blue ground, to his own. The letters patent that authorized the display cited the young nobleman's "high and commendable services." It was an extremely rare honor that was usually accorded to communities instead of individuals.[37]

In the spring of 1430, months after an abortive attempt to take Paris from the enemy, Jeanne went to Compiegne in northern France to confront the Burgundians. Gilles de Rais was not present for this particular campaign. During the skirmish, she was thrown off her horse and captured by the enemy. After several months, she was delivered to the English for 10,000 livers and imprisoned at Rouen, which was the main English stronghold in France.

Gilles de Rais may have planned a rescue. He spent the winter of 1430 at Louviers, which was around fifteen miles from Rouen. He also had an army with him, which was to be expected in occupied Normandy. At one point he was joined by Jean de Dunois, another French military leader, who had also fought alongside Jeanne at the battle of Orléans.
The presence of two French commanders in Louviers is not especially unusual, as the region had been taken from the English the previous year and was in a state of guerrilla warfare. But that winter, an attempt to rescue Jeanne had been initiated by the Armagnacs, a political party that supported Charles VII, and one pro-Rais website suggests that Gilles and Dunois were also plotting to liberate her.[38] If they actually tried, the attempt was beaten back like all others that took place during the winter of 1430-31.

Charles VII, whose coronation was largely due to the Maid's battlefield valor, made no attempt to secure her release. Historian Pierre Champion wrote that he threatened to exact vengeance upon captured Burgundian troops for the way the English had treated Jeanne. But otherwise he did nothing when Jeanne, whose actions had actually been against the English military, was turned over to church officials to be tried as a heretic.

---

[37] Benedetti, Jean (1971), Gilles de Rais, p.101
[38] http://gillesderaiswasinnocent.blogspot.ca/

Her trial for heresy, witchcraft, and dressing like a man (among other allegations) was initially public, but when Jeanne's responses outdid her accusers, the proceedings went private lest she arouse public sympathy and support. On May 28, 1431, the tribunal found her guilty of heresy and two days later, on May 30, she was brought to the marketplace in Rouen and burned at the stake in front of an estimated 10,000 people. She was nineteen years old.

******

Contrary to what some historians have assumed, Gilles de Rais did not retire from the battlefield, disheartened and disillusioned, after Charles VII essentially allowed the English to execute Jeanne. He may have been upset, and even mourned her loss, but he was, above all else, a military leader.

He was present at Beauvais in 1432, when French forces drafted a plan to storm Rouen and kidnap the young English monarch, Henry VI. The scheme came to nothing, but in early August, he got the action he craved when his army encountered the English near Lagny. Rais attacked the besieging forces, who were led by the duke of Bedford, with such skill and enthusiasm that one author described the battle as a repeat of the Orléans victory.

This conflict was different from than his previous ones, however. Rais allowed his men to pillage and plunder in the wake of the battle, something he had never done before.[39] The devastation, which was typical of some military commanders, was abnormal for him.

Gilles' grandfather, Jean de Craon, appears to have sensed a shift in the young noble's behavior, one that worried him. Relations between the two men had been strained for at least three years by that point. In 1429, soon after the birth of his only daughter, Marie, Rais sold his estate in Blaison to an outsider. Craon was furious: after swiftly buying the estate back, he publicly hurled so much abuse at his grandson that local residents still remembered his tirades thirty years later.[40]

A formerly close relationship was now soured. Before dying on November 15, 1432, Craon left his sword and breastplate to Gilles' younger brother René de la Suze. It was a highly public sign of disappointment and dismissal that ultimately broke whatever sense of self-restraint Rais had left.

---

[39] Villalon, L. J. Andrew. *The Hundred Years War (Part III): Further Considerations*, p.164
[40] Ibid, p.165

Fall from Grace

Gilles de Rais continued to be active on the military front, but he had clearly changed. In 1434, after assembling troops to liberate the town of Grancy from the Duke of Burgundy, Gilles suddenly refused to actually participate in the battle and relinquished the command of his detachment to his brother, René.

Another atypical act occurred in 1435, when Gilles' cousin, Georges de la Trémoille, asked for his help in a battle against Jean de Luxembourg, who had delivered Jeanne d'Arc into English hands. Rais agreed, but with a fraction of his usual energy, and when his troops protested that they were not getting paid enough, he simply washed his hands of the entire affair.

The military dishonor no longer troubled him like it might have at one time. By that point, he had gradually withdrawn from both public and military life and instead dedicated his energies to the construction of an opulent Chapel of the Holy Innocents, where he officiated in robes he designed himself.

At the time, churches, chapels, sermons, and plays were dedicated to the Holy Innocents all over Europe. Based on verses in Matthew 2: 16-18, the story of the "Massacre of the Innocents" relates how King Herod ordered the slaughter of all male children in an effort to eliminate his rival as King of the Jews. Then he supposedly took the bloodshed further by killing all children who were two years and under in Bethlehem and the surrounding coasts.

Some books and articles about Gilles de Rais point out that his choice of chapel name reflected a guilty conscience, given the crimes he later died for. While that is possible, it must be pointed out that many French chapels and churches were dedicated to these child saints, and Gilles may have been following the dictates of fashion instead of guilt.

Not long after Jean de Craon died, Rais began selling property to finance an increasingly extravagant lifestyle. His retinue, which accompanied him wherever he traveled, consisted of 25 to 30 people: servants, chaplains, young clerks, singers from his chapel, and children who served as pages. In the chapel itself, he employed a dean, archdeacons, cantors, vicars, a schoolmaster, and more. Occasionally he would be so pleased with one of them that he gave them legacies as well as wages. A choirboy from Poitiers received an annuity worth two hundred livres, and Rais provided a bonus of two hundred crowns for his parents.

By the late winter of 1433 he had sold all his holdings in Maine and every estate in Poitou except those owned by his wife Catherine. Half of the proceeds were spent financing the production of *Le Mistère du Siège d'Orléans*, a theatrical spectacle with more than 20,000 lines of verse, requiring 140 primary actors and 500 extras. It called for six hundred costumes, and Rais directed that after each performance, these costumes be discarded and replaced by new ones. He also ordered and paid for unlimited supplies of food and drink for the spectators who attended the inaugural performance in Orléans on May 8, 1435, and every show thereafter.

It has been suggested that Jean de Craon had served as a moderating influence on his wild-natured grandson, preventing him from committing the deeds that later made him infamous. When the old man died, Gilles gave free rein to his hedonistic impulses.

While he only went into serious decline after 1432, he was already somewhat of a spendthrift, having tried to sell his Blaison estate for unknown reasons in 1429. He was also showing signs of indifference to military honor, evidenced by the failure to stop his men from running rampant at Lagny in August 1432.

Gilles de Rais had never been a paragon of compassion and virtue. He (with full support from his grandfather) had kidnapped his mother-in-law and threatened to drown her. He had also beaten up the royal emissary who had come to ensure that Béatrice de Montjean got her property back. But such Machiavellian violence was common among the nobility, whose primary means of ascension and gain were breaking the backs of others. On the other hand, squandering family money and jeopardizing his military career were definitely not the norm.

Was Gilles de Rais bipolar? During this period of his life, many of his actions could be interpreted as manic: a tendency to show poor judgment, inflated self-esteem or grandiosity, lavish spending sprees, and sexual indiscretions. Some people gripped by mania even see themselves as having superhuman skills and powers. Or could he have incurred a battlefield injury to the head, causing errant behavior to manifest itself later on?

Whatever the cause, 1432 was the beginning of the end for several reasons, one of which was that his earliest alleged victims disappeared.

******

The consensus is that the first child to be murdered by Gilles de Rais was the twelve-year-old son of a man named Jean Jeudon. Sometime in 1432, the Baron's cousins, Gilles de Sillé and Roger de Briqueville, approached a local furrier, Guillaume Hillairet, to whom the boy was apprenticed. They asked if they might briefly employ young Jeudon to take a message to the Rais castle at Machecoul.

Hillairet assented, but when the boy did not return, he questioned the two noblemen. They claimed to know nothing of his whereabouts and suggested that he might have been kidnapped by child stealers at nearby Tiffauges to be made into a page.

The furrier was alarmed but had no cause to doubt the idea. Kidnapping was common in France during the Middle Ages. If a man wanted to marry a woman who refused him, he merely stole her, forced a marriage, and raped her, making the union legal. (A consummated marriage could not be undone.) Landlords also kidnapped children to populate their own villages with young workers and residents.[41] In the latter instance, tracing the abductor was next to impossible, as the children were usually taken out of their home districts. Only if the missing boy or girl was a member of the nobility was any official effort made to recover them.

---

[41] "Medieval Information." Medieval Crimes. Accessed December 2, 2015. http://medieval-castles.org/index.php/medieval_crimes_thieves_burglars_kidnapp.

Les empocheurs.

Illustration of medieval 'child thieves' (*Author's Collection*)

While young Jeudon's parents were despairing, Jeannot Roussin learned that her nine-year-old son had disappeared. Someone recalled seeing Gilles de Sillé speaking with the boy, but if Rais' cousin was questioned at all, he probably told the same story about an abduction.

Jeanne Edelin, a widow living near the Baron's castle at Machecoul, reported that her eight-year-old son, whom she described as a "comely lad, white of skin and very capable" was gone. Local efforts to find him were still underway when the sons of Mace Sorin and Alexandre Chastelier vanished.

Although these disappearances were not officially tied to Gilles de Rais until eight years later, they did take place at a time when his downward spiral increased in velocity.

******

In June 1435, his alarmed relatives cooperated to prevent Rais from descending into total bankruptcy and dragging the family name down with him. An unsuccessful appeal was made to Pope Eugene IV to denounce the Chapel of the Holy Innocents. His brother, René de la Suze, and his cousin, André de Laval-Lohéac, also reached out to Charles VII, who obliged in July by issuing a royal edict in Orléans, Tours, Angers, Pouzauges, and Champtocé-sur-Loire. Not only was Gilles de Rais forbidden from selling any more property; those who oversaw his castles were also prohibited from selling them on his behalf, and no subject of the King was allowed to enter into any such sales contract with him.

Predictably, Rais was outraged. When he discovered that a childhood teacher, Michel de Fontenay, had overseen the publication of the King's edict in Champtocé, Rais abducted and imprisoned him at Machecoul. He had no authority to do so, but he didn't care. De Fontenay might have come to the same end as Gilles Meschin had in 1423 had the Bishop and officers from the University in Champtocé not protested until he was released.

Angry and desperate, Rais used his personal property, such as rare books, valuable clothing, and works of art, as security for loans. He also freely disposed of his holdings in Brittany, where the King's edict did not apply, and the reigning Duke, Jean V, ignored the family's pleas to enforce it. He gladly accepted whatever Rais offered to sell him, with the understanding that Rais would be allowed to try buying these holdings back within six years.

These resources brought in some money, but nowhere near the amount Gilles felt he needed to support the lifestyle he wanted. His initial reaction was to retreat under a gloomy cloud of self-pity and depression. Then, when his coffers became dangerously low, he decided on a possible solution that flew in the face of the Catholicism he professed to embrace.

Black magic.

Black Magic

In *The Mammoth Book of True Crime,* Colin Wilson wrote that when Gilles de Rais first went to the Dauphin's court in 1425, he borrowed a book on alchemy from an Angevin knight incarcerated for heresy. The fact that it was illegal enhanced its appeal. Now, a decade later, the beleaguered nobleman thought that alchemy might be the way out of his predicament.

In 1439, he sent a priest in his entourage, Eustache Blanchet, to Italy to find him a genuine magician, someone who could restore his fortune. According to Wilson, he had tried several local prospects who couldn't conjure a bird, let alone piles of gold. In May, Blanchet returned from Florence with a "clerk in minor orders" named François Prelati, a good-looking and charming young man whom Rais was attracted to on sight.

Prelati, who was supposedly a former priest, told his new employer that only Satan could help a mere mortal transmute base metals into gold. To arouse Satan's interest and support, the worst possible crimes had to be dedicated to his name. Children had to be killed, and their hearts, eyes, and sexual organs offered as sacrifices.

A year later Poitou and Henriet Griert told their interrogators (after rounds of heavy torture) that Gilles de Rais quickly kidnapped, raped, and murdered a young peasant boy in honor of the Devil. The body was mutilated and the aforementioned body parts offered up. But when he refused to actually take the final step of selling his soul, Prelati said that he could not participate in the actual conjurations.

These sessions, which took place at Tiffauges, were pure theater. During one of them, Gilles and his cousin Gilles de Sillé heard a deafening series of thumps from inside the room where Prelati was supposedly appealing to the Devil. The two noblemen looked in and found the magician so badly injured he was on the verge of collapse. Asked what had happened, he blurted that the demon Barron had beaten him out of displeasure.

Prelati could just as easily have been hurling himself against the wall to achieve a convincing effect. He was bedridden for several days, and he enjoyed the direct and tender ministrations of his employer the entire time.

Another time, he hurried to tell Rais that Barron had taken mercy on him and empowered him to conjure a pile of gold. Elated, the Baron raced back to the conjuration room, but Prelati got there first. He opened the door, peered in, and yelled that a huge green serpent was guarding the coins. Both men fled, and when they returned, there was no gold, only piles of dust.

To ensure that the nobleman did not lose heart and abandon the experiments, Prelati would tell him wonderful stories and make significant gestures. When Rais spent a month in Bourges during the late summer of 1439, the magician sent him a present supposedly from the Devil himself: black powder on a slate stone. Gilles put the powder in a small silver box and wore it around his neck for days.

Poitou and Griert recalled that after the conjurations and talisman failed to work, Gilles de Rais was so discouraged and depressed that only a return to his murderous debauchery could cheer him up. Sometime in August, the aunt of a young boy named Colin Avril was approached by one of Rais' men (likely Poitou) asking her if they might borrow the child to "show him the house of the Archdeacon of Merles," as she later testified. It was understood that the boy would be given a loaf of bread too.

The aunt must have been uneasy about sending Colin off, because she insisted on accompanying him. But the next day the boy went to the Hotel de la Suze, where he occasionally received bread. Gilles de Rais and his entourage were staying at the hotel at the time.

Colin Avril never came home. Henriet Griert said at his trial that he brought the child to his master, who "had intercourse" with the boy. Colin, he added, was later "killed and burned."

Soon afterward, on the evening of August 26, Poitou brought fifteen-year-old Bernard Le Camus, a good-looking and intelligent teenager, to Rais' new quarters in Bourgneuf. Le Camus, a Breton who was in Bourgneuf to learn French, had caught Poitou's attention at the home of a local resident, where the boy was temporarily staying.

The chambermaid saw Poitou speaking to Le Camus in a way that she must have found suspicious, because afterward she asked Bernard what had been said. The youth shrugged and insisted that Poitou had not told him anything. Then he left and was never seen again.

Poitou said that around this time, he saw Rais put a dead child's hand and heart in a glass, cover it with a linen, and tuck it inside his long sleeve before walking to Prelati's room. The items were apparently offered to Barron, who failed to appear, so Prelati buried them in sacred soil, close to the castle's chapel.

******

On November 1, All Saint's Day, Eustache Blanchet left Rais' castle at Tiffauges after an argument with one of the Baron's favorite minions, Robin Romulart. The underlying reason was supposedly that he was opposed to the child sacrifices (although apparently not enough to report them). He took rooms at an inn in Montagne.

At the beginning of December, Jean Mercier, castellan[42] of La Roche-sur-Yon, traveled to Montagne and took rooms at the same inn. When the innkeeper asked his guest for news from Nantes and Clisson, Blanchet heard Mercier say that public rumor in those areas accused the Baron de Rais of killing a large number of children so he could write a book using their blood as ink. When the book was finished, the gossips said, Rais could seize all the fortresses he wanted, with no one able to stop him.

The next day, one of Rais' emissaries came to the inn to try and persuade Blanchet to return. The priest refused, insisting that the crimes had to stop because public rumor was mounting against them. When the emissary returned to his master without Blanchet, Rais was supposedly so angry that he threw the man into the prison of his castle at Saint-Étienne-de-Mer-Morte.
At the beginning of December, Charles VII's son (the future Louis XI, presently the Dauphin) came to the region of Poitou to put an end to the armed bands of marauders who were

---

[42] Governor of a castle

ransacking the area. A visit to Gilles de Rais at Tiffauges was on his agenda, so the Baron frantically destroyed all the alchemical ovens in the fortress. After the Dauphin left, Rais went briefly to Brittany, where he enjoyed the hospitality of his old friend Duke Jean, before going to Machecoul in December. It was a move that supposedly proved fatal to two young boys.

******

Two weeks before Christmas, Jeanette Drouet, who resided with her husband and children in Saint-Léger, sent two of her sons, aged seven and ten, to ask for alms at Machecoul. She later testified that she "had heard that Lord de Rais had them distributed there, and that, moreover, the men in that village willingly gave charity."

During the days that followed, several people recalled seeing the boys in the area, but when Madame Drouet went there herself, she found no trace of them.

The hunt for the missing brothers was still underway when Isabeau Hamelin sent two of her boys, aged seven and fifteen, to Machecoul on Christmas Day to buy bread. They never returned. The next day, Prelati and another man, the Marquis de Ceva, came to her door. She recognized both as members of the Baron de Rais' entourage.

Seeing her daughter and another one of her sons, the men asked if they were her only children. Madame Hamelin said there were two more, but she did not mention their disappearance. As they left, she heard one man remark to the other, "Two had come from that house."

Gilles de Laval, baron de Retz. Illustration pour L'Histoire de la magie (1870) de Pierre Christian (Pierre Pitois).

Double Jeopardy

The new year of 1440 was ushered in with blood if Henriet Griert is to be believed. He said that Prelati's friend, the Marquis de Ceva, engaged a teenaged boy, who was supposedly from the Dieppe region and of good family, to serve Prelati as a page. The boy remained at Machecoul two weeks before vanishing. When someone outside the castle asked what had happened to him, Prelati grumbled that the boy had stolen two crowns from him and run away.

Henriet told two versions of the boy's death. In his first forced confession, he said that he murdered the teenager at Machecoul, while in the second he denied remembering who did the killing, as he "wasn't there.... but Gilles abused him just like the others."

Two more boys vanished and were allegedly killed at Machecoul around this time. One was the page of a nobleman named Daussy, while the other was the nephew of a priest who had sent him off to learn to read and write.

Eustache Blanchet, who was finally persuaded to rejoin the Rais household, said that one morning before Easter (March 27), he saw Poitou enter the castle, accompanied by sixteen-year-old Guillaume Le Barbier, son of the village pastry cook. The boy was supposed to serve Jean Péletier, Catherine de Rais' tailor, but soon vanished.

Between March 27 and May 15 (Pentecost), two more boys left their homes, never to be seen again. One was the fifteen-year-old son of a mason from Nantes, whose widow turned the boy over to Poitou after the latter persuaded her. The other was the ten-year-old son of Thomas Aisé and his wife, poor people who sent the boy to Machecoul to beg for alms. Their disappearances added to the rapidly spreading gossip that Gilles de Rais was a fatal force for children.

******

On May 15, 1440, Gilles de Rais made the move that sealed his fate. Earlier, he had sold his estate at Saint-Étienne-de-Mer-Morte to Geoffroy de Ferron, treasurer to the Duke of Brittany. For reasons that have never been made clear, Rais decided to repossess the castle, which had not yet been occupied by Ferron. In the interim, the latter's brother, a priest named Jean de Ferron, was taking care of the premises.

Accompanied by sixty men-at-arms, Rais waited outside the local church, where Jean de Ferron was celebrating High Mass. When it concluded, he ran into the building, a double-sided axe gripped in his hands. He ambushed the bewildered Ferron, yelling, "Ha, ribald! You beat my men, and extorted from them. Come outside the church, or I'll kill you on the spot!"

The shaken priest agreed to surrender the castle to its former owner. Instead of being beaten, he was marched back to the estate and imprisoned in its dungeon.

By barging into a church and forcing Ferron to give up the castle, Gilles de Rais violated both ecclesiastical privilege and the rights of Jean V, the Duke of Brittany. The latter slapped him with a fine of 50,000 gold crowns, but Rais tried to escape paying by moving (and taking Jean de Ferron with him) to Tiffauges, which was outside the Duke's control.

Although the disrespect he had shown the Catholic Church did not appear to trouble the Baron, he soon realized that antagonizing Jean V had not been a wise move, given the fact that the Duke was the only one who would help him liquidate his assets when he needed money. Before setting out on a reconciliation meeting, he ordered Prelati to ask Barron if it was safe to travel into the Duke's territory. Henriet Griert said that three children were killed in a field to ensure a response from the demon.

When Prelati reported that Barron had approved the journey, Rais set out on a mission of reconciliation. He had no idea that his old protector had turned against him. By 1440, Jean V owned most of the Baron's holdings, and if Gilles were convicted of sacrilege (a capital offense) and executed, there was no chance of his retrieving them in six years as per their agreement. The Duke reported the church assault to the Bishop of Nantes and started proceedings for sacrilege, adding a charge of heresy for good measure.

Unaware of the treachery, Gilles de Rais and his party stopped overnight in the town of Vannes after leaving the Duke's household. He wanted to find André Buchet, who had been a choirboy in his entourage in 1434. While there, he was purported to have encountered the ten-year-old son of a local resident named Jean Lavery. Since his present lodging was not private enough for what he had in mind, the boy was taken to another house near the market. There, Poitou said, he was raped, murdered, and decapitated. The body was thrown into the latrines, where the smell of decomposition would be effectively masked.

Rais committed his last canonical murder on August 15. Poitou obtained a young boy by telling the child's mother that he needed a page. He made the story more believable by paying twenty sous for a doublet. According to Poitou, the child was killed and burned.

******

In response to Jean V's allegations and complaint, Jean de Malestroit, the Bishop of Nantes started a private investigation that turned up "evidence" that Gilles de Rais was murdering children and invoking demons. All of his findings were based on public rumor, but for Malestroit, it was enough. On July 29, he published his findings in the form of letters patent and obtained the prosecutorial cooperation of Jean V.

The Duke secured the assistance of his brother Arthur de Richemont, the Constable of France, by promising him two lands that still technically belonged to Gilles de Rais. The Baron had not even been tried yet, but Jean V was apparently so confident of the trial's outcome that he distributed the spoils in advance.

Because he was one of the crown's principal officers, Richemont was empowered to enter Tiffauges, seize it, and free Jean de Ferron. As soon as the Constable entered the estate, Gilles de Sillé and Roger de Briqueville fled for parts unknown. They could see what was coming, even if their master couldn't, and decided to escape rather than go down with him.

On September 13, without his knowledge, Gilles was indicted before the ecclesiastical tribunal of Nantes on charges of sodomy, murdering children, invoking demons, heresy, and offending Divine Majesty. Two days later, he was arrested.

Arrested

Gilles de Rais was at Machecoul when the Duke of Brittany's men, accompanied by a notary public, appeared at its portal with the captain of arms in the lead. When they announced that they were there to arrest him, he gave them no trouble. He probably believed that the arrest was a mere formality in connection with the uproar at St-Etienne-de-Mer-Morte.

Prelati, Blanchet, Poitou, and Henriet were taken into custody too. The latter was not as calm about the situation as his master. On the road to Nantes prison, the terrified servant gave serious thought to cutting his own throat.

******

The trial of Gilles de Rais began on September 19, 1440, on the large upper hall of the castle of La Tour Neve. The proceedings were opened in an ecclesiastical court, which focused on his religious crimes and did not mention the civil charges of sodomy and murder.

The Baron had no idea that the day before, the secular proceedings against him had begun. Authorized by Magistrate Pierre de l'Hôpital and overseen by a cleric, Jean de Touscheronde, they started off with the testimonies of Peronne Loessart, who had last seen her son in La Roche-Bernard in 1438, and a Port-Launay man named Jamet Brice, who had also lost a son.

Oblivious to this second action, Rais listened as the ecclesiastical prosecutor read out the religious offenses he was being charged with. When he was ordered to appear before the Vice-Inquisitor, Jean Blouyn and the Bishop of Nantes on September 28, he did not protest their authority to try him. He was still confident that a heresy charge could be easily dealt with.

When the 28th rolled around, however, Rais failed to appear as ordered. The heresy proceeding was swiftly joined by the concurrent civil one, as the Bishop and the Vice-Inquisitor listened to a parade of parents and relatives who had lost children in recent years. There were so many of them that the proceedings had to run until October 8 to hear everyone.

The judges also heard the testimonies of Henriet and Poitou, who had been tortured before telling their stories. They had been identified by so many witnesses as being associated with the missing children that the authorities deemed it necessary to apply extra force to get at the "truth."

Poitou said that his master had started killing boys at the Champtocé castle during the lifetime of Jean de Craon. He supplied a date of 1426, although he himself did not enter Rais' service until 1427. Both he and Griert said that boys – and occasionally, girls – would be lured to the castle on some pretext, and once inside the Baron's chamber, be hung from the ceiling on a rope or chain. But before he (or rarely, she) could lose consciousness, they were taken down, stripped, and raped. Once the assault was over, Rais or one of his accomplices would cut their throats or decapitate them.

Sometimes murder was not enough to sate the Baron, who would go on to sexually abuse the child's corpse, sometimes cutting open the stomach and masturbating over the entrails.

320

Afterward, Poitou or Griert would dismember and burn the body in Gilles' fireplace. The ashes were then tossed into the moat, cesspit, and other hiding places.

Poitou recalled that when Gilles' brother, René de la Suze, and cousin came to Machecoul in 1437, Gilles de Sillé and another accomplice removed over forty children's skeletons from the castle. Apparently two had been overlooked and were left in the lower tower. When one of Lord de la Suze's captains asked Poitou and Griert if they knew anything about this, they denied it.[43]

These allegations resulted in the transcript being so lurid that the judges later ordered the worst portions to be stricken from the record.

******

On October 8, 1440, Rais finally made an appearance in the upper hall of La Tour Neve castle. He seemed nonchalant and unconcerned. When the prosecutor read the civil charges against him — murder and sodomy — his genteel demeanor evaporated instantly. Rais exploded in a raging denial and, despite four demands and a threat of excommunication, refused to take an oath.

On October 14, the prosecutor read out the bill of indictment he had prepared. Standing before the Bishop, the Vice-Inquisitor, and several Nantes officials, he formulated the charge as it was laid out in the forty-nine articles of the indictment. According to the lengthy document, the Baron de Rais had started killing children in 1426, and his total victim count was 140 boys and girls. They had been "shamefully tortured" and in the case of the girls, he had disdained their "natural vessel" in favor of sodomizing them. Other crimes included invocations of demons and violating the Church's immunity, which he had done by kidnapping Jean de Ferron.

Interrogated by the Bishop and the Vice-Inquisitor on the forty-nine articles in the indictment, Gilles de Rais became combative. He called his judges simoniacs (those who buy and sell ecclesiastical privileges) and ribalds (those who are vulgar or indecent in speech or language), who had no right to sit in judgement on him.

"I would much prefer," he snarled, "to be hanged by a rope around my neck than respond to such ecclesiastics and judges."

A few minutes after this outburst, a peremptory excommunication took place. He protested, but the Bishop of Nantes stood firm, in view of what the record called "the nature of the case and the cases of this order, and also on account of the monstrous and enormous crimes" brought against the nobleman.

The next day, Rais changed his perspective. The excommunication had greatly upset him, as evidenced by a tearful apology to his judges and his humble acceptance of their authority. He also declared that he was guilty of all the charges against him except invoking of demons, which he suspected that the Church regarded as a more serious crime than murder. At one point, he even collapsed to his knees and begged for the excommunication to be lifted. He seemed so distraught and contrite that the Bishop assented.

---

[43] For whatever reason, this captain was not called to testify.

Rais' relief must have been palpable. Even when desperate for money, he had refused to sell his soul, and if the ecclesiastical judges wanted to hear a confession in order to lift their excommunication, he would give them one, even if it may not have been true. For by then, he knew that he was doomed.

Miniature painting of the interrogation of Gilles de Rais

Guilty

In his confession, which he formally made in court on October 22[44], Rais said that he had started murdering children sometime in 1432 or 1433. He corroborated most of the nauseating testimony supplied by Poitou and Griert. The court record indicates that the Baron spoke "with great contrition of heart and great grief, according as it appeared at first sight, and with a great effusion of tears."

Many times he faced the parents in the audience and begged them to forgive him. They wept too and declared that he was forgiven, a strange response from a group that should have been baying for his blood. Still sobbing, he urged them to watch over their children and ensure they were not "too finely dressed" or lazy.

The next day, October 23, the ecclesiastical court found Rais guilty of heresy, while its secular counterpart declared him guilty of kidnapping and torture and raising armed forces without the Duke of Brittany's permission. The former handed down a sentence of excommunication, which was later lifted after Rais expressed the appropriate level of contrition.

On October 23 the secular court condemned Poitou and Henriet to death by hanging and burning. The same sentence was passed on Gilles de Rais two days later, on the 25 of October. The Baron, who accepted the punishment humbly, asked for a favor. He wanted to die first, so that Poitou and Henriet could see that he had not gone unpunished.[45]

The court, deeply moved, consented, and told him that instead of being burned afterward, his body could be buried in a church of his choice. The Baron was allowed to make confession, and his request to be buried in the church of the monastery of Notre-Dame des Carmes in Nantes was granted.

---

[44] After Rais admitted to the charges on 21 October, the court canceled a plan to torture him into confessing.

[45] The other accused men got off relatively lightly. It is not known what Eustache Blanchet's punishment was, but François Prelati was sentenced to life in prison instead of death because there was no proof he had actually participated in any murders. He escaped, but was later caught forging checks and hanged.

The execution of Gilles de Rais

The execution was set for Wednesday 26 October. Because of his high position, Gilles de Rais was granted the comparative mercy of being strangled to death before the flames consumed his body.

At nine o'clock, Gilles and his two convicted accomplices made their way in procession to the place of execution on the Ile de Biesse. Gilles is said to have addressed the crowd with contrite piety and exhorted Henriet and Poitou to die bravely and think only of salvation. Instead of hooting and jeering, which was routine at public executions, people wept and loudly prayed for his soul.

As Rais made his final confession to a friar who had accompanied the execution party, assistant hangmen tested the nooses and their attached chains. When everything was ready, the condemned nobleman ascended the long wooden ladder propped against the gibbet. He paused while the hangman looped the noose tightly around his neck.

In 1440, condemned felons did not wear hoods or blindfolds, so as he stood on the ladder, Gilles de Rais gazed at the staring crowd below, the broad expanse of sky above, and the Nantes countryside all around him. Together, it all comprised his final glimpse of the world.

At eleven o'clock, the brush at the platform was set afire. Gilles either stepped off the ladder voluntarily or was pushed by the hangman. Sometimes the sudden drop broke the victim's neck and caused instant death, but more often death came after slow strangulation. Whatever the case with Rais' execution, he was dead and his body cut down before the flames could reach him. Henriet and Poitou were not so lucky: although hanged first, they were partly burned alive.

Four women identified as "ladies of high rank" claimed the body of Gilles de Rais, which had been cut down after the flames had given it a cursory singeing. As promised, the church permitted his burial in a Catholic cemetery.

Aftermath

Of Catherine de Rais, Rais biographer Jean Benedetti wrote, "It is difficult to imagine that she didn't know about the crimes that the trial of 1440 had succeeded in revealing."

One myth that rapidly became part of Gilles de Rais folklore states that Catherine and her sister discovered blood, a dead child, and other evidence of murder in a Champtocé tower they had been forbidden to enter. The two terrified women alerted their brothers, who led armed forces to the castle and rescued them.

This episode is taken straight from a chapter of *La Barbe bleue*, a French folktale written by Charles Perrault and published in 1697. In the story, it is the butchered bodies of her predecessors that Bluebeard's wife and her sister discover. Although many commentators suggest that Gilles de Rais was the original Bluebeard, the crimes of the real and mythical personages were too different in terms of victim profile and count, and the gruesome tower discovery by Catherine de Rais never happened.

Whether or not she knew anything about the missing children is impossible to answer now, but what is known is that soon after her husband's execution, she married again, this time to Jean de Vendôme, who became the Duke of Brittany's chamberlain in 1441. Although Gilles had squandered many of his own holdings, Catherine retained Tiffauges, Pouzauges, and the other assets she had brought into the marriage.

For a while, she also controlled the holdings of her daughter, Marie. But the child's possessions were so numerous and valuable that their oversight was passed to Admiral Prégent de Cöetivy, a high-ranking nobleman who was also one of the King's most able advisors. Charles VII actually arranged a marriage between thirteen-year-old Marie and the much older Admiral in the spring of 1442. It was celebrated three years later. The couple had no children at the time of his battlefield death on July 20, 1450.

Marie's second husband was her father's cousin André de Laval-Lohéac, who had worked with René de la Suze to stop Gilles from destroying the family fortune. After their wedding at Vitré in February 1451, he helped her fight to reclaim Champtocé, which her first husband's family insisted was theirs under her marriage contract with the Admiral.

Marie de Rais believed so strongly in her father's innocence that she erected a monument at his execution site years later. It became a place of pilgrimage and remained one for three hundred years, until it was destroyed in the Terror. There, women would pray to the small statue of the Virgin Mary for enough milk to feed their babies. Tradition says that these prayers were answered. It raises an interesting question: If the local people really believed that Gilles de Rais had preyed on and desecrated local children, why was the monument so revered?

Marie de Rais died on November 1, 1457, aged thirty-seven. Because she had no children, her father's legacy passed to his brother René, who officially became Baron de Rais. Being more direct than his cousin or Marie, he seized Champtocé and ignored the indemnification demands made by the Cöetivy family. He died in 1473, leaving everything to his daughter, Jeanne.

******

In January 1443, Gilles de Rais' old benefactor, King Charles VII, sent letters patent to Pierre de l'Hôpital, who had been in charge of the secular investigation, and François I, who had succeeded Jean V as Duke of Brittany. He ordered their appearance before the Parliament of Paris to account for what he saw as the wrongful execution of Gilles de Rais. His anger is detectable in the language used, even centuries later. He refers to the "seizure, arrest, and detention of [the Baron's] person and refusal and denial of justice, and other wrongs and grievances to be declared more plainly at the appropriate time and place, against him and to his prejudice, wrongly, unduly and without reason.... The said late Lord de Rais was condemned and put to death by the said de l'Hôpital, unduly and without reason."

Pierre de l'Hôpital and François I never made the requested appearance, and for some reason the King did not press them. In the letter he insisted that restitution had to be made, and subsequently Gilles de Rais' estates (at least the ones that Jean V had confiscated) were restored to his daughter, Marie.

Like the case with Jeanne D'Arc, Charles got involved too late to do any good. Perhaps the gesture made to Marie was a salve for a guilty conscience.

« 1443 (nouveau style), 3 janvier. – Lettres d'adjornement en cas d'appel, [du procès du mareschal Gilles de Rays], adroissantes au duc [de Bretagne]... – Original en parchemin jadis scellé sur queue simple.

» Charles, par la grâce de Dieu, roy de France, à nostre très chier et très ami nepveu le duc de Bretaigne, salut et dilection.

» Comme feu Gilles, en son vivant seigneur de Rays, mareschal de France, de certaines condempnacions, exploiz, mainmise, arrest et détencion de sa personne et reffus et dené de droit, et autres tors et griefs à déclarer plus à plain en temps et lieu, contre lui et à son préjudice, à tort, indeuement et contre raison, faiz et donnez par feu nostre frère et cousin vostre père, maistre Pierre de Lhospital, soy disant ou portant président de Bretaigne, et autres ses officiers, au prouffit, pourchas, requeste ou instance du procureur de nostredict feu frère et cousin, ou autrement indeuement, eust appelé à nous et nostre court de parlement comme de nulz, et, se aucuns sont ou estaient, comme de faulx et mauvais, iniques et déraisonnables ; après lequel appel, et dedans ung mois après ce que ledit appel fut interjecté, ledict feu seigneur de Rays fut condamné à mort et fait mourir par ledict de Lhospital, indeuement et sans cause, le XXVIJ^e (*sic pour XXVI*) jour du mois d'octobre l'an mil CCCC quarante.

» [...] Si vous enjoignons que vous ayez avec vous audict pour ledict de Lospital, soy portant vostre président de Bretaigne, et autres nos officiers, pour soustenir et deffendre lesdits exploiz, sentences et autres appointements ; les veoir corriger, réparer, amender et mestre au néant se estre le doivent, procéder et avant aller en oultre selon raison. Et vous deffendons que pendant ladicte cause d'appel, contre ne ou préjudice d'icelle ne de nozdictz conseiller et cousine, vous ne eulx actemptez ou innover au contraire, mais tout ce qui fait, actempé ou innové auroit esté, réparez et remectez ou faictes réparer et remectre tantost et sans délay au premier estat et deu.

» Donné à Montalban, le IIIJ^e jour de janvier, l'an de grâce mil CCCC quarante et deux, et de nostre règne le XXIe, soubz nostre scel ordonné en absence du grant.

» Par le roy en son conseil. »

CHEVALIER

Conclusion

Was Gilles de Rais guilty? Or did he confess to those terrible crimes to save his soul after being forced to acknowledge that he would never be believed innocent?

The historians who believe that he was guilty insist that the proof against him was overwhelming. He and his accomplices had confessed, and a slew of grieving parents came forward to give evidence against him. But it can also be argued that the confessions had been given under duress, and while Poitou, Henriet, and Prelati had been seen courting victims, Rais can't be tied to them directly.

Today, a good defense lawyer would argue that these procurers had committed the crimes for their own entertainment, and Rais knew nothing about them. He might have been aware that young people were brought to his castles to serve as pages and general servants, but his households were so large that he could never have kept track of their appearances and disappearances even if he had wanted to.

There is no official record of human remains being found at any of Gilles de Rais' castles at any time. Poitou talked about bones being removed from Machecoul prior to the arrival of René de la Suze and the discovery of two skeletons that had been missed, but the captain who allegedly found them never gave evidence at the trial.

It is also a fact that several other children vanished in France during the time that Gilles de Rais was supposedly reveling in young blood, and he could not have been involved in any of their disappearances. They included:

- An eight-year-old orphaned pauper's son (surname Brice), last seen in his home of Saint-Étienne-de-Montluc in February 1439. The Rais household was not in the area, which was a considerable distance north of the Baron's Loire holdings.

- In August 1349, the thirteen-year-old pupil of Jean Toutblanc (also from Saint-Étienne-de-Montluc) vanished. Once more, Gilles de Rais was elsewhere in the country.

- Two months later, in October 1439, two sons of a man named Robin Pavot, who lived near Rennes, attended a fair in Rais. When they didn't come home, their parents made frantic inquiries, and one of their older brothers traveled to neighboring regions, but he could learn nothing. At the time, Rais was at Tiffauges.

To compound the issue, the crowd at the execution site wept and prayed when Gilles de Rais was led out to the gallows. One would think that a vicious child killer would have merited howls and jeers.

The proprietor of a pro-Rais blog[46] made the following observation about the trial judges:

---

[46] http://gillesderaiswasinnocent.blogspot.ca/

The judges, too, were not as impartial as they ought to have been in a capital case. Jean de Malestroit had engaged in numerous business deals with the accused, buying his estates at knockdown prices. He was the cousin of Jean V, Duke of Brittany, who had also illegally bought properties from his vassal, including the strategic border castles of Champtocé and Ingrandes. These fortified castles were vital to Brittany´s defense, and Jean V´s father had coveted them before him. Although the Duke finally obtained them, when Gilles´ finances were on the verge of collapse and he could no longer hold on to them, they were sold on condition that Gilles could repurchase them within six years if he wished. Neither Jean V nor de Malestroit was willing to risk such an eventuality.

The question of guilt or innocence has proved to be so troubling over the centuries that in 1992, Gilles de Rais was retried in an official process of rehabilitation.[47] A French arbitration court consisting of lawyers, historians, politicians, and writers was assembled to determine whether there was sufficient evidence to prove he might have been framed.

Historian Gilbert Prouteau, who led the campaign, said, "The case for Gilles de Rais's innocence is very strong.... No child's corpse was ever found at his castle at Tiffauges, and he appears to have confessed to escape excommunication....The accusations appear to be false charges made up by powerful rival lords to benefit from the confiscation of his lands."

Former Justice Minister Michel Crepeau seemed to agree. He said that the trial's true motivation appeared to be political.

The court studied the minutes of the Baron's trial at the hands of Jean de Malestroit and heard arguments that he was the victim of circumstantial evidence. The presiding judge, Henri Juramy, later said that the primary motive was to ascertain whether French history had been deliberately damaged by the original condemnation.

Some French newspapers reported that the Roman Catholic Church, unwilling to reopen a ruling by the Inquisition, accused Freemasons of being behind the creation of the arbitration court.[48]

When the hearing concluded, Juramy declared that Gilles de Rais was not guilty of murder. The ruling spawned a documentary called *Gilles de Rais ou la Gueule du loup*, which was narrated by Prouteau.

Two lobbies protested the acquittal. One was the Catholic Church. The other was the local residents living in the vicinity of Tiffauges, Machecoul, and Champtocé. For them, vindicating Gilles de Rais posed a serious threat to their livelihood, given the number of tourists who visited the ruined castles every year. Tiffauges guide Georges Gautier declared, "We're not interested in reopening the affair."[49]

---

[47] http://www.theguardian.com/theguardian/2013/jun/17/bluebeard-gilles-de-rais-france
[48] Riding, Alan. "Bluebeard Has His Day in Court: Not Guilty." The New York Times. November 16, 1992. Accessed December 6, 2015. http://www.nytimes.com/1992/11/17/world/bluebeard-has-his-day-in-court-not-guilty.html.
[49] Ibid

Because the trial and verdict took place before the Internet exploded, the acquittal is not generally known, and most history and serial killer sites continue to refer to Gilles de Rais as the "original Bluebeard" whose guilt is beyond question. The gruesome details of his alleged crimes are too shocking and morbidly appealing for many true crime writers and fans to even want him to be innocent.

At the same time, his complete innocence doesn't seem possible. Even if the crimes were the private perversions of Gilles de Sillé, Poitou, or Henriet Griert, could they really have taken place at Tiffauges, Machecoul, and Champtocé without Rais knowing or suspecting anything?

The debate will go on for a while yet, for after all this time, all anyone can do is conjecture. When a person's crimes are as sensational and iconic as those attributed to Gilles de Rais, his guilt or innocence will always be like beauty: in the eye of the beholder.

Bibliography

The Casanova Killer

Douglas, John E., and Mark Olshaker. *Journey into Darkness: Follow the FBI's Premier Investigative Profiler as He Penetrates the Minds and Motives of the Most Terrifying Serial Killers*. New York: Scribner, 1997.

Fawkes, Sandy. *Killing Time*. New York: Taplinger Pub., 1979.

Schechter, Harold. *The Serial Killer Files: The Who, What, Where, How, and Why of the World's Most Terrifying Murderers*. New York: Ballantine Books, 2004.

Newspapers

Augusta Chronicle
Boca Raton News
Ocala Star-Banner
Sarasota Herald-Tribune
The Evening Independent
The Telegraph

The Butcher Baker

Andrews, Laurel. "'Frozen Ground' serial killer Hansen dead." Alaska Dispatch News. August 21, 2014. Accessed August 15, 2017. https://www.adn.com/crime-justice/article/infamous-alaska-serial-killer-robert-hansen-dies/2014/08/21/.

"Antisocial Personality Disorder." Psychology Today. April 19, 2017. Accessed August 19, 2017. https://www.psychologytoday.com/conditions/antisocial-personality-disorder.

"Bipolar Affective Disorder (Manic Depression)." MyVMC. September 30, 2015. Accessed August 19, 2017. https://www.myvmc.com/diseases/bipolar-affective-disorder-manic-depression/.

Blanco, Juan Ignacio. "Robert Hansen." Murderpedia, the encyclopedia of murderers. Accessed August 15, 2017. http://murderpedia.org/male.H/h/hansen-robert.htm.

Bonnie. "Serial Killer: *Butcher Baker* Robert Hansen." My Life of Crime. August 24, 2014. Accessed August 15, 2017. https://mylifeofcrime.wordpress.com/2014/08/23/serial-killer-butcher-baker-robert-hansen-killed-at-least-17-women-sentenced-to-years-in-prison-died-8212014/.

Brennan, Tom. *Murder at 40 below: true crime stories from Alaska*. Kenmore, WA: Epicenter Press, 2001.

Connell, Richard. "The Most Dangerous Game." 1924.

Coppock, Michael. "Alaska's serial killer: Hunting strippers in the bush." Juneau Empire. April 11, 2008. Accessed August 15, 2017. http://juneauempire.com/stories/041108/nei_267504580.shtml#.WZNgUXG1vDc.

"Denied by Hansen, Pt. 1: Megan Emerick." Butcher, Baker. January 12, 2017. Accessed August 19, 2017. http://butcherbaker.net/wordpress/denied-by-hansen-pt-1-megan-emerick/.

Douglas, John E., and Mark Olshaker. *Mindhunter: Inside the FBI's Elite Serial Crime Unit.* New York: Pocket books, 1996.

DuClos, Bernard. (1993). *Fair game.* NY: St. Martin's. (ISBN 0-312-92905-6)

Dunham, Mike. "Grisly legacy of 'Eklutna Annie'." Alaska Dispatch News. September 29, 2016. Accessed August 19, 2017. https://www.adn.com/alaska-news/article/grisly-legacy-eklutna-annie/2012/07/15/.

Etherealairhead, ***. "Ode to Doe: Horseshoe Harriet." A Kitten's Curiosity. February 26, 2017. Accessed August 19, 2017. https://etherealairhead.wordpress.com/2017/02/26/ode-to-doe-horseshoe-harriet/.

Ferri, Jessica. "Robert Hansen: The Alaskan Serial Killer Who Hunted Human Game." The Line Up. December 09, 2016. Accessed August 15, 2017. https://the-line-up.com/robert-hansen-the-serial-killer-who-hunted-human-game.

Gilmour, Walter & Hale, Leland E. (1991). *Butcher, baker: A true account of a serial murderer.* NY: Onyx Press. (ISBN 0-451-40276-6)

Good, Meaghan Elizabeth. "The Charley Project." The Charley Project. Accessed August 19, 2017. http://www.charleyproject.org/.

H, Reva. Sue Luna. July 18, 2000. Accessed August 19, 2017. http://www.murdervictims.com/voices/sue_luna.htm.

Hale, Leland E. "Unsolved Murder: Did Alaskan Serial Killer Robert Hansen Kill Beth van Zanten?" The Line Up. July 19, 2017. Accessed August 19, 2017. https://the-line-up.com/unsolved-murder-did-alaskan-serial-killer-robert-hansen-kill-beth-van-zanten.

"Hansen v. State." Justia Law. Accessed August 19, 2017. http://law.justia.com/cases/alaska/supreme-court/1978/3412-1.html.

"If film makes Hansen's victims real, the story's worth retelling." Alaska Dispatch News. April 28, 2016. Accessed August 19, 2017. https://www.adn.com/voices/article/if-film-makes-hansens-victims-real-storys-worth-retelling/2011/08/01/.

Krajicek, David J. "Serial killer's sick 'revenge' in the Alaskan frontier." NY Daily News. August 31, 2014. Accessed August 15, 2017. http://www.nydailynews.com/news/crime/serial-killer-sick-revenge-alaskan-frontier-article-1.1922167.

Lundberg, Murray. "Robert Hansen A Serial Killer in Alaska." ExploreNorth.com—Your Gateway to the North. February 11, 2000. Accessed August 15, 2017. http://www.explorenorth.com/library/crime/alaska_serial_killer.html.

McLaughlin, Emily, Megan Donnelly, Carrie Draper, and Jennifer Duncan. PDF. Radford, VA: Department of Psychology Radford University. https://www.google.com/url?sa=t&rct=j&q=&esrc=s&source=web&cd=12&cad=rja&uact=8&ved=0ahUKEwjRqpaljNrVAhWE4iYKHZpGD3c4ChAWCCwwAQ&url=http%3A%2F%2Fmaamodt.asp.radford.edu%2FPsyc%2520405%2Fserial%2520killers%2FHansen%2C%2520Robert%2520-%2520fall%2C%25202005.pdf&usg=AFQjCNEemgH1T4oty4gguzFo1I3_3IGDwQ

"Missing girl tips revive Alaska cold case." UPI. September 28, 2008. Accessed August 19, 2017. http://www.upi.com/Missing-girl-tips-revive-Alaska-cold-case/15701222624602/.

"Never Forget Me." Facebook . 2014. Accessed August 19, 2017. https://www.facebook.com/pg/WeWontForgetThem/photos/?tab=album&album_id=922946237719414. Eklutna Annie Images

Olshaker, Mark. "Robert Hansen: Good Riddance." Mindhunters. August 25, 2014. Accessed August 15, 2017. http://mindhuntersinc.com/robert-hansen-good-riddance/.

"Photos." Butcher, Baker, the True Story of a Serial Killer: Photos. Accessed August 15, 2017. http://butcherbaker.net/photos.html.

"Robert Hansen Archives Map." Butcher, Baker. November 8, 2013. Accessed August 19, 2017. http://butcherbaker.net/wordpress/tag/robert-hansen/.

Roberts, Sheila. "Director Scott Walker Talks THE FROZEN GROUND, His Feature Directorial Debut, and Upcoming Werewolf Comedy BULLET BLOOD WILD." Collider. February 09, 2015. Accessed August 19, 2017. http://collider.com/scott-walker-frozen-ground-interview/.

"Serial Killers: Nature vs. Nurture." National Center of Crisis Management. Accessed August 19, 2017. http://www.nc-cm.org/article213.htm.

"Sue Luna remembered." Sue Luna remembered—Democratic Underground. May 16, 2008. Accessed August 23, 2017. https://www.democraticunderground.com/discuss/duboard.php?az=view_all&address=341x12804.

Townsend, Catherine, and Mike McFadden. "Serial Killer And "Butcher Baker" Robert Hansen Hunted Women Down In The Woods." CrimeFeed. February 15, 2017. Accessed August 15, 2017. http://crimefeed.com/2017/02/crime-history-robert-hansen-who-hunted-women-in-alaska/.

The Horrific Crimes of Gilles de Rais

Bataille, Georges. *The Trial of Gilles De Rais*. Los Angeles: Amok, 1991.

Benedetti, Jean. *Gilles De Rais*. New York: Stein and Day, 1972.

MacCulloch, Diarmaid. *A History of Christianity*. Penguin Books, 2010.

Villalon, L. J. Andrew. *The Hundred Years War (Part III): Further Considerations*. Brill, 2013.

Wolf, Leonard. *Bluebeard, the Life and Crimes of Gilles De Rais*. New York, N.Y.: C.N. Potter, 1980.